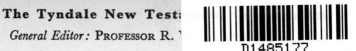

The Tyndale New Testa...

General Editor: PROFESSOR R. ...

220.3
MOR

THE GOSPEL ACCORDING TO ST. LUKE

THE GOSPEL ACCORDING TO ST. LUKE

AN INTRODUCTION AND COMMENTARY

by

THE REV. CANON LEON MORRIS
M.Sc., M.Th., Ph.D.

Principal, Ridley College, Melbourne

The Training Centre

© INTER-VARSITY PRESS, LONDON

Inter-Varsity Fellowship
39 *Bedford Square, London WC1B 3EY*

First Edition—August 1974
HARDBACK EDITION 0 85111 619 1
PAPERBACK EDITION 0 85111 820 8

Made and printed in England by
STAPLES PRINTERS LIMITED
at their Rochester, Kent, establishment

GENERAL PREFACE

ALL who are interested in the teaching and study of the New Testament today cannot fail to be concerned with the lack of commentaries which avoid the extremes of being unduly technical or unhelpfully brief. It is the hope of the editor and publishers that this present series will do something towards the supply of this deficiency. Their aim is to place in the hands of students and serious readers of the New Testament, at a moderate cost, commentaries by a number of scholars who, while they are free to make their own individual contributions, are united in a common desire to promote a truly biblical theology.

The commentaries are primarily exegetical and only secondarily homiletic, though it is hoped that both student and preacher will find them informative and suggestive. Critical questions are fully considered in introductory sections, and also, at the author's discretion, in additional notes.

The commentaries in this New Testament series have been based hitherto on the Authorized (King James) version. It was felt desirable, however, that this final volume, published some eighteen years after the launching of the first volume, should be based on the Revised Standard Version, since this is now so widely used by Bible students. No one translation, however, is regarded as infallible, and no single Greek manuscript or group of manuscripts is regarded as always right! Greek words are transliterated to help those unfamiliar with the language, and to save those who do know Greek the trouble of discovering what word is being discussed.

It is a matter for thankfulness that interest in this series of commentaries, now completed, has been steadily maintained through the years of their production, and that they continue to be found helpful by Bible students in many parts of the world.

R. V. G. Tasker.

CONTENTS

CONTENTS

CHIEF ABBREVIATIONS

AG   *A Greek-English Lexicon of the New Testament and Other Early Christian Literature* edited by William F. Arndt and F. Wilbur Gingrich, 1957.

ANF   *The Ante-Nicene Fathers* (American reprint of the Edinburgh edition), n.d.

Arndt   *The Gospel according to St. Luke* by William F. Arndt (*Bible Commentary*), 1956.

AV   English Authorized Version (King James), 1611.

Barclay   *The Gospel of Luke* by William Barclay (*Daily Study Bible*), 1967.

Bengel   *The Gnomon of the New Testament* by John Albert Bengel, translated, revised and edited by Andrew R. Fausset, 1873.

BJRL   *Bulletin of the John Rylands Library.*

Blaiklock   *St. Luke* by E. M. Blaiklock (*Scripture Union Bible Study Books*), 1967.

Browning   *The Gospel according to Saint Luke* by W. R. F. Browning (*Torch Bible Commentaries*), 1965.

BS   *Bible Studies* by Adolf Deissmann, 1901.

Caird   *Saint Luke* by G. B. Caird (*Pelican Gospel Commentaries*), 1963.

CBQ   *The Catholic Biblical Quarterly.*

Creed   *The Gospel according to St. Luke* by John Martin Creed, 1950.

Ellis   *The Gospel of Luke* by E. Earle Ellis (*Century Bible, new series*), 1966.

ET   *The Expository Times.*

Farrar   *The Gospel according to St Luke* by F. W. Farrar (*Cambridge Greek Testament*), 1893.

Ford   *A Reading of Saint Luke's Gospel* by D. W. Cleverley Ford, 1967.

Geldenhuys   *Commentary on the Gospel of Luke* by Norval Geldenhuys (*New London Commentary*), 1952.

Godet   *A Commentary on the Gospel of St. Luke* by F. Godet, 2 vols., 1889.

GT   *A Greek-English Lexicon of the New Testament* being Grimm's Wilke's *Clavis Novi Testamenti*, translated, revised and enlarged by Joseph Henry Thayer, 1888.

Harrington	*The Gospel according to St Luke* by Wilfrid J. Harrington, 1968.
HDAC	*Dictionary of the Apostolic Church* edited by James Hastings, 2 vols., 1915–18.
JB	The Jerusalem Bible, 1966.
JBL	*The Journal of Biblical Literature.*
JTS	*The Journal of Theological Studies.*
Leaney	*A Commentary on the Gospel according to St. Luke* by A. R. C. Leaney (*Black's New Testament Commentaries*), 1966.
Lenski	*The Interpretation of St. Luke's Gospel* by R. C. H. Lenski, 1961.
LS	*A Greek-English Lexicon* compiled by H. G. Liddell and R. Scott, new edition revised by H. S. Jones and R. McKenzie, 2 vols., 1940.
LT	*The Life and Times of Jesus the Messiah* by Alfred Edersheim, 2 vols., 1890, reissued 1953.
LXX	The Septuagint (pre-Christian Greek version of the Old Testament).
Manson	*The Gospel of Luke* by William Manson (*Moffatt New Testament Commentary*), 1937.
Melinsky	*Luke* by Hugh Melinsky (*Modern Reader's Guide to the Gospels*), 1966.
mg.	margin.
Miller	*Saint Luke* by D. G. Miller (*Layman's Bible Commentaries*), 1966.
MM	*The Vocabulary of the Greek Testament* by James Hope Moulton and George Milligan, 1914–29.
Moorman	*The Path to Glory* by John R. H. Moorman, 1963.
Morgan	*The Gospel according to Luke* by G. Campbell Morgan, n.d.
MS(s)	manuscript(s).
NBD	*The New Bible Dictionary* edited by J. D. Douglas et al., 1962.
NEB	The New English Bible, Old Testament, 1970; New Testament, Second Edition, 1970.
NTS	*New Testament Studies.*
Plummer	*A Critical and Exegetical Commentary on the Gospel according to S. Luke* by Alfred Plummer (*International Critical Commentary*), 1928.

RSV	American Revised Standard Version, Old Testament, 1952; New Testament, Second Edition, 1971.
RV	English Revised Version, 1881.
Ryle	*Expository Thoughts on the Gospels, St. Luke* by John Charles Ryle, 2 vols., 1856, reissued 1969.
SE, i	*Studia Evangelica*, vol. i, edited by K. Aland *et al.*, 1959.
SE, iv	*Studia Evangelica*, vol. iv, edited by F. L. Cross, 1968.
SB	*Kommentar zum neuen Testament aus Talmud und Midrasch* by Herman L. Strack and Paul Billerbeck, 4 vols., 1922–28.
SJ	*The Sayings of Jesus* by T. W. Manson, 1949.
SLA	*Studies in Luke-Acts* edited by Leander E. Keck and J. Louis Martyn, 1966.
TDNT	*Theological Dictionary of the New Testament*, a translation by Geoffrey W. Bromiley of *Theologisches Wörterbuch zum neuen Testament*, vols. 1–4 edited by G. Kittel, 5– edited by G. Friedrich, 1964– .
TEV	Today's English Version: the New Testament, 1966.
THB	*A Translator's Handbook on the Gospel of Luke* by J. Reiling and J. L. Swellengrebel, 1971.
Thompson	*The Gospel according to Luke* by G. H. P. Thompson (*New Clarendon Bible*), 1972.
Tinsley	*The Gospel according to Luke* by E. J. Tinsley (*Cambridge Bible Commentary*), 1965.
TNTC	*Tyndale New Testament Commentary*.
ZNW	*Zeitschrift für die Neutestamentliche Wissenschaft.*

The following translations are cited by the translator's surname: Goodspeed, Knox, Moffatt, Phillips, Rieu. Philo and Josephus are cited from the Loeb edition, the Mishnah from Danby's translation and the Talmud and the Midrash from the Soncino translation.

INTRODUCTION

UNTIL recently very little attention seems to have been paid to the remarkable fact that Luke is the only one of the four Evangelists to write a sequel to his Gospel.[1] Why did he do it? The other three wrote books which concentrated on the life, death and resurrection of Jesus. Evidently they felt that this story could stand by itself. It needed no supplement. But Luke wrote Acts. Why?

His second volume, of course, takes us on into the history of the early church. It tells us of those first days in Jerusalem and of the way the preachers went abroad with the gospel, Peter and John, Stephen the martyr, Philip and others, but especially Paul and his helpers.

The great thought Luke is expressing is surely that God is working out His purpose.[2] This purpose is seen clearly in the life and work of Jesus, but it did not finish with the earthly ministry of Jesus. It carried right on into the life and witness of the church. The church does not represent a new, completely unrelated act of God. Luke seems to be saying that the work of Jesus led, and in the plan of God was meant to lead, to the life of the church. Some writers like to bring this out by speaking of Luke's theme as 'salvation history', or by drawing attention to the promise and fulfilment motif.[3]

This divine purpose Luke sees as intimately bound up with the love and mercy of God. A feature of this Gospel is the way God's love is portrayed as active in a variety of ways and among

[1]In the last two decades (especially in Germany) the importance of linking Luke with Acts has been increasingly emphasized. W. D. Davies points out that 'The recognition that Luke and Acts belong together is the decisive factor in recent interpretation of Luke' (*Invitation to the New Testament* (London, 1967), p. 219). This is part of a flurry of activity in recent Lucan studies which, however, has produced very little agreement, so that W. C. van Unnik could write an essay not so long ago with the title, 'Luke-Acts, a Storm Center in Contemporary Scholarship' (*SLA*, pp. 15ff.).

[2]Notice Luke's frequent use of the word *dei* to convey the thought of a divine necessity in Jesus' ministry (2:49; 4:43; 9:22; 13:16, 33; 17:25; 19:5; 22:37; 24:7, 26, 44). So also he uses *boulē*, 'purpose', twice in Luke and seven times in Acts, a total of nine out of the twelve occurrences of the term in the New Testament. S. Schulz has emphasized the importance of the plan of God in Luke's theology (*ZNW*, liv, 1963, pp. 104–116).

[3]*Cf.* Nils A. Dahl, *SLA*, pp. 150ff.

a variety of people. This is not an occasional theme, but one which runs through the whole writing. As A. H. McNeile put it, whereas in Matthew the keynote may be said to be royalty, and in Mark power, in Luke it is love.[1] It is perhaps this that gives to the Third Gospel its peculiar attractiveness. The writer was obviously a man of culture, with an appreciation of the beautiful, and he certainly could write well. But it is not any or all of these that accounts for the beauty of this writing. Rather it is the way the love of God shines through in parable and saying and story of Jesus.[2]

Luke's theme is a grand one and he treats it at some length. His Gospel is the longest of the four, and when Acts is added he has written more of the New Testament than any other single writer. Clearly a study of his writings is important for the student of the New Testament.

I. AUTHORSHIP

It is usually agreed that the author of our Gospel is to be identified with the writer of Acts. The Preface to Luke (1:1–4) is addressed to Theophilus and Acts 1:1 appears to be a kind of secondary preface. It is addressed to the same person and is apparently intended to recall the former.[3] Style and vocabulary favour unity of authorship.

Tradition unanimously affirms this author to be Luke. This is attested by the early heretic Marcion (who died *c.*

---

[1]A. H. McNeile, *An Introduction to the Study of the New Testament*, 2nd edn, rev. C. S. C. Williams (Oxford, 1953), p. 14.

[2]Many have paid their tribute to the attractiveness of the book. E. Renan spoke of it as 'the most beautiful book there is (le plus beau livre qu'il y ait)' (*Les Évangiles* (Paris, 1877), p. 283), a verdict which caused C. K. Barrett to remark that Luke 'was more concerned with truth than beauty' (*Luke the Historian in Recent Study* (London, 1961), p. 7). W. Manson pays the tribute: 'Luke has cast his net wide, and produced a gospel the most voluminous and varied, the most vibrant and sympathetic, the most beautiful and sweetly reasonable of all that we possess' (Manson, p. xxvii). F. C. Grant sees Luke as 'the most valuable of our four' and Luke-Acts as 'the most valuable writing in the New Testament' (*The Gospels* (London, 1957), p. 133).

[3]H. Conzelmann and E. Haenchen take the view that the Preface to Luke is not meant to refer to Acts. But most scholars see the Preface as applying to both books. See, for example, the discussion by A. J. B. Higgins in *Apostolic History and the Gospel*, ed. W. Ward Gasque and Ralph P. Martin (Exeter, 1970), pp. 78–91.

AD 160; Luke was the only Gospel in his canon), the Muratorian Fragment (a list of the books accepted as belonging to the New Testament; it is usually held to express Roman opinion at the end of the second century), the anti-Marcionite Prologue to Luke (which also says that Luke was a native of Antioch, that he was a physician, that he wrote his Gospel in Achaia, and that he died at the age of 84, unmarried and childless),[1] Irenaeus,[2] Tertullian,[3] Clement of Alexandria[4] and others.

Sometimes this tradition is dismissed as no more than guesswork, but this is too cavalier. Luke was not, as far as we know, a person of such prominence in the early church as to have two such considerable volumes as these fathered on to him without reason. If people were guessing, would they not be much more likely to come up with an apostle? Or Epaphras? Or Mark? The fact that a non-apostolic man of no known prominence is universally held in antiquity to have been the author must be given weight.

We should not overlook the point made by Martin Dibelius that this book is unlikely to have been published without the author's name attached. He points out that the address to Theophilus presupposes that there was the desire to circulate the book among the educated. For such readers the name of the writer would necessarily have been included. If the prologue 'gave the name of the person to whom the dedication was addressed, the name of the author could hardly be omitted from the title'.[5] Tradition would not uniformly ascribe to Luke

[1]The text is given in Greek in Albert Huck, *A Synopsis of the First Three Gospels*, English edn. ed. F. L. Cross (Tübingen, 1936), p. VIII, and in English in Ellis, p. 41. The Prologues are dated by Huck AD 160–180. Most recent scholars, however, regard them as much later and as of little value. See, for example, the note in E. Haenchen, *The Acts of the Apostles* (Oxford, 1971), pp. 10–12. Ellis is more respectful (Ellis, *loc. cit.*), as is R. G. Heard, who finds some early and valuable biographical material here (*JTS* n.s., vi, 1955, pp. 9–11).

[2]*Adversus Haereses* III. i. 1.

[3]*Adversus Marcionem* iv. 2.

[4]*Stromateis* i. 21.

[5]M. Dibelius, *Studies in the Acts of the Apostles* (London, 1956), p. 148. H. J. Cadbury points out that when the title and author of the book were named on a separate tag (which he thinks was probably the case with Luke-Acts) neither appeared in the text of the roll (*The Making of Luke-Acts* (London, 1958), p. 195). Cadbury thinks the evidence that Luke was the author is not conclusive. But he does not explain how Luke could have displaced another name so completely.

a book known from its publication to have been written by someone else.

The tradition accords with the Preface which shows us that the author was not an eyewitness of the things he records, though he had searched out evidence from those who were. He was clearly a careful writer and a cultured man, but not one of Jesus' first followers.

The internal evidence agrees. In Acts there are four passages in which the writer uses the pronoun 'we' (Acts 16:10–17; 20:5–16; 21:1–18; 27:1 – 28:16). These appear to have been taken from the diary of one of Paul's companions. One of the 'we' sections yields the information that the writer stayed for some time in Caesarea with Philip the evangelist and his four daughters (Acts 21:8ff.). It was not until more than two years later (Acts 24:27) that he and Paul sailed for Rome (Acts 27:1). This period spent with such companions must have given opportunity for discovering much about Jesus and the early church.

The vocabulary and style of the 'we' passages are the same as those of the rest of the book, from which the natural conclusion is that one author wrote the whole. It is true that some critics deny this. They hold that the author of Acts has copied a few passages from someone else's diary as his way of supplying information about part of the events he is describing.[1] Or they think that the 'we' is simply a literary device.[2] Such arguments are not impressive. The use by the author of extracts from his own notes is intelligible, that by someone else much less so. We might pose the dilemma in this way: If the author is not trying to use the prestige of the writer of the earlier document, why should he retain the 'we'? If he is, why does he not use that writer's name? That would have been far more effective. Indeed, without the name the 'we' proves little, as the variety of explanations proves. Nothing so far adduced is nearly as natural an explanation of these passages as that which holds that a companion of Paul used extracts from his own diary.

[1]For example, H. Windisch holds that the author of Acts was not Luke, 'but he used as a source a diary of Luke's' (*The Beginnings of Christianity*, ed. F. J. Foakes Jackson and K. Lake, vol. ii (London, 1922), p. 342).

[2]Ernst Haenchen, following Dibelius, takes this line. He suggests that the use of 'we' is a way of indicating that 'for some of the trips he (i.e. the author of Acts) was able to depend upon reports from an eyewitness' (*SLA*, p. 272).

If we can accept this we shall see the author as one of those who were with Paul at the times indicated by the use of 'we' but who are not named in the narrative (the author would not give his own name but include himself in the 'we'). Acts ends with Paul in Rome and the author is perhaps to be looked for among those named in the captivity Epistles or 2 Timothy as being with him, but not mentioned in Luke-Acts. This leaves us with a small group: Titus, Demas, Crescens, Jesus Justus, Epaphras, Epaphroditus and Luke. There seems no reason for thinking of any of those apart from Luke as being our author.[1]

Paul speaks of Luke as 'the beloved physician' (Col. 4:14) and in earlier days the case for the Lucan authorship was held to be strongly supported by the medical language which many discerned in Luke-Acts.[2] But H. J. Cadbury has convinced most people that the language is not especially medical,[3] by pointing out that most of the examples cited can be paralleled in writers who were not medicos. It seems generally agreed now that there was no special technical medical language in our sense of the term, for writers such as Hippocrates and Galen seem to have used the ordinary language of educated men. But if Cadbury has made it difficult to think of the language of Luke-Acts as proving that the writer was a physician, he seems to have turned up nothing inconsistent with the hypothesis. At least on occasion there are indications of

[1] Luke is mentioned in the New Testament only in Col. 4:14; Phm. 24; 2 Tim. 4:11. Some have identified him with Lucius of Cyrene (Acts 13:1) or with the Lucius whom Paul calls his kinsman (Rom. 16:21), but the names are slightly different and there seems no reason for identifying either with Luke. Some of the early church Fathers thought Luke was 'the brother, whose praise is in the gospel throughout all the churches' (2 Cor. 8:18, av; *cf.* the collect for St. Luke's day in the Book of Common Prayer), but this seems fanciful.

[2] The case was strongly argued by W. K. Hobart, *The Medical Language of St. Luke* (London, 1882), and more cautiously by A. Harnack, *Luke the Physician* (London, 1907).

[3] H. J. Cadbury, *The Style and Literary Method of Luke* (Harvard, 1920). A. Q. Morton however sees a weakness in Cadbury's approach, when he compares Luke's language to that in Josephus and the Septuagint: 'There are 18,000 words in the Gospel of Luke and 1,500,000 in the works of Josephus and in the Septuagint.' This could mean that the words in question are a hundred times more common in Luke than in Josephus (A. Q. Morton and G. H. C. Macgregor, *The Structure of Luke and Acts* (London, 1964), p. 3; Morton is not arguing for Hobart's hypothesis, which he castigates as 'a lunatic assertion', but indicating a weakness in Cadbury's refutation).

medical interest. Thus where Matthew and Mark speak only of a fever, Luke particularizes it as a 'high' fever (Mt. 8:14; Mk. 1:30; Lk. 4:38). Similarly he speaks of a certain man not simply as having leprosy, but as 'full' of leprosy (5:12, *i.e.* he was an advanced case). Again, if he was a medical man it was a very human touch that he omits the statement that the woman with the haemorrhage had spent all her money on doctors (8:43; *cf.* Mk. 5:26).

The most serious objection to the Lucan authorship is the allegation that Acts differs in some important respects from the Pauline writings. The inference is drawn that no-one who was a close companion of Paul's could have written Acts. Thus the speaking with 'tongues' on the Day of Pentecost seems different from what Paul means by 'tongues' in 1 Corinthians 14. Again, it is not easy to reconcile the statements about Paul's visits to Jerusalem in Acts 9:26; 11:30; 15:2 with those in Galatians 1:18; 2:1. Some draw attention to problems in reconciling the movements of Paul's companions in Acts 17:16; 18:5 and in 1 Thessalonians 3:1, 6, or in reconciling the statements about the guarding of Damascus (Acts 9:24; 2 Cor. 11:32). Close examination reveals little of substance in such objections. Difficulties of this type may well show that Acts was written in independence of the Pauline Epistles, but they scarcely show more. There are no real contradictions.

The real strength of the objection, however, concerns theology rather than narrative. The theology of Acts, objectors say, even in speeches attributed to Paul, is so very different from that of the apostle that it is out of the question that Acts could have been written by one of his companions. The classic expression of this argument seems to have been given by Philipp Vielhauer, who makes four main points.

1. In the Areopagus speech Luke makes Paul express the Stoic idea of natural theology. 'Due to its kinship to God the human race is capable of a natural knowledge of God and of ethics (Acts 10:35) and has immediate access to God. The "word of the cross" has no place in the Areopagus speech.'[1]

2. In Acts Paul is 'a Jewish Christian who is utterly loyal to the law'. More precisely he is 'a true Jew . . . in contrast to

---

[1]*SLA*, p. 37. This is from a translation of his essay of 1950–51 which seems to have set the pattern for much subsequent German thinking. Vielhauer's view has been further developed by Götz Harbsmeier, who holds that the church must always face the fixed alternative between Paul and Luke (*SLA*, pp. 68f.).

the Jews who have been hardened'.[1] He circumcises Timothy (16:3) and takes action to show that he conforms to the law (Acts 21:21ff.). The real Paul is implacably opposed to the doctrine of the law set forth in Acts.

3. The Christology of Acts is adoptionistic and pre-Pauline.

4. In Acts, 'Eschatology has been removed from the center of Pauline faith to the end and has become a "section on the last things." '[2]

But not all go along with this point of view. Vielhauer is scarcely just to all the evidence. Thus in the Areopagus passage he overlooks the fact that the speech follows much the same three points as Paul makes in 1 Thessalonians 1:9f., namely the importance of turning from idols to serve the true God, of the return of Christ for judgment, and of the resurrection of Jesus.[3] Again, it is not really fair to Luke to say that his report of the speech teaches that natural man is able to come to a saving knowledge of God.[4] The hearers of Paul's address did not come in fact to know God and in Luke-Acts ignorance of this kind is regarded as culpable. Thus Jesus prays for His ignorant executioners – their ignorance does not justify them (Lk. 23:34). Luke repeats that these executioners were ignorant, but guilty (Acts 3:17 with 2:23; 13:27f.). Again, Vielhauer does not give sufficient weight to that strand of Pauline teaching in which the apostle can say, 'To the Jews I became as a Jew, in order to win Jews' (1 Cor. 9:20). Nor does he allow sufficient weight to the consideration that it is highly unlikely that the apostle's mission preaching was in the same vein as his letters to churches.[5] It is also true, as Ellis

[1] *SLA*, p. 38.
[2] *SLA*, p. 45.
[3] J. Rohde reports U. Wilckens as making essentially this point (*Rediscovering the Teaching of the Evangelists* (London, 1968), p. 207).
[4] Ellis cites B. Gärtner and E. Norden as agreeing that this speech does not contradict Pauline teaching (Ellis, p. 46).
[5] *Cf.* C. F. D. Moule, 'it needs to be remembered that it is a priori likely that there should be differences between a speaker's initial presentation of the gospel to a non-Christian audience, and the same speaker's address to those who have already become Christians; and that, with rare exceptions, the Acts speeches belong to the former, while the Pauline epistles belong to the latter class' (*SLA*, p. 173). In the rare exceptions Acts 20:17ff. has Paul speaking to Christians and verse 28 has a very 'Pauline' reference to redemption. Passages in the Epistles such as Rom. 1:3, 4; 1 Cor. 15:1ff.; 1 Thes. 1:9f. recall evangelistic preaching and they approximate to the *kerygma* of Acts. G. Bornkamm finds some conflict between Acts and Paul, but he finds the incident of the vow (Acts 21:17ff.) authentic (*SLA*, pp. 204f.).

points out, that Paul 'never disparages the voluntary keeping of the Law by Jewish Christians'.[1] Vielhauer's point about Christology seems to be met by C. F. D. Moule's study, 'The Christology of Acts', in which he argues that the Christology of Acts is not uniform, but that Luke is apparently reproducing his sources pretty faithfully.[2]

As for eschatology, Ulrich Wilckens examines the view of many of our contemporaries that, in his endeavour to portray redemptive history, Luke has lost the emphasis on eschatology so typical of other early writers. He agrees that there is something in this. Luke is indeed interested in history and he does not have the same eschatological views as do some other New Testament writers. But he comes to this conclusion: 'It is Paul, interpreted existentially, who is so sharply set against Luke as the great but dangerous corrupter of the Pauline gospel. But the existentially interpreted Paul is not the historical Paul. And the essential points of theological criticism levelled against Luke are gained not so much from early Christian tradition itself as from the motifs of a certain modern school of theology which disregards or misinterprets essential aspects of early Christian thought.'[3] We are not compelled to choose between Luke and Paul.

This is a very important conclusion. The question is not whether there is a difference between Acts and the Epistles, but whether the right conclusion is being drawn from it. In history it has happened not infrequently that a close companion of a great man has given a picture of him different from that man's self-disclosure in his letters. Granted that the writer of Acts may well not have penetrated deeply into the distinctive Pauline theology, he is yet capable of reporting what Paul said and did, and he seems to have done so. All that the objection proves is that Luke was not another Paul, perhaps also that he had not seen any of Paul's Epistles. He was writing independently of the apostle.

We should, moreover, not overlook the fact that there is no evidence that Luke was converted by Paul. The probability is that he was not, and that he had reached Christian maturity

---

[1] Ellis, p. 44. He cites Rom. 14:20f.; 1 Cor. 7:18ff.; 9:20 and draws attention to Kirsopp Lake's view that 'in this respect Acts gives a faithful representation of St. Paul's own view' (*HDAC*, i, p. 29).

[2] *SLA*, pp. 159–185.

[3] *SLA*, p. 77.

before coming under Paul's influence. If so, we must not expect his theology to be a kind of diluted Paulinism. Moreover, if, as seems almost certain, he was a Gentile,[1] he may well have found some of Paul's rabbinic method of argument difficult to follow.

The differences between Acts and Paul may be used as an argument in favour of the Lucan authorship just as easily as against it. An author who was not one of Paul's companions would scarcely dare to write so extensively of the apostle without taking care to use the Epistles.[2] If it be contended that he did not know the Epistles, the further question arises, Why then did he write of Paul? Someone who knew neither Paul nor his letters would not make Paul the central figure in the Gentile mission. It is not sufficient to counter that he relied on a diary of a companion of Paul's, for 'Heroes are seldom made by reading other people's diaries'.[3]

A similar objection points out that in Acts 15 Paul accepts the decrees of the Council, including food laws, an attitude which is difficult to reconcile with his failure to mention these things in Galatians. However, if Galatians was written before the Council the objection loses its force. Paul could not have mentioned non-existent decrees. We cannot regard as decisive an objection which depends for its force on a particular view of the dating of Galatians.[4] Even if Galatians were

---

[1]His good Greek is not evidence for this, as a cultured Jew might well have a good grasp of the language. The case rests on the reference to Luke in distinction from those 'of the circumcision' (Col. 4:11, 14). This probably does mean that Luke was a Gentile, though some argue that the expression means Jews who were 'zealous for the law' in distinction from those who were lax. But to most this seems far-fetched. And apart from *amen* he avoids Semitic words. Again, he has little about the dispute between Jesus and the Pharisees over the law, a topic which would be interesting to a Jew, but less so to a Gentile. Reicke, however, thinks that Luke was probably Jewish (*The Gospel of Luke* (London, 1965), p. 22), as does Ellis (pp. 52f.).

[2]Morton S. Enslin, in his article 'Luke the Literary Physician' in *Studies in New Testament and Early Christian Literature*, ed. D. A. Aune (Leiden, 1972), pp. 135–143, contends that Luke did use these Epistles. Many will find his arguments unconvincing. But even if they are accepted it remains that there is no obvious use of the Epistles and this is significant. One would expect attention to be drawn to the use of the Epistles as a means of accrediting the writing.

[3]Ellis, p. 51.

[4]For the date of Galatians see the discussions in R. A. Cole, *The Epistle of Paul to the Galatians* (*TNTC*) (London, 1965), pp. 20–23, and in George S. Duncan, *The Epistle of Paul to the Galatians* (London, 1939), pp. xxi–xxxii.

written subsequent to the Council it is more than doubtful whether the objection will stand. More than one scholar has seen in the difference of viewpoint and interest an adequate explanation of the difference.[1]

From all this it seems that there is good reason for holding that Luke is the author of our Gospel (and of Acts). While the evidence falls short of final proof it is quite strong, and no suitable alternative has been suggested.

II. DATE

Three dates for this Gospel have been suggested with some seriousness, namely around AD 63, about AD 75–85 and early in the second century. The date is bound up with that of Acts, for Luke must be earlier than its sequel.[2]

For the early date the following considerations are relevant.

1. Acts ends with Paul in prison. If Luke knew of Paul's release or martyrdom he would probably have mentioned it.

2. The Pastorals seem to show that Paul visited Ephesus again. If Luke wrote after that date he would surely not have left Paul's prophecy that the Ephesians would not see him again (Acts 20:25, 38) stand without comment.

3. Luke notes the fulfilment of the prophecy of Agabus (Acts 11:28). If he were writing after AD 70 it is logical to expect him to mention somewhere the fulfilment of Jesus' prophecy that the city would be destroyed (Lk. 21:20).

4. Acts shows no knowledge of the Pauline Epistles so must be early. The fact that they were preserved shows that these letters were treasured and it is a fair inference that they would have become known not very long after they were written. Any Christian interested enough in Paul to write about him would have made use of them.

5. In Acts no event after AD 62 is mentioned. There are no references, for example, to the deaths of James (AD 62) or of Paul, or to the destruction of Jerusalem.

---

[1]For example, J. B. Lightfoot, *Saint Paul's Epistle to the Galatians* (London, 1902), p. 125; Herman N. Ridderbos, *The Epistle of Paul to the Churches of Galatia* (London, 1954), pp. 78f.

[2]Perhaps we should note that a few scholars have thought Acts earlier than Luke, at least in its present form. Thus C. S. C. Williams argues that Proto-Luke appeared first, then Acts, then our present Luke (*ET*, lxiv, 1952–53, pp. 283f.). Pierson Parker supports such a view (*JBL*, lxxxiv, 1965, pp. 52–58).

Not all evaluate this evidence the same way. It can be argued that these points mostly depend on our view of what Luke is or is not likely to have included and we may be wrong. Some accordingly hold that these considerations do not stand in the way of a latish date (W. G. Kümmel favours a date between AD 80 and 90,[1] and A. F. J. Klijn c. 80[2]). But to others the considerations adduced are weighty and E. M. Blaiklock, for example, thinks of a date c. AD 62,[3] F. F. Bruce not very long after c. AD 61 (which he sees as the date of Luke),[4] and Pierson Parker AD 62 or 63.[5] Bo Reicke holds that when Luke wrote Acts he knew nothing of events later than AD 62, so that Luke must be earlier than this.[6]

Those who favour a date c. AD 75–85 argue as follows.

1. Some sayings of Jesus, particularly in the eschatological discourse, seem to show that Luke was writing after the fall of Jerusalem (19:43; 21:20, 24). Thus, whereas Mark says, 'when you see the desolating sacrilege set up where it ought not to be' (Mk. 13:14), the Lucan equivalent is, 'when you see Jerusalem surrounded by armies' (21:20). But if this kind of reference is to be taken as a 'prophecy' manufactured after the fall of Jerusalem, it might equally be argued that other passages are unfulfilled or mistaken 'prophecies' uttered before it, *e.g.*, 'then they will see the Son of man coming in a cloud with power and great glory' (21:27). There is also the well-known fact that, in response to revelation, the Christian community fled from Jerusalem to Pella as the Romans approached.[7] This seems to show that, before the siege began, Christ's words were known and the command 'flee to the mountains' (21:21) was taken literally. Kümmel takes it as certain that 'Luke looks back upon the fall of Jerusalem' and he regards this as 'decisive' against an early date.[8] But he does not take 21:27 into account.

2. Luke used Mark and therefore must be later than *c.*

[1]W. G. Kümmel, *Introduction to the New Testament* (London, 1965), pp. 132f.
[2]A. F. J. Klijn, *An Introduction to the New Testament* (Leiden, 1967), p. 66.
[3]E. M. Blaiklock, *The Acts of the Apostles* (*TNTC*) (London, 1959), p. 17.
[4]F. F. Bruce, *The Acts of the Apostles* (London, 1951), p. 14.
[5]*Art. cit.*, p. 55.
[6]Aune, *op. cit.*, p. 134.
[7]Eusebius, *Historia Ecclesiastica* III. v. 3.
[8]W. G. Kümmel, *op. cit.*, p. 105. By contrast C. F. D. Moule is not impressed by the argument that Lk. 21:20 was written after the event (*The Birth of the New Testament* (London, 1962), p. 122).

AD 68, the earliest date most critics will allow for Mark (personally I think Mark should be dated somewhat earlier).

3. There is no good reason for dating Luke far from Matthew, and as the First Gospel is usually put into the 80s a similar date is required for Luke.

4. Luke tells us that many had written before him (1:1). But this could scarcely have taken place earlier than AD 70.

The argument usually relied on is that from prediction. Critics feel that a prophecy such as that about the fall of Jerusalem is likely to have been given its precise shape after the events, not before them. But this is very dubious. If Luke was shaping the prophecy after the event and making it fit the facts, why did he leave it so general? After all, to speak of a city as surrounded by armies shows no great knowledge. Even if we throw in the reference to casting up a bank (19:43) we get no farther, for this was normal siege technique.[1] The further question arises: If Luke is re-shaping the narrative in the light of events, why does not Matthew do the same? A much more likely explanation is that Jesus spoke both of 'the desolating sacrilege' and of the armies which would surround the city.[2] Matthew and Mark retain one expression and Luke the other. The interests of the authors probably explain their choice. Matthew speaks of the fulfilment of prophecy which would carry conviction to his readers, while Luke, writing for the Gentiles, chooses rather the words which speak of armies.[3]

The other points are no more convincing. A few scholars hold that Luke did not, in fact, use Mark. Most agree that he did, but the date of Mark is not known and not all scholars put it as late as AD 68. Again, there is no good reason for tying Luke's date to Matthew's. Even if we do it is far from certain that Matthew was written in the 80s. As for the view that 'many' could not have written before Luke unless we date him

[1]Bo Reicke is scathing about the view that this prophecy is *ex eventu*, calling it 'an amazing example of uncritical dogmatism in New Testament studies'. He argues that in none of the Synoptists does the prophecy correspond to what is known about the Jewish war and the destruction of Jerusalem (Aune, *op. cit.*, p. 121).

[2]F. Blass made this suggestion long ago. He regarded it as 'self-evident' that Jesus' speech was longer than the report of it in any one Gospel. See *Philology of the Gospels* (London, 1898), p. 46.

[3]Donald Guthrie reminds us that history knows of accurate predictions and he cites Savonarola's prophecy that Rome would be captured (*New Testament Introduction*[3] (London, 1970), p. 114). We should not minimize Jesus' ability to predict.

after about AD 70, this depends on the view that Christians took about forty years to start writing. But Paul was writing in the early 50s, probably indeed in the late 40s, and there is no reason for thinking he was the only one. Thus none of these arguments proves much. They turn out to be subjective estimates of the possibilities.

Recently some scholars have argued for a second-century date (*e.g.* J. Knox, J. C. O'Neill). Such views put the Gospel dangerously close to the time of Marcion, who based his canon on an expurgated version of Luke. Knox holds that Marcion did not use Luke but an earlier writing, which as it happens was also used by Luke.[1] But the orthodox based their attack on Marcion on the view that his Gospel was based on the canonical Luke. They were highly vulnerable if it was not. Those who hold to a late date but yet see Marcion as using Luke are faced with the difficult problem of explaining how Luke's Gospel could, within ten to twenty years, have gained enough authority for Marcion to be able to gain a following by relying on it alone.

The view that Luke is late is sometimes bolstered by an appeal to statements in Acts which are thought to have been taken from the Jewish historian Josephus. His *Antiquities* was published *c.* AD 93, so that if Luke depended on it he wrote late. The first of such passages is that in which Josephus says that Theudas rebelled during the governorship of Fadus, 44–46. He was overthrown and the next governor, Alexander (46–48), executed some of the sons of Judas the Galilean. Luke reports Gamaliel as speaking of Theudas followed by Judas. Notice it is Judas, not the sons of Judas, and Gamaliel is speaking some twelve years before Theudas rebelled. If Luke is depending on Josephus here he has misquoted him.

The other statement concerns Lysanias (Lk. 3:1). A man of this name was tetrarch of Abilene, but was executed by Mark Antony in 36 (or 34) BC. Again Luke has made a mistake if he is relying on Josephus. However there is some evidence that there was another Lysanias[2] and it will be this man to whom Luke refers.

[1] *SLA*, p. 287, n. 8. J. C. O'Neill has argued his case in ch. I of *The Theology of Acts*[2] (London, 1970).
[2] W. Ramsay cites an inscription from Abilene referring to this Lysanias between AD 14 and 29. He sees 'absolutely no justification for the unreasonable charge that this dating in Luke III. 1 was wrong' (*The Bearing of Recent Discovery on the Trustworthiness of the New Testament* (London, 1895), p. 298). See further the note on 3:1.

Clearly neither of these examples shows that Luke had read Josephus. Hans Conzelmann rejects the idea that Luke is dependent on Josephus (though he is not averse to a later date for Acts).[1] Indeed, the presumption is all the other way, for Luke is normally accurate in the places where he can be tested. It is unlikely that he will have taken these two statements from Josephus and made an error both times.[2] I cannot see that the evidence for a second-century date has much to be said for it.

On the whole, then, there seems most to be said for a date in the early 60s. The evidence comes short of complete proof, but there seems more to be said for this view than for either of the others.

III. LANGUAGE

Linguistically this Gospel falls into three sections. The Preface (1:1–4) is written in good classical style. It shows what Luke was capable of,[3] but thereafter he forsakes this style altogether. The rest of chapter 1 and chapter 2 have a strongly Hebraic flavour. So marked is this that a number of scholars have come to the conclusion that we have here a translation from an original Hebrew. If so we have no way of knowing whether Luke or someone else did the translating.

From 3:1 on the Gospel is written in a type of Hellenistic Greek which is strongly reminiscent of the Septuagint, the translation into Greek of the Hebrew Old Testament. The vocabulary is extensive, and Luke uses 266 words (other than proper names) which are not found elsewhere in the New Testament, quite a remarkable number when we consider that

---

[1] *SLA*, p. 299.

[2] F. J. Foakes Jackson makes the point that there is little in Josephus that is relevant to Luke's purpose. It is hard to see why he should spend time on a book which would give him so little information (*The Acts of the Apostles* (London, 1937), pp. xivf.). There is no reason for thinking that Luke had ever read Josephus.

[3] For the conventions adopted in writing prefaces see H. J. Cadbury, *The Style and Literary Method of Luke*, pp. 194ff. He points out that the preface shows that the work was meant for a public (*ibid.*, p. 204). It stamps the work as literature, and shows that it was not originally intended, for example, for liturgical purposes.

he shares much of his subject-matter with Matthew and Mark.[1]

The most interesting thing about all this is the way the style is so constantly reminiscent of the Septuagint. Luke's Old Testament quotations are commonly from that version, and he normally uses the forms of proper names found there. Much of his characteristic vocabulary is apparently drawn from the Septuagint, as are some of his striking phrases.[2] It seems that Luke thought of the style of the Septuagint as good biblical style and most appropriate for the kind of narrative he was composing.

But this does not explain everything. Sometimes Luke's language contains Hebraisms and sometimes Aramaisms.[3] Again, in some places his language is more Semitic than others.[4] Both sets of facts seem better explained as reflecting Luke's sources.[5] As E. Earle Ellis points out, 'it is difficult to see why the story of the Palestinian Church (Ac. 1–12) should be more "flavoured" than Jesus' Galilean mission or Paul's Jerusalem speech (Ac. 22).'[6] It seems much more likely that in such places Luke is keeping close to a Semitic source.[7]

[1]The corresponding figures for Matthew and Mark are 116 and 79 respectively. See R. Morgenthaler, *Statistik des Neutestamentlichen Wortschätzes* (Frankfurt am Main, 1958), p. 170. Luke has another 60 words which are found elsewhere in the New Testament only in Acts, while Acts has 415 peculiar to itself. The figures differ only slightly from those given by Sir John Hawkins in *Horae Synopticae* (Oxford, 1909), pp. 198ff.

[2]See the examination by H. F. D. Sparks, *JTS*, xliv, 1943, pp. 129ff.

[3]Sometimes we can speak only of Semitisms where the two languages have similar constructions. But in some points they differ, and Luke reflects both. See Creed, pp. lxxix–lxxxi.

[4]X. Léon-Dufour stresses this variability. He thinks that Luke 'to a Greek ear was at once refined and often vulgar' (*Introduction to the New Testament*, ed. A. Robert and A. Feuillet (New York, 1965), p. 223). He notes that Luke sometimes corrects Mark's vulgarisms, but now and then alters good Greek into what is worse. He wonders whether Luke is reproducing a source (*ibid.*, p. 224).

[5]So F. F. Bruce, *The Acts of the Apostles*, pp. 18–21; M. Wilcox, *The Semitisms of Acts* (Oxford, 1965), pp. 180–184.

[6]Ellis, p. 3.

[7]E. P. Sanders, in a careful examination of the evidence, shows that Semitisms can be late as well as early (*The Tendencies of the Synoptic Tradition* (Cambridge, 1969), pp. 190–255). He concludes that no argument as to date can safely be drawn from Semitisms. In the light of the evidence he adduces it is difficult to see how his conclusion is to be resisted. But he agrees that 'it would be impossible completely to invalidate' the position that in the New Testament Semitisms are more likely to be 'remnants of the original language' than features introduced into an original Greek relatively free from Semitisms (*ibid.*, p. 199). In the present case it is not unlikely that Luke's Semitisms point us to an early source or sources.

Perhaps this is the place to notice that we must always bear in mind that our Evangelists are reporting in a language other than that originally used by Jesus and the disciples. It is usually agreed that Jesus' native tongue was Aramaic (though this is not quite certain).[1] Some of the differences between the Synoptists are no doubt due to different ways of translating from the original, and some of the unusual Greek constructions are no doubt reflections of constructions which were quite at home in the original Semitic.

IV. LUKE THE THEOLOGIAN

People used to write books and articles with titles such as 'Luke the Historian'. Discussion centred round the question of whether Luke was a good or a bad historian, but that he did intend to write history was normally accepted. But in recent times many scholars have given attention to the deep theological purpose that plainly underlies Luke-Acts. Luke is now commonly regarded as one of the theologians of the New Testament[2] and he is seen as more interested in conveying religious and theological truth than he is in writing a history. Indeed, so far has the pendulum swung that many suggest that Luke's interest in theology was so great that he allowed it to sway his historical judgment. In other words they say that Luke was prepared to alter his history a little if it would bring out his theological points.

We might begin our discussion of this point by noticing that Luke has not left us in the dark about what he is trying to do. He tells us that he has followed 'all things' closely for some time and that he now writes to Theophilus 'that you may know the truth concerning the things of which you have been informed' (1:4). 'This', F. C. Grant writes, 'is as clear and straightforward as the codicil in John 20.30f . . . his business was to clear up points of misunderstanding or misrepresenta-

[1] Some hold that Jesus would have spoken Hebrew. See, for example, the discussion by James Barr, *BJRL*, 53, 1970–71, pp. 9–29. It is not unlikely that He knew Greek, and if so some of His sayings may be reported in the language in which they were originally spoken. But there is every reason for holding that in most cases the original was Aramaic or Hebrew.

[2] James D. G. Dunn, for example, regards Luke as one of 'the three major New Testament theologians' (*ET*, lxxxiv, 1972–73, p. 7; Paul and John are the others).

tion which had (presumably) arisen in the pagan world and even (perhaps) in the courts of Roman magistrates.'[1]

But not all have seen his role in this way. Some of the Form Critics, for example, have seen Luke as little more than a compiler, an editor who wrote down a series of unconnected incidents and sayings (they see Matthew and Mark the same way).

Form Criticism was called by Vincent Taylor 'the child of disappointment'.[2] It arose after critics felt they had taken the two-document hypothesis[3] as far as they could. It was a serious attempt to go behind the written sources to the time when information about Jesus circulated only in oral tradition. Parts only of the information about Jesus and His teaching would be preserved out of the very large mass of material at first available. As stories and sayings were told and re-told they assumed certain fixed forms. It is the study of these forms which gives Form Criticism its name. Some stories, for example, culminate in a striking saying and appear to be told for the sake of the saying. The details of the story are not important, but the saying is. R. Bultmann calls these 'Apophthegmata' and Vincent Taylor, 'Pronouncement Stories'. Such stories are manifestly different in form from miracle stories. Other 'forms' are also detected.

The study of the forms in which oral tradition circulated is obviously of value. But most Form Critics go further than that. They assume that the purveyors of oral tradition were so interested in the needs of their own day that they saw Jesus not as He was,[4] but as He spoke to their own contemporary needs. In other words they read back into the teaching of Jesus what they saw was needed in their own situation.[5]

---

[1]F. C. Grant, in *Current Issues in New Testament Interpretation*, ed. W. Klassen and G. F. Snyder (London, 1962), p. 83.

[2]V. Taylor, *The Gospels* (London, 1930), p. 16.

[3]For a discussion of this hypothesis see pp. 48ff.

[4]They usually overlook the point made by W. Barclay, 'their (i.e. the Form Critics') one mistake is their failure to see that the gospel writers sought to awaken faith by showing Jesus as he was' (*The First Three Gospels* (London, 1966), p. 115).

[5]Joachim Rohde includes among the 'most important insights and presuppositions of the form-critical method' the following statement: 'The Synoptic gospels are not biographies in the historical sense, but testimonies to the faith of primitive Christianity', and further, 'The Easter faith of the community did not remain without influence on the accounts of Jesus' life' (*Rediscovering the Teaching of the Evangelists*, p. 5).

This is clearly going beyond a study of the forms. A further assumption of these critics is that the tradition was transmitted in isolated units: there was no connected narrative. The Form Critics speak of the destruction of the framework of the life of Jesus. When the Evangelists began to write their Gospels, on this understanding, they were confronted with a series of unconnected units which they perforce put together like beads on a string. This took away all possibility of seeing movement and development in the story of Jesus. The Form Critics are usually somewhat sceptical. They are so sure that what we have in oral tradition is Jesus as the early church saw Him that they often conclude we have no means of knowing what the historical Jesus really was like at all.

These critics have rendered the church a service by drawing attention to the importance of the oral stage in the transmission of the life and teaching of Jesus. There is also much that can be learnt by the study of the forms in which the narratives are cast. But the Form Critics seem to have made some serious errors. For example, their insistence that the church read back its own concerns into the teaching of Jesus overlooks the fact that the topics of the Gospels are not the topics that occupied the early church, topics such as the place of the Gentiles in the Christian church, what to do in persecutions, the place of ministers, the exercise of the gifts of the Spirit and the like. Again, these critics ascribe to the community the power to create the memorable sayings of the Gospels, quite ignoring the fact that in history it is great individuals, not committees, that produce striking language. Moreover Paul at any rate was careful to distinguish between his own teaching and that of the Lord (1 Cor. 7:10, 25), a fact that creates the presumption that the early church did not indiscriminately read back its own teaching on to the lips of Jesus. The Form Critics took little account of the way first-century Palestinian teachers went to work. The rabbis used to cast their teaching into forms suitable for memorization and insist that their pupils learn it by heart. It is accordingly relevant that much of Jesus' teaching has a poetic form suitable for this purpose.

For such reasons many recent scholars, while thankfully acknowledging the contribution the Form Critics have made, feel they have gone too far. The evidence does not sustain their sceptical conclusions.

More recently there has emerged a new discipline, namely Redaction Criticism, or Editorial Criticism. This insists that the Evangelists must be understood as real authors, not simply as scissors-and-paste men, who did no more than take material from their sources and string it together. The Evangelists had their reasons for their arrangements and they had their reasons for the particular way in which they worded their incidents and reports of teaching.

As far as Luke is concerned the great name is that of Hans Conzelmann. He argues that Luke is concerned to write about the story of salvation and this he sees in three stages:

1. The period of Israel (16:16).

2. The period of Jesus' ministry (4:16ff.; Acts 10:38).

3. The period since the ascension, *i.e.* the period of the church.[1]

The German title of Conzelmann's work, *Die Mitte der Zeit* ('The Middle of Time'), sums up the author's position admirably. He holds that Luke sees Jesus as absolutely central and that he writes his Gospel out of that conviction. Conzelmann sees it as a work dominated by theology. Luke's geography, for example, is not to be taken seriously. Conzelmann doubts whether Luke knew Palestine at first hand, but in any case he sees his use of geographical terms as symbolic and theological. Thus the Jordan is simply the sphere of John the Baptist.[2] Again, it is 'pointless to attempt to locate' the desert in which the temptation took place, since this is only a symbol of the separation between Jordan and Galilee.[3] This approach to geography is a major emphasis of Conzelmann's and he develops it throughout Part One of his book.

This kind of approach is open to legitimate criticism. Many feel, for example, that Conzelmann's structure is an artificial one which Luke would never have recognized. It is further objected that he builds far too confidently and far too much on his exegesis of a particularly difficult verse in Luke 16:16.

Again, Conzelmann's strictures on Luke's geography are made without reference to Acts. Here we find that the Mount of Olives is a sabbath day's journey from Jerusalem (Acts

---

[1] H. Conzelmann, *The Theology of St Luke* (London, 1960), p. 16.
[2] *Ibid.*, p. 20.
[3] *Ibid.*, p. 27.

1:12) and that the field where Judas perished bore the name Akeldama (Acts 1:19). The author knows of the Beautiful Gate of the Temple and of Solomon's colonnade (Acts 3:10, 11). He refers to an official called 'the captain of the temple' (Acts 4:1), and again to the road from Jerusalem to Gaza which he knows is a desert road (Acts 8:26). His description of the prison from which Peter escaped seems to presuppose local knowledge (Acts 12:10), as does his awareness of the meeting-place of the local group of Christians (Acts 12:12). He knows that the seat of Roman government was Caesarea (Acts 12:19; 23:23–26) and that there was a cohort stationed in Jerusalem (Acts 21:31). He speaks quite naturally of the steps leading up to the tower of Antonia (Acts 21:40). He can locate Caesarea as two days' journey from Jerusalem (Acts 23:23, 31, 32; the distance is 62 miles). There are not as many verifiable references in the Gospel, but while all his references cannot be checked, Luke does speak consistently as though he knows where the places of which he is writing are located (see 1:26, 39; 4:31; 7:11; 8:26; 9:10; 19:29, 37). It is perhaps worth noting that Bultmann discerned no such geographical scheme as Conzelmann postulates, for he says, 'Luke's *geography* for the Galilean ministry is throughout the same as Mark's.'[1]

But when full allowance has been made for just criticism, the new approach is to be welcomed insofar as it takes seriously the work done by the Evangelists. It can help us to look for those dominant theological considerations that swayed the Gospel writers and induced them to write. It is surely important that we see with them what God has done, as well as what happened on what day so long ago.

But the new movement can be as sceptical as the old. It is possible to argue that, whereas the Form Critics hid Jesus behind the community, the Redaction Critics have hidden Him behind the authors. In other words, the Gospels can now be approached with the assumption that we cannot see Jesus as He was, but only as Matthew or Mark or Luke or John saw Him.

But this kind of scepticism is not necessary. It is possible to see the Evangelists as theologians and still as men with a

---

[1]R. Bultmann, *The History of the Synoptic Tradition* (Oxford, 1963), pp. 363f. (Bultmann's emphasis). I. Howard Marshall examines and rejects Conzelmann's conclusions on geography (*Luke: Historian and Theologian* (Exeter, 1970), pp 70f.).

profound respect for history. I have elsewhere argued that in the Fourth Gospel John the Baptist is beyond all doubt depicted from one point of view only, that of a witness to Jesus. The Evangelist is certainly making a theological point in his references to the Baptist. But one consequence of the study of the Dead Sea scrolls has been to show that there is some parallel there to practically every piece of teaching ascribed to John in the Fourth Gospel. This has convinced some hard-headed critics that that Gospel must now be regarded as a valuable historical source for John the Baptist.[1] The same I suggest is true elsewhere.

Specifically it is the case with Luke. His writings, and more particularly Acts, have been subjected to a very close scrutiny. They have been compared with those of other early writers and the results of archaeological research have been taken into account. While it would not be true to say that all the problems have been solved, there is widespread recognition that Luke is a reliable historian.[2] His theological purpose is real. We should not miss it. But his theology does not run away with his history. Even Rudolf Bultmann can say, 'he does not permit his dogmatic conceptions to exercise any essential influence on his work.'[3] It is well known that Sir William Ramsay began his researches convinced that Luke was a poor historian, but he was led by the facts to see him as first rate. These words of his should not be overlooked: 'No writer is correct by mere chance, or accurate sporadically. He is accurate by virtue of a certain habit of mind. Some men are accurate by nature: some are by nature loose and inaccurate. It is not a permissible view that a writer is accurate occasion-

---

[1] See my *Studies in the Fourth Gospel* (Exeter, 1969), pp. 110ff.

[2] This is far from universal and many recent critics, particularly among the Germans, would demur.

[3] R. Bultmann, *op. cit.*, p. 366. He goes on to say, 'that can hardly be called meritorious, for he has obviously not adopted a strongly marked position with specific tendencies.' I do not agree with this, but the interesting thing is that, whether it be meritorious or not, Luke has not allowed his 'dogmatic conceptions' to dominate his work. He is too good a historian. Nils A. Dahl has this to say about Luke's history and theology: 'He keeps rather close to his sources and wants to respect what he assumes to have been the historical facts. Yet, by means of redaction, rearrangement, and some minor changes, he is able to write history in such a way that he simultaneously sets forth his theology' (*SLA*, p. 154). J. H. Ropes also insists that Luke does not 'distort the history' (*The Synoptic Gospels* (London, 1960), p. 84).

ally, and inaccurate in other parts of his book. Each has his
own standard and measure of work, which is produced by
his moral and intellectual character.'[1] As Luke can be
demonstrated to be accurate often (as in the tricky nomen-
clature of officials in Acts), we should see him as one of Ramsay's accurate writers.

Some find valuable a distinction between different kinds
of historian. Thus C. K. Barrett makes the point that Luke was
not a historian 'of the modern scientific kind . . . but a historian
of the Hellenistic age'. This appears to mean that he was
interested in things other than facts. But Barrett goes on to
say that this 'does not mean that Luke is not to be taken
seriously as a writer of history; the distinction between fact
and fiction was understood long before he wrote'.[2] Thompson
brings out this point by emphasizing that Luke does conform to
the accepted canons for history writing. He points out that
Lucian wrote an essay entitled 'How to Write History', and
that, while he is later than Luke (c. AD 170), he does show us
the kind of thing educated people would have looked for in
New Testament times. It is therefore important that his
criteria include truth and impartiality. Thompson sums up,
'Judged by the criteria for historical writing that Lucian lays
down, Luke would in his contemporary world be thought to
attain a high standard as a historian, and would compare
favourably with other literary men of his day.'[3] Luke then was
a good historian, though it is helpful to bear in mind that he
was not trying to write the kind of history our modern scientific
historians try to write. As Barrett further says, he was 'one of
the biblical writers who confront us with a more than human
testimony to Jesus Christ'.[4] This does not mean carelessness

[1]W. Ramsay, *The Bearing of Recent Discovery on the Trustworthiness of the
New Testament*, p. 80. He further says, 'The present writer takes the view
that Luke's history is unsurpassed in respect of its trustworthiness' (*ibid.*,
p. 81). We should not, of course, understand Ramsay to mean that if a
writer can be shown to be accurate in some places he is to be trusted
everywhere. Obviously even a careful writer can make a mistake. But his
point is valid against those who see Luke as careless about accuracy. When
at point after point a writer can be shown to be accurate, this must be taken
to indicate his cast of mind.
[2]C. K. Barrett, *Luke the Historian in Recent Study*, p. 9. This does not
prevent Barrett from thinking of Luke as in error on some points, for example
in giving a picture of the early church which lacks controversy among its
leaders (*ibid.*, p. 74).
[3]Thompson, p. 16.
[4]C. K. Barrett, *loc. cit.*

about fact, but it does mean that the facts are recorded not
for their own sake, but in fulfilment of a religious and theological purpose. We may see something of that purpose from
the following points.

1. *Salvation history*. It is usual to see Luke as the theologian
of what the Germans call *Heilsgeschichte*.[1] He sets his narrative
in the context of secular history more firmly than does any
of the other Evangelists (2:1f.; 3:1), and he sees God's action
in Christ as the great, central intervention of God in the
affairs of men whereby man's salvation is worked out (Acts
2:36; 4:10-12; 17:30f.). Jesus Christ is the focus of all history
(*cf.* the title of Conzelmann's work, *Die Mitte der Zeit*, 'The
Middle of Time').[2] Luke emphasizes that salvation has become
present in Christ with a frequent use of the adverbs 'now' and
'today'. He uses 'now' 14 times (Matthew 4 times, Mark 3
times) and 'today' 11 times (Matthew 8 times, Mark once). In
Jesus the time of salvation has come.

Luke's view of salvation history does not stop at the ascension. He sees God's act as continuing in the proclamation
of the gospel and in the life of the church. The Jews have a
special place in the divine economy and to the end it is 'the
hope of Israel' that the gospel preachers proclaim (Acts
28:20). But the Jews rejected their Messiah. This did not
mean that God was defeated. Indeed, it was the occasion
for an enlargement of His triumph in the proclamation of the
gospel to the Gentiles. But the gospel had first to be offered
to the Jews. It was their refusal of God's good gift which
meant that the church became predominantly Gentile (Acts

[1]It is difficult to find an adequate English equivalent. C. K. Barrett
objects that ' "Redemptive history" suggests that history redeems, and
"history of salvation" suggests that salvation is an institution' (*From First
Adam to Last* (London, 1962), p. 4, n.). As to what Luke was doing, H.
Flender sees him as confronted with a threefold task: 'First, he had to
preserve the unique character of the Christ event in on-going history.
Secondly, there was the problem of historical continuity between Israel
and the Church. Thirdly, there was the problem of how to describe the
presence of salvation in the Christian community as it passes through time'
(*St Luke, Theologian of Redemptive History* (London, 1967), p. 91). *Cf.* also
the discussion by J. Reumann (*SE*, iv, pp. 86–115).
[2]C. F. Evans sees Luke as bringing out the truth that Jesus was the
prophet like Moses of Dt. 18:15 by modelling his great central section
(9:51 – 18:14) on Deuteronomy ('The Central Section of St. Luke's
Gospel' in *Studies in the Gospels*, ed. D. E. Nineham (Oxford, 1967), pp.
37–53).

13:46ff.). James specifically includes Gentiles in 'a people for his name' (Acts 15:14).

All this springs from the love and the grace of God. Luke delights to bring out the way God's love is shown to a variety of people. As noted in the opening section, it is possibly this which makes the Third Gospel such an attractive piece of writing. God's salvation is not rootless. It springs from His great love for men.

2. *Universality of salvation*. We see the breadth of that great love of God in the universality of the salvation of which Luke writes. The very word 'salvation' is absent from Matthew and Mark and occurs but once in John. Luke, however, used *sōtēria* four times and *sōtērion* twice (another seven examples of the two words occur in Acts, a total of thirteen). He also uses the term 'Saviour' twice (and twice more in Acts), and he employs the verb 'to save' more often than does any other Evangelist. I. Howard Marshall sees this interest in salvation as critically important: 'It is our thesis that the idea of salvation supplies the key to the theology of Luke.'[1]

Nor is it only a matter of statistics. Luke tells us that the message of the angel concerned men in general, not specially Israel (2:14). He takes the genealogy of Jesus right back to Adam (3:38), the progenitor of mankind, and does not stop at Abraham, the father of the Jewish nation (as Matthew does). He tells us about Samaritans, for example when the disciples wanted to call down fire on them (9:51–54), or in the well-known parable of the good Samaritan (10:30–37), or in the information that the grateful leper was of this race (17:16). He refers to Gentiles in the song of Simeon (2:32) and tells us that Jesus spoke approvingly of non-Israelites such as the widow of Zarephath and Naaman the Syrian (4:25–27). He tells us about the healing of a centurion's slave (7:2–10). He records words about people coming from all the directions of the compass to sit in God's kingdom (13:29) and the great commission that the gospel be preached to all nations (24:47). It is generally held that his story of the mission of the seventy (10:1–20) has relevance to the Gentiles. It is clear that Luke has a deep interest in God's concern for all people.

We should not, however, understand this as though he meant that all will be saved. He sees the church as existing in a

[1] I. H. Marshall, *Luke: Historian and Theologian*, p. 92.

hostile world. He distinguishes 'the sons of this world' from 'the sons of light' (16:8; *cf.* 12:29f., 51ff.). The gospel is freely offered to all men, but they have a responsibility to repent and they will be judged in due course (Acts 17:30f.). Judgment is a not infrequent theme in this Gospel (*cf.* 12:13ff.; 17:26ff.).

Nor should we understand it as though it means a playing down of the importance of Israel in God's purpose. One of the fascinating things about Luke's writing is the way this Gentile emphasizes the importance of the Temple and of Jerusalem. He begins and ends his Gospel with people in the Temple at Jerusalem in contrast with the 'Jewish' Gospel of Matthew whose opening scene stresses the place of the Gentile magi and who ends with a commission in Galilee to go into all the world. He speaks of Jesus as presented in the Temple as a baby and visiting it as a boy. It recurs as the climax of Luke's temptation narrative and as the place for the climax of Jesus' work for men. In between, a considerable section of the Gospel is taken up with a journey to Jerusalem (9:51 – 19:45; note the emphasis on Jerusalem as the destination, 9:51, 53; 13:22; 17:11; 18:31; 19:28; *cf.* 13:33f.). All told he refers to Jerusalem 31 times as against 13 times in Matthew, 10 times in Mark and 12 times in John. The universalism of Luke is real, but we should not let it hide from us a very real 'Jewishness'.[1]

3. *Eschatology*. Luke writes of a great salvation and a salvation that avails through eternity as well as through time. Some scholars, it is true, hold that he plays down the eschatological motif.[2] The other Gospels, they hold, are written in the expectation that Christ would return soon and set up the kingdom of God, an expectation shared by Paul and others. But Luke writes when the vivid expectation has died down. For him the return of Christ is no longer imminent. 'One does not write the history of the church if one daily expects the end of the world.'[3]

This whole thesis should, however, be looked at more

[1]This is stressed in G. W. H. Lampe's Ethel M. Wood Lecture, *St Luke and the Church of Jerusalem* (London, 1969).

[2]Thus E. Käsemann says that, in Luke, 'Eschatology is replaced by a salvation history which is remarkably well organized and connected but which, in spite of the sheen imparted to it by miracles, remains confined within the limits of immanence' (*New Testament Questions of Today* (London, 1969), p. 21).

[3]Käsemann, cited in *SLA*, p. 24.

critically than it often is. In the first place it is not clear that the thought of the near return of Christ did in fact dominate the thinking of the first Christians. No doubt they looked for the Lord's coming, but we must always bear in mind the point made so neatly by W. C. van Unnik, 'The faith of the early Christians did not rest on a date but on the work of Christ.'[1] The church certainly looked for an interval before the return of Christ, as is shown, for example, by the fact that no Christian ever advocated that the preaching of the gospel should cease when Christ died. Jesus called men to preach the gospel and there is not the slightest hint that this was to be only during His lifetime. On any showing the church expected an interval, and its duration is nowhere specified. While the delay of the parousia was a problem, it seems to have been less so to the members of the early church than to some modern expositors.

Then, in the second place, it is not at all clear that Luke was not interested in eschatology. The contrary is demonstrated by passages such as 12:35ff.; 17:22ff.; 21:25ff., *etc.* He has the thought of imminent judgment (3:9, 17; 18:7f.) and of the nearness of the kingdom (10:9, 11; in the latter verse Luke includes the words 'the kingdom of God has come near' which are not in the Matthean parallel, Mt. 10:14).[2] Luke may not have quite the same emphasis as some other New Testament writers, but the point must not be overstated. Bo Reicke will not concede even so much. He can say, 'It is a mystery how Luke can be accused of "de-eschatologizing" in his Gospel'; and again, 'it is not at all true that Luke represents Jesus and the kingdom of God in a lesser eschatological light than the other Synoptists.'[3] He develops the point that Luke stresses the

[1] *SLA*, p. 28. Rohde cites Hans-Werner Bartsch for the view that Luke is concerned not to oppose the imminent expectation of the parousia, but the identification of the resurrection with the parousia (*Rediscovering the Teaching of the Evangelists*, p. 187). While I would not wish to endorse Bartsch's thesis, the fact that he can take up such a position shows that Luke's abandonment of the imminent expectation of the parousia is not nearly as obvious as some critics suppose.

[2] *Cf.* C.F.D. Moule, 'It is not that Luke does not expect a Day of Judgment and a coming of the Lord: about these he is as explicit as anybody' (*The Birth of the New Testament*, p. 170; he goes on to note that Luke is 'primarily concerned with a positive estimate of the intervening period').

[3] B. Reicke, *The Gospel of Luke*, pp. 77, 76. A. J. Mattill, Jr. is another who stresses Luke's eschatological interest. Indeed he argues that Luke saw himself as helping forward the Pauline mission and thus expediting an essential part of the eschatological plan (*CBQ*, xxxiv, 1972, pp. 276–293).

idea of joy at the closeness of salvation and he finds in this genuine eschatology. C. H. Talbert is another who insists that Luke is interested in eschatology. He finds 'two dominant eschatological emphases in Luke-Acts. One is the proclamation that the End is near ... the other ... is the attempt to prevent a misinterpretation of the Jesus-tradition ... to the effect that the eschaton had been and could be fully experienced in the present'.[1]

It thus seems a misreading of the evidence to see Luke as uninterested in eschatology. On the contrary, he looks for the coming of the End when the salvation of which he writes will reach its consummation.

4. *Early Catholicism.* Some miss the thrust of what Luke is saying by holding that he has institutionalized Christianity, or at least that he writes as a representative of institutional religion. In course of time the church did, of course, settle down as an institution. It lost the first fine flush of enthusiastic proclamation of the gospel and eager expectation of the Lord's return. It became interested in questions of order and sacramental practice, and generally in all that makes for the institutional side of Christianity. The result is called 'early Catholicism' by many scholars and they see Luke as one of its first exponents. Unfortunately not all are agreed as to what the term means. This makes it very difficult to say whether this is a feature of Luke's treatment or not. What can be said is that many competent critics have come to the conclusion that Luke is very faithful to his sources,[2] so that he is carefully depicting what the sources say rather than what happened in his own day. Talbert sees Luke as crystallizing the apostolic tradition in his two volumes and as writing in careful order with a view to refuting certain heretical views.[3]

[1]C. H. Talbert, *Jesus and Man's Hope* (Pittsburgh Theological Seminary, 1970), p. 191.
[2]For example, Nils A. Dahl, *SLA*, p. 154; *cf.* Henry J. Cadbury, 'Luke evidently reproduced his sources faithfully, in general purport though not in wording' (*The Making of Luke-Acts*, p. 365). The whole argument of Vincent Taylor's *The Passion Narrative of St Luke* (Cambridge, 1972) presupposes that Luke is faithful to his sources; otherwise they could not be disentangled. *Cf.* also Caird, 'We thus arrive at the interesting and important conclusion that, where Luke's modern detractors have thought him a careless historian, the sum of his fault has usually been that he was meticulously following his sources' (p. 29).
[3]C. H. Talbert, *op. cit.*, pp. 206ff.

We may agree that Luke was writing to meet the needs of his day without drawing the conclusion that he reflects only his own situation. As Talbert also reminds us, we must not be so busy asking why Luke added Acts to his Gospel that we forget to ask why he prefixed his Gospel to Acts. Clearly he was interested in Christianity's historical base. It will not do simply to see Luke as setting out a conventional treatment of the institutional religion of his own day. He saw God's plan in the church around him, but he saw it also in the Old Testament and in the coming of Jesus. He was not so much an institution man as a man who included the institution in the over-arching purpose of God.

5. *The plan of God.* Luke saw God as working out a great plan in the affairs of men. We have already noted his frequent use of various words to denote 'purpose' to bring out the thought of a divine necessity as operative in Jesus' ministry.[1] The purpose was seen supremely in the cross (Acts 2:23; 3:13; 5:30f., *etc.*). Luke also brings it out with his many references to the fulfilment of prophecy (Lk. 4:21; 24:44, *etc.*). He was clear that men do not defeat God. He was clear also that God is not some remote Olympian, aloof from men and careless as to their fate. The God Luke knows is interested in men's salvation and He is constantly operative in the affairs of men to bring to pass His redemptive purpose.

6. *Individuals.* In working out that great redemptive purpose Luke thought of God as concerned with people. He did not think of the divine purpose as appearing only in great movements of nations and peoples: it operated in the lives of humble men and women, for even the little people matter to God. So he has much to say about individuals, often people not mentioned elsewhere. He tells us of Zechariah and Elizabeth, of Mary and Martha, of Zacchaeus, of Cleopas and his companion. He tells of the woman who anointed Jesus' feet in the home of Simon the Pharisee, and of others. An interesting point emerges from the study of the parables he records. Whereas in Matthew the parables centre on the kingdom, in Luke they tend to stress persons. Luke is interested in people.

7. *The importance of women.* An important part of God's concern for people is that it is manifested towards groups not

[1] See above, pp. 13f.

highly esteemed in first-century society, women, children, the poor, the disreputable. For example, he gives a significant place to women. In the first century women were kept very much in their place. But Luke sees them as the objects of God's love and he writes about many of them. In the infancy stories he tells of Mary, the mother of Jesus, and of Elizabeth and Anna. Later he writes also of Martha and her sister Mary (10:38–42), of Mary Magdalene and Joanna and Susanna (8:2f.). He refers to women whom he does not name, such as the widow of Nain (7:11f.), the sinner who anointed Jesus' feet (7:37ff.), the little old bent woman (13:11), the widow who gave all she had to God (21:1–4) and the 'Daughters of Jerusalem' who lamented for Jesus as He went to the cross (23:27ff.). Sometimes women turn up also in the parables, as in that of the lost coin (15:8ff.) or the unjust judge (18:1ff.).

8. *Children*. The most obvious example of Luke's concern for children is the infancy stories. Of course, an interest in children is not the only reason for these stories. Luke is concerned to emphasize that God's plan was being fulfilled in the birth and early life of John and of Jesus. He reminds us of the fulfilment of prophecy in connection with these events. But it is interesting that he finds God's plan in events that concern children. Matthew tells us something of the birth of Jesus and he alone relates the visit of the wise men, but Luke gives us most of our information about those early days. He also tells us something of the circumstances surrounding the birth of John the Baptist. He gives us the only story we have of Jesus' boyhood, and he tells us from time to time about the 'only son' or 'only daughter' of people of whom he writes (7:12; 8:42; 9:38).

9. *The poor*. Jesus came to preach the gospel to the poor (4:18), and it is noteworthy that Luke reports a blessing on the poor (6:20; by contrast there is a woe for the rich, 6:24), whereas Matthew speaks of 'the poor in spirit' (Mt. 5:3). Preaching good news to the poor is characteristic of Jesus' ministry (7:22). The shepherds to whom the angels came (2:8ff.) were from a poor class. Indeed the family of Jesus Himself seems to have been poor, for the offering made at the birth of the Child was that of the poor (2:24; *cf.* Lv. 12:8). In general Luke concerns himself with the interests of the poor (1:53; 6:30; 14:11–13, 21; 16:19ff.).

The other side of this coin is an emphasis on the danger of riches. Luke has a 'Woe' for the rich (6:24), and he tells us that God sends rich men away empty (1:53). There are parables warning the rich, such as the rich fool (12:16ff.), the unjust steward (16:1ff.), Dives and Lazarus (16:19–31). There are warnings for the rich in the stories of the rich young ruler (18:18–27), of Zacchaeus (19:1–10), and of the widow's mite (21:1–4).

10. *The disreputable.* Luke tells us that on one occasion 'the tax collectors and sinners were all drawing near to hear' Jesus (15:1). This is not an isolated incident in the Third Gospel, for Luke finds occasion to mention many who were scarcely respectable. Thus he tells us of Zacchaeus (dismissed by the bystanders as 'a sinner', 19:7), and of the feast Levi made for a crowd described by the Pharisees as 'tax collectors and sinners' (5:30). In the same strain he recounts the story of the sinful woman who wept over Jesus' feet and anointed them and of whom Jesus said that her many sins were forgiven and that 'she loved much' (7:37–50). The prodigal son was not exactly a model of rectitude and the unrighteous have a way of turning up in the parables in this Gospel (7:41f.; 12:13–21; 16:1–12, 19–31; 18:1–8, 9–14).

11. *The passion of Christ.* Supremely is God's purpose worked out in the passion of our Lord. Luke writes from the conviction that God has acted in Christ to bring men salvation. Sometimes commentators have reacted too hastily to the fact that Luke has omitted some important Marcan statements about the cross (*e.g.* Mk. 10:45)[1] and have affirmed that he has no theology of the cross.[2] In fact the cross dominates the

---

[1] Rudolf Otto holds that Luke retains the essence of this saying in his passion narrative: 'the idea of a ransom for many was precisely the meaning of the distribution of the bread, and by the act of distributing the meaning had just been fixed' (*The Kingdom of God and the Son of Man* (London, 1943), p. 272).

[2] This view is fashionable in some quarters. But it is worth noting that in earlier days the same evidence was viewed differently. Plummer reminds us that the four symbols, the Man, the Lion, the Ox and the Eagle, were assigned to the Gospels in a variety of ways, but always the Ox was the symbol of Luke. He cites Isaac Williams, 'This sacerdotal animal implies Atonement and Propitiation; and this exactly corresponds with what is supposed to be the character of St. Luke's Gospel' (Plummer, p. xxii). We should also notice the point made by Marshall that in this respect Luke does not differ significantly from Matthew and Mark (*Luke: Historian and Theologian*, pp. 170f.).

whole.[1] Quite early Luke refers to 'the days . . . for him to be received up' (9:51), and he adds that Jesus 'set his face to go up to Jerusalem'. Jesus refers to His death as a baptism and adds, 'how I am constrained until it is accomplished!' (12:50). He sends a message to Herod, 'I cast out demons and perform cures today and tomorrow, and the third day I finish my course' (13:32; He goes on to speak of perishing in Jerusalem). In one of the Q passages Luke has a prediction of the passion which is absent from Matthew (17:25). Similarly he tells us in his transfiguration narrative, as the others do not, that Moses and Elijah spoke of Jesus' death (9:31). And, of course, the passion narrative occupies a large space at the end of the Gospel. Luke has a number of references to the fulfilment of Scripture in connection with the passion which gives his account a special flavour (see 18:31; 20:17; 22:37; 24:26f., 44, 46; probably also 9:22; 13:33; 17:25; 24:7). In the passion God's will is done.

It is true that Luke does not stress the connection of the cross with salvation in the manner of Paul or John. This makes it possible to understand Luke's references to the cross, as a reader of this book in manuscript says, as though he saw it as 'the divinely ordained path on the road to resurrection and exaltation as a Prince and Saviour'. This may be possible, but it is not at all obvious. There is no hint at ultimate triumph in most of the Lucan references and where the triumph does come in it tends to be without emphasis (*cf.* 'on the third day he will rise', 18:33; there is no more, not one word about triumph or exaltation). In any case the reader gave his case away in the final word. It is that that is important. Luke sees Jesus as men's Saviour and that by way of the cross. If the atoning significance of Christ's suffering is not stressed at least it is there, and it is worth reflecting that Luke does not hint at any other significance. In view of his clear interest in salvation the question may well be asked, Why does Luke so stress the cross unless because of its saving significance?

[1]Bo Reicke thinks that the passion story in Luke 'is important and illuminating because together with the prelude it encompasses the whole drama and gives it a distinctive character, but especially because it represents the climax of the whole drama' (*The Gospel of Luke*, p. 60). Cf. Bishop Cassian, 'from the prophecy of Simeon in the temple, (2, 25–35), there is a certain accent on the coming Passion' (*SE*, i, p. 137; Cassian does not see this as what he calls 'the building principle' which is rather universalism). *Cf.* also Tinsley, p. 13.

Nor should we allow our thoughts to stop with the Gospel. In his second volume Luke continues to emphasize the importance of the cross. He brings out the fact that the early church concentrated on what Jesus had done for man's salvation and specifically on the cross and resurrection. Here we find that the death of Jesus took place in accordance with 'the definite plan and foreknowledge of God' (Acts 2:23). There is much more.[1] The death of Jesus was central.

12. *The Holy Spirit.* God's purpose does not stop at the cross. It continues in the work of the Holy Spirit which meant so much in the church of Luke's day. But this Evangelist's interest in the Spirit goes back to early days. The Spirit is prominent in this Gospel from the beginning. There is a prophecy that John the Baptist would be filled with the Holy Spirit from his mother's womb (1:15), while both Elizabeth and Zechariah are said to have been filled with the Spirit (1:41, 67). The same Spirit was 'upon' Simeon, revealed to him that he would see the Christ, and led him into the Temple at the appropriate time (2:25–27).

The Holy Spirit was active in connection with the ministry of Jesus. This goes right back to the original conception, for the angel Gabriel informed Mary that 'The Holy Spirit will come upon you, and the power of the Most High will overshadow you' (1:35). When Jesus was about to begin His ministry there are several references to the Holy Spirit. John the Baptist prophesied that Jesus would baptize with the Holy Spirit and with fire (3:16). When our Lord was baptized the Holy Spirit came upon him 'in bodily form, as a dove' (3:22), and the same Spirit filled Him and led Him in the wilderness at the time of the temptation (4:1). When the temptation was over and He was to enter into His ministry He 'returned in the power of the Spirit into Galilee' (4:14). Then when He preached in the synagogue at Nazareth Jesus applied to Himself the words, 'The Spirit of the Lord is upon me' (4:18). There are not many references to the Spirit during the ministry, though on one occasion Jesus 'rejoiced in the Holy Spirit' (10:21) and we should probably take this to indicate that the Spirit was with Him continually. Again, He

[1]See further my *The Cross in the New Testament* (Exeter, 1965), chs. 2, 3. Michael Green draws attention to seven points which show Luke's concern for the truth that Christ's death has atoning significance (*Evangelism in the Early Church* (London, 1970), pp. 73f.).

told His followers that in emergencies the Holy Spirit would give them what they needed to say (12:12) and it is not easy to think that they would have the Spirit and Jesus not. Blasphemy against the Spirit is the gravest of sins (12:10). Jesus told His disciples that the Father would give the Holy Spirit to those who asked (11:13). After the resurrection He said, 'behold, I send the promise of my Father upon you' and went on to assure the disciples that they would be 'clothed with power from on high' (24:49). This is a clear reference to the coming of the Holy Spirit, a prophecy fulfilled at Pentecost.

But, important as this Gospel's teaching about the Spirit is, it is in Acts that we receive the full thrust of Luke's emphasis. That book is full of the Spirit and it has well been called 'The Acts of the Holy Spirit'. The Spirit is constantly at work from the Day of Pentecost on.

It is abundantly clear, then, that one of Luke's great emphases is the Holy Spirit. He does not think of God as leaving men to serve Him as best they can out of their own resources. God's love is seen in the Spirit who enters and empowers and guides the followers of Jesus.

Some have seen Luke's emphasis on the Holy Spirit as a substitute for the eschatology which means so much to the other Evangelists. Helmut Flender notes the contention of Conzelmann and Schweizer that redemptive history and eschatology are mutually exclusive. Against this he contends, in my judgment rightly, that this is not a true understanding of the work of the Spirit. Flender sees the exaltation of Christ and the outpouring of the Spirit as genuine eschatological events, but he denies that this makes the church 'equally eschatological'. He goes on: 'To understand redemptive history in this way would be to confound divine with human activity, which would be intolerable. When we speak of the Spirit as eschatological we mean that it is eschatology made present.'[1] What ensures the genuine sense of imminence, of continuous expectation, is that the gift of the Spirit is not something institutional, as though the church had the Spirit in its control and could produce the gifts of the Spirit any time it chose. The Spirit might be given at Pentecost, but He could fill the same people again a little later in response to prayer (Acts 4:31). The presence of the Spirit 'is still a super-

[1]H. Flender, *St Luke, Theologian of Redemptive History*, p. 142.

human gift, for which the faithful must wait, and which they must be ready to receive'.[1] The Spirit may not be presumed on. The church may not say, 'We have the Spirit safely in our keeping. We need not look for the coming of our Lord.'

The Lordship of the Spirit over the historical process is amply brought out in Acts. And as we noted in an earlier section, Luke has more to say about the Spirit in his Gospel than does any of the other Evangelists. This forms a bond of continuity.[2] Both in the ministry of Jesus and in the life of the early church the Spirit of God is at work.

13. *Prayer*. In his teaching about the Spirit, then, Luke shows us that God effects His purpose. This demands a right attitude on the part of the people of God and it accords with this that Luke stresses the importance of prayer. There are two principal ways in which this interest is brought out. The first is in recording the prayers of Jesus (3:21; 5:16; 6:12; 9:18, 28f.; 10:21f.; 11:1; 22:41ff.; 23:46; seven of these are in Luke alone and they show Jesus at prayer before each great crisis of His life). This Gospel alone records that Jesus prayed for Peter (22:31f.). Luke tells us that Jesus prayed for His enemies (23:34) and for Himself (22:41f.). The second is in the parables which teach so much about prayer, the friend at midnight (11:5ff.), the unjust judge (18:1ff.), the Pharisee and the publican (18:10ff.). In addition Luke records some exhortations to the disciples to pray (6:28; 11:2; 22:40, 46), and he has a warning about the wrong kind of prayer (20:47).

14. *Praise*. Luke's is a singing Gospel. He records some of the great hymns of the Christian faith: the glory song of the angels (2:14), the *Magnificat*, the *Benedictus* and the *Nunc Dimittis* (1:46ff., 68ff.; 2:29ff.). Quite often people who receive benefits praise God or glorify God or the like (2:20; 5:25f.; 7:16; 13:13; 17:15; 18:43). The verb 'rejoice' and the noun 'joy' are found often (*e.g.* 1:14, 44, 47; 10:21). There is laughter in this Gospel (6:21) and merry-making

---

[1] Flender, *loc. cit.*

[2] G. W. H. Lampe can say, 'The connecting thread which runs through both parts of St. Luke's work is the theme of the operation of the Spirit of God' (*Studies in the Gospels*, ed. D. E. Nineham, p. 159). I cannot follow him, however, when he claims that in these two writings 'the Spirit is still, generally speaking, non-personal' (*ibid.*, p. 163).

(15:23, 32). There is joy in Zacchaeus's reception of Jesus (19:6). There is joy on earth over the finding of the lost sheep and the lost coin and there is joy in heaven over the finding of lost sinners (15:6f., 9f.). And this Gospel finishes, as it had begun, with rejoicing (24:52; *cf.* 1:14).

From all this it is clear that Luke has written with a profoundly theological purpose. He sees God as at work bringing men salvation and it is his pleasure to bring out a variety of aspects of this great saving work.

V. THE RELATIONSHIP OF LUKE TO THE OTHER GOSPELS

a. The Synoptic Problem

A problem is posed by the resemblances between certain passages in our first three Gospels. Sometimes they are in all three Gospels, sometimes in two of them. The resemblances are often very close and the passages may be almost word for word. Even minute and unimportant particles may be the same in all three accounts. If this occurred only in Jesus' words we might possibly think of faithful reporting as the explanation. But it is found also in narratives of events. The problem is how to account for these facts and to explain the relationship between these Gospels. We may set out the principal facts as follows:

1. The general scheme of these three Gospels is similar. There is a ministry of Jesus in Galilee, followed by a journey to Jerusalem where the passion is located. There is a quite different approach in John, where we see Jesus making a number of visits to Jerusalem.

2. There are passages in all three Gospels which resemble each other closely, *e.g.* Matthew 9:6 = Mark 2:10 = Luke 5:24.

3. Matthew and Mark often agree in wording where Luke differs, and Mark and Luke similarly agree against Matthew. Matthew and Luke more rarely agree against Mark.

4. There are passages in Matthew and Luke which are absent from the corresponding sections of Mark, *e.g.* Matthew 3:7–10 = Luke 3:7–9; *cf.* Mark 1:2–8.

5. Some material is found in Matthew and Luke which is similar, but not identical, *e.g.* Matthew 5:3 and Luke 6:20.

6. The common matter may be placed in different con-

texts, *e.g.* the healing of the centurion's servant (Mt. 8:5ff.; Lk. 7:1ff.).

7. Each Gospel has material which neither of the others shares.

It cannot be said that any explanation has been offered which accounts for all the facts. But much can be learnt from looking at the solutions which have been offered. In earlier days the usual explanation was oral tradition: 'an original oral Gospel, definite in general outline and even in language, which was committed to writing in the lapse of time in various special shapes, according to the typical forms which it assumed in the preaching of different Apostles.'[1] Nowadays this is felt to be inadequate. The tradition would have begun in Aramaic and it is hard to see why the Greek would be so close. The dependence extends even to Greek particles. It is also difficult to see why an oral tradition should have produced so much in the way of a common order. Matthew and Luke may deviate from Mark's order, but they always return to it.

We may agree that oral tradition will not explain all the facts; but it must be remembered that on any showing the Gospel material was handed down orally for quite some years. It is not improbable that too little attention has been paid to oral tradition. There seems no reason why the Evangelists should not have taken notice of the oral tradition that undoubtedly existed when they wrote. Form Criticism has emphasized for us the importance of the pre-literary period. So from another direction has the work of Scandinavian scholars such as H. Riesenfeld and B. Gerhardsson.[2]

But most critics these days agree that we must think of written sources. The two-document theory holds that Mark was the first of the Gospels to be written and that Matthew

---

[1] B. F. Westcott, *Introduction to the Study of the Gospels* (London, 1875), p. 188.

[2] These men have emphasized the role of oral transmission among the rabbis and have suggested that the early Christians must be seen against this background. They think it likely that the first Christians would have used much the same methods as the rabbis for carrying on the tradition. See H. Riesenfeld, *The Gospel Tradition* (Oxford, 1970); B. Gerhardsson, *Memory and Manuscript* (Uppsala, 1961); *Tradition and Transmission in Early Christianity* (Lund, 1964). It must be borne in mind that the Christians differed from the rabbis as well as resembled them, but this approach surely has value.

and Luke used Mark and also another source usually designated Q.[1]

Reasons given for the priority of Mark are as follows:

1. Almost the whole of Mark is contained in the other two. Matthew has the substance of more than 600 of Mark's 661 verses and he retains about 51% of Mark's actual words even though his style is more condensed. It is harder to be accurate about Luke, but he seems to have about 350 verses in common with Mark and in these about 53% of the words are Mark's.[2] About 90% of Mark is in Matthew and about half in Luke. Only four paragraphs of Mark do not appear in one or other of these two.

2. The way this matter is used seems to show that Mark can scarcely have employed the other two as his sources. F. B. Clogg comments on the healing of the paralytic (Mt. 9:1-8; Mk. 2:1-12; Lk. 5:17-26): 'after the introduction, which is peculiar to each Evangelist, there is nothing in Matthew and Luke which is not found in Mark, but Mark has much pictorial detail which is wanting in the other two. It is hardly possible that Mark should have compiled his narrative from the other two, and yet should be the freshest and most lifelike of the three.'[3] A similar comment could be made again and again.

3. Both Matthew and Luke sometimes omit what Mark has, but they do not often agree in their omissions.

4. Matthew and Luke generally follow the Marcan order. When one departs from Mark's order the other normally supports it. They rarely agree in detail against Mark.

5. Mark is franker than the others in depicting Jesus'

---

[1] Q is the initial letter of the German word *Quelle*, 'source', and it is usually said confidently that this is the reason for the symbol. According to R. H. Lightfoot, however, Armitage Robinson, when lecturing in the nineties of the last century, used to refer to Mark as P (Peter's reminiscences) and the sayings document as Q. He thought someone carried the method to Germany where Q was related to *Quelle*. He had the idea that it was first used in Germany by Wellhausen in 1903 (*History and Interpretation in the Gospels* (London, 1935), p. 27, n. 1). However, W. F. Howard pointed out that the symbol was used by J. Weiss in an essay published in 1891 and again in a book published in 1892 (*ET*, l, 1938-39, pp. 379f.). The question cannot be said to have been resolved.

[2] B. H. Streeter, *The Four Gospels* (London, 1930), pp. 159f. W. G. Kümmel says that Matthew and Luke between them have 8,189 out of Mark's 10,650 words (*Introduction to the New Testament*, p. 45).

[3] F. B. Clogg, *An Introduction to the New Testament* (London, 1940), p. 183.

humanity. For example he tells us that in the synagogue, after He had asked whether it is lawful to do good or harm on the sabbath, preparatory to healing the man with the withered hand, Jesus 'looked around at them with anger, grieved at their hardness of heart' (Mk. 3:5). But Matthew and Luke both omit the references to anger and grief.

6. Mark is more prone to report the failings of the Twelve. Thus he tells us that, on the occasion of the discussion of the 'leaven of Herod', Jesus asked them, 'Are your hearts hardened? Having eyes do you not see, and having ears do you not hear?' (Mk. 8:17f.). But in his report of the incident Matthew omits this (Mt. 16:9).

7. In Mark there are vivid touches (which look very much like the recollections of an eyewitness), which Matthew and Luke omit in their parallel accounts. These include points such as Jesus' sitting down and calling the Twelve (Mk. 9:35), His looking round on His disciples (Mk. 10:23), and the unusual word for the 'groups' in which the people sat down at the feeding of the five thousand (Mk. 6:40; the word is used of garden beds).

8. While Matthew and Luke are independent of one another in their infancy stories, they start agreeing with one another (and with Mark) at the point where Mark begins his Gospel.

9. There seems a tendency for Matthew and Luke to refine Mark's account. They seem to adopt a more reverential tone (see points 5 and 6), they amend awkward and ungrammatical constructions and they omit Aramaic expressions. Beside them Mark's account seems more primitive.

10. Some detect in Matthew and Luke attempts to clear up Marcan ambiguities. Thus where Mark has, 'that is why I came out' (Mk. 1:38), which might mean 'came out from God', or 'came out from Capernaum', Luke reads, 'I was sent for this purpose' (Lk. 4:43). Similarly Mark 11:3 might mean that the owner would send the ass back to Jesus, or that, when He had finished with it, Jesus would return the ass to the owner (RSV does not reflect the ambiguity of the Greek). But Matthew 21:3 makes the point clear.

Not all these points carry the same weight. Thus points 5–7 are surely only matters of the different approaches of the different authors. Again, point 4 can be stated too strongly. Sanders maintains that 'the facts of order as they are usually stated are misleading; the phenomenon of order has yet to be stated and explained adequately. The argument from order is not adequate to prove the two-document hypothesis with the degree of certainty which would be necessary in order to justify the procedure followed by Bultmann and Taylor.'[1] But some of the others build up a weighty case. Against it are urged principally two points.

1. There are some agreements of Matthew and Luke against Mark. For example, in the saying about putting new wine into old wineskins Matthew and Luke both say the wine will be spilt, whereas Mark says only that the wine and the skins perish (Mt. 9:17 = Mk. 2:22 = Lk. 5:37).[2] Similarly in the passion story Matthew and Luke both have 'saying' and 'Who is it that struck you?', neither of which is in Mark (Mt. 26:67f. = Mk. 14:65 = Lk. 22:63f.). This kind of thing is strange if Matthew and Luke depend on Mark. To explain it some have thought that Mark was revised: there was an original Mark (an *Ur-Marcus*) and a revised version. If so our Mark must be the original and Matthew and Luke used the revision. But most scholars agree that the evidence for an *Ur-Marcus* is insufficient.

Many of the arguments are unconvincing. Thus both Matthew and Luke often independently omit unimportant words characteristic of Mark's more verbose style. It is not surprising that they sometimes coincide. It is the same with grammatical changes, such as changing the historic present (in Mark 151 times, but in Matthew 78 times and Luke 4–6 times)[3] to the imperfect or aorist. But when full allowance is made for this many scholars feel that a problem remains.

2. If Matthew and Luke are depending on Mark, it is asked why they omit whole sections of their source. But it is fairly countered that both were entitled to make a selection. They were under no compulsion to reproduce the whole of any source they may have had. And in any case surprisingly little of Mark is in fact omitted. It is however puzzling that Luke should omit everything in Mark 6:45 – 8:26. Perhaps this

[1]E. P. Sanders, *The Tendencies of the Synoptic Tradition*, p. 277. In a footnote he points out that the argument from order is true only for longer, complete units. In smaller units there are places where neither Matthew nor Luke follows Mark's order and he cites Mk. 9:50; Mt. 5:13; Lk. 14:34.

[2]See the list in F. Crawford Burkitt, *The Gospel History and its Transmission* (Edinburgh, 1907), pp. 42ff.

[3]The passages are listed in Hawkins, *Horae Synopticae*, pp. 144–149.

omission was accidental. It was not easy to locate a passage in an ancient scroll and it has been suggested that Luke could well have passed accidentally from the feeding of the multitude in Mark 6:42–44 to the similar words in 8:19–21. Or he may have felt that he had sufficiently close parallels to most of the matter in this section.[1]

Such objections are not held to be decisive. Most scholars accordingly hold that Mark was the first of our four Gospels to be written. They think that this Gospel was used by both Matthew and Luke. This does seem the most likely reading of much of the evidence, but we cannot say more than that. It is not completely proven,[2] and we must bear in mind that some scholars hold to the priority of Matthew[3] and a few even to that of Luke.[4]

We turn now to Q, the other source in the two-document theory. The following points are relevant.

1. There are about 250 verses common to Matthew and Luke but absent from Mark.

2. The degree of resemblance varies. Some passages are almost word for word (*e.g.* the 'brood of vipers' section, Mt. 3:8–10; Lk. 3:7–10: in the Greek 60 out of 63 words are identical in the two accounts; so also Mt. 6:24 is similar to Lk. 16:13; Mt. 7:3–5 to Lk. 6:41–42; Mt. 7:7–11 to Lk. 11:9–13; Mt. 11:4–6, 7b–11 to Lk. 7:22–23, 24b–28; Mt. 11:21–23 to Lk. 10:13–15; Mt. 11:25–27 to Lk. 10:21–22; Mt. 12:43–45 to Lk. 11:24–26; Mt. 23:37–38 to Lk. 13:34–35; Mt. 24:45–51 to Lk. 12:42–46). Agreements can reach to unusual words and phrases and grammatical peculiarities. But in others the differences are as striking as the resemblances (*e.g.* the Beatitudes, Mt. 5:3–11; Lk. 6:20–22).

3. The common matter occurs in different contexts.

[1]Creed finds a variety of explanations (p. lxi).

[2]David Wenham draws attention to a number of difficulties in his article 'The Synoptic Problem Revisited' in *Tyndale Bulletin*, 23, 1972, pp. 3–38.

[3]*Cf.* B. C. Butler, *The Originality of Matthew* (Cambridge, 1951); M. L. Loane, *A Brief Survey of the Synoptic Problem* (Melbourne, n.d.); W. R. Farmer, *The Synoptic Problem* (New York, 1964).

[4]E. P. Sanders cites W. Bussmann for the view that 'a source document G (*Geschichtsquelle*) lay behind the synoptic triple tradition, but had been used by our evangelists in different recensions. Luke used the earliest form and Matthew the second, while Mark itself is actually the third recension of the source G' (*op. cit.*, p. 95).

According to Streeter, subsequent to the temptation narrative there is not one case in which Matthew and Luke insert a piece of Q material into the same Marcan context.[1] Not surprisingly accordingly the order in which the Q material occurs is different in the two Gospels. It is usually held that Luke has preserved something of the order of the original, while Matthew arranged his matter topically.

4. There is little narrative material in the common matter. Q is mostly a sayings source.

Theoretically the common matter might be due to direct dependance rather than to the use of the same source; but few feel that there is any justification at all for holding that Matthew copied from Luke. Some scholars do think that Luke is dependent on Matthew. Against them, however, is the fact already noted that, after the temptation story, we never find the common matter in the same context. Why should Luke systematically take Matthew's matter out of its context and place it elsewhere?[2] Again, there seems no reason why Luke should have taken up none of Matthew's additions to Mark's text. This seems inexplicable. A rather subjective point is that scholars usually feel that, where there are slight differences in the common matter, Luke's is the fresher account and seems more original. Thus it does not seem likely that either of these Gospels depends directly on the other.

Most scholars hold that such a source as Q existed, though there is little agreement as to what was in it. James Moffatt cites sixteen different reconstructions of Q and gives another of his own.[3] Streeter gives yet another.[4] The problem is of course with the passages which show differences as well as resemblances. Are they to be included in Q? Some hold that

---

[1] B. H. Streeter, *The Four Gospels*, p. 183.

[2] As an example of the difficulty we may take W. H. Blyth Martin's contention that, in the Woes on the Scribes and Pharisees, if Luke used Matthew he omitted several verses and arranged the others in the order Mt. 23:25-26, 23, 6-7, 27, 4, 29-31, 34-36, 13 (*Theology*, lix, May 1956, pp. 187f.). Harold A. Guy has also stressed the significance of Luke's very different order (*ET*, lxxxiii, 1971-72, pp. 245ff.). K. Peter G. Curtis has an argument from vocabulary in support of the Q hypothesis (*ET*, lxxxiv, 1972-73, pp. 309f.).

[3] J. Moffatt, *An Introduction to the Literature of the New Testament* (Edinburgh, 1927), pp. 197ff.

[4] B. H. Streeter, *op. cit.*, p. 291.

they are and that there were different recensions of that document. Then Matthew used one form of Q and Luke another. Others think that Q was an Aramaic source (perhaps the *logia* of Matthew referred to by Papias[1]) and that our Evangelists are using different translations into the Greek. Some of the differences between Matthew and Luke could be explained from slight differences in Aramaic words or from Aramaic words with two meanings. Another complicating factor is the probability that at times one only of our Evangelists used Q. Scholars differ when they try to identify such passages.

Those who feel that the existence of Q has not been satisfactorily demonstrated point out that no example of the kind of literature postulated can be shown to have existed. Perhaps the Gospel of Thomas comes closest, but this is a second-century document, probably Gnostic. Nothing like it is known in New Testament times. The agreements of Matthew and Luke do indeed present a problem, but it is not incapable of solution. Some think Matthew is earlier than Luke and that Luke used both it and Mark.[2] Such views are not without difficulties of their own, but their very existence shows that the hypothesis that Mark and Q lie behind our first and third Gospels has not been proved.

It is difficult to escape the impression that many critics are trying to cram too many eggs into one Q basket. They are ignoring Luke's express statement that many had written before him (1:1). The best way of accounting for the problem of the differences and resemblances seems to be to take this statement of Luke's seriously. Where Matthew and Luke are nearly word for word we need not doubt that they are using a common source. There may well have been more than one such common source. But where the differences are as great as the resemblances it seems better to think of different

---

[1] Cited in Eusebius, *Historia Ecclesiastica* III. 39. 16.

[2] See for example the essay by A. M. Farrer, 'On Dispensing with Q' in *Studies in the Gospels*, ed. D. E. Nineham, pp. 55–86. W. H. Blyth Martin replied with an article called 'The Indispensability of Q', *art. cit.*, pp. 182–188. J. H. Ropes maintains that it has never been shown to be impossible that Luke used Matthew (*The Synoptic Gospels*, p. 93). N. Turner has argued that the agreements of Matthew and Luke against Mark seem best explained by Lucan dependence on Matthew (*SE*, i, pp. 223–234). But R. McL. Wilson urges some considerations which point the other way (*SE*, i, pp. 254–257).

sources.[1] It is not without its interest that in recent times there seems to be a tendency to be less dogmatic about Q.[2] Many scholars regard it as no more than a convenient way of referring to the matter common to Matthew and Luke which they obtained from the same source or sources. We shall use the symbol in just this way.

Since B. H. Streeter's great work many have been attracted to the four-document theory. Streeter accepted Mark and Q as two basic documents, but pointed out that in addition both Matthew and Luke have considerable amounts of material peculiar to themselves. He postulated special sources to explain this, giving to Matthew's special source the designation M, and to Luke's L. He thought that each of the great centres in early Christianity would have had its own cycle of tradition and he links the sources with those centres: Mark with Rome, Q with Antioch, M (which has a Jewish colouring) with Jerusalem and L with Caesarea. When these traditions were enshrined in the Gospels there was no longer a need for their separate existence and they were allowed to perish. This part of his theory is open to question, for the early church did not allow Mark to perish when almost all of it was included in Matthew or Luke.

An interesting development of Streeter's theory is his view of the way Luke's Gospel was composed. He thinks that when Luke began writing he relied chiefly on Q and L and that only

---

[1]W. L. Knox uses the suggestive expression, 'Q tracts' (*The Sources of the Synoptic Gospels*, ii (Cambridge, 1957), pp. 45ff.). He thinks that short tracts were quite early, 'Probably even in the late thirties, and certainly by the early fifties' (*ibid.*, p. 139). C. K. Barrett argues for a number of sources rather than a single Q document (*ET*, liv, 1942–43, pp. 320ff.). Olof Linton thinks that there was a Q document, but that Matthew and Luke also made use of material that had been passed on orally ('The Q-Problem Reconsidered' in *Studies in New Testament and Early Christian Literature*, ed. D. A. Aune, pp. 43–59). E. P. Sanders has demonstrated again the complexity of the problem and has argued for multiple sources which sometimes overlap ('The Overlaps of Mark and Q and the Synoptic Problem', *NTS*, 19, 1972–73, pp. 453-465).

[2]Ropes sees the Q hypothesis as having been 'modified, refined, and complicated to such a degree as, for that reason if for no other, to arouse doubts of its validity' (*loc. cit.*). M. Dibelius thinks we are warranted in speaking 'rather of a stratum than of a document' (*From Tradition to Gospel* (London, 1934), p. 235). R. H. Fuller also thinks of Q as 'shorthand for a common layer of tradition, partly written and perhaps partly oral' (*A Critical Introduction to the New Testament* (London, 1966), p. 72). Of course, many find it a profitable working hypothesis.

after he had combined these into a first draft of a Gospel (which Streeter calls Proto-Luke) did he come across Mark. He then inserted Marcan matter into Proto-Luke and formed the present Gospel. Up till Streeter the usual view was that Luke took Mark as basic and inserted his non-Marcan matter into the Marcan framework. But Streeter breaks with the view that Mark was a primary source for Luke and he denies that Mark provided Luke's framework. Caird points out that the resolution of this question is of more than merely academic interest, for it involves our view of the historical value of this Gospel. If Luke took Mark as his basis, then it follows that he 'used wide editorial freedom in rewriting his sources'.[1]

The principal evidence for Proto-Luke is as follows.

1. Luke has alternate Marcan and non-Marcan blocks of material. He makes very little use of Mark in the sections 3:1 – 4:30; 6:20 – 8:3; 9:51 – 18:14; 19:1–27, and his passion narrative seems basically independent of Mark's. He gives no appearance of combining his Marcan and non-Marcan matter in anything like the way he has combined the different strands in his non-Marcan material. For some reason he has nothing from Mark 6:45 – 8:10.

2. Luke 3:1 looks like the opening of a book. If it was, then the position of the genealogy, coming after the first mention of the name Jesus, is natural. Those who hold the Proto-Luke hypothesis, of course, normally believe that this document did not include the infancy narratives.

3. Sometimes when Luke is apparently following Mark a particular incident is omitted. But we find it in a different form in a different place. Such incidents include the Beelzebub controversy (Q), the mustard seed (Q), the rejection at Nazareth (L), the anointing (L), *etc.* Caird lists seventeen places where Luke departs from the Marcan order in Mark 1: 1–14:11.[2] It looks as though Luke preferred his non-Marcan source, even when Mark's version is more vigorous. This is intelligible if he had earlier incorporated that source into his work, less so if he is operating with Mark as his basis. In fact it seems that when Luke is not following Mark's order he is not freely correcting the other Evangelist, but simply following another source.

[1]Caird, p. 23.
[2]Caird, pp. 24f.

4. Q+L would make a document considerably longer than Mark.[1] It is difficult in the light of this to see Mark as Luke's framework.

5. This hypothesis would explain why Luke omits so much more of Mark than does Matthew.

6. The use of 'the Lord' rather than 'Jesus' in narrative is not found in Matthew or Mark. Nor does it occur in Luke's Marcan material. But it is found fifteen times in the rest and in roughly proportionate numbers in Q and L. Similarly the address *Kyrie*, 'Lord' or 'Sir', is found only once in Mark (the Syrophenician woman), but sixteen times in Luke, fourteen of which are in Proto-Luke (eight in L and six in Q). It is also found nineteen times in Matthew.[2] It is clear that the use of the term does not characterize the final writing of the book, else it would be in the Marcan sections. The inference is that it belongs to an earlier stage of Luke's writing.

7. Luke's passion narrative is not a recasting of Mark's. When Luke is using Marcan material he normally has about 53% of Mark's words, but in the passion narrative only 27%,[3] including many words without which a passion story could scarcely have been told at all. Luke has also a dozen variations from the Marcan order.[4] Again, Luke's resurrection appearances are located in Jerusalem. Scholars are divided as to whether Mark's Gospel originally ended where it does in our copies, in which case he had no resurrection appearances, or whether there was an ending which has now been lost, in which case most agree the appearances must have been in Galilee (Mk. 16:7). In either case Luke is not depending on Mark.[5]

8. When Luke uses Q material he does not simply insert it into a Marcan framework, but combines it with L.

Streeter concludes from this kind of evidence that Luke probably completed a first draft of his Gospel before he sighted

---

[1]Streeter, *The Four Gospels*, pp. 211f. He estimates the non-Marcan matter in Lk. 3:1 – 22:14 at 671 verses and in the passion narrative at 135 verses, a total of 806 (*ibid.*, p. 209; there are about 660 verses in Mark).

[2]*Ibid.*, pp. 213f.

[3]Caird, p. 25.

[4]Caird, *loc. cit.*

[5]See further the detailed discussion in Vincent Taylor, *The Passion Narrative of St Luke*. Taylor makes it very difficult to hold that Mark was Luke's basic source for the passion narrative, though he agrees that Luke has used Mark in some sections.

Mark. If this is so, then Proto-Luke is very old indeed. Scholars have been in the habit of attaching special value to Mark and to Q, for documents that precede both Matthew and Luke and which were thought of highly enough to be relied on by both must be both ancient and reliable. Streeter thinks that Proto-Luke must be thought of as in the same class. His theory enhances the value of much in Luke.

Not all have been convinced by him, however. Scholars usually feel that not enough evidence has been produced to show that M and L existed as documents. That Matthew and Luke had special sources of information is clear enough. That these were embodied in two documents is not. Moreover, if we separate out the passages assigned to Proto-Luke some are not impressed. J. M. Creed calls the result 'an amorphous collection of narrative and discourse'.[1] It is not a well-rounded Gospel.

But those who reject Proto-Luke seem never to have given a convincing explanation of two facts: 1. Luke habitually combines his special matter with Q, but never with Mark, and 2. Luke departs from Mark so often in the passion story. He seems to have attached great importance to his combination of Q and L. It appears to have been his basic source for his passion narrative, and at the other end of his Gospel there is a block of non-Marcan matter right after the infancy stories (3:1 – 4:30). There are, it is true, some expressions in common with Mark in this section, and some critics regard Luke as dependent on Mark throughout it. This, however, scarcely seems justified, for the bulk of this section is clearly non-Marcan. There is evidence that Mark and Q overlapped. For example, Luke 8:16 appears in a Marcan context (Mk. 4:21) and the very similar 11:33 is usually assigned to Q (*cf.* Mt. 5:15). It seems that Luke has taken this saying from both his sources. The same phenomenon is repeated several times and this leaves scholars almost uniformly convinced that Mark and Q overlapped. This being so, Luke need not have derived what seems like Marcan matter in 3:1 – 4:30 from Mark. It may have come from Q and, considering the nature and extent of the differences, this seems to be what has in fact happened.

[1]Creed, p. lviii n. While objecting to the Proto-Luke hypothesis Creed is ready to allow the possibility that Q and some of Luke's special material 'may have been already combined, and may have lain before Luke as a single document' (*ibid.*).

Many have pointed out that if we detach the Marcan sections from Luke's Gospel there is little cohesion in them. They do not look like the framework of the longest of our Gospels. This makes it look as though Luke used Mark late rather than early in his composition.

Certainty is impossible in such a situation, but it does seem as though Luke had been busy long before he came across Mark. It may be saying too much to claim that he had produced Streeter's Proto-Luke. The facts seem best accounted for if he had been collecting material from a variety of sources, both oral tradition and such writings as he came across, and working it into a tentative document. The frequent combination of Q and L seems to indicate no less. Then when he came across a copy of Mark he inserted such extracts as he thought suitable into his partially-written document, rewording them where necessary. In some such way he produced the present volume.

In concluding this section of our study let me stress that much remains uncertain. To read some accounts of the Synoptic problem, one would never gather that there are so many exceptions to the rules scholars lay down. The facts are extraordinarily complex and nothing more than a tentative hypothesis is justified. The problem must be pursued. We cannot work on these Gospels without hypotheses of some sort. But in the present state of our knowledge we must not be too dogmatic.[1]

b. Luke and John

An interesting and puzzling feature of this Gospel is the large number of points of contact it has with the Fourth

[1]A. Wikenhauser is somewhat pessimistic: 'up to the present no real solution has been found which explains the highly complex facts of the synoptic problem, nor is it likely that such a solution will be found' (*New Testament Introduction* (New York, 1958), pp. 231f.). D. G. A. Calvert refers to 'the growing feeling that the synoptic problem is still with us, and that the two-source theory is no longer adequate' (*NTS*, 18, 1971–72, p. 218). J. A. Fitzmyer holds that 'the history of Synoptic research reveals that the problem is *practically insoluble*' (*Jesus and Man's Hope* (Pittsburgh Theological Seminary, 1970), p. 132). W. D. Davies thinks it unlikely that the four-document hypothesis will be completely discarded: 'Nevertheless, in recent scholarship, the neat lines of Streeter's source analysis are being rubbed faint, if not entirely rubbed out' (*Invitation to the New Testament*, p. 96). In E. P. Sanders' study, *The Tendencies of the Synoptic Tradition*, the complexity of the evidence is made clear, as also the fact that there is no real trend.

Gospel. There are far more than in either of the other Synoptic Gospels. Thus several people are mentioned by Luke and John only, namely Mary and Martha (John speaks of their brother Lazarus, and Luke uses this name in a parable), a disciple named Judas who is distinct from Judas Iscariot, and Annas. These two writers show an interest in Samaria and in Jerusalem much greater than anything in Matthew and Mark and the same can be said of their references to the Temple. There are other links, especially in the passion narrative. Both, for example, speak of the role of Satan in the betrayal (Lk. 22:3; Jn. 13:27); both tell us that it was the *right* ear of the slave that Peter cut off in the Garden (Lk. 22:50; Jn. 18:10); that Pilate said three times over that Jesus was innocent (Lk. 23:4, 14, 22; Jn. 18:38; 19:4, 6); that Joseph's tomb had not been previously used (Lk. 23:53; Jn. 19:41); that there were two angels on the resurrection morning (Lk. 24:4; Jn. 20:12); and that resurrection appearances took place in Jerusalem (Luke refers briefly to a visit to the tomb which John describes more fully, Lk. 24:12, 24; Jn. 20:3–10).

Some have explained this sort of thing by maintaining that John used Luke as one of his sources.[1] But there is other evidence which makes this unlikely.[2] Thus both these Gospels have stories of an anointing of Jesus by a woman, but whereas Luke speaks of a prostitute performing the action in the house of a Pharisee (Lk. 7:36ff.), John describes the action of Mary, a friend of Jesus, in her own home (Jn. 12:1ff.). Again both tell of a miraculous catch of fish, Luke early in Jesus' ministry and John at one of the resurrection appearances (Lk.5:1ff.; Jn. 21:1ff.). Other examples could be cited of incidents which are somewhat similar, but where the differences are as important as the resemblances. They make it very difficult to think of direct dependence or the use of a common source. Under the circumstances Caird's conclusion is not too strong: 'The unavoidable inference is that Luke and John were relying on two allied streams of oral tradition.'[3]

---

[1]*Cf.* J. A. Bailey, *The Traditions Common to the Gospels of Luke and John* (Leiden, 1963).

[2]I have examined the relationship of John to the Synoptic Gospels generally in chapter 1 of *Studies in the Fourth Gospel*, and come to the conclusion that there is no convincing evidence for dependence.

[3]Caird, p. 21. P. Parker also sees the answer in oral tradition (*NTS*, ix, 1962–63, pp. 317–336).

ANALYSIS

PREFACE (1:1–4)

I. THE INFANCY NARRATIVES (1:5 – 2:52)
- a. The birth of John foretold (1:5–25)
- b. The birth of Jesus foretold (1:26–38)
- c. Mary's visit to Elizabeth (1:39–45)
- d. The song of Mary (1:46–56)
- e. The birth and naming of John (1:57–66)
- f. The song of Zechariah (1:67–80)
- g. The birth of Jesus (2:1–7)
- h. The angels and the shepherds (2:8–20)
- i. The baby Jesus (2:21–40)
- j. The boy Jesus in the Temple (2:41–52)

II. THE MINISTRY OF JOHN THE BAPTIST (3:1–20)

III. THE BEGINNING OF JESUS' MINISTRY (3:21 – 4:13)
- a. Jesus' baptism (3:21, 22)
- b. Jesus' genealogy (3:23–38)
- c. Jesus' temptations (4:1–13)

IV. JESUS IN GALILEE (4:14 – 9:50)
- a. The sermon at Nazareth (4:14–30)
- b. Jesus healing (4:31–41)
- c. A preaching tour (4:42–44)
- d. Jesus' miracles (5:1–26)
- e. The calling of Levi (5:27–32)
- f. Fasting (5:33–39)
- g. The right use of the sabbath (6:1–11)
- h. Choosing the Twelve (6:12–16)
- i. The sermon on the plain (6:17–49)
- j. Healing the centurion's slave (7:1–10)
- k. The widow of Nain's son (7:11–17)
- l. John the Baptist's questions (7:18–35)
- m. The anointing of Jesus by a sinful woman (7:36–50)
- n. Women who helped Jesus (8:1–3)
- o. The parable of the sower (8:4–15)
- p. The lamp and the cover (8:16–18)
- q. Jesus' mother and brothers (8:19–21)
- r. The stilling of the storm (8:22–25)
- s. The Gerasene demoniac (8:26–39)

COMMENTARY

PREFACE (1:1-4)

The opening paragraph is one sentence in good Greek style, with classical vocabulary, rhythm and balance. Luke has a feeling for style and clearly he sees a somewhat Semitic accent as right for the kind of book he is writing. But this excellently rounded sentence is equally right for a literary opening. And a literary opening, of course, implies that what follows was meant for circulation. Some of our oldest MSS incidentally give the book the simple title: 'According to Luke'.

1. Luke begins by drawing attention to those who had written before him. *Many*, he tells us, had set out to compose a *narrative*. He uses a general term which leaves it open whether they had written gospels or some other kind of narrative. He gives no indication who they were, but most agree that Mark was one of them. The verb *accomplished* can be used of being fully persuaded (hence AV, 'most surely believed'), but this meaning is unlikely here. The word has about it the air of fulfilment (*cf.* 2 Tim. 4:5) and thus Luke may be hinting at the working out of God's purpose, a thought which will be so much before him throughout his Gospel and its sequel.[1]

2. Luke has good authority for what he writes. He was not himself an eyewitness, but had consulted others who were. Some have thought the reference to *eyewitnesses* to be nothing more than conventional, but, as Creed says, 'an ancient writer would no more claim the authority of eye-witnesses without expecting his statement to be believed than a modern'. The eyewitnesses were also *ministers of the word*. This unusual expression, which is not found elsewhere in the New Testament, appears to mean 'men who preached the Christian gospel'. But we should not overlook the facts that in the opening of his Gospel John speaks of Jesus as 'the Word' and that elsewhere Luke seems to regard preaching Jesus and preaching

---

[1] H. J. Cadbury thinks there is probably nothing more to it than a desire for a long and sonorous word (*The Beginnings of Christianity*, ii (London, 1922), p. 496). But this is unlikely to be correct.

the word as much the same thing (Acts 8:4; 9:20; *cf.* also Acts 10:36ff.). He is approaching John's thought, for these men were servants of the Word as well as of the word. He is also implying that his authorities were not so much academic historians as men who knew and lived by the word they preached. *From the beginning* takes us back to the ministry of John the Baptist. Luke was not missing out on anything essential but going back to the very roots of the Christian movement. *Delivered* is wide enough to cover both oral and written tradition and Luke may have both in mind.

3. He claims to have *followed all things closely*. Some (*e.g.* Cadbury) hold that this means that he was personally present (as he was at some of the events in Acts). But this seems to read too much into his verb. We should take it rather in the sense 'track down', 'investigate', for, on his own admission, Luke was not an eyewitness of some at least of what he narrates. MM think that the verb implies, not that Luke had 'investigated' all his facts afresh, but that he had acquired such familiarity with them and had so kept in touch with them 'that his witness is practically contemporary witness'. He claims to have followed the events 'accurately' (as mg., rather than *closely*). He is saying that his information is good. He knows what he is talking about. He goes on to say that he has traced the story from its beginning (*for some time past* should rather be 'from the very first' as AV). There has been a good deal of discussion of the word translated *orderly* (*kathexēs*), used by Luke alone in the New Testament. Some hold that it means 'in chronological order' but this seems to be reading too much into it. Geldenhuys, while not overlooking the chronological possibilities, sees in the word 'logical and artistic arrangement' and some such view is probably correct. *Theophilus* is unlikely to be a symbolic name (despite its meaning, 'lover of God'). It points to a real person who would probably, as Luke's patron, have met the costs of publishing the book. The epithet *most excellent* probably indicates a person of rank (*cf.* Acts 23:26; 24:3; 26:25), though the possibility remains that it is only a courtesy title.

4. The verb *informed* is often used of the instruction of Christian converts or inquirers (*katēcheō*; see Acts 18:25; 1 Cor. 14:19, *etc.*). Some deduce that Theophilus was a

believer, and support this with the contention that he was
unlikely to have been Luke's literary patron if he was not. But
against that it is urged that he would probably have been
called 'brother' if he was. In any case the verb may be used
of a report both hostile and wrong (*e.g.* Acts 21:21, 24), so
we must keep open the possibility that he was no more than
an interested outsider. He certainly knew something about the
Christian faith and Luke wants him to know *the truth* of it.
Ned B. Stonehouse sees truth as specially important in the
Prologue. The 'main impact' of the Prologue is 'that Christianity is true and is capable of confirmation by appeal to what
had happened'.[1]

I. THE INFANCY NARRATIVES (1:5 – 2:52)

In this section (peculiar to Luke) we have our only information
about the origins of John the Baptist and some unique information about the birth of Jesus. There are some notable parallels
between the two birth stories. In both the angel Gabriel
brought news of what was to happen, in both the circumstances
of the birth and circumcision are narrated, and in both this is
followed by prophetic utterances. Luke is bringing out the
wonder of the Messianic age. Prophecy had ceased at the close
of the Old Testament period; but now God was sending His
Messiah and the prophetic gift was renewed. John is shown
to have a special place in the Messianic happenings. There is
no possibility of confusing him with the Messiah in Luke's
account, for he is but the forerunner (1:17). But there is no
possibility either of missing his true greatness.

Both the language and the ideas of these chapters reflect a
Semitic background. Some scholars hold that Luke is translating a Hebrew or Aramaic document, while others think he is
writing in imitation of the style of the Septuagint. On the whole
it seems likely that Luke is reflecting his sources and that these
come from Palestine.

a. The birth of John foretold (1:5-25)

5-7. Luke dates his narrative from the reign of Herod the
Great (37-4 BC). What he describes comes somewhere near
the end of that reign. He tells of *Zechariah*, a priest from the

[1] N. B. Stonehouse, *The Witness of Luke to Christ* (London, 1951), p. 44.

country (39f.), who took his turn in ministering in the Temple. There were many priests, but only one Temple. So they served on a roster (1 Ch. 24:1–6). The priests were divided into twenty-four divisions of which that of *Abijah* was the eighth (1 Ch. 24:10). Actually only four divisions returned from the Exile (Ezr. 2:36–39), but the four were subdivided to make up twenty-four again with the old names. Each division was on duty twice a year, for a week on each occasion. Zechariah was married to *Elizabeth*, herself a priest's daughter. A priest was required to marry an Israelite virgin (Lv. 21:14), but not necessarily one of a priestly family. To have a wife of priestly stock was an added blessing for a priest. The piety of this couple is brought out with the adjectives *righteous* and *blameless*. This means, of course, that they served God faithfully, not that they were sinless. It made their childless state hard for them to understand, for men held at that time that God would bless faithful servants by giving them children. The mention of their age is probably to make it clear that they could expect no change in the situation. Zechariah might have been very old, for there was no retiring age for priests (as there was for Levites).

8–10. There were many priests and not enough sacred duties for them all, so lots were cast to see who would perform each function. The offering of incense was regarded as a great privilege. A priest could not offer incense more than once in his entire lifetime (Mishnah, *Tamid* 5:2), and some priests never did receive the privilege. Thus the time when Zechariah offered the incense was the most important moment in his whole life. Luke does not say whether he offered at the morning or the evening sacrifice. In either case he would go into the holy place with other priests. But they would retire, leaving him alone. When the signal was given he would offer the incense. The worshippers waited in the outer court until the priest discharged this duty (10).

11, 12. Luke gives us no description of the angel. He simply tells us that the heavenly visitor stood *on the right side of the altar of incense*. As directions are often given in the Bible from the standpoint of a man facing east, this probably means the south side. The angel would then be standing between the altar of incense and the golden candlestick.

13. The angel first reassured Zechariah: *Do not be afraid.*
Then he went on, *your prayer is heard.* The aorist tense seems
to indicate prayer on one specific occasion, rather than
habitual prayer. If so, it will surely be the prayer Zechariah
offered at the time of the incense. Our first thought is that
he had prayed for a child. But, even allowing for the lack of
faith with which we so often pray, Zechariah's blank incredu-
lity when told he would have a son seems hard to reconcile
with this. Moreover a priest might have thought it unseemly
to make his private concern the object of prayer at such a
moment. Thus there is much to be said for the idea that he
prayed for the redemption of Israel. Now he was told that this
prayer was to be granted. But that was not all: in addition he
would have a son. The child's name was to be John (='The
Lord is gracious').

14–17. In a poetic passage the angel speaks first of the joy
that would come to Zechariah and many others at the birth of
the child, and then of the destiny the boy would fulfil. That
Zechariah would have *joy and gladness* was only to be expected.
But this child was to be *great before the Lord*, so that his birth
would be a cause of happiness to many others as well. He
was to abstain from *wine* and *strong drink* (like Samson's
mother, Jdg. 13:4). Some have deduced that he would be a
life-long Nazirite (Nu. 6:1–8); but this is never said, and the
absence of a reference to the hair (a Nazirite's hair was not
cut) seems against it. It may be better to see John as having a
unique position, neither Nazirite nor priest, though with
points of connection with both. The most important thing is
that from the very first John was to be *filled with the Holy Spirit.*
Thus early Luke begins his references to the Spirit,[1] without
whose help God's work cannot be done effectively. For the
contrast between the stimulation caused by wine and that of
the Spirit *cf.* Ephesians 5:18.

The child would *turn* many Israelites *to the Lord their God*
(which makes it clear that they had gone away from Him).
His ministry is likened to that of *Elijah* (*cf.* Mk. 9:13) and the
prophecy of Malachi 3:1; 4:5f. is invoked. This brings out
both John's greatness and his subordinate place. The fulfilment
of prophecy and the comparison with Elijah emphasize the
greatness of the man. But on the other hand he was no more

[1]See Introduction, pp. 44ff.

LUKE *1:18–22*

than a forerunner, one who could prepare men for the coming
of the Lord. The meaning of *to turn the hearts of the fathers to the
children* is not immediately obvious. It may be that John
was to remedy disunity among families. Or *the fathers* may
refer to the patriarchs, the great ancestors of the present
sinners. From their vantage-point in the next world they
looked at their descendants and were displeased. But John's
work would bring about such a change that the fathers would
look with favour on Israel (*cf.* Is. 29:22f. for a similar thought).
Similarly John would change *the disobedient* so that they
accepted *the wisdom of the just.* The result would be *a people
prepared* for the Lord.

18. Zechariah refused point blank to believe the angel. His
question is identical with that asked centuries before by
Abraham (Gn. 15:8), but it is asked in a different spirit. It
amounts to a demand for a sign. Gideon and Hezekiah, it is
true, asked for signs (Jdg. 6:36–39; 2 Ki. 20:8), but again in a
very different spirit. Zechariah is speaking from a position of
unbelief, as he goes on to remind the angel that both he and
his wife are old. He does not need to add that children do not
come to such as them.

19, 20. The angel replies by disclosing his name and
position. *Gabriel* means 'man of God'. His place *in the presence
of God* shows something of his dignity. Zechariah would be in
no doubt as to the importance of his informant. And this
great Gabriel *was sent* (*i.e.* by God) to bring to the old priest
good news. Luke emphasizes the point by employing a verb
later to be used characteristically of preaching the good news of
the gospel. Zechariah's refusal to believe must be seen in the
light of God's condescension in sending such a messenger with
such a message. To reject him was serious and it would have
its consequences. Zechariah would get his sign all right, though
not the kind of sign he wanted. He would be *silent*, quite
unable to speak until such time as Gabriel's words were fulfilled. Gabriel leaves no room for uncertainty. What God has
said will come to pass.

21, 22. It did not take long to offer the incense and priests
normally came out quickly from the holy place (lest they be
punished there for some act of presumption). The people had

no way of knowing what was keeping Zechariah so long beyond the normal time, and they *wondered at his delay*. *Temple* would be better translated 'sanctuary'. People and priests were all in one part or other of the Temple, but Zechariah was ministering in the holy place. When he came out he should have joined the other officiating priests in pronouncing the benediction (Mishnah, *Tamid* 7:2). His making of signs and remaining dumb made it evident that something unusual had happened in the sanctuary. The people could not know exactly what it was, but they concluded *that he had seen a vision*.

23–25. Zechariah evidently remained at the Temple until the end of his week of service, then went home. In due course Elizabeth *conceived*, thus affording him evidence of the truth of what Gabriel had said. It is not clear why Elizabeth hid herself for *five months*. But during this time her pregnancy would not have been noticeable. It may be that she did not want to be seen until it was obvious to all that the Lord had *looked on* her *to take away* her *reproach* (*cf.* Gn. 30:23). Childlessness was usually considered a punishment from God, and Elizabeth had evidently had to put up with reproaches from people who did not recognize her piety (6). Now she would know this no more.

b. The birth of Jesus foretold (1:26–38)

The virgin birth is a distinctive Christian doctrine. Some commentators, while they agree that there is no Jewish parallel, suggest that the idea came from the Greek world. There were similar birth stories among the Greek legends, they say, and Christian apologists produced the story in a spirit of 'Anything they can do we can do better!' But none of the parallels adduced is really relevant. They usually tell of a divine person having sexual intercourse with a human (usually a god with a woman). A truly virgin birth is unique. Ellis notes that the subject is absent from the writers to the Hellenistic church, such as Paul and Mark. He thinks it is a Palestinian tradition which was publicly avoided by Christians 'to prevent Jewish offence and "Greek" misunderstanding of Jesus and his messiahship'. Some commentators think Luke is here combining sources, some of which do not speak of the birth as from a virgin, and use this to throw doubt on the whole idea. But it is precarious to reason from what may have been the content of a hypothetical source. The evidence of the Gospel as we have it is plain.

26, 27. The *sixth month* will refer to the sixth month of Elizabeth's pregnancy. Luke tells us first of the city to which Gabriel was sent and then of the maiden in that city to whom he came. Nazareth is called *a city*, perhaps because Greek has no word for a 'town' and the alternative is 'village'. But it was not a metropolis. *Mary* is described as *betrothed*, a state which was much more binding among the Jews of that day than is an engagement with us. It was a solemn undertaking to marry, so binding that divorce was necessary to break it.

28, 29. Gabriel greeted Mary as *favoured one*, but even the addition, *the Lord is with you!* does not make it clear in what the favour consisted. Nor is it quite clear what caused Mary to be *greatly troubled*. We might understand it had she been frightened at the sight of an angel (as Zechariah was). But her distress is linked with *the saying*. Evidently in her modesty she did not understand why a heavenly visitant should greet her in such exalted terms.

30, 31. Gabriel reassures her, as he had done with Zechariah (13). He tells Mary not to be afraid, for she has *found favour with God*. It is, of course, a complete misunderstanding which translates the words, 'Hail Mary, full of grace', and understands them to mean that Mary was to be a source of grace to other people. Gabriel is saying simply that God's favour rests on her. He goes on to explain that she will *conceive* and *bear a son* (*cf.* Is. 7:14). As with John earlier, the angel names the child: *you shall call his name Jesus* (=Heb. Joshua='The Lord is salvation').

32, 33. In poetic words Gabriel goes on to speak of Jesus and first says He will be *great*. Earlier he applied this word to John (15), but he uses it now with a fuller meaning, for Jesus *will be called the Son of the Most High*. This sets Him apart from all others and makes Him Son of God in a special sense. Gabriel goes on to speak of Him as the recipient of *the throne of his father David*. The Messiah was expected to be of David's line (*cf.* 2 Sa. 7:12ff.; Ps. 89:29) and it is clearly this that is in mind. This is further brought out in the reference to *his kingdom* as never-ending. In current Messianic speculations the Messianic kingdom was often seen as of limited duration. It was God's final kingdom that would have no end. Jesus is thus brought into relation with this kingdom of God, a kingdom that is not to be understood as a temporal kingdom, an earthly realm; rather it is God's kingly rule, as Jesus would in due time make clear.

34. Where Zechariah had been disbelieving, Mary was puzzled, though why is not immediately obvious. She was soon to be married, so there seems no insuperable difficulty in the thought of her bearing a son. Some exegetes hold that her question implies that she had made a vow to remain a virgin perpetually. But in the first instance this reads something into the text (and into other passages also, for we read of brothers of Jesus). And in the second instance there seems no reason why she should get married, if she planned to remain a virgin. The solution of the difficulty rather is that Mary understood Gabriel to mean that she would bear a child without the intervention of a man, perhaps even that conception would be immediate.

35. Speaking with reverent reserve Gabriel says that the Holy Spirit will *come upon* Mary and that *the power of the Most High will overshadow* her. This delicate expression rules out crude ideas of a 'mating' of the Holy Spirit with Mary. Gabriel makes it clear that Mary's conception will be the result of a divine activity. Because of this the child to be born would be *holy, the Son of God.* We should not miss this explanation of what *the Son of God* means.

36, 37. Evidently Mary had not heard of Elizabeth's experience. Gabriel now informs her that it is *the sixth month* of her pregnancy. Mary will see that *with God nothing will be impossible* (*cf.* Gn. 18:14). She must be encouraged by Elizabeth's experience. Some have concluded from the fact that Elizabeth is Mary's *kinswoman* that Mary must have been of the family of Aaron, as Elizabeth was (5). They conclude that, if we accept the virgin birth, Jesus was not descended from David. But this is to go too far too fast. All the conditions are satisfied if one of Mary's parents was of David's family and the other of Aaron's. The reference to Jesus as descended from David (32), made when Joseph's reaction was as yet undetermined, shows that Mary must have been able to claim Davidic descent.

38. Mary's response is one of quiet submission. *Handmaid* (*doulē*) means 'slave-girl'. It expresses complete obedience. The slave-girl could not but do the will of her Master. This is reinforced with *let it be to me according to your word*. We are apt to take this as the most natural thing and accordingly we miss Mary's quiet heroism. She was not yet married to Joseph. His reaction to her pregnancy might have been expected to be a strong one and Matthew tells us that he did in fact think of divorcing her (Mt. 1:19). Again, while the death penalty for adultery (Dt. 22:23f.) does not seem to have been carried out often, it was still there. Mary could not be sure that she would not have to suffer, perhaps even die. But she recognized the will of God and accepted it.

c. Mary's visit to Elizabeth (1:39-45)

39, 40. Mary lost no time in paying a visit to her kinswoman. Gabriel visited her in Elizabeth's sixth month (36) and she returned home after a visit of about three months (56), apparently before the birth of John. She must therefore have set out almost immediately after the angel's visit. *The hill country* of Judah does not locate the home of Zechariah and Elizabeth with any precision, but it does make it clear that they were country folk. Attempts to identify the place where they lived have not been successful.

41, 42. At the moment that Mary greeted her relations the baby moved in Elizabeth's womb. Movements of the foetus are not, of course, uncommon. But on this occasion Elizabeth was *filled with the Holy Spirit* and under His inspiration interpreted the movement as the expression of her unborn baby's joy (44). The *loud cry* (or 'shout', *kraugē*) shows her excitement. Her words are printed as prose in our Bibles, but actually they form a little poem. She greets Mary as *Blessed . . . among women* (which reflects a Hebrew construction meaning 'the most blessed of women'). There may be a contrast with Zechariah, who had had a visit from an angel but who had responded very differently.

43-45. The use of the title *my Lord* indicates that Elizabeth recognized that Mary's child would be the Messiah (*cf.* Ps. 110:1). She goes on to explain that at Mary's greeting her own baby *leaped for joy* (the word denotes 'exultation') in her womb. It was this that enabled her to recognize Mary for what she was. She concludes with a further blessing of Mary. We should probably take her words to mean 'Blessed is she who believed, for there will be . . .' (the Greek is ambiguous, but 'for' seems better than 'that'). Elizabeth is affirming that the *fulfilment* will certainly take place, not simply that Mary believed it would.

We should not miss the absence of all jealousy in Elizabeth's attitude to Mary. The older woman, who had been the recipient of such a signal blessing from the Lord, might well have tried to guard her position jealously. But in genuine humility she recognized the superior blessing God had given to Mary. A further point of interest is the fact that John the Baptist did not recognize Jesus as Messiah until the baptism (Jn.1:32f.). Apparently Elizabeth's recognition that He is *Lord* was an inspired but personal affair. John had to find it out for himself.

d. The song of Mary (1:46-56)

The song of Mary (called the *Magnificat* from its opening words in the Latin translation) is an outburst of praise largely in Old Testament language. In particular there are quite a number of resemblances to the song of Hannah (1 Sa. 2:1-10). But we should notice a difference in tone. Hannah's song is a shout of triumph in the face of her enemies, Mary's a humble contemplation of the mercies of God. Ford asks whether some later poet may have composed the song and attributed it to Mary; but he thinks it more likely that Mary on her four days' journey to Elizabeth brooded over the story of Hannah and then uttered her own inspired song.

46-48. A few Latin MSS read 'Elizabeth said' instead of *Mary said*, and some commentators (*e.g.* Creed) accept this. But the textual evidence in support of Mary is overwhelming.

There is also a marked difference in tone between this song and the one just considered. Elizabeth's words are excited and tumultuous, these are calm and measured. It is not easy to think of the one singer as uttering these two songs on the same occasion. We should accept *Mary* as the true reading.

Her song begins with an expression of praise. We should not make a difference between *soul* and *spirit*, the change being due to the requirements of poetic parallelism. RSV misses a change of tense which may be significant: *magnifies* denotes the habitual act (Mary keeps on magnifying the Lord), but *rejoices* is rather 'rejoiced', the aorist pointing to a special act of rejoicing, probably when the angel brought his message. The word is a strong one and could be rendered 'exulted' (*cf.* the corresponding noun in verse 44). *God my Saviour* shows that Mary recognized her need—she was a sinner like other people. Some take *low estate* to signify 'humiliation'. This probably goes too far, but the word is expressive of humility, as is *handmaiden* (='slave-girl'; see on 38). Goodspeed brings out the meaning with 'he has noticed his slave in her humble station'.

49, 50. From thankfulness for what God has done for her Mary turns to contemplation of God Himself. She dwells on three things, His power, His holiness and His mercy. She sees herself as insignificant, but that did not matter, for 'the Mighty One' (Rieu) is at work. But God is not to be thought of only in terms of power. He is *holy*. The *name* in antiquity was used in a fuller sense than with us: it stood for the whole person. So this verse means not simply that God's name is a holy name and must be used reverently; it means that God is a holy God. Further, He is merciful. In every generation *his mercy* is certain for those who reverence (so, rather than *fear* in our sense of the term) Him.

51-53. The impression left by an English translation is that Mary continues to recite God's habitual actions. But we have a series of six aorist tenses in the Greek which are most unlikely to have this meaning. There are other possibilities. Mary may be looking back to specific occasions in the past when God has done the things she enumerates. Ford takes this view and comments, 'Only because the mighty Lord has done mighty things is there good news to tell, only because of the past tenses which speak out God's deeds is there a gospel to proclaim.' Or Mary may be referring to acts still future but which have begun to be realized. It is perhaps more likely that she is looking forward in a spirit of prophecy and counting what God will do as so certain that it can be spoken of as accomplished (this is frequent in the Old Testament prophets). This section of the song tells of a complete reversal of human values. It is not *the proud* or *the mighty* or *the rich* with whom is the last word. Indeed, through His Messiah, God is about to overthrow all these. *The proud* are spoken of with reference to *the imagination of their hearts*, *i.e.* it is proud thoughts that are in mind and not simply arrogant actions. *The mighty* are on *thrones*. Mary is speaking of those actually ruling (NEB, 'monarchs'), not simply of powerful people. There is a revolutionary note about filling *the hungry* and sending *the rich* away *empty*. In the ancient world it was accepted that the rich would be well cared for. Poor people must expect to be hungry. But Mary sings of a God who is not bound by what men do. He turns human attitudes and orders of society upside down.

54-56. Mary now sings of God's help for His people. The verb *helped* is not explained. But the aorist is probably still prophetic and Mary seems to be thinking of the help that will come through Messiah. We should probably understand *as he spoke to our fathers* as a parenthesis (there is a change of construction in the Greek, with *pros* before *fathers* but a simple dative with *Abraham*; it is certainly difficult to take *fathers* as in apposition with *Abraham*). Mary is saying that God's action in the Messiah is not so much completely new as a continuation of His mercy to Abraham. It is also in accordance with His promises to the fathers of old time.

The song concluded, Luke tells us that Mary's visit lasted *about three months*, after which she went home. He may simply be finishing this part of Mary's story before returning to Elizabeth; but it seems more likely that he means that Mary left before John was born. There would then be much excitement and many visitors. Mary, in her condition, might not wish to be there for that.

e. The birth and naming of John (1:57-66)

57, 58. As the angel had prophesied, Elizabeth's child was a boy. The birth was clearly of widespread interest among the mother's family and friends, and many of them came to share her joy. Luke describes the happy event in terms of the Lord's *mercy*, a topic that runs through these opening chapters.

59. It was provided in the law that a male child should be circumcised on *the eighth day* of his life (Gn. 17:12; Lv. 12:3). In the Old Testament the name was apparently given at birth and it does not seem in any way connected with circumcision. SB note this passage and 2:21 as the early witnesses for the practice, it being found next in eighth-century Jewish writings. Some scholars, impressed by the lack of contemporary Jewish evidence, hold that the custom is later than New Testament times and that Luke is influenced by prevailing practices in the Roman empire. But it is not easy to find clear evidence for naming boys on the eighth day anywhere in the ancient world. The Romans, for example, named boys on the ninth day and the Greeks on the seventh or the tenth. There seems no reason for rejecting SB's view that Luke happens to be the first to mention a custom that the Jews had developed.[1] It is curious that the relations try to name this child, as that was the privilege of the parents. Perhaps they simply took it for granted that the child would be named after his father. This was far from inevitable (few New Testament men seem to be so named). But in some Jewish writings it is taken as customary (*e.g. Genesis Rabbah* 37:7).

60-63. Elizabeth decisively rejected the idea (her *Not so* is emphatic). Her statement that the child would be called *John* drew the immediate objection that this was not a family name. For the friends that ruled it out altogether. But they were under the disadvantage that they had no right to name the child themselves. So they tried to enlist the father. It is curious that they *made signs* to him. In their excitement they forgot that Zechariah was able to hear, or else the old priest was deaf as well as dumb (the word *kōphos* which describes his ailment in verse 22 can mean 'deaf and dumb'). His response when they gave him *a writing tablet* (a board covered with wax, SB) was definite enough. He did not say, as had Elizabeth, that the child would be called John, but *His name is John*. In the Greek

---

[1] For the naming of children among the Jews see H. Daniel-Rops, *Daily Life in Palestine at the Time of Christ* (London, 1962), pp. 106-109.

John comes first with emphasis, and we should not overlook the force of the present. The angel had already named the child and Zechariah accepts the name as an accomplished fact.

64. The result was an immediate end to Zechariah's dumbness. It is a measure of the thinking he had doubtless been engaging in throughout the silent months that his first words were the praise of God.

65, 66. The neighbours were awe-struck (*fear*=deep reverence rather than fear in our sense of the term). Some think that Elizabeth had been supernaturally informed of the name and that it was this that impressed the friends. But there is no reason for thinking that Zechariah had not communicated his whole story to his wife, including the name of the child. Surely that writing tablet had been much in use during Zechariah's prolonged silence! These strange events formed a topic of conversation *through all the hill country of Judea*. But these country people did not simply gossip. They *laid . . . up in their hearts* the content of what was being said, and wondered about the destiny of this child. Plainly the events that had just occurred portended some mighty action of God.

f. The song of Zechariah (1:67–80)

Zechariah's joy overflows in an inspired song (known as the *Benedictus* from its opening word in the Latin). It may be divided into four strophes: thanksgiving for the Messiah (68–70), the great deliverance (71–75), the place of John (76, 77), and the Messianic salvation (78, 79). Farrar speaks of it as 'the last Prophecy of the Old Dispensation, and the first of the New'. Some see the song as primarily political with an emphasis on the overcoming of Israel's enemies (71, 74), and add that a Christian at the end of the century would not have composed so Jewish a poem. We may agree that there is an authentic Jewish note, but it should not be overlooked that the deliverance from enemies is specifically related to serving God (74). The song is religious rather than political.

67. Zechariah's words must be understood as the result of the Holy Spirit's coming upon him. They are words of prophecy, words which express God's revelation.

68–70. *Blessed be the Lord God* was a common way of introducing a thanksgiving (*cf.* Pss. 41:13; 72:18; 106:48). Zechariah's song is thus one of thanks. He speaks first of God as visiting (a common Old Testament way of speaking, but only in Luke and Heb. 2:6 in the New) and redeeming (*i.e.* saving at cost; *cf.* Melinsky, ' "rescue" at a high price'). The *horn* was a symbol of strength (as with the horn of a bull), so that *a horn of salvation* means 'a mighty salvation' or 'a strong saviour' (Moffatt). The reference to *the house of his servant David* shows that Zechariah is singing about the Messiah (*cf.* Ps. 132:17). It reveals incidentally that Mary probably had Davidic connections, for at this time Zechariah could not have known whether Joseph would marry her or not. The reference to the *holy prophets* stresses the divine purpose. God is working out His plan, a thought which is further emphasized in the references to His dealing mercifully with the fathers, to the 'holy covenant' and to the oath to Abraham (72f.).

71–75. The salvation the Messiah will bring is spoken of first as deliverance (71), then as mercy to the fathers (not only to the living; *cf.* verse 17), and then in terms of the covenant. There are several covenants in the Old Testament, but that with Abraham stands out. The *oath* was a significant part of any covenant, and here it is emphasized. God will not go back on what He has sworn. The covenant with Abraham will be brought to its consummation. There is a religious aim behind the deliverance from the enemies. It is so that God's people may *serve him without fear*. They will serve in *holiness* (they will belong to God), and *righteousness* (they will live as God's people should).

76, 77. We might have expected that Zechariah's song would be all about his little boy. He surprised us by beginning with the Messiah whom God was about to send. But he was very pleased about John, and in this part of his song he prophesies the child's future. He addresses him directly, and says that he will be called *the prophet of the Most High*. There had been no prophet among the Jews for centuries, so the words should not be taken too calmly. John represented a radical departure from what had become customary. And not only was he to be a prophet, but he was to prepare the Lord's way. He would be forerunner to the Messiah. Specifically he would tell people about the coming of salvation *in the forgiveness of their sins*. John could not save men. No man could. But he would call men to repentance and tell them about One who could.

78, 79. Zechariah finishes his song by dwelling on the coming salvation. It will come through God's *tender mercy*. The compassion of God is a constant theme of the New Testament. The old priest goes on to speak of salvation in terms of *light*. The contrast between light and darkness is a natural one, but none the less powerful for that. It is possible to understand the Greek as 'the dayspring' and see an unusual name for the Messiah (so RSV mg.; *cf.* Mal. 4:2; 2 Pet. 1:19; Rev. 22:16). But it seems more natural to take it as *day*, or better, 'sun' (*anatolē* means the 'rising' of the sun or a star, and hence the sun or star itself; RSV's *day* does not seem to be attested) and see the contrast between light and darkness (*cf.* Is. 60:1f.). The concluding note is that of *peace*, that peace of God that calms men's hearts and makes them strong to live for God. It 'does not mean merely freedom from trouble; it means all that makes for a man's highest good' (Barclay).

80. John's upbringing is described very briefly. Many points in the later teaching of John remind us of similar points in the Dead Sea scrolls. Some scholars point out that there were Essenes who brought up other men's children and they suggest that perhaps John's aged parents died or were not able to bring up their child themselves, so that he was brought up by some such sect. This is very hypothetical, but many things about John would be explained if he had in fact been brought up by some such desert sect but had broken away from it in adult life. Caird reminds us also that the wilderness was 'the traditional home of prophetic inspiration'. Luke may mean us to see John as a true prophet from the beginning.

g. The birth of Jesus (2:1-7)

1. There are difficulties posed by the facts that our knowledge of the times is imperfect and that what Luke says is not easy to fit in to what we do know. Thus there is no record of any law of Augustus that a universal census be held. But he did reorganize Roman administration, and there are records of censuses held in a number of places. In Egypt, where the

custom is unlikely to have differed significantly from neigh-
bouring Syria of which province Judea was a part, a census
was held every fourteen years. Actual documents survive for
every census from AD 20 to 270 (Barclay). When Augustus
died he left in his own handwriting a summary of information,
such as statistics on direct and indirect taxation, which would
most naturally have been derived from censuses.[1] The
evidence seems best satisfied if we understand the *decree* of
which Luke writes, not as a formal law, but as an administrative direction which set the whole process in motion and had
its effect in distant Judea.

It was not, of course, necessary for Luke to mention the
point (none of the other Evangelists does). But it seems to be
part of his plan to set his story in the secular context (*cf.* 3:1).
He sees God as Lord of history, and the actions of the emperor
in far-away Rome do but set forward the divine plan and
purpose.

2. There is a further difficulty about the part *Quirinius*
played. As governor of Syria he carried out a census in AD 6
(Josephus, *Antiquities* xviii. 26; this is mentioned in Acts 5:37).
This aroused violent opposition and Judas of Gamala led a
rebellion (*Antiquities* xviii. 3ff.). But that census is too late for
the present passage. However, certain inscriptions indicate
that between 10 and 7 BC Quirinius performed military
functions in the Roman province of Syria. If the interval
between censuses was fourteen years, this brings him into the
area in an official capacity at the right time. There is no
record outside Luke for a census at this time, but there is
nothing improbable about it. Josephus tells us that at about
this time 'the whole Jewish people' swore an oath of loyalty to
Caesar (*Antiquities* xvii. 42), which possibly reflects a census.
It is also worth noting that Tertullian says that the census
was carried out under Saturninus, who was governor of Syria
9–6 BC (*Adversus Marcionem* iv. 19). This is not in the Bible, so,
if the statement can be relied on (which some scholars doubt[2]),
Tertullian must be relying on other evidence. Justin, in the
middle of the second century, assures the Romans that they

[1] Tacitus, *Annals* i. 11; Suetonius, *Octavian* 101.
[2] C. F. Evans, in an article, 'Tertullian's References to Sentius Saturninus
and the Lukan Census', argues that Tertullian's statement does not refer
to the census in Luke (*JTS*, n.s., xxiv, 1973, pp. 24–39).

can see the registers of Quirinius's census (I *Apology* 34). Some
hold that the census of AD 6 must have been the first, for
people rebel at the unfamiliar, whereas once a census had been
held a second would be accepted. But it is fairly contended
that at the time of which Luke writes Herod would have
arranged the details and 'it would be quite like Herod's skill in
governing Jews to disguise the foreign nature of the command
by an appeal to tribal patriotism' (Easton, cited in Manson).
This is supported by the fact that in Luke's census people
returned to their family homes, whereas a Roman registration
would have been at the place of residence.

3. It seems to us a rather curious way of taking a census to
order everyone to return to his own home. But at least one
such direction is preserved from antiquity, namely an edict of
the governor of Egypt in AD 104 ordering everyone to return
home for enrolment.[1]

4, 5. Since Joseph was of the family of David he had to
report at Bethlehem, called *the city of David*, though David is
not recorded as having contact with it after he left it. Similarly
Jesus is never said to have visited it after His birth there.
Mary's attendance was probably not necessary. Little is
known of the regulations governing such a contingency, but
the probability is that, even if she had property, Joseph's
attendance would suffice. Perhaps Joseph did not care to leave
her at Nazareth. She had been with Elizabeth for three months
after her pregnancy began (1:56) and we have no means of
knowing how much later the wedding took place. To have
remained behind may have exposed her to calumny. Luke
refers to Mary as *his betrothed*, perhaps because, though they
were married (Mt. 1:24), the marriage was not yet consummated (Mt. 1:25).

6, 7. The birth of God's Son is described very simply.
Swaddling cloths are long strips which could wrap the child
round and round. That Mary wrapped the child herself points
to a lonely birth. That He was laid in a manger has traditionally been taken to mean that Jesus was born in a stable. He

---

[1]See A. Deissmann, *Light from the Ancient East* (London, 1928), p. 271.
Deissmann says that Luke uses official 'departmental language' in reporting
the order (*ibid.*, p. 270, n. 5).

may have been. But it is also possible that the birth took place
in a very poor home where the animals shared the same roof as
the family. A tradition going back to Justin says it occurred in
a cave (*Dialogue with Trypho* 78) and this could be right. Some
have thought that the birth took place in the open air (possibly
the courtyard of the inn), that being where a manger would
most likely be. We do not know. We know only that everything points to obscurity, poverty and even rejection. *There
was no place for them in the inn.* Joseph may have left his journey
too late. Or the innkeeper may not have wished to have them.
Another possibility is that the word does not mean *inn* here,
but a room in a house (as in 22:11). It had been meant for
Joseph and Mary, but was occupied by others by the time they
arrived.

We should perhaps reflect that it was the combination of a
decree by the emperor in distant Rome and the gossiping
tongues of Nazareth that brought Mary to Bethlehem at just
the time to fulfil the prophecy about the birthplace of the
Christ (Mi. 5:2). God works through all kinds of people to
effect His purposes.

h. The angels and the shepherds (2:8-20)

8. It is not unlikely that the *shepherds* were pasturing flocks
destined for the temple sacrifices. Flocks were supposed to be
kept only in the wilderness (Mishnah, *Baba Kamma* 7:7;
Talmud, *Baba Kamma* 79b–80a), and a rabbinic rule provides
that any animal found between Jerusalem and a spot near
Bethlehem must be presumed to be a sacrificial victim
(Mishnah, *Shekalim* 7:4). The same rule speaks of finding
Passover offerings within thirty days of that feast, *i.e.* in
February. Since flocks might be thus in the fields in winter
the traditional date for the birth of Jesus, December 25, is not
ruled out. Luke, of course, says nothing about the actual date
and it remains quite unknown. As a class shepherds had a bad
reputation. The nature of their calling kept them from observ-
ing the ceremonial law which meant so much to religious
people. More regrettable was their unfortunate habit of confusing 'mine' with 'thine' as they moved about the country.
They were considered unreliable and were not allowed to give
testimony in the law-courts (SB). There is no reason for
thinking that Luke's shepherds were other than devout men,

else why should God have given them such a privilege? But
they did come from a despised class.

9. The *angel* (the word means 'messenger') is not identified.
But his appearance struck terror into the shepherds as 'the
splendour of the Lord blazed around them' (Phillips).

10, 11. The angel first reassures his hearers (*cf.* 1:13, 30).
He goes on to explain that he has come with good and joyful
news (the verb translated *bring . . . good news* was later to be
used characteristically of the good news of the gospel). Thus
early the note of *great joy* is struck. *The people* (*laos*) normally
means 'the people of Israel', not people in general. The news
of the Saviour would mean much to men in every land, but
it came in the first instance to God's ancient people. The
Saviour (a title used of Jesus here only in the Synoptic Gospels;
it is found once in John) is called *Christ the Lord*. This renders a
Greek expression found nowhere else in the New Testament
and meaning, literally, 'Christ Lord'. Perhaps we should
understand it as 'Christ and Lord' (*cf.* Acts 2:36; 2 Cor. 4:5;
Phil. 2:11). The term *Christ* is Greek for 'Anointed one', just as
'Messiah' is our transliteration of a Hebrew term with a
similar meaning. Anointing was for special service like that of a
priest or a king. But the Jews expected that one day God
would send a very special deliverer. He would be not simply
'an' anointed but 'the' anointed, the Messiah. It is this one
whom the angel announces. *Lord* is used in the Septuagint of
God (it is used in other ways as well, but it is the translation
of the name Yahweh). *Christ the Lord* thus describes the child in
the highest possible terms.

12. The angel completed his message by giving the shepherds *a sign*. This would help them recognize the baby, but it
would also attest the truth of the angel's words. In Bethlehem
that night there might be one or two babies *wrapped in
swaddling cloths*, but surely only one *lying in a manger*.

13, 14. The message ended, there suddenly appeared a
multitude of other angels praising God. They are called a *host*,
i.e. 'army', paradoxically an army that announces peace, as
Bengel sagely remarks. First they speak of *Glory to God*, a
necessary preliminary to real peace on earth. There are

problems both of text and translation in the expression translated *among men with whom he is pleased* (more literally, 'among men of (his) good pleasure'). But RSV is right over against 'peace, good will toward men' (AV), a reading supported by many late MSS. The angels are saying that God will bring peace 'for men on whom his favour rests' (NEB). There is an emphasis on God, not man. It is those whom God chooses, rather than those who choose God, of whom the angels speak. *Peace*, of course, means peace between God and man, the healing of the estrangement caused by human evil.

15–18. The shepherds hurried to see for themselves. It is not easy to convey in English the sense of urgency imparted by the particle *dē*, but Leaney tried with, 'Come on, let us go. . . .' They found all as the angel had said, with the baby *lying in a manger*. Luke records the wonder with which everybody received the news of why they had come.

19. Luke's *But* places Mary in some contrast with the shepherds. Where they spoke out she *kept all these things, pondering them in her heart* (*cf.* Gn. 37:11). She treasured all this, and retained it in the inmost recesses of her being.

20. Luke rounds off the story with the return of the shepherds. They were full of praise to God 'for the news they had heard and the sight that had confirmed it' (Rieu).

i. The baby Jesus (2:21–40)

Luke proceeds to tell us something of the baby Jesus. His store of information is greater than that in any of the other Gospels.

i. The circumcision (2:21). Jesus was circumcised on the eighth day in accordance with Jewish law (Gn. 17:12). He was 'born under the law, to redeem those who were under the law' (Gal. 4:4f.) and was thus subjected to the requirements of the law. Luke puts no emphasis on the circumcision and in fact does not say explicitly that it took place. His emphasis is on the naming of the child with *the name given by the angel*. The divine purpose is to be seen in the name.

ii. The presentation in the Temple (2:22–24). Two quite separate ceremonies are involved here, the presentation of the

child and the purification of the mother. The attendance of
the child was not necessary, but it was natural when the parents
were close enough to Jerusalem. The presentation of the baby
follows from the fact that *every male that opens the womb* (*i.e.* the
first-born son of a mother, not necessarily of the father) *shall
be called holy to the Lord* (Luke's quotation is not exact but gives
the sense of several passages: Ex. 13:2, 12, 15; Nu. 18:15).
Though Luke does not mention it, doubtless the usual five
shekels were paid to redeem the first-born (Nu. 18:15f.).

The Levitical law provided that after the birth of a son a
woman would be unclean for seven days leading up to the
circumcision and that for a further thirty-three days she should
keep away from all holy things (for a daughter the time was
doubled; Lv. 12:1–5). Then she should offer a lamb and a dove
or pigeon. If she was too poor for a lamb a second dove or
pigeon sufficed instead (Lv. 12:6–13). Mary's offering was
thus that of the poor. The reference to *their* purification is a
little strange. Some think Jesus is included, but it seems more
likely that *their* refers to the same people as the following *they*,
i.e. Joseph and Mary. If Mary was ceremonially unclean it was
almost a certainty that Joseph would contract defilement and
they would both need cleansing.

iii. The song of Simeon (2:25–32). Luke records the
inspired reaction of Simeon to the bringing of Jesus into the
Temple. We seem always to think of this man as old, though
there is no evidence apart from his cheerful readiness to die
(29). Attempts to identify him as a priest or an important
citizen are without foundation. The name was a common one.
We know nothing about him apart from this story.

25, 26. Simeon was an upright man. *Righteous* shows that he
behaved well towards men, while *devout* (*eulabēs*; used by Luke
alone in the New Testament) signifies 'careful about religious
duties' (in the classics it means 'cautious'). *The consolation of
Israel* for which he looked is another name for the coming of
the Messiah (*cf.* SB). This was expected to be preceded by a
time of great suffering ('the woes of the Messiah'), so that he
would certainly bring comfort. In days when the nation was
oppressed men of faith looked all the more intensely for the
Deliverer who would solve their problems. The Holy Spirit
was upon him, which seems to mean on him continually. In the

old dispensation we read of the Spirit as coming upon people
on special occasions, but a continuing presence is rare.
Simeon's endowment was something special. The Spirit had
indicated to Simeon in some way not specified that he would
see the Messiah, *the Lord's Christ* (*cf.* 2:11) before his death.

27, 28. In fulfilment of the promise the Spirit brought
Simeon into the Temple at the same time as Joseph and Mary.
Simeon was 'in the Spirit' (*cf.* Rev. 1:10, *etc.*), which includes
inspired by the Spirit but seems also to indicate something more,
a special sensitivity. Joseph and Mary are called *the parents*.
This does not mean that Luke has forgotten that he has just
told us of the virgin birth, nor that he is here using a source
which was ignorant of it. 'The word *parents* is simply used to
indicate the character in which Joseph and Mary appeared
at this time' (Godet). *The custom of the law* will refer to the
offering of the five shekels on behalf of the child rather than
the sacrifice for the mother, for Luke says they do it *for him*.
Simeon *blessed God*, *i.e.* offered up a prayer of thanksgiving
(which would normally begin, 'Blessed be thou, O Lord').

29–32. As with the hymns in chapter 1 this little song is
known by its opening words in the Latin, namely *Nunc
Dimittis*. Simeon's *now* is important. He is ready to die peace-
fully *now* that he has seen God's *salvation*, *i.e.* the Baby through
whom God would in time bring salvation. His language is that
used of the freeing of a slave and he may be thinking of death
as 'his release from a long task' (Plummer). Simeon goes on to
show that this salvation is not for any one nation but for all.
This is clear enough in *all peoples*, but Simeon spells it out by
speaking of both *the Gentiles* and *thy people Israel*. It is probably
only the poetic structure that links *a light for revelation* with the
former and *glory* with the latter, for he would bring revelation
to Israel as to others. But there is appropriateness in linking
glory with Israel. There is much about glory in the Old Testament, particularly in connection with God's manifestations of
Himself to His people. But Israel will see glory in its truest and
fullest sense when it sees the Son of God. His being a light to
Gentiles means no diminution of Israel's glory but rather its
full realization.

iv. Simeon's prophecy (2:33–35). Some argue, from the
fact that Joseph and Mary *marvelled*, that Luke has imported a

narrative from a source lacking the preceding, for they would not be amazed after the visit from the shepherds. But this does not follow. There is matter for wonder that Simeon knew all this, and in any case what he says goes far beyond anything the shepherds said. We now find that the whole story is not sweetness and light. Salvation will be purchased at heavy cost and Simeon sombrely records this. He invokes a blessing on *his father and his mother* (see the note on 'the parents' in verse 27). Then in enigmatic words he goes on to speak of Jesus as *set for the fall and rising of many in Israel* (elsewhere in the New Testament the word rendered *rising* is always used of resurrection). It is not certain whether Simeon has in mind one group of people or two. In the former case he is saying that, unless men lose all pride in their own spiritual achievement, there is no hope for them. They must fall and take the lowly place; then they can rise (*cf.* the publican in the parable, 18:9–14). In the latter he means that Jesus will divide men. Those who reject Him will in the end *fall* (*cf.* Is. 8:14f.). Those who accept Him will rise, they will enter into salvation. Not surprisingly, He will be *spoken against*. That He will also be *a sign* is not so obvious. The expression means that He will point to the action of God. Simeon goes on to the cost to Mary. The *sword* (*rhomphaia* denotes a large sword, not the small *machaira* of 22:36, 38, 49, 52) that *will pierce* Mary's soul is the death of Jesus. His suffering will not leave her untouched. Simeon's final words point to the revelatory function of Jesus' work. Men declare themselves by their attitude to Him. They cannot ultimately be neutral. When men see Christ suffer, their reaction shows on which side they stand.

v. Anna's thanksgiving (2:36–38). To Simeon's prophecy Luke now adds the thanksgiving of another representative of organized religion, a prophetess named Anna. While many religious people failed to accept Jesus, this early recognition came from those who faithfully observed the requirements of their religion. Nothing more is known of Anna than we read here.

36, 37. There had been no prophet for hundreds of years, so it is noteworthy that God had raised up this *prophetess*. The Jews counted seven prophetesses only (Talmud, *Megillah* 14a), so this was no ordinary distinction. *Asher* was one of the lost ten tribes, but evidently some members of it survived and kept their genealogies. Anna had been married for seven years and remained a widow. It is not quite clear whether she was in fact eighty-four or whether she had been a widow for that length of time. If the latter she would have been a very old lady indeed, so many favour the former. *She did not depart from the temple*, which may mean that she had quarters within the Temple precincts or, more probably, that she was constantly at worship ('she never missed a service'! *cf.* 24:53). *Fasting and prayer*, practices which could be performed by individuals quite apart from corporate worship, point to a disciplined life.

38. Anna came up at the critical moment and thanked God, presumably for sending His Messiah. Luke however gives no indication of the content of the thanksgiving, nor of the further comments of Anna. *The redemption of Jerusalem* is another way of referring to the deliverance to be effected by the Messiah. A group within the old religion was thus expecting Messiah.

vi. The return to Nazareth (2:39, 40). Luke rounds off this part of his narrative with the return of Joseph and Mary to Nazareth. He makes no reference to the flight into Egypt (Mt. 2:13ff.) and there is no way of knowing whether Luke knew of it or not, and whether it preceded or followed the visit to Jerusalem. He speaks of the completion of the law's requirements after which *they returned into Galilee*. Jesus' childhood is described briefly in terms of development. There was growth, physical and mental and spiritual.

j. The boy Jesus in the Temple (2:41-52)

We know nothing of Jesus' boyhood apart from this one incident which Luke alone relates.

41. For *his parents*, see on verse 27. All male Jews were required to attend at the Temple three times in the year, at Passover, Pentecost and Tabernacles (Ex. 23:14-17). The Mishnah expressly exempts women from the obligation (*Hagigah* 1:1), but some rabbis appear to have thought they should go up and some, of course, did. Attendance at all three festivals was difficult with Jews scattered all over the Roman world and beyond, but many made the effort once a year. It was the custom of Joseph and Mary to go up at Passover, the feast that commemorated the deliverance of the nation from Egypt (Ex. 12).

42–45. They followed their custom on the occasion when Jesus was *twelve years old*. It was at thirteen years of age that a Jewish boy could become a 'son of the law' or full member of the synagogue (*cf.* Mishnah, *Aboth* 5:21; *Niddah* 5:6). He would then assume all the responsibilities implied in his circumcision. For some observances at any rate the Mishnah provides that a boy should be taken to the observance a year or two before he turned thirteen so that he might be prepared (*Yoma* 8:4), and there may have been something of this on the present occasion (though it is equally possible that Jesus went up every year; we do not know). On this occasion Jesus was left behind when His parents returned. In a large 'caravan' (Rieu) parents might well not know where a child was. If the later practice was followed, the women and small children went ahead and the men followed with the bigger boys. Joseph and Mary may each have thought that Jesus was with the other. For a full day they journeyed, looking for Him among the travellers before they concluded He must still be in Jerusalem and so returned thither. The description of Jesus as *the boy, pais*, may be in intentional contrast with 'baby', *brephos*, and 'little boy', *paidion*, in verses 16, 40. There is a record of development.

46, 47. *After three days* probably means three days from the time they first missed Jesus. It should not have taken three days to find Him in a place the size of Jerusalem, all the more so since He was in a prominent place, not hidden away. They found Him *among the teachers* in the Temple precincts. This was a customary place for teaching and evidently there was no problem in an unknown boy attaching himself to the circle. He was *listening to them and asking them questions*, which indicates a thirst for knowledge. There would have been few good teachers in Nazareth, and Jesus was making the most of the opportunity of learning while in the capital city. The educational system of the day appears to have put some emphasis on the discussion of problems (SB). This gave scope for a bright pupil both to ask and answer questions. The teachers *were amazed at his understanding and his answers*.

48. Joseph and Mary *were astonished*. Clearly they had expected nothing like this. There is reproach in Mary's question, *Son, why have you treated us so?* and in her reference to their anxious search.

49, 50. For Jesus it was a matter of surprise that there should have been any difficulty. The natural place for Him to be was *in my Father's house*. The Greek could be rendered 'about my Father's business' (AV). But RSV is probably right, for the Father's business could be done in many places and His parents' problem was where He was, not what He was doing. His answer shows that thus early Jesus had a clear idea of the importance of the service of God. Probably He also knew that He stood in a special relationship to God. The expression *my Father* is noteworthy and no parallel appears to be cited (the Jews added 'in heaven' or used 'our Father' or the like).[1] The first recorded words of the Messiah are then a recognition of His unique relationship to God and of the necessity (*must*) of His being in the Father's house. There is a Jewish midrash which speaks of the Messiah as knowing God directly, without human assistance, a distinction shared only by Abraham, Job and Hezekiah (*Midrash Rabbah, Numbers* xiv. 2). But Luke is saying more than this. Jesus had a relationship to God shared by no other. Joseph and Mary did not understand this. They learnt what Jesus' Messiahship meant bit by bit.

51. As a dutiful son Jesus returned to Nazareth and *was obedient to them* (this is Luke's last reference to Joseph; was he dead before Jesus' ministry began?). It was not yet time for Him to engage on His mission, so He remained in the home. As before with the shepherds (19), Mary did not forget. She might not understand, but she remembered.

52. A further summary in the manner of verse 40 rounds off the section. Jesus continued to advance intellectually and physically. *In favour with God and man* (*cf.* 1 Sa. 2:26; Pr. 3:4) points to spiritual and social progress. In the similar summary in the case of John the Baptist (1:80) there is nothing equiva-

[1] See G. Dalman, *The Words of Jesus* (Edinburgh, 1902), pp. 184–194. Of Jesus' general use he says, 'The usage of family life is transferred to God: it is the language of the child to its father' (*ibid.*, p. 192).

lent to *in favour with . . . man*. Probably there was an early difference in personality. John's sternness precluded him from anything like attractiveness.

II. THE MINISTRY OF JOHN THE BAPTIST
(3:1-20)

All the Gospels make it clear that the ministry of John the Baptist prepared the way for that of Jesus and that it was characterized by a call to repentance. But Luke alone tells us how John replied to questioners anxious about the way repentance affected their particular callings. His answers are simple and practical, though without the depth of insight that marked Jesus' teaching. Where John, for example, did not go past individual acts Jesus called for 'nothing less than the complete surrender of the soul to the indwelling power of the divine Spirit' (Manson, on 3:10-14). John's answers, however, reveal a recognition that each calling in life has its own temptations and that it is the mark of the truly penitent to resist them.

1. Luke begins with an elaborate dating, set, not at the beginning of Jesus' ministry, but at the beginning of that of John. It thus reflects the critical importance of the revival of prophecy. And it sets what follows firmly in the context of secular history. As Augustus died on 19 August AD 14, *the fifteenth year of the reign of Tiberius Caesar* was August AD 28–August AD 29. Some argue that the starting-point should be that of Tiberius's co-regentship with Augustus, AD 11-12; but no example appears to be cited of anyone ever dating from this point. Dates are always from the time Tiberius became emperor. Others hold that Luke is using the Syrian method whereby the year began on 1 October. The period 19 August–30 September would be counted as the first year of the reign, with the second beginning on 1 October. This brings us to the year beginning 1 October AD 27. If he followed a similar Jewish system the year would be that beginning Nisan 1 (March–April) AD 28.[1] It does not seem as though we can get closer than about AD 27-29.

[1] See G. Ogg in *NBD*, p. 223; J. Finegan, *Handbook of Biblical Chronology* (Princeton, 1964), pp. 272f.

Pontius Pilate was *governor*. This word is quite general, but an inscription shows that his title was 'prefect' (not 'procurator', as has often been held). *Judea* was part of the region assigned by Herod the Great to Archelaus, but he ruled so badly that his subjects petitioned the Romans to remove him. They did so and installed their own governor in AD 6. Pilate held this office AD 26–36. *Herod* is Herod Antipas, son of Herod the Great. He became tetrarch of Galilee and Perea on his father's death in 4 BC and held office until AD 39. He thus ruled during most of Jesus' lifetime over the territory in which most of Jesus' time was spent. The word *tetrarch* strictly means a ruler over a fourth part of a region, but it came to be used of any petty prince (Herod the Great in fact divided his kingdom into three parts). Herod's brother *Philip* ruled his tetrarchy (which was north-east of the Sea of Galilee) 4 BC–AD 33 or 34. *Lysanias* is a problem. Josephus mentions a man of this name who ruled extensive territory from his capital Chalcis until his death in 36 (or 34) BC (*Antiquities* xv. 92) and some have concluded that Luke is mistaken. There are, however, inscriptions which refer to a Lysanias at a later time who ruled as tetrarch in Abilene, which is to the north of the other regions mentioned (see the Additional Note in Creed). It seems best to hold that Luke is independent of Josephus and is writing about this later Lysanias. Nothing more is known of this man.

2. Luke proceeds to add a dating of peculiar importance to Jews, namely with reference to *the high-priesthood*. *Annas* was high priest AD 6–15, when the Roman governor Gratus deposed him. Five of his sons became high priest in due course, and *Caiaphas*, who held the office AD 18–36, was his son-in-law. Luke uses the singular, which shows that he knew there was only one high priest. He appears to mean that Caiaphas was officially in office but that Annas still exercised great influence, perhaps even was regarded by many Jews as the true high priest (*cf.* Acts 4:6). It may be worth pointing out that when Jesus was arrested He was first brought to Annas (Jn. 18:13).

At the time so impressively marked out then *the word of God came to John*. The expression is very like that used in LXX of the way the prophets got their message (*cf.* Je. 1:2). It is probably meant to place John in the true prophetic succession.

3. *He went into all the region about the Jordan* appears to mean that John travelled about in the Jordan valley. Unlike Matthew and Mark, Luke says nothing about John's appearance and dietary habits. He goes straight to his message. John preached *a baptism of repentance for the forgiveness of sins*. This means a baptism which follows repentance and is a sign of it. John called on men to turn away from their sins. The acceptance of baptism was a sign that they had done this. The purpose was *forgiveness*. Baptism was a rite of cleansing in a number of religions. It seems certain that at this time the Jews used proselyte baptism. They regarded all Gentiles as unclean, so baptized them when they became proselytes (as well as circumcising the males). The sting in John's practice was that he applied to Jews the ceremony regarded as suitable for unclean Gentiles. Many Jews expected that in the judgment God would deal hardly with Gentile sinners, but that the Jews, the descendants of Abraham, the friend of God, would be safe. John denounces this attitude and removes the fancied security.

4–6. In all four Gospels Isaiah 40:3 is applied to John the Baptist, but only Luke adds verses 4, 5. All four see John as regarding himself as no more than a voice ('The whole man was a sermon', Plummer), and so as preparing the Lord's way. But Luke goes on to the filling of the valleys, *etc.* (the imagery points to the making ready of a road before the approach of a king) and to the climax, *all flesh shall see the salvation of God* (the word *salvation* is derived from LXX, not the Hebrew; it may be an interpretation of the word for 'glory'). This fits in with Luke's purpose of bringing out the universality of the gospel.

7–9. Where Matthew mentions Pharisees and Sadducees as John's hearers, Luke names *the multitudes*. John's message was for the whole nation. His words as recorded here are almost identical with those in Matthew 3:7–10. Of sixty-three words in the Greek the only differences are Luke's *fruits* and *begin* (8) where Matthew has 'fruit' and 'presume'. The paragraph is heavy with judgment. John condemns his hearers as *vipers* trying to flee *the wrath to come*. The wrath of God is an important topic in both Testaments. It stresses the continuing divine hostility to all evil.[1] With this we take *the axe* lying by

[1] See my *The Apostolic Preaching of the Cross*[3] (London, 1965), chs. V, VI.

the root of the trees. The trees are not yet cut down. But the warning is clear. In between John reminds his audience that repentance must be shown by the appropriate *fruits*. He warns them against relying on Abrahamic descent. Jews were apt to think that God would ultimately be kind to them because of Abraham's merits, if they had none of their own. John reminds them that we stand before God as individuals. There is a play on words between *stones* and *children*, Aramaic *'abnayya'* and *b^enayya'*.

10, 11. John's teaching was rejected by Jewish leaders (7:30), but it led others to ask questions. People wanted to know what was expected of them. John's first answer is intensely practical: people should share what they have with those who have nothing. *Coats* (*chitōnes*) are properly 'tunics'. Normally one was worn under the outer garment (*himation*), but a man might wear more than one for extra warmth (Mk. 6:9) or have an extra tunic he was not wearing.

12, 13. The Romans taxed people by farming out the taxing rights to the highest bidder. The successful man would pay Rome the amount he bid, but he would collect more than that to pay expenses and to give him his legitimate profit. But it was a strong temptation to levy more tax than was strictly necessary and to pocket the extra. This provoked resentment, especially among the patriotic, who in any case did not like to see Jews helping the Romans by collecting their taxes for them. So the tax collectors were hated. And the more they were hated the more they tended to overtax. It was a vicious circle. The *tax collectors* who came to John's baptism were certainly the agents of the tax farmers, not the tax farmers themselves. John's preaching had convinced some of them that what they were doing was wrong and they wanted to express their repentance in baptism. John's advice is *Collect no more than is appointed you*.

14. Luke does not say whether the *soldiers* were Jewish or Roman. Most agree that they were probably Jewish and some think they may have been associated with the tax collectors in providing the backing which enabled them to do their work. Either way they were in a privileged position over against the

general public. Citizens could have little redress when troops
used violence or false charges to rob them. The word rendered
rob . . . by false accusation is a picturesque term meaning literally
'show figs'. It has been conjectured that this referred originally
to denouncing people for exporting figs from Attica (a
prohibited practice), but this and other suggestions are dismissed by LS as 'mere guesses'. John told the soldiers not to
presume on their position but *be content with your wages*, an
injunction with wide application. Notice that John does not
call on either group to leave their jobs. Rather he wants them
to act uprightly in them.

15. Such activities raised in men's minds the question
whether John might perhaps be the Christ (*cf.* Jn. 1:20, 25).
Messianic expectations were in the air and John's activities
were such as to make people wonder whether he might be the
one they were looking for.

16. But John repudiates the idea. He makes two points: he
is inferior to Someone who is yet to come and his baptism is
likewise inferior. This Successor, says John, *is mightier than I.* In
sheer power He surpasses John. And when it comes to worth,
John sees himself as unfit to loose *the thong of* His *sandals.*
Palestinian teachers were not paid, but pupils used to show
their appreciation with a variety of services. A rabbinic saying
(in its present form dated *c.* 250 but probably much older) runs,
'Every service which a slave performs for his master shall a
disciple do for his teacher except the loosing of his sandal-
thong' (SB, i, p. 121). Untying the sandal-thong was just too
much. But John selects precisely this duty, which the rabbis
regarded as too menial for a disciple, as that for which he was
unworthy. This is genuine humility.

John's other point is that his own baptism is *with water,*
whereas the mightier one *will baptize . . . with the Holy Spirit and
with fire.* This second baptism is clearly metaphorical. The
figure of speech emphasizes that the Mighty One will give the
Spirit in generous measure. The reference to *fire* is taken by
some to be in apposition with *Spirit,* 'the fire of the Spirit'
(Harrington), by some to mean testing (Creed), by others to
point to judgment. The context favours the last-mentioned,
and W. H. Brownlee has drawn attention to a passage in the

Dead Sea scrolls referring to an eschatological fire of judgment which he thinks supports this interpretation.[1] But it is the same people who are baptized with the Holy Spirit as with fire (and the two are governed by one *en* in the Greek). It seems best to see John as thinking of positive and negative aspects of Messiah's message. Those who accept Him will be purified as by fire (*cf.* Mal. 3:1ff.) and strengthened by the Holy Spirit.

17, 18. The judgment theme is developed. Winnowing was the process wherein, the grain having been loosened from the husks (as by treading it with oxen), the whole was thrown into the air against a breeze. The wind carried the chaff away, but the grain fell straight down. The *winnowing fork* (*ptuon*) was the fork or shovel by which the grain was tossed into the air. By this means the *threshing floor* was cleared. The *wheat* was brought into the barn, but the chaff burnt *with unquenchable fire*. This strong expression emphasizes the certainty and completeness of judgment. Luke rounds off the section by adding that John preached many such things. Notice that he includes this in the *good news* John preached. Judgment is not at first sight very good news; but it is an integral part of the gospel. Unless we can be sure that in the end evil will be decisively overthrown there is no ultimate good news.

19, 20. John was a fearless preacher of righteousness and he rebuked *Herod the tetrarch* for having married his brother's wife. *Herodias* was the daughter of Aristobulus, half-brother to Herod Antipas, and she was married to Herod, another half-brother and a private citizen. Herod Antipas persuaded Herodias to leave her husband and marry him, though it involved his divorcing his own wife also. It was a very unsavoury business. Luke mentions other evils of Herod (as Matthew and Mark do not) and goes on to say that he added to all the rest this further example, that he imprisoned John. From Josephus we learn that this was in the fortress Machaerus (*Antiquities* xviii. 119). Luke is not writing chronologically, for John continued at work during the early part of Jesus' ministry. He is simply finishing his story of John, after which he concentrates on the ministry of Jesus.

---

[1] *The Scrolls and the New Testament*, ed. K. Stendahl (London, 1958), p. 42.

III. THE BEGINNING OF JESUS' MINISTRY
(3:21 – 4:13)

a. Jesus' baptism (3:21, 22)

Luke begins his account of Jesus' ministry with our Lord's
baptism by John (though without mentioning John's name; he
has moved from John to Jesus). This is the one occasion on
which the Baptist is recorded to have been with Jesus. The
story is told briefly, but it is very important. It marks the call of
Jesus to His public ministry, a call accompanied by the gift of
the Holy Spirit and confirmed by a voice from heaven.
Unexpectedly, Luke refers to Jesus' baptism only in a subordinate clause. He prefers to emphasize the opening of
heaven and the descent of the Holy Spirit. The opening of
heaven means that a revelation from God follows. All four
Evangelists mention the descent of the Spirit *as a dove*.
Matthew and Mark tell us that Jesus saw this and John that
the Baptist saw it. Each might have been speaking of a subjective vision, but Luke's *in bodily form* shows that there was
an objective reality. The symbolism is puzzling, as the dove
was not an accepted symbol of the Holy Spirit (though a few
late Jewish writings do use it). Rather the dove stood for
Israel. However there is no doubt that here it is a sign of the
coming of the Holy Spirit. This must be taken as a piece of
early Christian symbolism, not as something taken over from
Jewish or Hellenistic sources. Luke is the only one of the
Evangelists who tells us that the descent of the Spirit occurred
as Jesus *was praying*.[1] It thus happened not at the baptism but
just after it.

It is at first sight puzzling that Jesus should have accepted
baptism at the hands of John, for this baptism was 'a baptism
of repentance' (3:3). Since Luke depicts Jesus as without sin it
is not obvious why he tells us He was baptized in this way. But
Jesus saw sinners flocking to John's baptism. Clearly He
decided to take His place with them. At the outset of His
ministry He publicly identified Himself with the sinners He
came to save.

Luke next tells us of the Father's approval given in the *voice
. . . from heaven*. This refers to Jesus as *my beloved Son* (in the

[1]For Luke's interest in prayer see Introduction, pp. 46f.

similar voice at the transfiguration He is 'my Son, my Chosen', 9:35). *With thee I am well pleased* means 'On you my favour (or pleasure) rests' rather than 'I am delighted with you'. Tasker points out that the significance of the words is 'on whom my plan for the salvation of mankind is centred'.[1] We may see in them also a combination of some words from Psalm 2:7 and an echo of Isaiah 42:1. At the threshold of His ministry, the heavenly voice directed Jesus' thoughts to the unusual combination of the Son of God and the Suffering Servant. This combination was to determine much of His ministry.

b. Jesus' genealogy (3:23–38)

Luke's genealogy differs greatly from that in Matthew. Luke gives the line from Adam to Abraham, as Matthew does not; they are practically the same from Abraham to David, and they diverge from that point on. There are three chief explanations of the difficulty.

1. Some suggest that Matthew gives us the genealogy of Joseph, the legal father of Jesus, while Luke gives that of Mary, the actual line of Jesus. This understands *Joseph, the son of Heli* as 'Joseph, the son of Heli by marriage'. Against this approach it is urged that this is not what Luke says and that in any case genealogies were not traced through the female line. Luke, however, is speaking of a virgin birth, and we have no information as to how a genealogy would be reckoned when there was no human father. The case is unique.

2. Africanus (*c.* AD 220) suggested that there was a levirate marriage. He thought that when Heli died childless Jacob, who had the same mother but a different father, married the widow and Joseph was born. On this view Matthew gives us Joseph's genealogy through Jacob, his actual father, while Luke gives it through Heli, his legal father.[2]

3. J. Gresham Machen argued Lord Hervey's view that Matthew gives us 'the *legal* descendants of David – the men who would have been legally the heir to the Davidic throne if that throne had been continued – while Luke gives the descendants of David in that particular line to which, finally, Joseph,

---

[1] *TNTC* on Mt. 3:17.
[2] *ANF*, vi, p. 126.

the husband of Mary, belonged'.[1] On this view Jacob, the father of Joseph in Matthew, and the heir to David's throne, died without issue. The succession then passed to the line represented by Eli.

In the present state of our knowledge it is impossible to say which of these is to be preferred, or whether there is a better explanation.

Luke's insertion of the genealogy at this point, after the baptism that marked Him out as Son of God and before the temptation which helped define the nature of His Messianic task, may be meant to help us see something of Jesus' Messianic significance. That the genealogy is recorded at all shows Him to be a real man, not a demi-god like those in Greek and Roman mythology. That it goes back to David points to an essential element in His Messianic qualifications. That it goes back to Adam brings out His kinship not only with Israel but with the whole human race. That it goes back to God relates Him to the Creator of all. He was the Son of God.

23. It is to Luke that we owe the information that Jesus *was about thirty years of age* at the beginning of His ministry. This was the age when the Levites began their service (Nu. 4:47) and was evidently regarded as the age at which a man was fully mature. The Greek is a trifle difficult, there being no object to the verb *began*. AV could render 'Jesus himself began to be about thirty years of age'. This, however, is most unlikely. We should accept RSV. The parenthesis *as was supposed* shows that Luke is bearing in mind that Jesus was really the son of Mary, not of Joseph.

24–38. Luke simply lists the names in his genealogy, in each case preceded by the genitive of the article, rendered 'son of'. Where Matthew takes the list back to Abraham Luke goes right back to Adam, in accordance with his interest in mankind generally. Miller thinks there may also be a reference to Jesus as the 'last Adam' (*cf.* 1 Cor. 15:22, 45). Luke adds *the son of God*, for we must see Jesus ultimately in His relationship to the Father. In this the genealogy harmonizes with the preceding and the following narratives, both of which are concerned with Jesus as the Son of God.

[1]J. G. Machen, *The Virgin Birth of Christ* (London, 1958), p. 204.

c. Jesus' temptations (4:1–13)

Jesus had just been baptized and now looked forward to the public ministry to which He had set His hand. But first He spent time in quiet reflection in the wilderness. What sort of Messiah was He to be? Was he to use His powers for personal ends? Or for the establishing of a mighty empire that would rule the world in righteousness? Or for working spectacular, if pointless, miracles? He rejected all these for what they were, temptations of the devil. That they were temptations implies that Jesus knew He had unusual powers. 'It is no temptation to us to turn stones into bread or leap from a Temple pinnacle' (Barclay). But Jesus was not bound by our limitations. He knew He had powers other men do not have and He had to decide how He would use them. This whole story has another interest for believers, namely that it must have come from none other than Jesus Himself. Matthew has the second and third temptations in the reverse order, a fact that has never been satisfactorily explained (the reasons suggested are all subjective).

1, 2. Matthew and Mark tell us that Jesus was brought into the wilderness by the Spirit, but Luke alone says that Jesus was *full of the Holy Spirit*. He also says that it was 'in (rather than *by*) the Spirit' that Jesus was led. Satan indeed tempted Jesus, but there was more to the story than that. It was in God's plan that right at the outset Jesus should face up to the question of what kind of Messiah He was to be.

3, 4. Satan began with Jesus' hunger and went on to raise a doubt as to His divine Sonship. Jesus had just heard a voice from heaven call Him 'Son' (3:22). Satan suggests that He verify His Sonship by turning a stone into bread. The problem for Jesus was to know whether the voice He now heard came from the same source as the heavenly voice. His answer came in a passage from the Bible (Dt. 8:3). What does not agree with Scripture does not come from God. The essence of the temptation may have been to use miraculous powers to supply bread to the hungry, *i.e.* to become a social worker. But there were no hungry men with Jesus in the wilderness, so it is perhaps more likely that the temptation was to use His powers for the supply of His own personal needs. The words in which the temptation was rejected have a wide application. Man must be concerned with many things besides bread (*cf*. Jn. 4:34). He is not simply an animal, living on the level of physical needs.

5-8. Luke does not say, as Matthew does, that the devil took Jesus to a high mountain to show Him *all the kingdoms of the world*. He emphasizes not the place from which the vision came but the fact that the evil one brought before Jesus all this world's pomp. He claimed it as his own (for Satan as 'the ruler of this world' *cf*. Jn. 12:31; 14:30; 16:11), and promised to give it to Jesus if only He would worship him. This means that Jesus saw the possibility of setting up a kingdom that would be mightier far than that of the Romans. It is not difficult to see how such a vision might be regarded as a legitimate aim. It would mean government concerned only with the genuine welfare of the people and the way would be opened for much good. But it meant compromise. It meant using the world's methods. It meant casting out devils by Beelzebub. For Jesus it meant turning His back on His calling. His kingdom was of a very different kind (Jn. 18:36f.). He had already identified Himself with the sinners He had come to save (3:21). That meant the lowly path, not that of earthly glory. It meant a cross, not a crown. To look for earthly sovereignty was to worship wickedness and Jesus decisively renounced it. Once again He appealed to the Bible (Dt. 6:13), pointing out that the worship of God is exclusive. None other is to be worshipped than He.

9-12. The third temptation is located in Jerusalem. Jesus is invited to throw Himself from *the pinnacle of the temple*. The article shows that a definite pinnacle is in mind, but we cannot identify it with certainty (suggestions include the apex of the sanctuary, the top of Solomon's portico and the top of the Royal portico). The temptation may have been to perform a spectacular, but pointless, miracle in order to compel wonder and belief of a kind. But since nobody else is said to have been present the temptation may rather have been, as Jesus' answer seems to indicate, that of presuming on God instead of trusting Him humbly. Farrar draws attention to an important point when he cites Augustine's comment that Satan can do no more than suggest: only the tempted person can perform the wrong act (throw *yourself* down). The evil one on this occasion quotes Scripture (Ps. 91:11f.) to assure Jesus that He would be safe enough. But this is a wrong use of the Bible. It is twisting a text to suit a purpose. Jesus rejects this temptation as He had the other two by appealing to the real meaning of the Bible (Dt. 6:16). It is not for man to put God to the test, not even when the man in question is the Son of God incarnate.

Notice that on all three occasions Jesus countered the temptations by quoting from Deuteronomy and in fact from the restricted area between 6:13 and 8:3. These chapters refer to the wilderness experiences of Israel, the people of God. It may well be that Jesus had given a lot of thought to these passages as He reflected on the mission to which God was calling Him. There were parallels in the experience of the ancient people of God to those in His own experience. He was one with the people of God.

13. Throughout these temptations no special resource is open to Jesus. He met temptation in the same way as we must, by using Scripture, and He won the victory. Luke rounds off the narrative with Satan decisively beaten. He had 'finished tempting Jesus in every way' (TEV), but Jesus had not yielded. This does not mean that from this point on Jesus was not subjected to further temptation. Conzelmann maintains that Luke pictures Satan as absent during Jesus' ministry, but this is not in accordance with the facts (*cf.* the work of Satan in 8:12; 10:18; 11:18; 13:16; 22:3, 31, and references to temptation or to testing, which imply his activity, in 8:13; 11:4, 16; 22:28). The devil left Him only 'till a fresh occasion should present itself', as Rieu translates. There is no freedom from temptation in this life. There was not for Jesus and there is not for us.

IV. JESUS IN GALILEE (4:14 – 9:50)

Luke proceeds to deal with Jesus' ministry in Galilee. Much of the material in this long section is shared by Matthew and Mark, but Luke gives it all his own stamp.

a. The sermon at Nazareth (4:14–30)

Luke appears to be referring to an incident put later by
Matthew and Mark. He does not regard it as the beginning of
Jesus' ministry, for he knows of earlier work (14, 15), though
he does not choose to describe it. But right at the outset Luke
shows that Jesus fulfils the prophecy of Isaiah. This was the
kind of ministry that Jesus would exercise. These are the
themes that would recur.

14, 15. It is not quite clear why *a report* about Jesus began
to circulate, for He has not yet been described as doing anything. But He came back from Jordan *in the power of the Spirit*
(notice Luke's interest in the Spirit). Evidently it could be
seen that Jesus was filled with the Spirit and this caused comment. Jesus proceeded to add to His reputation by teaching
in the synagogues and Luke tells us that He was *glorified by all*.
The plural, *synagogues*, points to a preaching tour. For *Galilee*
as the starting-point of Jesus' mission, *cf.* 23:5; Acts 10:37.

16. Luke reminds us that Jesus had been *brought up* at
Nazareth, and he tells us that in that city Jesus went to worship
on the sabbath *as his custom was*. There are many references to
Jesus' attendance at worship, but this is the only one that tells
us that it was His habit. Many commentators tell us how
synagogue services were conducted and point out where Luke
agrees. But we should bear in mind that this is the earliest
description of a synagogue service we have, so that this passage
is of critical importance for the study of the synagogue. We
may assume that some customs, which we know from later
times, were as old as this, but we should be clear that this is
assumption. Luke is our only authority for what was done at
this time. If later custom was begun as early as this, the service
would have commenced with prayer and there would have
been a reading from the Law (the books from Genesis to
Deuteronomy) before Jesus read from the prophets. There
were no ministers as we understand the term, but the local
synagogue authorities would invite people to read and to
preach. Scripture seems always to have been read in the
original Hebrew, though a translation into Aramaic would
have been made by the reader or someone else. From Acts it
is plain that it was not uncommon for distinguished visitors to

be invited to preach. The synagogue was used for instruction as well as for worship; indeed teaching may be held to be its primary function (*cf*. 13:10). The synagogue was of uncertain antiquity, but in Palestine it was not highly developed before the destruction of the Temple. There appear to be no certain ruins of synagogues in Palestine from pre-Christian times.[1] Jesus *stood up to read*, a mark of respect for the Word of God. Preaching seems usually to have been done sitting down (20; *cf*. Mt. 26:55; so SB). Paul however stood on at least one occasion (Acts 13:16) and Philo speaks of this custom (*de specialibus legibus* ii.62).

17. Apparently Jesus did not select the book from which He read, for the Isaiah scroll *was given to him*. But this does not mean, as some think, that He read from a fixed lectionary. We cannot authenticate a lectionary as early as this. The passage may have been selected by the ruler of the synagogue or Jesus may even have picked it Himself. This would fit in with Luke's words, *He opened the book and found the place where it was written. . . .*

18, 19. He read from Isaiah 61:1f. followed by 58:6. The words prophesy of the Messiah's ministry to people in distress, *the poor, the captives, the blind*, and the *oppressed*. Jesus' application of the words to Himself shows that the sense of vocation that came with the heavenly voice at His baptism remained strong (for the Spirit's anointing, *cf*. Acts 10:38). Jesus saw Himself as coming with good news for the world's troubled people. The *acceptable year of the Lord* does not, of course, represent any calendar year, but is a way of referring to the era of salvation.

20. Jesus rolled up the scroll (*closed the book*) and returned it to the attendant. He *sat down*, thus taking the posture for preaching. With everyone now looking at Him expectantly all was ready for the sermon.

21, 22. Jesus *began* by saying that the prophecy He had just read was being fulfilled. The words of Isaiah applied to the ministry He was beginning (*cf*. 7:22). *Today* is important. Jesus' contemporaries did not doubt that God's kingdom

[1] See further my *The New Testament and the Jewish Lectionaries* (London, 1964), pp. 11ff.

would come some day. Jesus' teaching was different, in that
He saw God as acting in the present, in His own work. 'Not
in a future age but *now* is the captive power of sin to be broken,
communion with God to be established, and the will of God
to be done' (Manson). *All spoke well of him* is more literally 'all
witnessed to him'. Rieu's 'they soon began to recognize his
power' is a paraphrase, but it tells us what happened. As He
spoke the villagers came to see that what they had heard about
Him was true and they said so. They were impressed by His
gracious words, i.e. His attractive way of speaking. They were
astonished that someone from their own town, one whom they
could call *Joseph's son,* could speak like this. Notice that Luke
speaks of astonishment, not admiration or appreciation. They
wondered at His preaching, but they did not take it to heart.

23. Jesus knew that His reputation had spread to Nazareth
and that those among whom He had grown up would want
Him to live up to that reputation. He cited a proverb (otherwise unknown, though similar proverbs are found) whose point
is clear. The immediate application, however, is not so plain,
for there was no question of Jesus healing Himself. Perhaps the
thought is that the working of miracles would benefit Him by
saving His reputation. Or Nazareth may be regarded as an
extension of the Man from Nazareth (though 'Heal your
fellow-townsmen' is not the same as 'Heal yourself'). Notice
that they say *what we have heard you did at Capernaum,* not 'what
you did . . .'. They do not believe. Mark gives this as the reason
that Jesus did not work miracles at Nazareth (Mk. 6:5). Luke
does not say as much, but he probably implies it.

24. They wanted proof. But instead (*de* should be rendered
'But', not *And*) Jesus took a line of His own. His rejoinder
begins with *amēn, truly.* This word is used only six times in Luke
(he prefers to translate the Aramaic term), but in Matthew
and John it is frequently on Jesus' lips. It gives emphasis and
marks the following words as specially significant. Jesus goes
on to affirm that prophets are not accepted in their own
locality. People are always more ready to see greatness in
strangers than in those they know well.

25, 26. Jesus illustrates His point with reference to two
great prophets. Elijah was succoured, not by one of the many

Israelite widows of his day, but by a woman of Zarephath of
Sidon (*cf.* 1 Ki. 17:8ff.). The addition, *who was a widow*, is not
strictly necessary (it is implied in the reference to widows in the
previous verse), but it brings out the comparative unimpor-
tance of this foreigner. Yet it was to her that Elijah was sent.
The length of the famine is given as *three years and six months* (as
in Jas. 5:17), which is a trifle longer than 'in the third year'
(1 Ki. 18:1). The 'third year' may, of course, refer to the
length of Elijah's time in Zarephath (1 Ki. 17:8) rather than to
that of the famine, in which case there is no problem. If it
does refer to the famine there are various possibilities. Tasker
thinks the three and a half years may be a deduction from the
passage in Kings.[1] Or Jesus may have had some other source
of information. And in any case the famine would have continued for some time after the drought broke.

27. The example of Elijah is reinforced with that of Elisha,
who healed, not one of the many lepers in Israel, but Naaman
the Syrian (2 Ki. 5:1-14).

28-30. This was too much for them. It was bad enough
when one of their own showed that He did not belong in the
ruck with them. Now that He appealed to God's dealings with
Gentiles, that was too much. Anger swept over the whole
congregation ('God for the Jews'!) and they set out to lynch
Jesus. The attempt to throw Him down from *the brow of the hill*
looks like an endeavour to cast Him over a precipice (though
it may be simply a prelude to stoning). The identification of
the spot is not easy, but the general meaning is plain enough.
So is the majesty of the presence of Jesus. He simply passed
through the midst of them and *went away*. He spoke no angry word,
nor did He work any spectacular miracle. He simply walked
through the mob. Some have felt that this was itself a miracle—
though not the kind of miracle the Nazarenes wanted! As far
as is known Jesus never returned to Nazareth. Rejection can
be final.

In all this we have a commentary on the third temptation.
The people tried to put Jesus into the position Satan had
suggested. But He did not let them.

[1] *James* (*TNTC*), p. 141.

b. Jesus healing (4:31–41)

Luke begins his account of Jesus' mission with some miracles of healing and a preaching tour. This is one of his Marcan sections.

i. The man with an unclean spirit (4:31–37). 31, 32.
Here we have the first of five healings on the sabbath narrated in this Gospel (*cf.* 4:38f.; 6:6ff.; 13:10ff.; 14:1ff.). Clearly the right use of the sabbath interested Luke. From Nazareth Jesus *went down* to Capernaum (*down* because the lakeside city was on a lower level; the site is not known for certain, though many advocate Tell Hum). Jesus' teaching caused astonishment, because He taught *with authority*. Originality was not highly prized among the rabbis and it was usual to accredit one's words by citing illustrious predecessors. For example, R. Eliezer piously disavowed novelty: 'nor have I ever in my life said a thing which I did not hear from my teachers' (*Sukkah* 28a; a similar statement is made about R. Johanan b. Zakkai, and the attitude was common). Jesus did no such thing and the authority with which He spoke impressed men.

33, 34. In the synagogue there was *a man who had the spirit of an unclean demon*. This last expression is nowhere explained. Some take it literally and think the man was dirty and dishevelled. Others hold the reference to be moral and think of a wicked spirit. It is possible that both are in mind. In the ancient world it was widely held that many troubles are caused by evil spirits. The Bible says little about demon possession before or after the incarnation, but much during Jesus' ministry. In Scripture then this phenomenon is part of the conflict between Jesus, who came to destroy the works of the devil (1 Jn. 3:8), and evil. (See further the Special Note in Geldenhuys, pp. 174f.) On this occasion the demoniac 'shrieked at the top of his voice' (NEB). *Have you come to destroy us?* is usually taken as a question, but it might be a statement, 'You have come . . .'. The demon recognized the opposition between Jesus and all of his kind. *The Holy One of God* (elsewhere only Mk. 1:24; Jn. 6:69) is an unusual title, stressing the thought of consecration to God's service. In this place we should see it as an example of what James had in mind when he wrote 'the demons believe—and shudder' (Jas. 2:19). Ryle comments that the demon's knowledge was 'unaccompanied by faith, or hope, or charity'.

35. Jesus performed the exorcism simply, without the spells so beloved of His contemporaries. He *rebuked* the demon, which implies that it ought not to have possessed the man, and commanded it, *Be silent* (lit. 'Be muzzled'; MM note that the word was sometimes used in the sense 'bind with a spell', but this is not the meaning here). Jesus added, *come out of him!* The demon threw him down (Mark says it convulsed him). But that was all. It came out *having done him no harm.*

36, 37. The people were amazed at *this word* and proceeded to comment on the *authority and power* with which Jesus commanded the spirits. Their tense implies that He did this habitually. They are not commenting on this one miracle. Not unnaturally *reports* went out into the *surrounding region*. Jesus was becoming a public figure.

ii. Peter's mother-in-law (4:38, 39). From the synagogue Jesus went to the home of Simon (Mark adds 'and Andrew' and tells us that James and John went along; Luke omits all reference to them, perhaps because he has not yet told of their call). All three Synoptists mention the *fever*, but only Luke says that it was *a high fever* (apparently a medical term), that Jesus *rebuked* it (does this mean that He saw Satan behind the disease?), and that, when the woman was cured, she got up and served them *immediately* (thus showing the completeness of the cure).

iii. Many healings (4:40, 41). The end of the day saw *any that were sick with various diseases* brought to Jesus. They could not be carried on the sabbath, but with its end at sundown people lost no time. There is a personal touch in that Jesus *laid his hands on every one of them* as He healed them. Luke is the only one to tell us this and also that the demons who were expelled cried out, *You are the Son of God!* The Galileans may have thought Jesus no more than a man, but the evil ones did not make that mistake. Mark shares the information that Jesus did not allow them to speak, but not that Jesus *rebuked* them (*cf.* 4:35, 39). Jesus did not countenance evil. It is interesting that Luke tells us that thus early the demons recognized *that he was the Christ*. It took the disciples a long time to learn this lesson. The refusal to allow the demons to disclose that Jesus was the Christ was probably to forestall nationalistic Messianic movements. Popular enthusiasm would have made a rebel hero out of any messiah!

c. A preaching tour (4:42–44)

Next morning Jesus *went into a lonely place* (interestingly Mark, not Luke, tells us it was to pray). But clearly *the people* had been impressed by the happenings just recounted and they did not want to lose Jesus. However, when they found Him (Mark tells us that Peter took the lead in this) Jesus refused to stay with them. He said He *must* preach the gospel elsewhere. Notice the compelling necessity. This is Luke's first mention of *the kingdom of God*, which was to become the favourite theme in Jesus' teaching. It is an exceedingly large subject. Here it must suffice to say that it is God's rule in action. The Jews looked forward to a time when God would assert Himself as King over the nations. Jesus taught that God's kingdom had already come in Him, in the authority with which He combated evil. In a sense the kingdom was a present reality. In another sense it was yet to come in all its fullness. There is a further note of purpose in Jesus' words, *I was sent for this purpose* (for the idea of Jesus being sent *cf.* 9:48; 10:16). There is a problem about *the synagogues of Judea*, for the Synoptists say nothing elsewhere of such a tour. AV has 'the synagogues of Galilee', but this has inferior attestation and RSV is to be accepted. We should perhaps understand *Judea* here in the broad sense of 'Palestine', which would include Galilee (as it does in 23:5, *etc.*; Luke, however, sometimes uses the term of Judea proper, *e.g.* 2:4). Or Luke may be speaking, as he often does, of something we find in John. In that Gospel we find that Jesus had an extensive ministry in Judea.

d. Jesus' miracles (5:1–26)

Luke narrates a trio of miracles: first a nature miracle, then a couple of healings. They emphasize Jesus' mastery of the situations in which He found Himself, and show His compassion.

i. The miraculous catch of fish (5:1-11). Some scholars hold that this is a variant of the story in John 21, a post-resurrection appearance of Jesus. But the differences are too many and too great. Luke is telling us about an incident in Jesus' ministry, John of a quite different happening after Jesus was raised. A similar remark should be made about the story of the call of the disciples in Mark 1:13-20. It is just possible that Mark tells of the incident without the miracle (though even then there are not inconsiderable differences). But it is more likely that Luke is referring to a different incident.

1-3. Luke sets the scene. The crowd, eager *to hear the word of God* (which may mean 'the word that comes from God' or 'the word that tells of God'), pressed in on Jesus as He stood by *the lake of Gennesaret*. Luke, incidentally, always calls this sheet of water a lake, whereas the other Evangelists follow the Old Testament in calling it a sea. It measures roughly 13 miles by 7 miles and is situated about 700 feet below sea-level. This is the only place where it is called Gennesaret, the usual name being Galilee (Chinneroth in the Old Testament; Tiberias twice in John). Jesus saw two little boats from which the fishermen had gone out to wash their nets. After each fishing trip the equipment had to be checked and cleaned in readiness for the next. So Jesus got into one of the boats, which belonged to Simon, and asked him to thrust out a little from the shore. Jesus then *sat down*, taking the customary position for teaching, and taught the people from the boat.

4, 5. The lesson over, Jesus suggested to Peter that they go fishing. In reply Peter addresses Jesus as *Master* (*Epistata*), a word found in this Gospel only in the New Testament. In all seven of its occurrences it is used in addressing Jesus. The term is not specific like 'Rabbi' (which Luke never uses), but denotes anyone in authority. Peter goes on, *we toiled all night and took nothing!* There is perhaps an implied rebuke. Night was considered the best time for fishing, and Peter may be suggesting that, when experts, fishing at the right time, had caught nothing, it was useless to try at the request of a Carpenter. If that is the way of it, Peter's willingness to act on Jesus' suggestion shows a realization that His word was not to be ignored on any subject. Peter might not agree but he could obey.

6, 7. Obedience brings results! Peter and his friends let down the nets and *enclosed a great shoal of fish.* There were too many for the nets to hold. Even when the fishermen signalled to their partners in the other boat and they too came up, there was still not the necessary capacity. They *filled both the boats, so that they began to sink.* The number of fish is not given (as it is in the story in John), but clearly the catch was abnormal. It was not to be explained along the usual lines of fishing techniques.

8. Here only in his Gospel Luke uses the compound name *Simon Peter.* Up till 6:14 (apart from this verse) he always calls this man Simon. Afterwards, except in passages where he is quoting other people, Luke always calls him Peter. Perhaps surprisingly Peter did not welcome the great catch. He recognized the miracle and reacted as one in the presence of God. It is not easy to see the meaning of *fell down at Jesus' knees.* But perhaps we should take *Iēsou* as dative and render with Phillips 'fell on his knees before Jesus'. Peter's next words, *Depart from me, for I am a sinful man, O Lord,* remind us of the experience of great saints in the immediate presence of God, such as Abraham (Gn. 18:27), Job (Jb. 42:6), or Isaiah (Is. 6:5). *Cf.* also Israel's 'let not God speak to us, lest we die' (Ex. 20:19). Peter recognized the hand of God and that drove him to realize his own sinfulness. The address, *Lord,* replaces 'Master' of verse 5 and this is probably connected with this heightened apprehension. While it can be used as no more than a form of polite address (like our 'Sir'), the word is also used consistently of God in the Septuagint, and is common in many religions in referring to deity. On the change Plummer comments, 'It is the "Master" whose orders must be obeyed, the "Lord" whose holiness causes moral agony to the sinner (Dan. x. 16).' This reaction, when nothing is recorded as taking place after earlier miracles, is probably not due to Luke's recording the miracle out of order, as some have suggested. Rather it will be because this was a miracle in Peter's own area of expertise. He knew fishing; and therefore he knew what this haul implied.

9–11. Luke brings out the extraordinary nature of the

catch by referring to the astonishment of the fishermen. He particularizes with Peter first, then those with him, and then he names Peter's *partners* (the word, incidentally, is different from that in verse 7; Moffatt distinguishes with 'mates' and 'partners').

Then Luke goes on to the important thing, the sequel to the miracle. First Jesus reassures Peter. *Do not be afraid* means 'Stop being fearful' rather than 'Don't get scared'. It calms an existing fear. Peter was evidently awe-struck, as his whole reaction shows. *Henceforth* introduces a new set of circumstances. A turning-point has been reached. From now on things will be different with Peter. The nature of the new life to which Jesus is calling him comes out in the final words: *you will be catching men*. The tense is continuous: a habitual practice is in mind. And Peter will no longer be concerned with fish but with men. *Catching* is, of course, used in a different sense, catching for life not for death (*zōgreō* means 'catch alive', 'catch for life'). When the fishing party got to land *they left everything*. They left the greatest catch they had seen in all their lives. The catch was not as important as what it showed them about Jesus. They realized this and they *followed him*. They became disciples in the fullest sense.

ii. Healing a leper (5:12–16). *Leprosy* in biblical times was the name given to a variety of diseases, some curable and some not. In its worst form it was a greatly dreaded and very dreadful disease. It was both disfiguring and fatal and the ancient world's only defence against it was quarantine (Lv. 13:46). Sufferers were forbidden to approach other people. To prevent accidental contact they were required to call out 'Unclean' (Lv. 13:45). They had no way of earning a living and had to depend on charity. The psychological effects of all this seem to have been as serious as the physical. People had (and often have) an attitude to leprosy different from that to any other disease. It was defiling. People were ashamed of it, though it was no fault of their own. Jesus healed lepers and saw in this one of the signs of His Messiahship (Lk. 7:22).

12. Luke does not locate the incident with precision. But in some town there was a man *full of leprosy*. Luke alone has *full of*; it is apparently a medical term for an advanced case, though Creed notes that there is no exact parallel to *full of*

leprosy. It was against the law for a leper to come into the city
(Lv. 13:46). Luke may mean that the encounter took place
on the outskirts. Or the man, desperate in his misery, may have
ignored the regulation. At any rate he came close enough to
Jesus to prostrate himself before Him and to address Him.
He had no doubt about Jesus' ability to heal, but was not so
sure whether He was willing. Notice that he does not speak of
being healed but says, *you can make me clean*. Leprosy was a
dirty disease. It defiled. To be healed meant to be cleansed.

13. Jesus' compassion comes out in the fact that He *stretched
out his hand* (was the man keeping his distance?), *and touched
him*. Men shunned lepers and we are safe in saying that
nobody but other lepers had touched this man in years. That
touch spoke volumes. Then Jesus pronounced words of healing:
I will; be clean. The result was immediate cure.

14. Jesus had already forbidden demoniacs to speak of
Him (4:35, 41). Similarly He now commands the leper to be
silent. He does not say why. Perhaps it was to prevent the
kind of popular enthusiasm that would try to make Jesus into
the Messianic conqueror nationalists looked for. Instead
Jesus told him to perform a quiet religious rite. The procedure
for a man claiming to be cured of leprosy was to go to the
priest, who acted as a kind of health inspector. If the priest
was satisfied, a sacrifice was offered, after which the healed
man was able to take his place in the community (see Lv. 14).
The Greek translated *for a proof to the people* means 'for a
testimony to them'. Everything depends on the meaning of
them. Phillips renders, 'as evidence to the authorities'. He may
be right, but perhaps RSV is more likely. The words probably
point to a safeguard for the healed man. People would know
that he had been a leper and would be slow to accept him.
But if a priest had inspected him and accepted his offering,
there was proof that he had been healed. It would also show
that Jesus upheld the law. And it would be a testimony to
people in general that the power of God was at work in Jesus.

15, 16. Jesus' request for silence was not heeded. Luke tells
us that *so much the more the report went abroad concerning him* (Mark
says that the healed man himself took the lead in this). The
inevitable result was that crowds flocked round Jesus. But

this was not in His plan. He had rejected the devil's temptation to become a popular wonder-worker. So He forsook the
cities and went to *the wilderness*. Characteristically Luke tells
us that there He *prayed*. In the midst of pressing duties He
found it necessary to be quiet and pray.

iii. Healing a paralytic (5:17-26). The fascinating story
of the healing of the paralytic lowered through the roof is in
all three Synoptists. Jesus meets the objection to His forgiving
sins by working a miracle expressly 'that you may know that
the Son of man has authority on earth to forgive sins' (24).
And the people reacted as those in the very presence of God.

17. Once again Luke does not locate the incident (Mark
tells us it was in Capernaum). Jesus had quite a reputation by
now, for Pharisees had come even from *Judea and from Jerusalem*, as well as locally. The *Pharisees* took their religion very
seriously. They were so anxious not to break God's commandments that they 'put a fence about the law'. For example,
when the law said, 'Thou shalt not take the name of the Lord
thy God in vain' they went further by refusing to pronounce
the name at all. This hedge of all the provisions of the law
('the tradition of the elders') had the unfortunate result of
externalizing religion. Men then put a great deal of effort into
the outward without necessarily coming to love God in their
hearts. The Pharisees were not numerous (Josephus put the
number at something in excess of 6,000, *Antiquities* xvii. 42),
but they were very influential. They were the unofficial
religious leaders of the day and they spearheaded the opposition to Jesus. Luke further tells us that *the power of the Lord* (*i.e.*
God) *was with him to heal*.

18, 19. Some men (Mark tells us there were four) brought
a paralysed man on his bed. Because of the crowd they could
not *lay him before Jesus*, so they took him up to the roof. Houses
usually had flat roofs, often with external staircases leading up
to them. So the crowd did not prevent these men reaching the
roof. There they *let him down with his bed through the tiles*. Mark
says nothing about the tiles (he does not say what the roof
was made of), but says that they 'unroofed the roof' and that
they 'dug it out'. Most commentators say that Palestinian
houses did not have tiled roofs and that Luke has described

houses he knew elsewhere, not a Palestinian house. But according to *NBD*[1] the tiled roof 'came into use before New Testament times'.

20. Apparently nothing was said, but the action was a mute appeal. It showed *their faith*. Notice that the faith of the friends is important (for other examples of faith availing for others *cf.* 7:9f.; 1 Cor. 7:14). Indeed, some hold that it is only their faith that is in mind. But this seems unlikely. First, the unqualified plural *their* seems meant to include the whole party, the sick man as well as his friends, and secondly, it is impossible to think that the man's sins were forgiven if he had no faith of his own. Jesus' first words have to do with sin, not sickness. In authoritative language He said, *Man, your sins are forgiven you*. This is very important. Manson maintains that 'what the incident is intended primarily to bring out is that the authority of Jesus in religion starts with the forgiveness of sins. He comes to deliver souls from the paralysis of moral and spiritual energy.' He rejects Bultmann's contention that the forgiveness of sins is a late doctrinal accretion and sees it (in my judgment, rightly) as rather 'the core of the original narrative'.

21. These words provoked a reaction from *the scribes and the Pharisees*. The *scribes* were men learned in the law (*cf.* 'teachers of the law', 17) and might be Pharisees or Sadducees (Luke links them with the Pharisees five times and with the chief priests seven times). This opposition group correctly sees that only God can forgive sin, but incorrectly assumes that Jesus is guilty of blasphemy. They do not stop to ask whether Jesus' relationship to the Father is such that He can in fact forgive. Luke, incidentally, is rather fond of questions which begin with 'Who?' and refer to Jesus (7:49; 8:25; 9:9, 18, 20; 19:3).

22, 23. Jesus *perceived their questionings*. This seems to mean that He read their thoughts rather than that He heard what they were saying (*cf. in your hearts* and also Mk. 2:8). Jesus replied by posing some questions also. On the surface it is easier to say *Your sins are forgiven you* than *Rise and walk*. The latter may be put to an immediate and obvious test, whereas the onlooker does not know whether sins are forgiven or not. This may be the sense of it. But it is not improbable that Jesus

[1]*NBD*, art. 'House'.

is saying that it is much harder really to pronounce the word of forgiveness than the word of healing. He was doing more than the healers of the day could do.

24. Jesus performs the cure that they *may know that the Son of man has authority on earth to forgive sins*. His words about forgiveness and healing go together. If He can do the one He can do the other. The Jews of the day thought that all sickness was due to sin (*cf.* Jn. 9:2). 'R. Alexandri said in the name of R. Ḥiyya b. Abba: A sick man does not recover from his sickness until all his sins are forgiven him' (*Nedarim* 41a). Had they been consistent accordingly they must have accepted the man's forgiveness!

This is Luke's first use of the expression *the Son of man*, which he will use in all twenty-six times. It is Jesus' favourite self-designation, being found in the Gospels over 80 times, and in all the strata critics discern in all four Gospels. It is used only by Jesus (except for Stephen, Acts 7:56). It appears to be His way of referring to His Messiahship with the use of a term which would not arouse the wrong associations in men's minds.[1] The Son of man, then, spoke the word of healing and told the paralytic to take up his bed and go home.

25, 26. The cure took place immediately. The man did as Jesus told him. Bengel comments on *took up that on which he lay*, 'A happy expression. The couch had borne the man: now the man was bearing the couch.' Luke alone tells us that he went off *glorifying God*. The healing did not centre on the human Jesus: it was God that the man glorified. Luke proceeds to tell of the reaction among the onlookers. They, too, saw the hand of God, for they *glorified* Him and *were filled with awe* (the appropriate emotion in the presence of deity). Their comment was, *We have seen strange things today*, where *strange* means 'beyond expectation'; *cf.* Moffatt, 'We have seen incredible things to-day.' Human achievement could not explain what had happened.

e. The calling of Levi (5:27–32)

27, 28. Jesus *went out*, perhaps from the house, though some think from the city, for they hold that the toll-booth would

---

[1] See further, Leon Morris, *The Lord from Heaven*[2] (London, 1974), ch. 2.

have been outside the town. He saw Levi *sitting at the tax office,*
which probably means sitting in front of it; had he been in the
office it would not have been easy for Jesus to see and call him.
His name is given as Matthew in our First Gospel (and in the
lists of apostles in Mark and Luke). For *tax collector (telōnēs)*
see note on 3:12, 13. The Roman system of farming out the
taxing rights would have been in force, though the taxes in
this area were paid to Herod Antipas to whom the Romans
had assigned the revenues (Josephus, *Antiquities* xvii. 318).
The taxes that Levi collected are likely to have been toll or
customs duties rather than poll tax or the like. The tax collectors were heartily disliked both as collaborators and as
extortioners. As a class they were regarded as dishonest and the
Talmud classes them as robbers (*Sanhedrin* 25b). Jesus saw
Levi and said no more than *Follow me.* Levi *left everything* (a
detail found in Luke only) *and followed him.* This must have
meant a considerable sacrifice, for tax collectors were normally
wealthy. Matthew must have been the richest of the apostles.
We should not miss the quiet heroism involved in this. If
following Jesus had not worked out for the fishermen, they
could have returned to their trade without difficulty. But
when Levi walked out of his job he was through. They would
surely never take back a man who had simply abandoned his
tax office. His following of Jesus was a final commitment.

29. But clearly he took the step not in a spirit of grim
resignation but with banners flying. He had no regrets, but on
the contrary gathered *a large company* for *a great feast* in cele-
bration (for Luke's dinner scenes see 7:36; 9:12ff.; 10:38ff.;
11:37; 14:1; 19:7; 22:14; 24:30, 41ff.). Clearly Levi found it
an exhilarating thing to forsake wealth for Christ. And he
probably wished to introduce some of his associates to his new
Lord. 'A converted man will not wish to go to heaven alone'
(Ryle).

30. *The Pharisees* would not have been at the reception.
Perhaps the house was open and they perceived what was
going on; or Luke may be giving us a later reaction when they
came to hear what had happened. They and *their scribes* (some
scribes were Sadducees, but many belonged to the Pharisaic
party) *murmured against, i.e.* complained about, the disciples.
With their strict rules of ceremonial purity it was unthinkable

that they would have eaten with people such as Levi and his associates. Some members of such a company were bound to be ceremonially unclean and there was no surer way of contracting defilement than by associating with *sinners*. Moreover to eat with a man meant friendship, full acceptance. So they criticize the disciples. How could people who professed to be religious countenance sinners like these?

31, 32. It was the disciples who were addressed, but Jesus who replied. With unanswerable logic He pointed out that it is the sick, not the well, who need the physician. His business was with sinners. He did not, however, come to leave them in their sin. He called them *to repentance*. Jesus' reference to *the righteous* is, of course, ironical. But the Pharisees saw themselves that way and on their own premises Jesus' conduct was justified. Their failure to become disciples is perhaps connected with the fact that repentance is not easy for the respectable and the self-righteous. Luke is very interested in the theme of repentance and develops it much more fully than either Matthew or Mark (see 3:3, 8; 10:13; 11:32; 13:3, 5; 15:7, 10; 16:30; 17:3, 4; 24:47).

f. Fasting (5:33-39)

33. Jesus' disciples were too cheerful. They did not practise mournful fasts and this puzzled some. Though the only fast prescribed in the law was that on the Day of Atonement, fasting was practised by John the Baptist's followers and by those of the Pharisees. So they asked Jesus why His disciples did not conform to this widespread practice. The reference to offering prayers probably means set prayers at fixed hours. Luke makes it very clear that Jesus and His followers prayed often. And indeed here, though Jesus agrees that His followers do not fast, He does not say the same about prayer.

34, 35. 'Wedding guests don't fast' is the gist of Jesus' answer. His presence brings joy like that of a wedding party. Really to follow Christ is to enter a happy experience. While He is with them His disciples cannot fast; but He does envisage a day when He will be *taken away from them*. This surely refers to the cross. There may be the notion of violence in the verb *aparthē*. When this happens *they will fast*. Jesus does not say 'will be made to fast' (cf the question in verse 34), and He seems to refer to voluntary fasting.

36. He adds *a parable* (the word can denote a short, pithy saying as well as a story). He takes it from the homely practice of patching clothes. To patch an old garment with a piece torn from a new one is to spoil both, the new by being torn and the old by having a patch that does not match. Mark's version is slightly different. He speaks of a piece of 'unshrunk cloth' used as a patch, when its greater strength will make it tear away from the old, thus making a worse tear than the one it mended. Clearly the illustration was used more than once in slightly different forms.

37–39. Another illustration is taken from *wineskins*. The flesh and bones of animals, usually goats, were removed, leaving the skins intact. They could then be used as containers for liquids. At first they were fairly elastic, but when old they lacked this quality and could easily burst under stress. Jesus says that new wine put into old skins means burst skins and spilled wine. *New wine must be put into fresh wineskins.* Both this and the previous illustration drive home the point that Jesus is not simply patching up Judaism: He is teaching something radically new. If the attempt is made to constrict this within the old wineskins of Judaism (*e.g.* by imposing fasting), the result will be disastrous. He sees that this teaching will not be palatable to some. A man drinking old wine does not want even to try the new. *The old is good*, he says (not 'better', as the margin). He is not even comparing them. He is so content with the old that he does not consider the new for a moment.

g. The right use of the sabbath (6:1–11)

All four Gospels make it clear that a chief point in the conflict between Jesus and the Jewish authorities concerned the right way to keep the sabbath. The Jews took the sabbath seriously (a whole tractate in the Mishnah is given up to it). Many students of rabbinics hold that the sabbath was a delight, but the rules for keeping it were certainly elaborate and repressive. The interesting thing about Jesus' approach is that He was not simply arguing that repressive regulations should be relaxed and a more liberal attitude adopted: He was saying that His opponents had missed the whole point of this holy day. Had they understood it they would have seen that deeds of mercy such as His were not merely permitted—they were obligatory (*cf.* Jn. 7:23f.).

i. Lord of the sabbath (6:1–5). The disciples' action in plucking and eating grain began a dispute which led up to Jesus' notable pronouncement that He is Lord of the sabbath.

1, 2. One sabbath, as Jesus went through grainfields, His disciples *plucked and ate some heads of grain*. Wayfarers were permitted to help themselves to satisfy their hunger (Dt. 23:25). Objection was being made, not to the action in itself, but to its being performed on the sabbath. The Pharisees would find in the plucking of the ears a breach of the regulation which forbade reaping and in the rubbing in their hands that which prohibited threshing. Throwing away the husks probably represented winnowing, while eating showed that they had prepared food. Four distinct breaches of the sabbath in one mouthful! The Talmud regards reaping and grinding corn no greater in bulk than a dried fig as culpable (*Shabbath* 70b), so that small quantities were significant.

3, 4. Jesus replied by directing the attention of the Pharisees to the action of David in eating *the bread of the Presence* (1 Sa. 21:3–6). This was bread prepared in a prescribed manner and meant for use only in the service of the Temple (Lv. 24:5–9). David's action was technically a breach of the law, for only the priests should eat this bread (Lv. 24:9). But the need of his band overrode the legal nicety and no-one blamed him. Human need must not be subjected to barren legalism.

5. Jesus now adds a further and very different justification. He claims that He, the Son of man, is *lord of the sabbath*. This is a staggering claim, for the sabbath was of divine institution (Ex. 20:8–11). To be lord of a divine ordinance is to have a very high place indeed. Some take *Son of man* to mean 'man' (as the Aramaic original often does). They take the verse to mean that man is supreme over the sabbath. This would fit neatly with the preceding; but there are difficulties. Jesus never taught that man is lord over a divine institution. Again, in the Gospels *Son of man* invariably refers to Jesus. He is surely referring to His Messianic function. It may be significant that this follows a reference to David's action. It is the Son of David who is Lord. If David could override the law without blame, how much more could the much greater Son of David do so?

ii. Healing the withered hand (6:6–11). Luke emphasizes his point by adding a story of a miracle Jesus worked on the sabbath. It is a demonstration in action of His lordship over the day and over disease. The rabbis did not object to healing on the sabbath if there was any danger to life and they interpreted this liberally. 'Whenever there is doubt whether life is in danger this overrides the Sabbath' (*Yoma* 8:6). But if there was no danger they were adamant. Such healing was not allowed.

6. Luke sets the stage. Once more he does not date his incident with precision, simply locating it *on another sabbath*. Jesus was teaching in the synagogue when there was a man present with a crippled hand. Typically Luke tells us that it was the *right hand* that was affected. *Withered* is a word used of plants or dried wood. Here it seems to mean some form of muscular atrophy.

7. Again the opposition comes from *the scribes and the Pharisees*. They *watched him* (the verb means 'watched closely') in the hope of seeing Him heal and of thus finding matter for an accusation. They were interested in the accusation, not the healing.

8, 9. Jesus sensed the challenge and met it head-on. Luke does not tell us how He *knew their thoughts*. Probably this is part of the way he brings out the deity of our Lord. Jesus summoned the man with the useless hand to come and stand with Him, evidently in a prominent place where there would be no doubt as to what was happening. Then He addressed the opposition, challenging them with the question, *is it lawful on the sabbath to do good or to do harm?* He does not envisage the possibility of neutrality. 'Jesus will recognize no alternative to the doing of good except the doing of evil. The refusal to save life is tantamount to the taking of it' (Manson). There is no middle course. The man before Him was leading an impaired life. To do nothing on the sabbath was to destroy life. Jesus came to save.

10. Having posed His alternatives Jesus apparently paused a moment while He *looked around on them all*. This gave them an opportunity of answering Him, but they did not take it. So He told the man to stretch out his hand. He did so and found it *restored*.

11. The effect on the Pharisees and their allies was that they were *filled with fury* ('beside themselves with anger', NEB). We can understand that they were angry that Jesus had defied them and got away with it. But there seemed nothing they could do, which is probably the reason for their discussion. Jesus had laid the case before them, asked what was right, and had received no answer. He could justly claim that they had been given the chance to say what should have been done, but had declined to take it.

h. Choosing the Twelve (6:12–16)

12. Once more Luke's time reference is vague (*In these days*). He is not giving attention to exact sequence. Jesus was facing a momentous decision. The preceding incidents had shown that His enemies were increasing. One day they would kill Him. What was He to do? Characteristically Luke tells us that He prayed. And then He chose a little band of men who would carry on His work after Him.

13. At daybreak Jesus *called his disciples*. This will be a group of people who had attached themselves loosely to Him. A disciple was a learner, a student. In the first century a student did not simply study a subject; he studied under a teacher. There is an element of personal attachment in 'disciple' that is lacking in 'student'. From this larger number of adherents Jesus *chose . . . twelve*. This is the number of the tribes of Israel, a number which indicates that Jesus was establishing the people of God, the true Israel. In Jesus and His followers 'people could see a dramatization of the Old Testament picture of God bringing the twelve tribes of Israel to the promised land' (Tinsley). Jesus never set up an organization. These twelve men represent the total of His administrative machinery. Some of them were clearly outstanding men, but on the whole they seem to have been no more than average. Most have left very little mark on church history. Jesus preferred to work, then as now, through perfectly ordinary people.

These twelve Jesus *named apostles*. The term derives from the verb 'to send' and means 'someone sent', 'a messenger'. Luke uses the word six times (with twenty-eight more in Acts), whereas each of the other Evangelists uses it once only (Mark may have it twice, depending on the solution to a textual problem). In the Gospels the group is usually referred to simply as 'the twelve'. Mark explains that Jesus chose them 'to be with him, and to be sent out to preach and have authority to cast out demons' (Mk. 3:14f.). This brings out the notion of mission and the centrality of preaching in their function.

14–16. There are minor variations in the order, but if we divide the names into three groups of four the same names occur in each group in all our lists. The same name heads each group, though the order within the groups varies. The first name in all the lists is *Simon*. Jesus gave him another name, *Peter*, which means 'Rock'. From this point on Luke always uses this name, not Simon as hitherto. He does not say when the name was given (see Jn. 1:42). The later Simon is called *the Zealot*. He may have belonged to the radical group of 'Zealots' who were notorious for their violent resistance to Rome, or the name may suggest that he was characterized by fiery zeal. For *Judas the son of James* (again in Acts 1:13) Matthew and Mark have Thaddaeus, which appears to be another name for the same man. All three finish with Judas Iscariot and mention his betrayal, but only Luke says that he *became* a traitor. Apparently he was faithful at the beginning. *Iscariot* probably means 'man of Kerioth', a town in Judea (Jos. 15:25) or Moab (Je. 48:24). If so Judas was the only non-Galilean in the Twelve.

i. The sermon on the plain (6:17–49)

Matthew gives three chapters to the sermon on the mount. Luke's sermon 'on a level place' has many parallels, but is much shorter. However, in addition he has much similar matter scattered through his Gospel. Many feel that the same sermon lies behind both accounts, and they usually hold that Matthew has supplemented it by bringing together material from a variety of Q contexts. This is possible, but the differences are many. Preachers usually make use of the same or similar matter in different sermons, especially if they speak without a written script. This habit of preachers seems a better explanation of the combination of resemblances than extensive editorial activity.

This sermon begins with the beatitudes and the woes, and goes on to the kind of conduct appropriate to those in the kingdom, special stress being laid on love and on the importance of not judging others. The principle that the tree is known by its fruit is brought out and Jesus ends by likening the attitude of His hearers to that of a man building a house. Throughout we are reminded of what it means to be a disciple. It is not a matter of fine words only, but of a whole way of life.

i. The multitude (6:17–19). Luke tells us how a crowd assembled. Jesus stood *on a level place* (perhaps on the mountain side; it is not the usual word for a plain). He was joined by *a great crowd of his disciples*, but also by *a great multitude of people*. Some who had not as yet given their allegiance to Jesus were attracted by reports of His teaching and wanted to hear more. Some of them wanted healing. They came from great distances, as far south as *Jerusalem* and as far north as *Tyre and Sidon*. Sick people were healed and Luke particularly mentions those *troubled with unclean spirits* (see on 4:33). Jesus *healed them all*.

ii. The beatitudes (6:20–23). Together with the following woes these beatitudes make a mockery of the world's values. They exalt what the world despises and reject what the world admires.

20. Jesus looked at *his disciples*, to whom the following words are evidently addressed. He pronounced a blessing on them as *poor* (*cf.* 4:18). He is not blessing poverty in itself: that can as easily be a curse as a blessing. It is His disciples of whom Jesus is speaking. They are poor and they know that they are without resource. They rely on God and they must rely on Him, for they have nothing of their own on which to rely. It is in this spirit that in the Old Testament 'the poor' is often almost equivalent to 'the pious' (*e.g.* Pss. 40:17; 72:2, 4). Matthew brings out the meaning with 'poor in spirit'. The rich of this world often are self-reliant. Not so the poor. These humble men receive *the kingdom of God* (see on 4:43). Notice that Jesus says *yours is*, not 'yours will be'. The poor enter the kingdom now.

21. In Matthew there is the addition 'and thirst for right-eousness' after the blessing on those who *hunger*. This is to make explicit what is implicit here. But it is typical that Luke should emphasize the need. It is those who have the need who will be *satisfied*. Matthew has no equivalent to Luke's blessing on *you that weep now*. This fits in with the two previous beatitudes. It cannot mean those who cherish some personal grief, but will refer to people who are sensitive to evil, to the world's rebellion against God and the world's suffering in consequence. It is those who see these realities of life who will in the end *laugh*.

22, 23. Jesus continues with His unexpected blessings, this one reserved for the persecuted. It is not suffering in general of which He speaks, but suffering *on account of the Son of man*. Those who suffer in this way are not to be pitied: they are blessed. Jesus tells them to *rejoice* and to *leap for joy*. They have an eternal reward. And they are in a godly succession: *the prophets* were treated in the same way. God's people can expect nothing else. Jesus promised His followers that they would be absurdly happy; but also that they would never be out of trouble.

iii. The woes (6:24–26). These woes, which are found in Luke only, form the natural correlative to the beatitudes. They pronounce a surprising verdict on qualities and states which men have universally regarded as desirable. But the world's blessings may encourage an independent attitude over against God, an attitude of self-sufficiency which is fatal to spiritual growth. *Woe* does not convey the exact force of Jesus' *ouai*. It is more like 'Alas' (NEB) or 'How terrible' (TEV). It is an expression of regret and compassion, not a threat.

24. The first woe is for *you that are rich*. This is not addressed to the disciples, for they were not rich. It may be the natural correlative to 'you poor' (20). Or Jesus may have been addressing rich people in the 'great multitude' (17). Wealth predisposes men to think they have need of nothing. They then rely on riches, not on God. Their attitude is the very opposite of that commended (20). To the rich Jesus says, *you have received your consolation.* His verb is one often used in receipts with a meaning like 'Paid in full' (see MM). The expression 'they have had it!' is an interesting contemporary illustration of the meaning. When all that a man has is worldly wealth he is poor indeed. That kind of prosperity goes with an inner emptiness. We must never mistake comfort for blessedness.

25. *You that are full* means much the same as 'you that are rich', but there is more emphasis on the state of the persons concerned. They are not only rich but have all they want. They lack nothing. People who live thinking that what they have is all-sufficient, who allow material possessions to be all-in-all and who think they have no need of God, are assured *you shall hunger.* This does not necessarily refer to physical hunger. The satisfied often remain satisfied throughout life. Jesus is referring to ultimate reality. In the kingdom of God it is these men who are paupers. One day they will see this for themselves.

A similar comment must be made about *you that laugh now.* Obviously Jesus is not objecting to laughter as such. His whole ministry was a protest against the killjoy attitude. He enjoyed life and must have laughed often. So did His disciples. But there is a laughter that is the expression of superficiality and it is this shallow merriment that will have to give way to mourning and weeping.

26. It is a danger *when all men speak well of you*, for this can scarcely happen apart from some sacrifice of principle. There is, it is true, a sense in which being 'well thought of by outsiders' (1 Tim. 3:7) is important. But that is different from universal popularity. It is *the false prophets* who win wide acclaim (*cf.* Je. 5:31). A true prophet is too uncomfortable to be popular.

iv. Love (6:27–36). The heart of this sermon is the need for love. Jesus stresses that His followers must love the unlovely as well as those that appeal to them. There were several words for love in Greek. Jesus was not asking for *storgē*, natural affection, nor for *erōs*, romantic love, nor for *philia*, the love of friendship. He was speaking of *agapē*, which means love even of the unworthy, love which is not drawn out by merit in the beloved but which proceeds from the fact that the lover chooses to be a loving person.

27. *Love your enemies* is uncompromising. As Matthew reports in his equivalent saying, people have been ready to love their neighbour and hate their enemy (Mt. 5:43). But Jesus goes beyond that. His follower cannot be selective in his love. He must love all men, including his enemies, in the spirit of his Master. It is not enough to refrain from hostile acts. He is to *do good to those who hate* him. To men living in occupied territory such words must have sounded odd. Must not the Romans be opposed and hated and hurt? To men of strong nationalistic leanings Jesus' teaching was downright immoral. But, as Caird says, 'He who retaliates thinks that he is manfully resisting aggression; in fact, he is making an unconditional surrender to evil.'

28. The believer's love finds expression in his words. Some will *curse* him, but he will *bless* them, the opposite of what might have been expected and of what the world will do in a similar situation. Some will *abuse* him. He is not to retaliate in kind. He is to *pray for* such.

29. Jesus illustrates from physical violence. The *cheek* is *siagōn*, which is rather the jaw. Jesus is speaking of a punch to the side of the jaw rather than a light slap in the face. The natural reaction to such a blow is to strike back hard. Jesus enjoins His follower to *offer the other* side of the jaw. He is speaking about an attitude. When we receive an injury we must not seek revenge, but be ready if need be to accept another such injury. A literal turning of the other side of the face is not always the best way of fulfilling the command (*cf.* Jesus' own attitude to a blow, Jn. 18:22f.). One worldly wit advised, 'Always forgive your enemies. Nothing infuriates them more.' It is possible to be outwardly forgiving without showing real love. But it is love that Jesus looks for. This lies behind His words about the *coat* and the *shirt* (the *coat, himation*, was the normal outer garment, and the *shirt*, the *chitōn* or tunic, the usual undergarment). One must not react in anger against the man who takes the coat, but let him have the shirt as well.

30. Once again it is the spirit of the saying that is important. If Christians took this one absolutely literally there would soon be a class of saintly paupers, owning nothing, and another of prosperous idlers and thieves. It is not this that Jesus is seeking, but a readiness among His followers to give and give and give. The Christian should never refrain from giving out of a love for his possessions. Love must be ready to be deprived of everything if need be. Of course, in a given case it may not be the way of love to give. But it is love that must decide whether we give or withhold, not a regard for our possessions. *Give*, incidentally, is in a continuous tense. Jesus is talking about the habitual attitude, not the occasional generous impulse.

31. Jesus sums it all up in the golden rule, *as you wish that men would do to you, do so to them*. This principle covers all of life. If a man lives by it he needs little else as his guide. In its negative form the rule is pre-Christian. The great Hillel, for example, said to an inquirer, 'What is hateful to you, do not to your neighbour: that is the whole Torah, while the rest is the commentary thereof' (*Shabbath* 31a). The negative form is found also in the *Epistle of Aristeas* 207 and similar teaching is given by a variety of sages in many cultures. But significantly Jesus gives the rule in the positive form, which nobody else seems to have done. It is not enough for Him that His followers refrain from acts they would not like done to them. They must be active in well-doing.

32–34. The nature of the loving attitude is brought out with three illustrations of the way Christians must surpass *sinners*. Even men who own no allegiance to God practise some virtues. They *love those who love them*. They repay good deeds done to them. They lend to those in need if they can be sure of getting their money back or perhaps rely on getting loans in return when they themselves are in need (the verb for *lend*, incidentally, probably means 'lend on interest'). If Christians do these things they are doing no more than the world does. It is easy for the Christian to congratulate himself on some virtue he fancies he detects in himself. But before he can claim that he is obeying Christ's command he should ask whether he is doing anything more than *sinners* do in similar circumstances.

35, 36. Again there is the positive attitude, first *love your enemies*, then *do good*, then *lend*. There is a difficulty with the following expression. The context seems to require a meaning like *expecting nothing in return*, but the verb *apelpizō* never has this meaning elsewhere. It is used in the sense 'despair (of)', to give the meaning here 'never despairing' (RV), or 'despairing of no one' (Rieu). It is probably better to take the word in its normal meaning. Christians should lend, despairing of nothing and nobody. When His followers live like that, Jesus tells them, *your reward will be great*. He never urges men to serve for the sake of reward. To do that is no more than to exchange material selfishness for spiritual selfishness. But He insists that the reward is there: it is one of the facts of life. Browning draws attention to a point made by K. E. Kirk, that a refusal to contemplate reward tends to lead to a subtle self-centredness: 'It turns the mind from God and forces it back upon the self and its own successes and failures.' In any case Christian reward is to be understood in terms of communion with God and opportunity for further service. Jesus goes on to point out that it is in living in this spirit that we fulfil our calling as members of the heavenly family. God *is kind to the ungrateful and the selfish* (this last word is more general and means 'the wicked', TEV). He is *merciful*. His good gifts, like sunshine and rain, seedtime and harvest, are sent to all men, saint and sinner without distinction. And 'like Father, like son'. The qualities that are seen in the Father are the qualities the sons should make their aim.

v. Judging other people (6:37–42). A number of sayings are here loosely connected. The unifying theme is leadership. In more than one of them there is a possible double application and we cannot always be sure which Jesus meant or whether He had both in mind. In this section we find that a further application of the love for which Jesus looks is to be seen in our attitude to judging our fellows.

37. Jesus' opposition to our judging other people is put in a peremptory command, *Judge not*. He goes on to the conse-

quence, *you will not be judged*. A similar injunction to avoid
condemning follows and an instruction to forgive. In all this
Jesus is not of course rejecting legal processes. He does not
have law-courts in mind but the all-too-common practice of
assuming the right to criticize and condemn one's neighbours.
This, He says, we must not do. It is not quite clear whether
you will not be judged refers to the present judgment of men or
the future judgment of God or both. If we are harsh with our
judgments on other people we generally find that they return
the compliment and we find ourselves widely condemned,
whereas if we do not pass judgment on others our neighbours
are slow to condemn us. But the words apply also to more
permanent consequences. The man who judges others invites
the judgment of God upon himself. It is the man with the
forgiving attitude who is forgiven. This is not salvation by
merit: rather the thought is that the true disciple is not judg-
mental. When God accepts a man God's grace changes him.
A forgiving spirit is evidence that the man has been forgiven.

38. The forgiven man is open-hearted and open-hearted-
ness brings its consequences. Jesus commands His hearers to
keep giving and reminds them that when they do this men
respond in kind. And not only in kind, for He speaks of *good
measure, pressed down, shaken together, running over*. The metaphor
is from measuring out grain in such a way as to ensure that full
volume is given. Your *lap* is really your 'bosom' (*kolpon*) and
refers to a fold in the outer garment made as it hung over the
girdle. It was used as a kind of pocket. Jesus concludes this
section with a reminder that there is a reciprocity in the affairs
of life. We get back what we put into life. He is apparently
making use of a proverbial saying which in one form or another
turns up in a number of rabbinic sayings.[1]

39. Jesus now turns to the responsibility that rests on disciples to make more disciples. He uses a series of metaphors to
bring out the importance of living on the highest level as they
do this. First He speaks of *a blind man* trying to lead another.
As the leader can see no more than the led, the only future for
both is disaster. This spells trouble for those who put their
trust in such people as the Pharisees. It is a warning to be
careful whom we follow. But there is also a warning about the

[1] See SB, i, pp. 450ff.

leadership Jesus' followers will exercise. The Christian cannot hope to act as guide to others unless he himself sees clearly where he is going. Lacking love, he does not. If a man does not know the way of salvation himself he can lead others only to disaster.

40. The second illustration reminds the little group of their status as disciples. Somewhat similar statements are found elsewhere (22:27; Mt. 10:24; Jn. 13:16). Clearly it is a thought that Jesus expressed more than once and in different ways. The student's progress is limited by the teaching he gets: he cannot know more than his teacher. We must not understand this in terms of our own situation, where libraries and other facilities put endless possibilities before the student. Jesus is speaking of a time when the disciple had only his rabbi as his source of information. To claim that he was *above his teacher* was the height of presumption. The disciple's one aim was to be *like his teacher* and he attained this only when *fully taught*. This last expression translates the verb *katartizō*, which has a meaning like 'to render fit' or 'complete'. It is used of repairing what is broken (Mk. 1:19) or of supplying fully (as when the world was 'fully made', Heb. 11:3). The follower of Jesus must make it his aim to be like Him. He cannot lay aside the command to love, believing that he is past that. But the main thrust of the saying concerns human teachers. Since it is unreasonable to expect a disciple to know more than his teacher, it is important that the teacher be well advanced himself in the Christian way. Specifically he must be on his guard against spiritual blindness and lack of love.

41, 42. Jesus rebukes hypocrisy with the illustration of the *speck* and the *log*. This is another theme sometimes used by the rabbis.[1] We should not overlook the fact that Jesus is quite ready to make His point in humorous vein. We are so often impressed with the solemnity of the issues involved in much of His teaching that we forget that Jesus had a sense of humour. Here He chooses to use the method of burlesque. He pictures the hypocrite with a great log sticking out of his eye while he solicitously tries to remove a speck from his brother's eye. But the humorous illustration should not blind us to the seriousness of the lesson it teaches. The slight imperfection in other people

[1] SB, i, pp. 446f.

is often more apparent to us than the large one in ourselves. Jesus is exhorting to rigid self-examination before we engage in judgment. It is important to take the log out of our own eye. It is not important that we concern ourselves with the speck in our brother's. And it is impossible for us to put our brother right before we have dealt with our own shortcoming. We cannot see clearly enough for the job.

vi. The tree and the fruit (6:43-45). A man's deeds show what he is like at heart.

43, 44. Jesus does not explain what He means by a *good tree* or a *bad tree*, but the following statement shows that the type of fruit the tree produces is in mind. *Figs* and *grapes* are set over against *thorns* and the *bramble bush*. Where we are dealing with plant life it is clear that each tree has its characteristic fruit. One cannot pick a certain type of fruit from any tree but its own. All other trees yield different fruit.

45. Good men, like good trees, produce good fruit. The *good man* produces his fruit *out of the good treasure of his heart*. It is what he is in his inner nature that determines what fruit his life will yield. So also with *the evil man*. His inner evil can produce only evil. The principle is stated at the end: *out of the abundance of the heart his mouth speaks*. There is always a reason for the things we say. Our words reveal what is in our heart.

vii. Foundations (6:46-49). This sermon, like that in Matthew, concludes with an impressive reminder of the importance of acting on the teaching Jesus has given. There is a difference in detail: in Matthew the difference between the two men is that they chose different sites on which to build; here they differ in what they do on the sites.

46. Evidently some had already shown themselves to be false disciples. So Jesus asks why they call Him *Lord, Lord*, but do not obey Him. To call anyone 'Lord' is to admit that allegiance is owed. To repeat the address is to put a certain emphasis on the admission. But words are no substitute for obedience.

47, 48. Jesus speaks now of the man who takes notice of what He says. This man is like a builder who *dug deep, and laid* *the foundation upon rock.* This is an essential for sound building, but it is time-consuming and it is hard work. So some avoid it. But when the storms and floods come, a house built on rock will stand. The hard work is worth it. The parallel in the spiritual life is clear. When the final test comes at judgment day it is the foundation on which our lives are built that matters (*cf.* 1 Cor. 3:11ff.). The words certainly have an application to the storms of this life. The man with a good foundation is not easily upset by life's difficulties; but it is the supreme final test that is specially in mind.

49. It is different with the house built *on the ground without a foundation.* When *the stream broke* against the house built in this way, *immediately it fell.* It could not withstand the onslaught. So is the man who hears the teaching of Jesus but does not act on it. He is building his life without a foundation. He may have every outward appearance of respectability and he may be noted for his religious observances, but lacking a foundation he is nothing.

j. Healing the centurion's slave (7:1–10)

For a writer with an interest in the Gentiles this is a significant story. The Gentile officer is not said in Luke's account to have seen Jesus, but he approached Him through Jewish intermediaries and was commended for his faith. This was an encouragement for members of the Gentile churches who had not seen Jesus, but had received the gospel through Jewish messengers. Matthew also tells this story, though with some differences. Some hold that the healing of the nobleman's son (Jn. 4:46ff.) is a variant of the same story, but the evidence scarcely supports this.[1]

1, 2. His sermon ended, Jesus returned to Capernaum. Luke proceeds to tell of *a centurion* with a sick slave. Originally a centurion was an officer who commanded a hundred soldiers, but in time the number varied. Josephus speaks of a gradation of officers, with the decurion below the centurion (like an NCO below the captain) and the chiliarch and the

---

[1] See my commentary, *The Gospel according to John* (*New London Commentary*) (London, 1972), *in loc.*

hegemon above him (like the colonel and the general) (*Bellum*
v. 503). Moffatt translates 'army-captain' and this is probably
our nearest equivalent. Barclay cites the historian Polybius
for a list of qualifications looked for in centurions: they must
not be so much 'seekers after danger as men who can command, steady in action, and reliable; they ought not to be
over anxious to rush into the fight; but when hard pressed
they must be ready to hold their ground and die at their
posts'. Men of fortitude and integrity were clearly required
for this post. It agrees with this, that each of the centurions of
whom the New Testament gives us knowledge is a man of
character (*cf.* 23:47; Acts 10:22; 22:26; 23:17, 23; 24:23;
27:1, 43). This centurion was a Gentile (3, 9), possibly a
Roman seconded to serve with the forces of Herod Antipas.
This is not certain, for some centurions were of other races,
and again, there may have been a small detachment of
Romans in Capernaum. The story shows this man to have
been humane, wealthy and pious. Matthew tells us that his
slave was paralysed. Luke does not say what the illness was,
but he makes it clear that it was serious. The slave was *at the
point of death*. The centurion was concerned, for the slave *was
dear to him* (*entimos* means 'honoured', 'esteemed').

3-5. The centurion *heard of Jesus*. While the content of the
report is not given, it must have included something about
cures Jesus had performed. So the centurion sent some Jewish
elders with the request that Jesus would come and heal the
sick slave. It is at first sight surprising that a Roman centurion should have been able to command Jewish elders in
this fashion, but the reason becomes evident when they speak
to Jesus. This was no ordinary centurion. The elders agree
that he *is worthy* to have Jesus help him. They specify two
things: the centurion had a general goodwill towards the
conquered people, *he loves our nation*, and he had given expression to that goodwill by aiding local worship, *he built for us our
synagogue*. It is not certain that he was a worshipper of the true
God, but a man would scarcely have undertaken all that is
involved in building a synagogue without some interest in the
God who was worshipped there. It is true that some Romans
helped religion out of a cynical regard for the best interests of
the State; but this centurion was a man of faith (9), not a
cynic. Some have conjectured that he was a 'god-fearer', one

who worshipped God but declined to become a proselyte to Judaism, and this is not improbable.

6–8. Jesus responded to the request and *went with them*. But before He got to the house the centurion sent friends with a message to stop Him. This is a little curious, since the earlier request was for Jesus to 'come' (3). In Matthew's account the man spoke to Jesus direct and there is no mention of either elders or friends. There are different ways of handling the difficulty. Some think of irreconcilable differences in the two accounts, while others harmonize them by thinking of the man as sending messengers first and afterwards going himself. But it is better to see Matthew as abbreviating the story and leaving out details inessential to his purpose. What a man does through agents he may be said to do himself. So Matthew simply gives the gist of the centurion's communication to Jesus, whereas Luke in greater detail gives the actual sequence of events. Perhaps we can discern something of the differing purposes of the two Evangelists in their treatment of the messengers. Matthew was concerned primarily with the centurion's faith and nationality: to him the messengers were irrelevant, even a distraction. But Luke was interested in the man's character and specifically in his humility: to him the messengers were a vital part of the story.

The centurion's message began, *Lord, do not trouble yourself, for I am not worthy to have you come under my roof*. The centurion was plainly a humble man. He had not met Jesus but knew enough about Him to accord Him a high place. Probably also he realized that a religious Jew might have scruples about entering the house of a Gentile. He went on, *therefore I did not presume to come to you*, where *presume* renders a verb meaning 'count (*sc.* myself) worthy' (it is a different word translated 'worthy' in verse 6). The elders had already affirmed that he was worthy (4), but in his modesty he would not claim so much.

He went on to make it clear that he did not see it as necessary for Jesus to be present in person in order to effect a cure. All that was necessary was that He should *say the word* (lit. 'speak with a word'; he is regarding the word as the instrument whereby Jesus' purpose would be effected). The power was in the word Jesus spoke. Nothing more was needed. The centurion can illustrate from his own experience. He did not have to be present to have his command accomplish what he willed. He could say *Go* or *Come* or *Do this* and know that in each case his word would be obeyed. He does not say, 'I am a man with authority' as we might have expected, but *I am a man set under authority*. The humility of the man comes out in his reference to his place in a graded hierarchy, when he might well have spoken only of his superiority to those beneath him. His words may imply that Jesus, like himself, drew His authority from a higher source. There is probably no great significance in his referring to soldiers as people who go and come at his bidding, and of his slave as the one to whom he says *Do this*. The point is that in more than one way, with soldiers and with slaves, the centurion's commands are obeyed.

9. Jesus *marvelled at him*. Twice only is Jesus recorded as marvelling at people, here on account of faith and in Nazareth because of unbelief (Mk. 6:6). Jesus shared His astonishment with the crowd. He *turned*, perhaps to make sure they got the message. He prefixed His statement with *I tell you*, which appears to serve the same purpose. This was a most unusual situation and Jesus did not want this group of Israelites to miss the full impact of His commendation of the military man. He went on, *not even in Israel have I found such faith*. This is not a criticism of Israel, for the implication is that Jesus did find faith there, though not as great faith as that of the centurion. The surprising thing was that this Gentile should have such great faith, faith surpassing that among the Israelites, the people of God. An intriguing question is the nature of the faith the man had. Clearly he had faith that his slave would be healed. But is that all? In a Christian context to speak of faith without any qualification normally means more than that. It means trust in Jesus and acceptance of Him as Lord (*cf.* verse 6). It may be that what this man had heard about Jesus had brought home to him more than the certainty that He could cure sickness. It must always remain possible that the centurion had no more than a conviction that Jesus could heal and that to say more is to introduce the developed meaning of faith that became common among Christians. But the suspicion remains that Luke's emphasis on faith means more.

10. Luke does not refer to any word of healing that Jesus spoke (Matthew tells us that Jesus said, 'Go; be it done for you as you have believed', Mt. 8:13; but even this is scarcely a 'word of healing'). He simply says that when the centurion's messengers got back to the house *they found the slave well*. Matthew says that the healing took place while the men were with Jesus, but Luke leaves us to infer this. He puts no stress on it. His emphasis is on the centurion's faith. And he leaves us with the question, Did Jesus go beyond even that great faith and heal without so much as a word?

k. The widow of Nain's son (7:11–17)

This story of raising from the dead is peculiar to Luke, though elsewhere there are other raisings, those of Jairus's daughter and of Lazarus. Luke stresses the compassion of Jesus as well as His power. He probably includes the story at this point as a preparation for the reply to John's messengers (22).

11. *Soon afterward* connects the narrative quite loosely with the preceding. *Nain* is mentioned here only in the Bible. It is generally held that the site was the modern Nein, about six miles south-east of Nazareth on the slopes of the Little Hermon and a day's journey from Capernaum. For *city* see on 1:26. The *great crowd* that went with Jesus shows us how popular He was at this period of His ministry. As He moved from town to town people attached themselves to Him and went along.

12. Jesus' arrival at Nain coincided with the departure of a funeral procession. Luke puts the meeting near *the gate of the city*, a place which would normally have its quota of citizens, for it was the regular meeting-place. He sets the scene by telling us that the dead man was *the only son of his mother* and that *she was a widow*. This is a poignant situation. The woman was now all alone in the world. Without a male protector and provider she must have been in difficulties. There were few openings for a woman to earn her living in the first century. And besides the hardship and the sense of loneliness and sorrow there was the knowledge that the family line had ended. The *large crowd from the city* that accompanied her shows that her plight was widely appreciated and that there was a depth of sympathy for her. Luke does not mention profes-

sional mourners, but they would have been there: 'Even the
poorest in Israel should hire not less than two flutes and one
wailing woman' (*Ketuboth* 4:4).

13–15. For the first time in narrative Luke calls Jesus *the
Lord* (a title he uses frequently in non-Marcan contexts;
Matthew and Mark do not use it in this way; John uses it
occasionally). It has undoubted fitness in this scene in which
Jesus will show Himself to be Lord over death itself. Nobody
asked Jesus to do anything. Moved with compassion, He took
action on His own initiative. First He addressed Himself to the
weeping widow and told her to dry her tears. She would have
been walking in front of the bier,[1] so that Jesus would have
encountered her first. Then He approached *the bier* on which
the body lay, wrapped in a shroud. Some argue that *soros*
means 'a coffin', but MM show that it was also used for a bier.
And, while the Jews sometimes used coffins (*Shabbath* 23:4;
Moed Katan 1:6), it was their practice to use the open bier (*e.g.*
Josephus, *Antiquities* xvii. 197; *Vita* 323). Clearly this is pre-
supposed here. Jesus' touching it meant pollution according
to the ceremonial laws, but where human need was in question He never worried about ceremonial trifles. When He
touched the bier *the bearers stood still*. No word was spoken to
them, but plainly they saw that something unusual was happening. Jesus proceeded to address the corpse with the words,
Young man, I say to you, arise. And at the word of power *the dead
man sat up.* There is nothing elaborate. Jesus simply spoke the
word and the miracle took place. Luke adds that the dead
man *began to speak*, clear evidence of his return to life. Nothing
that he said is recorded, as is the case also in the other two
examples of resurrections. Jesus' concern for the widow comes
out in the detail that He *gave* the young man to his mother (as
Elijah did in a similar situation, 1 Ki. 17:23).

16, 17. Those who saw this reacted as men in the presence
of God. *Fear*, which we must understand as awe, took hold of
them. They *glorified God*, interestingly not Jesus. They recognized the hand of God in what had happened and gave praise
where it was due. But they did salute Jesus, naming Him *a
great prophet*. This is an inadequate view of Jesus, but it probably represented the highest title the townsmen could give

[1] *LT*, i, pp. 555, 557.

anyone. It may have been called forth by the reflection that Jesus had just done what two great prophets did in days of old (1 Ki. 17:17ff.; 2 Ki. 4:18ff.). The people further exclaimed, *God has visited his people!* This expression is not uncommon in the Old Testament, where it often denotes blessing, as here (*e.g.* Ru. 1:6; 1 Sa. 2:21), though sometimes also judgment. The inevitable result of all this was a further increase in the fame of Jesus as the news spread far and wide. *Judea* is probably used here in the wider sense of Palestine in general, while the mention of *the surrounding country* shows that Jesus' fame was very widespread indeed.

l. John the Baptist's questions (7:18–35)

i. The questions asked and answered (7:18–23). John the Baptist was in prison. Evidently he was expecting Jesus to do something spectacular. When nothing seemed to happen he sent men to Jesus to find out why and possibly to provoke some action.

18–20. What Jesus had been doing was known widely in the countryside and word was taken to John in prison as well. So he summoned two disciples and sent them to ask Jesus *Are you he who is to come, or shall we look for another?* He who is to come (*cf.* 3:16; 13:35; 19:38; Heb. 10:37) was not an accepted Messianic designation, but clearly John is using it in this sense. But as he had long since borne witness to Jesus as the Mighty One who would come (3:16), it is not clear why he should ask this question (though we should bear in mind that in this Gospel John does not specifically say that Jesus was that One). Perhaps the least likely solution is that which suggests that John himself had no qualms but his followers did. So he sent his disciples with a message, knowing that Jesus would give a satisfactory answer. This is too artificial to carry conviction. There seems likewise little to be said for the view that the questions mark a dawning faith in John. Up till this time, it is suggested, John had continued his own movement in opposition to Jesus, but now he began to wonder whether Jesus was the Great One he knew would come and whether he should accordingly abandon his own movement. Against this is the fact that John was in prison. He was certainly not at this time promoting any rival group. There is also the fact that our sources indicate that John did point men to Jesus (Mt. 3:13f.; Jn. 1:29ff., 35f.; 10:41; Acts 18:25; 19:4). Others think John's faith in Jesus had failed a little. Confinement in Herod's prison was no picnic and, with the uncertainty as to whether he would ever be released, even this stout-hearted man may have quailed. The objection to this is the character of the man. The explanation remains possible, but it scarcely fits in with what we know of John. A fourth suggestion is that it was not John's faith but his patience that failed. His questions may be in the spirit of, 'You are the One we are expecting, aren't You? Then why not do something?' This must always remain a possibility. But perhaps it is more likely that John was just plain puzzled. He had prophesied that the Coming One would do some striking works of judgment (3:16f.). But Jesus was doing nothing of the sort. He was engrossed in works of mercy. Would somebody else then do those works of judgment? John wanted to know.

21–23. Jesus' answer to John's men is to direct their attention to what was going on. Help was being given to the blind (Is. 35:5), the lame (Is. 35:6), lepers, the deaf (Is. 35:5), the dead and the poor (Is. 61:1). The Old Testament parallels seem to show that the healing miracles and the preaching to the poor have Messianic significance. They are the divine accreditation of Jesus' mission. It was in such works of mercy and not in spectacular victories over Roman armies that Messiah's work would be accomplished. Jesus had preached about this in the synagogue at Nazareth (4:18ff.). But this truth is not open to the perception of every man. So Jesus pronounces a blessing on him *who takes no offence at me*. The verb rendered *takes offence* is picturesque. It derives from the trapping of birds, and refers to the action that depresses the bait-stick and so triggers off the trap. It is a colourful way of referring to the causing of trouble.

ii. The greatness of John (7:24–30). Those who heard Jesus answer John's messengers may have thought that He was rebuking or even repudiating John. He removes any such impression by making it clear that John was the greatest of men.

24. After the messengers left Jesus addressed some questions to the onlookers, and made them face up to what John was and stood for. The first question was, *What did you go out into the wilderness to behold?* Crowds had flocked to hear John's preaching. Why? Jesus suggests as an answer, *A reed shaken by the wind.* This may be a proverbial reference to the commonplace, what might be seen anywhere. More likely Jesus is saying that John was no reed, easily swayed. The incongruity of this as a description of that stern man of the deserts is evident.

25. Jesus' second question was, *A man clothed in soft clothing?* Again there are two ways of taking it. Did they expect to find a courtier in the wilderness? Or is Jesus asking, 'Was John a courtier?' The word *soft* (*malakos*) means 'soft to the touch', but it acquires the secondary meaning, 'effeminate'. This clearly does not fit John. Jesus goes on to say that those who are *gorgeously apparelled and live in luxury* are to be found, not in John's wilderness, but *in kings' courts.* The very fact that John had lived a hard life on the simplest of fare in the roughest of places ruled out all such suggestions.

26, 27. The third question was, *A prophet?* This time the answer is right, for John was a prophet and more. The addition of the quotation from Malachi 3:1 shows that to John was given the honour of being the forerunner of the Messiah. Manson reminds us that this not only points to the greatness of John, but 'presupposes on Jesus' part . . . a consciousness of the *finality* of his own mission to Israel'.

28. Jesus goes on to accord to John the highest place possible: *among those born of women none is greater than John.* Jesus was not downgrading John. He put him in the highest place He could. John's office set him apart from all other men.

But Jesus did not stop there. *He who is least in the kingdom of God is greater than he.* Jesus' coming marked a watershed. He came to inaugurate the kingdom. And the least in that kingdom is greater than the greatest of men. This is a statement of historical fact. John belonged to the time of promise. The least in the kingdom is *greater*, not because of any personal qualities he may have, but because he belongs to the time of fulfilment. Jesus is not minimizing the importance of John. He is putting membership of the kingdom into its proper perspective.

29. It is often held that verses 29, 30 are a parenthesis inserted at this point by Luke. But such an insertion into a speech of Jesus is quite without parallel. The uncertainty arises from the fact that in the Greek there is no object for the verb rendered *heard*. RSV supplies *this*, which demands that the section be a parenthesis. But we could supply instead 'him' (Goodspeed) or 'John' (Phillips). Taken this way, Jesus follows a reference to John's greatness with one to the reactions to his preaching. This seems preferable. *All the people* seems inclusive enough to take care of *the tax collectors*. But the tax men were so hated and ostracized that they formed a race apart (see on 5:27), so they are emphasized (*cf.* Goodspeed, 'even the tax-collectors'). But these common people *justified God*. This means that they 'pronounced God just', they accepted the ways of God as they truly were and did not try to constrain Him into a mould of their own manufacture. This is seen in that they were *baptized with the baptism of John*, that baptism which was with a view to repentance and which pointed men forward to the work that Jesus would do.

30. Over against the penitent little people Jesus sets *the Pharisees and the lawyers*. These latter were men who gave themselves over to the study of the law of God. They were very good at understanding the minutiae of the law without ever coming to grips with its essential message. They were concerned with the law of God but not with the will of God. So they and the Pharisees *rejected the purpose of God for themselves*. Where simpler people had heard and responded to God's call to repent, these men in their complacency and smug self-satisfaction found nothing to repent of. They rejected God's way. They refused John's baptism. They put themselves outside the way of blessing and would not give Jesus an open hearing when He came. The closed mind leads to mistake on mistake.

iii. The reaction of the hearers (7:31–35). Jesus proceeds to bring out the unreasonableness of the men of His day by pointing to their rejection of both John the Baptist and Himself, but for precisely opposite reasons. There was no pleasing them.

31, 32. Jesus asks a rhetorical question about what *the men of this generation* are like and answers in terms of children at

play. He quotes a little couplet which children apparently
used when other children would not join their games. When
they *piped* cheerily their playmates refused to dance. But when
they went to the other extreme and *wailed* their friends would
not co-operate in that either. They would be neither cheerful
nor glum. It is not quite clear whether *the men of this generation*
are being likened to the children who *piped* and *wailed* or to
those who refused to *dance* or *weep*. In the first case the thought
is that they complained that John the Baptist would not be
merry, but changed their tune when Jesus came and blamed
Him for not being gloomy. In the second case they did not
respond to Jesus' cheerfulness or John's solemnity. Perhaps
there is slightly more to be said for the latter, but either way
the point is much the same. They would accept neither Jesus
nor John.

33. Jesus brings this out with reference to John. He was an
ascetic. He ate no bread (his food was 'locusts and wild honey',
Mk. 1:6) and drank no wine (presumably he drank water).
But, although this spartan approach to living was characteristic of holy men in many religions, it did not endear John to
his fellows. His teaching was too uncomfortable. So they wrote
him off with the verdict, *He has a demon.*

34. Jesus did not follow John's ascetic line. He ate and drank
like ordinary people did. People who rejected John for depart-
ing from the general rule ought to have accepted Jesus. But
not a bit of it. They called Him *a glutton and a drunkard,* and for
good measure complained about His dining companions. He
was *a friend of tax collectors and sinners*. We have already noticed
that religious people shunned such low company. But Jesus
despaired of no man. To win sinners for God He freely associated with them. And yet people complained. After their
attitude to John this was sheer perversity. There was no reason
in it.

35. But wise men will not be put off. *Wisdom is justified by all
her children.* The verb *justified* means 'declared just' or 'shown
to be just' or 'accepted as just'. Those who are really wise (the
children of wisdom) will pronounce right the right way,
whether it be ascetic or social. They will see the wisdom of God

in both John and Jesus. They will not walk in the critical ways of men who can never be pleased.

m. The anointing of Jesus by a sinful woman (7:36–50)

Each Gospel has a story of an anointing of Jesus by a woman (Mt. 26:6–13; Mk. 14:3–9; Jn. 12:1–8). There are good reasons for thinking that the other three are describing one and the same incident, but Luke a different one. They refer to an incident in the last week of Jesus' life, Luke to one much earlier. The 'sinner' of Luke's account wet Jesus' feet with tears, wiped them with her hair, kissed them and anointed them, which is different from what the others describe. And the ensuing discussion is different. In Luke it is concerned with love and forgiveness, and in the others with selling the unguent and giving to the poor. There is no reason for holding that the woman in the other Gospels was 'a sinner' (John says she was Mary of Bethany). Some have held that Luke's 'sinner' was Mary Magdalene, but this is sheer speculation.

36. A Pharisee named Simon (40) invited Jesus to a meal. In Matthew and Mark the host is also called Simon ('Simon the leper'), but the name was very common and does not establish identity. It is a mark of Jesus' broad sympathies that He dined earlier with a publican (5:29) and now with a Pharisee.

37, 38. *A woman of the city* described as *a sinner*, which probably means a prostitute, came to know of it and entered the house. A meal such as the one that Jesus was attending was not private. People could come in and watch what went on. At the same time a prostitute would not have been very welcome in Simon's house, so it took courage to come. The woman brought *an alabaster flask of ointment*. The word *alabastros* denoted a globular container for perfumes. It had no handles and was furnished with a long neck which was broken off when the contents were needed (AG, LS). Despite the name the container was not always made of alabaster, but Pliny says that containers made of this material were best (*Natural History* xiii. 19, xxxvi. 60). We may fairly deduce that this perfume was costly. Jewish ladies commonly wore a perfume flask suspended from a cord round the neck, and it was so much a part of them that they were allowed to wear it on the sabbath (*Shabbath* 6:3). The extensive use of perfumes may be gathered from the fact that the Sages allotted a certain woman an allowance of 400 gold coins for perfume (*Ketuboth* 66b; even at that she was dissatisfied!). *Ointment* is not a good translation, for what is meant is perfumed oil, not a solid. Such oils were common accompaniments of festive occasions. People did not sit at table, but reclined on low couches, leaning on the left arm with the head towards the table and the body stretched away from it. The sandals were removed before reclining. The woman was thus able to approach Jesus' feet without difficulty. Evidently she intended to anoint them, but as she stood there her emotions got the better of her and *her tears* began to fall on Jesus' feet. She promptly wiped them with her hair, a significant action, for Jewish ladies did not unbind their hair in public. Clearly she was completely oblivious of public opinion in the grip of her deep emotion. This will explain also her kissing of the feet. There are examples of the kissing of the feet of a specially honoured rabbi (*e.g. Sanhedrin* 27b), but it was far from usual. Finally she anointed Jesus' feet with the unguent. Normally this would have been poured on the head. Her using it on the feet is probably a mark of humility. To attend to the feet was a menial task, one assigned to a slave. It is a fair conjecture that Jesus had turned this woman from her sinful ways and that all this was the expression of her love and gratitude. It is not clear whether she had met Jesus. She may simply have been among the crowds who listened to His teaching and had been so convicted that her life had been changed. Or she may have had unrecorded contacts with Jesus. We do not know.

39. Jesus' host saw all this and engaged in a little disapproving conversation with himself. The form of conditional sentence he used implies in the Greek (a) that Jesus was not a prophet, and (b) that He did not know *who and what sort of woman* was touching Him.

40. Jesus proceeded to correct both misapprehensions. The Pharisee had not spoken aloud but Jesus answered his thoughts. He showed that He knew who and what sort of man Simon was. He began by announcing that He had *something to say*. This got Simon's undivided attention. The Pharisee's reply is rather 'Speak on' (NEB) than *What is it?* His words are polite but not encouraging.

41–43. Jesus began with a little story about two debtors who were excused their debts, the one *five hundred denarii*, the other *fifty* (a denarius was a day's pay for a labourer, Mt. 20:2). It did not need a great deal of insight to recognize which would love the benefactor the more. Yet Simon's reply is somewhat grudging, with his *I suppose* before his mention of the one who was forgiven. Jesus did not comment on this, but agreed that Simon had given the right answer.

44–46. Then He came to the application. He turned to the woman and asked Simon, *Do you see this woman?* Did he? It is an interesting point. 'Simon could not see that woman as she then was, for looking at her as she had been' (Morgan). Jesus proceeded to contrast her attitude with that of His host. It now comes out that, though Simon had invited Jesus to his home, he had not given Him the treatment due to an honoured guest. It would have been expected that the host would have provided water for his guests' feet (*cf.* Gn. 18:4; Jdg. 19:21). Jesus had not received this courtesy. But He had had His feet washed with the woman's tears. Similarly in place of the kiss of welcome that might have been anticipated from the host (*cf.* Gn. 29:13; 45:15) He had received kisses on His feet. And finally, whereas Simon had omitted to anoint Jesus' head (*cf.* Pss. 23:5; 141:5), the woman had anointed His feet (*oil* is olive oil, which was plentiful and cheap; there is a contrast with *ointment*, which was rare and expensive perfume).

47. Jesus goes on to tell Simon that the woman's sins are forgiven. He does not gloss over those sins: they *are many*. But it is consistent New Testament teaching that, no matter how many and how great the sins, God's grace can forgive them. We must understand carefully the words *for she loved much*. Jesus is not saying that the woman's actions had earned forgiveness, nor even that her love had merited it. In line with His little parable and His later words (50), He is saying that her love is proof that she had already been forgiven. It was her response to God's grace. JB brings out the meaning with 'her sins, her many sins, must have been forgiven her, or she would not have shown such great love'. By contrast, *he who is forgiven* *little*, *loves little*. It is natural to think of Simon. He certainly had shown little love and the implication is that he had not been forgiven very much.

48–50. Jesus now said to the woman, *Your sins are forgiven* (*cf.* 5:21–24). Luke tells us that this provoked a discussion among the guests. The forgiveness of sins was a divine prerogative. *Who is this*, men asked accordingly, *who even forgives sins?* But Jesus completely ignored them. His interest was with the woman. *Your faith has saved you*, He said. This is important as showing that the love spoken of earlier was the consequence, not the cause, of her salvation. As elsewhere in the New Testament it is faith that is the means of receiving God's good gift. Jesus dismissed her with *go in peace* (*cf.* 8:48). The Greek is literally 'go into peace' and it may be worth noting that the rabbis held that 'Go in peace' was proper in bidding farewell to the dead, but to the living one should say, 'Go into peace' (*Moed Katan* 29a).

n. Women who helped Jesus (8:1–3)

Soon afterward Jesus went on a preaching tour. There is no mention of synagogues and it may well be that increasing hostility on the part of the synagogue establishment led Him to concentrate on preaching and teaching in the open air. He did not lack for an audience, for there are repeated references to the crowds (*cf.* 7:11, 24; 8:4, 19, 40, 45). On this occasion He was accompanied by the Twelve and by *some women* whom He had healed. The rabbis refused to teach women and generally assigned them a very inferior place. But Jesus freely admitted them into fellowship, as on this occasion, and accepted their service. First to be mentioned is *Mary, called Magdalene* (a place-name, meaning 'of Magdala', *i.e.* 'The Tower'). The Christian imagination has made free with Mary Magdalene, mostly seeing her as a beautiful woman whom Jesus had saved from an immoral life. There is nothing whatever in the sources to indicate this. Luke says that *seven demons had gone out* from her, which shows that Jesus had rescued her from a very distressing existence. But there is no reason for connecting the demons with immoral conduct: they are more usually associated with mental disorder. *Joanna* is mentioned again in 24:10, but otherwise nothing is

known of her. Her husband *Chuza* is mentioned here only.
That he was *Herod's steward* shows that he was a man of substance, though the precise nature of his office is not clear. The
word translated *steward* may denote the manager of Herod's
estates, or it may point to a political office. Godet conjectures
that this man may have been the officer whose son Jesus
healed (Jn. 4:46ff.). If so, it would explain why Joanna was
numbered among Jesus' followers and allowed to go with Him
on this tour. Nothing more is known of *Susanna*. Luke does not
go into further detail; there were *many others*, but he adds only
that they *provided for them out of their means*. This is valuable as
giving us one of the few glimpses we have of the way Jesus'
needs during His ministry were met. We read of the apostolic
band as having a common purse from which purchases for
food were made and gifts given to the poor (Jn. 13:29), but
not of how it was supplied. Here we learn that these women
responded in love and gratitude for what Jesus had done for
them (*cf.* Mk. 15:40f.). It seems to have been not uncommon
for godly women to help religious teachers, and Jesus speaks
of some Pharisees who were evidently quite rapacious (20:47).
It is heart-warming to read of this group of women who supported Jesus. And it is worth reflecting that the Gospels
record no woman as ever taking action against Him: His
enemies were all men.

o. The parable of the sower (8:4–15)

The second of Luke's Marcan sections begins here and goes on
to 9:50. It is usually agreed that the parable with which the
section begins and which is given prominence in all three
Synoptists marks something of a turning-point. The crowds
were thronging about Jesus. He was becoming a popular
preacher. But He looked for more than a superficial ad-
herence, so He intensified His use of parables, stories which
yielded their meaning only to those who were prepared to
search for them. The parables demand thought and spiritual
earnestness. They separate the sincere seeker from the casual
hearer.

In earlier days the interpretation of the parables was heavily
overlaid with allegory. In modern times it is generally agreed
that this is the wrong approach. But perhaps the repudiation
is taken too far, as when the interpretation given to this

parable in all three Synoptists is rejected. After all it is known
that the Old Testament, contemporary Judaism and the early
church all used allegory. There seems no reason at all why
Jesus should not have made some use of it too. Recent scholarship is right in turning from the allegorical excesses sometimes
engaged in by popular piety. But when it goes on to claim that
most or all of the interpretations of the parables given in the
Gospels originate with the early church and not with Jesus,
it is a different matter. As Tasker reminds us, 'such attempts
to disentangle primary and secondary elements must always
be more subjective than scientific'.[1]

4. Luke does not tell us with any exactness when this
parable was delivered. It came from a time of Jesus' popularity, for there was *a great crowd* and *people from town after town
came to him*. But we can scarcely say more.

5–7. The Palestinian sower sowed first and ploughed afterwards (as he still does). Seed *along the path* may refer to that
which fell on a path the farmer planned to plough up, though
the reference to its being *trodden under foot* looks more like a
regular path. In either case birds could eat the seed. The *rock*
will mean stony ground where a light covering of soil rests on
rock and there is no depth of soil to hold moisture. Plants
growing there must soon wither. *Thorns* are prickly plants of
vigorous growth. They grow faster than wheat and choke out
the good grain.

8. By contrast with the previous seeds, some *fell into good
soil*, where they yielded an abundant crop. Matthew and
Mark speak of thirtyfold and sixtyfold yields as well as of a
hundredfold, but Luke's version is abbreviated. He simply
makes the point that in good ground there is an abundant
harvest. The story finishes with the injunction to him who has
ears to use them.

9, 10. Jesus began His reply to the disciples' request for an
interpretation of the story with some general remarks. He
contrasts the disciples with others. To them are revealed *the
secrets of the kingdom of God*. Secrets (*mustēria*) are truths which

[1] *NBD*, art. 'Parable', p. 932.

man could never discover for himself, but which God has revealed. The word is common in Paul, but is found only in this connection in the Gospels. But *for others* there is sight without seeing and hearing without understanding. They hear the parables, but do not penetrate into the meaning. Parables both reveal and conceal truth: they reveal it to the genuine seeker who will take the trouble to dig beneath the surface and discover the meaning, but they conceal it from him who is content simply to listen to the story. This is plainly the result of the parables, but Jesus says it is also their purpose (*so that . . .*). Parables are a mine of information to those who are in earnest, but they are a judgment on the casual and careless.

11–15. Now comes the explanation of this parable. *The word of God* is the word that tells of God, or, more probably, the word that comes from God. *The ones along the path* are those who never really took in the word. They heard but they did not heed. Satan whipped it away before they believed. *The ones on the rock* do a little better. They are happy to receive the word (*cf.* Ezk. 33:32; Mk. 6:20), but there is no depth in them. In time of testing (*temptation*) they fall away. *What fell among the thorns* stands for people who have the potential for spiritual advance. But life will hold just so much, and these people fill their lives with so many things that there is no room for spiritual fruit. Over against all these are those *in the good soil*. The *honest and good heart* may go with *hold it fast* (as RSV), but more likely with *hearing*, as NEB, 'those who bring a good and honest heart to the hearing of the word'. They really retain the word, and they *bring forth fruit*.

There are two ways of understanding this parable. One sees it as encouraging disciples with the contrast between the small beginnings and the ultimate rich harvest. Despite the vicissitudes of the seeds that fell in unproductive places, the final result was impressive. The other emphasizes the importance of a right reaction to hearing the word. If we take it in, a rich harvest results, but if we react like the path, the rock, or the thorns, we finish with nothing. There is more to be said for the second view.[1] Tinsley argues from the prominence given to this parable and its explanation in all three Synoptists that it

[1] See I. H. Marshall, *Eschatology and the Parables* (London, 1963), pp. 11, 30f.

is especially significant. Of the explanation he says, 'It is as
near as Jesus *ever* comes to "explaining" himself and his mission . . . Jesus sees his mission as a way of speaking and acting
which will give men the greatest opportunity to respond to the
word of God.'

p. The lamp and the cover (8:16-18)

16, 17. The purpose of *lighting a lamp* is to give light, and
thus a lamp is not hidden under *a vessel* (*cf.* 11:33) or *a bed*.
Jesus' followers must let the light that is in them shine forth
and illuminate men. This leads on to the thought that in due
course all that is hidden will be made public (*cf.* 12:2). Nothing can be concealed on judgment day.

18. This saying links up with the parable of the sower and
also with that of the pounds (19:26). It is important to hear
rightly and not be like the seed that came to nothing in the
parable. The same lesson is driven home with the reminder
that *to him who has will more be given*. This is not, of course, a
message of encouragement for the moneyed classes: it is connected with hearing the word of God. If we use what God
gives it will increase. And the next words underline the
opposite truth: if we do not, we will lose even what we think
we have. This is total loss.

q. Jesus' mother and brothers (8:19-21)

The other Synoptists place this little incident before the
parable of the sower (though neither says explicitly that it
preceded it in time). It is not unlikely that Luke has placed it
here because of the way it illustrates the parables. His account
is the shortest of the three and omits details such as Jesus
looking round on the disciples and stretching out His hand to
them. Luke concentrates on the saying. He tells us that Jesus'
mother and brothers came to see Him, but were prevented
from approaching by the crowd. The most natural understanding of Jesus' *brothers* is that they were children of Joseph
and Mary. Theologians in the Catholic tradition usually hold
that Mary was perpetually virgin and explain this as a reference to children of Joseph by an earlier marriage or perhaps
to cousins of Jesus. There is little evidence for such views and

we should hold to the natural meaning.[1] In the family's implied claim that Jesus ought to be available to them there is perhaps a hint of possessiveness. But Jesus makes it clear that He is now given over to the work of ministry. His mother and brothers are *those who hear the word of God and do it*. The reference to hearing (absent from Matthew and Mark) comes in appropriately after the parable of the sower. But the stress is on doing. Those who are near to Jesus are those who take seriously their duty to God. This does not mean that family ties are unimportant or can be ignored: Jesus is not disowning His family. He thought of His mother even when He hung on the cross in the agony of achieving the world's redemption (Jn. 19:26f.). His meaning is that our duty to God takes precedence of everything else.

r. The stilling of the storm (8:22–25)

Many who are ready to accept the healing miracles (feeling perhaps that these fit in with our knowledge of functional disorders) find difficulty with the nature miracles and look for other explanations. In the present narrative, for example, they prefer to hold that Jesus calmed the disciples rather than the waves. This kind of approach is completely subjective. If we are to trust our sources Jesus did sometimes perform miracles in the realm of nature. The great miracle is the incarnation. If God became man in Jesus, then we need not boggle over such narratives as this. If He did not, then the question scarcely arises.

22, 23. Luke does not locate this incident with any precision (Mark puts it on the evening of the day when Jesus told the parable of the sower). Jesus invited the disciples to cross the lake. As they journeyed, He fell asleep, which fits in well with Mark's account; He would have been weary after a full day's teaching. A sudden storm blew up. The lake of Galilee is subject to sudden storms, situated as it is some 700 feet below sea level and adjacent to mountainous regions. Cold air from the heights is apt to sweep down through the precipitous gorges to the east and it can whip up the seas in a short time.

[1] See further, Leon Morris, *The Gospel according to John* (*New London Commentary*), pp. 187f.

On this occasion the boat was being filled with water and the travellers were in great danger.

24. So the disciples woke Jesus with the words, *Master, Master, we are perishing!* Luke omits the rebuke implied in Mark's 'do you not care if we perish?' and the entreaty in Matthew's 'Save, Lord'. All three tell us that Jesus rebuked the wind (*cf.* Ps. 106:9). His verb may imply that there was an evil force behind the storm. Be that as it may, the result was *a calm*. Jesus' mastery over the elements was complete (*cf.* Ps. 89:9).

25. His inquiry, *Where is your faith?* implies that the disciples ought not to have been terrified. They should have trusted Him. To this they reacted as in the divine presence. They were filled with awe (*afraid*); they *marvelled*; and they asked, *Who then is this?* This is the significant question which Luke does not want his readers to miss.

s. The Gerasene demoniac (8:26–39)

i. The exorcism (8:26–33). This miracle took place in a predominantly Gentile environment. There were some Jews in the area but the population was mostly Gentile.

26, 27. The *country of the Gerasenes* presents us with a problem, for Gerasa was about forty miles south-east of the lake. Matthew has 'the country of the Gadarenes', but Gadara is six miles away and separated by the deep gorge of the Yarmuk. All three Synoptists have both variants and also a third, 'the country of the Gergesenes'. This last reading was favoured by Origen, who saw that the other two are too distant and thought that the readings had arisen only because scribes did not know of the small town Gergesa, so substituted names they knew (see, for example, Manson). Modern students point to the village of Khersa and think this may retain the ancient name. This may be right, but the suspicion remains that the reading is found in the MSS only because Origen originated it. If either of the others is correct, we must understand that the city in question controlled a tract of land bordering the lake. As Jesus reached land in this territory He was met by a demoniac. The unfortunate man wore no clothes and he lived among the tombs.

28, 29. The man was violent. He had been *bound with chains and fetters* (*i.e.* bonds for both hands and feet). But he *broke the bonds*, which shows his great strength. When Jesus commanded the demon to leave him he screamed and proceeded to a response like that of the demoniac in 4:34, except that Jesus is now greeted as *Son of the Most High God* in place of 'the holy One of God'.

30. Jesus inquired the man's name. The reply is *Legion*, which seems a way of saying that a whole regiment of demons had entered him (in a Roman legion there were about 6,000 soldiers). Some think there is a reference to the Roman legions and that some traumatic experience with the soldiery was the origin of the man's plight.

31-33. The demons recognized that they must leave the man and they asked that they be not sent *into the abyss*. This is a place of confinement for spirits, even Satan (Rev. 20:1ff.).[1] Instead, they asked that they might be permitted to enter *a large herd of swine* grazing nearby. Jesus gave them leave, whereat the demons left the man and entered the pigs. The animals rushed down a steep bank into the lake where they drowned. There is a difficulty in seeing how demons could enter swine and another why the pigs should act in this way. But as we know little about what demons can do we should probably not raise such questions. Some see a further difficulty in that Jesus cured the man at the expense of the owners of the animals. To this the basic reply must be that the cure of the man was more important than a herd of pigs. Can anyone seriously hold that the pigs should have been saved and the man left unsaved? Farrar points out that, as well, 'the freeing of the neighbourhood from the peril and terror of this wild maniac was a greater benefit to the whole city than the loss of this herd'. It is also to be remembered that Jesus neither sent the demons into the pigs (He did no more than give them permission), nor the pigs into the lake (the narrative does not say that He willed the destruction of the pigs).

ii. The reaction (8:34-39). Luke goes on to the way the miracle affected both the man in question and the people of the district.

[1]See the note in Leon Morris, *Revelation* (*TNTC*) (London, 1969), pp. 127f.

34-36. The herdsmen, not unnaturally, ran away and spread the news. People then came to see for themselves. They found the former demoniac at Jesus' feet, *clothed and in his right mind*. Obviously something strange had happened, and they *were afraid*.

37. With all the evidence that a great miracle had been wrought before them, these people proceeded to reject the greatest opportunity of their lives. They might have welcomed Jesus, the liberator of men from demons. Instead, *seized with great fear*, they asked Him to leave. So He left. Their fear may have been a superstitious reaction to the supernatural power that had so evidently been in operation. It may also have been associated with the material loss involved in the destruction of the pigs. If so, they saw Jesus as a disturbing person, more interested in saving men than in material prosperity. It was more comfortable to ask Him to go.

38, 39. With the healed man it was different. He *begged* to be allowed to go with Jesus. He could not be close enough to His benefactor. But there was work for him elsewhere. Jesus sent him back home with the instruction, *declare how much God has done for you*. In response the man proclaimed how much *Jesus* had done for him. Luke will want us to catch the allusion that what Jesus had done God had done. The command to tell of the miracle contrasts with the injunction to silence elsewhere (4:41). Perhaps in this predominantly Gentile territory there would be little danger of arousing Messianic speculations. And, now that Jesus had been asked to leave, it was more than ever important that in this region there should be somebody to witness to what God was doing in Him.

t. The daughter of Jairus (8:40-56)

All three Synoptists have the healing of the woman with the haemorrhage in the middle of the Jairus story. The two form a powerful illustration of the way Jesus healed and even exercised authority over death.

i. The request for healing (8:40-42a). When Jesus returned He found a welcome from a waiting crowd. Among them was a man named Jairus (the Old Testament name Jair,

Nu. 32:41). He was *a ruler of the synagogue, i.e.* the official who was responsible for the arrangements at the synagogue services. He would select, for example, those who would lead in prayer, read the Scripture and preach. He was thus a man of eminence in the community. This man prostrated himself before Jesus and *besought him to come to his house.* He *had an only daughter* (we owe to Luke the information that she was an only child), *about twelve years of age,* who *was dying.* Luke does not mention any specific request, but a plea for healing is clearly implicit in Jairus's words. Mark says that he asked Jesus to lay hands on her for healing. But the real problem lies with Matthew, who gives Jairus's words as 'My daughter has just died; but come and lay your hand on her, and she will live'. This is probably to be explained, not as contradicting Mark and Luke, but as arising from the very abbreviated character of Matthew's account. The other two speak first of Jairus as coming to Jesus and telling Him that his daughter was at the point of death. Later there came a messenger with word that the girl had died. Matthew shortens the story by running both into one.

ii. The woman with the haemorrhage (8:42b–48).
Now comes an interruption which must have been very frustrating to Jairus, though none of the accounts records one word of complaint.

42b–44. In the narrow streets of an ancient city it was inevitable that a crowd meant a crush. Luke says that the people *pressed* round Jesus, where his verb is that used of the thorns crushing out the wheat in the parable (8:14). It must have been quite a press. Included among the people was a woman *who had had a flow of blood for twelve years.* The malady itself must have been distressing and it had social consequences as well as physical. Because this complaint made her ceremonially unclean (Lv. 15:25ff.), the sufferer was not permitted to take any part in temple worship or the like. Her uncleanness was readily communicable to other people (a touch was all that was needed, Lv. 15:27). She would accordingly have been avoided lest others contract from her an uncleanness which, though temporary, was troublesome. Life must have been very difficult. It was probably the nature of her malady that caused her to make the furtive approach she did. Had she come openly, in the first instance people might not have allowed her to get close to Jesus (in the crowd it was easier), and in the second, she would have had to tell in front of all the people something of the illness of which she wanted to be cured. In her embarrassment she preferred the secret touch. Luke does not tell us, as Mark does, that she had suffered many things at the hands of many physicians. Nor that, though she had spent all her money, she was no better but rather worse. This is perhaps natural if he was a medical man. He omits also the information that the reason she came behind Jesus in the crowd was that she thought that if she could only touch Him she would be cured. Luke concentrates on the healing. The woman *touched the fringe of his garment*. The *fringe* will be the tassel on the end of the square garment that was thrown over the left shoulder and hung down the back (Nu. 15:38ff.). We should not think of the lower hem, as this could not be reached in the circumstances. Immediately she touched this tassel *her flow of blood ceased*.

45. Jesus asked, *Who was it that touched me?* This must have seemed a curious question to anyone in the jostling throng. At all events everyone denied being responsible. Some must have pushed against Jesus, but they had not tried to touch Him. Each would thus feel that he was not the one Jesus was looking for. Typically it was Peter who took it upon himself to point out that crowds of people were all round Jesus and pressing on Him. The implication is clear: so many had touched Jesus that the question became meaningless.

46. But Jesus persisted. He explained, *I perceive that power has gone forth from me* (*cf.* 6:19). There is mystery here. Could power go out of Jesus at any touch? Could power go forth in such a way that He was quite unaware of who received it and what the power was for? This seems unlikely. It is easier to hold that Jesus knew quite well what had happened and this seems to be the meaning of the later words 'the woman saw that she was not hidden' (47). He wanted to bring the woman out into the open. More than one reason is apparent. It was good for her, indeed it was necessary for her that her cure be widely known. All her acquaintances must have been aware of her permanent state of ceremonial uncleanness. If she was to be received back into normal religious and social intercourse, it was necessary that her cure become a matter of public knowledge. So Jesus took steps to see that people knew what had happened. It is probable also that He wanted to do something else for the woman. It is difficult to deny that there was an element of superstition in her idea that a touch of Jesus' tassel would bring healing. By having a conversation with her Jesus was able both to show the woman that it was her faith that counted and to establish a personal relationship. The words also seem to indicate that He did not heal without some cost to Himself. Power went out from Him.

47. The woman perceived *that she was not hidden*. She had thought that she could touch Jesus, be cured, and slip away unnoticed. Indeed she may already have started, for she *came*. She saw that Jesus knew and that there was nothing for it but to come forward. But she did so *trembling* in her nervousness. Had she done wrong in touching Jesus? Would her cure be taken away? What would all the people think? It must have been a bad moment for her. But Jesus waited, so she came forward and prostrated herself. She told *in the presence of all the people* what she had done, why she had done it and how she had been healed. This was a complete disclosure. Everyone now knew of her cure.

48. Jesus addressed her tenderly as *Daughter*. She is the only woman He is recorded as having addressed in this way. He went on to point out that it had been her faith that had saved her and He told her to go in peace. With the exception of the prefixed address, *Daughter*, the words are identical with those addressed to the sinner in 7:50 (where see note; RSV has a slight difference in wording, but the Greek is the same).

iii. Jairus's daughter raised from the dead (8:49–56).
The interruption halted Jesus' progress to the house of Jairus. But it did not stop it, and Luke proceeds to show how the little girl was raised.

49. Mark as well as Luke lets us know that while Jesus was still speaking to the woman there came news from Jairus's house that his daughter had died. The messenger went on, *do not trouble the Teacher any more*. He apparently had no thought that Jesus' power could extend beyond death. There is con-

sideration for the busy Teacher implied in the suggestion that
He should not come to the house, but there is also a limitation
of faith and understanding.

50. Jairus did not say anything. Jesus overheard the words
spoken to him and immediately told him to stop worrying.
Only believe, He said, *and she shall be well*. If we can press Luke's
use of the aorist tense, *believe* means something like 'make an
act of faith', 'put your trust in Me' (though we should not
overlook Mark's present, 'keep believing'; both stress the
importance of faith at this moment). Jesus certainly made it
clear to the ruler of the synagogue that in the face of the
disaster that had hit him he must have faith. Nothing else
mattered.

51. The previous miracle had taken place unobserved, but
Jesus had insisted that it be given full publicity. As we saw,
this marked His consideration for the woman. It is equally a
mark of His consideration for the little girl that when she was
raised from death she would not find herself the centre of a
gaping crowd. Jesus allowed nobody to enter the house with
Him except the inner circle of His disciples and the child's
parents. This is the first time He has singled out Peter, John
and James in this way, but the same three figure on other
occasions. For this order of mention *cf.* 9:28; Acts 1:13;
James precedes John in Luke 5:10; 6:14; 9:54.

52, 53. It is not quite clear who is meant by the *all* who were
weeping and bewailing her. They will certainly include the family
(apart from the parents who were with Jesus), and the neighbours. As we saw on 7:12, professional mourners were obligatory and, as Matthew speaks of flute players, it seems that
they had lost no time in beginning to ply their trade. To those
engaged in noisy grief Jesus said, 'Stop wailing' (*Do not weep*
employs a construction meaning to cease to continue an
action already in process, while the verb denotes noisy grief,
not quiet tears). He explained, *she is not dead but sleeping*. Some
feel that this is to be taken literally and think that Jesus'
diagnosis led Him to the conclusion that the girl was still in
fact alive. However this is hard to reconcile with Luke's
express statement, *knowing* (not 'thinking') *that she was dead*,
and with his later words, 'her spirit returned' (55). It is better

to see the word as meaning that what is death to men is no more than sleep for Jesus (*cf.* Jn. 11:11-14). In the New Testament believers are never said to die, but to sleep (*cf.* Acts 7:60). However, Jesus' words brought scornful laughter (curiously these mourners are the only people in the New Testament expressly said to have *laughed*). The mourners knew that the girl was dead and Jesus was not yet in the house.

54, 55. Presumably at this point Jesus entered the death chamber. He took the dead girl by the hand and said, *Child, arise*. Mark retains the Aramaic words that the girl's mother would have used in calling her in the morning. Luke normally translates Aramaic terms and does so here. He goes on to describe the miracle in very simple terms: *her spirit returned, and she got up at once*. Jesus went on to tell them to give her something to eat. Even at the moment of a stupendous miracle He does not overlook the importance of practical details. And, of course, the words show once again the consideration Jesus had for the ordinary needs of those with whom He came in contact.

56. As often, Luke rounds off the narrative with the effect of the miracle. The girl's parents *were amazed*. Jesus went on to charge them to tell no-one what had happened. This can scarcely be in order that no-one should know about it. After all a mourning group had already assembled, expecting a funeral, and they would have to be told that there would not be one. Jesus probably wanted to turn the child's parents from a natural tendency to give themselves over to talking about the wonderful thing that had happened. It was better for them to concentrate on the girl's welfare. Publicity was not needed.

u. The mission of the Twelve (9:1-6)

Some scholars (*e.g.* Bultmann) hold that this preaching tour is not historical. They see the early church as justifying its practices by reading them back into the time of Jesus. This, however, is highly subjective and others point out that there is not the slightest reason for thinking that Jesus did not send His disciples out in this way. There were signs that His ministry in Galilee would not last much longer and it was important both to spread the message of the kingdom and to give the disciples experience.

1. First Jesus *called the twelve together*. We should not exaggerate the amount of time the apostles spent together. Some of them had homes and families in Capernaum and we need not doubt that they spent some of the time at their homes. But on this solemn occasion Jesus called them all together. The other Synoptists tell us that Jesus gave the apostles *authority*, but Luke strengthens this with the reference also to *power* and with the information that it was over *all demons* (the others refer to unclean spirits, but there is probably no great difference). With this is coupled power *to cure diseases*. They were thus adequately equipped with power and the authority to use that power.

2. Equipped in this way they were sent forth (two by two, as Mark tells us). Jesus sent them to do two things: *to preach the kingdom of God and to heal*. This is clearly an extension of His own ministry, for these were the things that He Himself had been doing. They were to be concerned with men's bodies as well as their souls.

3. The Twelve were to travel light. Jesus told them to *take nothing* with them, and He spelt this out with *no staff*, *nor bag*, *nor bread*, *nor money*. They are to concentrate on the task in hand, not on elaborate preparations. In fact they are to forgo even what would have been regarded as normal preparations for a journey. God will provide what they need and they are to trust Him for it, a trust which they later agreed was vindicated (22:35). There is a problem in *no staff*, for in the first instance it is not easy to see how this would in any way hinder the effectiveness of their preaching and healing, and in the second in Mark's account they were to take nothing 'except a staff' (Mk. 6:8). Various attempts have been made at harmonizing the two, such as the view that Luke means 'no additional staff' (but why would they want a spare staff?), or that we have variant translations of an Aramaic original (which was perhaps elliptical and might be filled out in more than one way). But so far no explanation seems really satisfactory. Perhaps both ways of putting it mean 'Go as you are'. Jesus is instructing them to make no special preparation for this trip. The *bag* (*pēra*) was the 'knapsack, traveller's bag' (AG). As they were to make no preparation such a bag was not needed. The need was urgent: they must simply go. Some, however, see the *pēra* as the beggar's bag used, for example, by itinerant Cynic preachers. Some of them seem to have made quite a good living by appealing to the public in this way. Jesus' preachers were not to emulate such. The prohibition of a second tunic fits in with the rest of the instructions. They were not to make even the simplest of preparations for their trip. Edersheim connects all this with the rabbinic rule that one must not enter the temple precincts with staff, shoes and money-bag. 'The symbolic reasons underlying this command would, in both cases, be probably the same: to avoid even the appearance of being engaged on other business, when the whole being should be absorbed in the service of the Lord.'[1]

4. Now we find how they were to be maintained. In each place they visited they were to go into one home and *stay there*. Someone would be interested enough and hospitable enough to provide for them. They were not to go to other homes. When they left the town they were to depart from the house to which they came at the first. The limitation on their acceptance of hospitality to that of one householder imposed a limit on the length of their stay.

5. Next Jesus instructed them as to their procedure when they found no-one to welcome them. They must do no more than *shake off the dust* from their feet. There was a rabbinic idea that the dust of Gentile lands carried defilement,[2] and strict Jews are said to have removed it from their shoes whenever they returned to Palestine from abroad. The disciples' shaking of the dust from their feet was *a testimony against them*. It declared in symbol that Israelites who rejected the kingdom were no better than Gentiles. They did not belong to the people of God. For the practice *cf.* Acts 13:51.

6. Luke records the apostles' obedience. They *went through the villages*, which points to a country tour. Luke does not go into detail, but he does tell us that they preached and that they healed. That they did it *everywhere* shows that between them they covered a lot of ground.

We should perhaps add that the instructions given here are not to be regarded as applying universally. At a later time

[1] *LT*, i, p. 643.
[2] See SB, i, p. 571.

Jesus could command His followers to take purse, bag and sword (22:36). These instructions are for this one trip.

v. Herod the tetrarch (9:7–9)

While the apostles are away on their mission Luke tells us a little about Herod the tetrarch. This man had heard about Jesus and he was perplexed.

7, 8. For *Herod the tetrarch* see the notes on 3:1, 19. He was the ruler of the territory in which Jesus had done most of His work; so he would be interested in the reports that reached him. What he heard puzzled him. Some people thought that Jesus was John the Baptist, now *raised from the dead*. Matthew and Mark tell us that this was Herod's own view and Luke may mean that in the end he came round to it. Others saw Jesus as Elijah or another of the prophets. All this may mean Messianic speculation, for Elijah was expected to precede the Messiah (Mal. 4:5) and the Jews thought other prophets would also come. It is clear that Jesus' ministry had aroused a lot of interest and caused a lot of talking. It is not unlikely that Herod had heard also of the band of apostolic preachers who had gone forth in Jesus' name. But with all the talking and all the interest people did not know what to make of Jesus.

9. Herod did some talking to himself. 'John? I beheaded him' (Rieu), he said. But that he came back to John after canvassing the other suggestions shows that the thought that the Baptist might have risen from the dead disturbed him. His conscience was perhaps troubling him when he thought of that good man. So he wanted *to see* Jesus for himself, perhaps to check up on whether He was John.

w. The feeding of the five thousand (9:10–17)

This is the one miracle, apart from the resurrection, recounted in all four Gospels. Clearly it made a special appeal to the early church. But some in more recent times have found difficulty with it. They have suggested that perhaps the 'miracle' took place in men's hearts. When Jesus' disciples prepared to share all they had, others were ashamed and produced the food they had with them but had not wanted to share. When they did so there proved to be more than enough for all. Others think of a token meal, like Holy Communion, and point to the similarity of language with that used of that sacrament. The trouble with such views is that they are far too subjective. If it had no more to it than this, it is hard to see how the story should have left such a mark both on the biblical tradition and on that of the early church (*cf.* the motif of the loaves and fishes in Christian art). This is not what any of the Evangelists is saying. They all describe a miracle. 'It is impossible to reduce the event to ordinary human dimensions' (Melinsky). This does not mean that it was not symbolic. John speaks of it as a 'sign', and this should be taken with full seriousness. The incident brought home the truth that God in Christ can supply any need. We may even accept the view that there was something sacramental about the meal. It was perhaps an anticipation of the Messianic banquet, the feast of Messiah with His people. There may also be something of a 'farewell to fellowship' aspect to it, as Jesus realized that He would not be able to move freely for much longer in Galilee. But such ideas should not be held in such a way as to obscure the miraculous.

10. In due course the disciples returned from their journey and reported. It is a further example of Jesus' consideration that after their strenuous labours He took them away to a deserted place. Evidently He wished them to have the opportunity to relax and to refresh themselves. They went to *Bethsaida*, which must mean to a place in the general vicinity of that city, for Luke also tells us that it was 'a lonely place' (12), and thus not the city itself.

11. It must have been a disappointment to cross the lake in the search for privacy and then to find that they had not escaped the crowds (from Mark we learn that some of the crowd even went on ahead so that they were waiting when Jesus and His friends disembarked). It is curious that the people followed Jesus round the lake. It would have been simpler for them to have awaited His return as they did once before (8:40). But Bethsaida lay outside the jurisdiction of Herod and it may well be that some unrecorded action of Herod's had convinced people that Jesus might not appear much more in Galilee. The death of John the Baptist would have been quite recent and it showed Herod's hostility to the kind of preaching in which Jesus and now His followers were engaging. So the people went out to meet Him. Despite His seeking of privacy Jesus displayed no irritation. On the contrary, He *welcomed them*. And He continued the work He had so recently been doing through the disciples. He *spoke to them of the kingdom of God, and cured those who had need of healing*.

12. We do not know at what time all this began, but it lasted throughout the rest of the day. Towards evening the Twelve thought it was time to take action. So they called on Jesus to send the people away. In the *lonely place* where they were there was no food, so the crowd must go off to the surrounding countryside and villages if they were to eat.

13. Jesus responded by suggesting that the disciples give the people what they needed (*you* is emphatic). But they said they had no more than *five loaves and two fish*. From John we learn that they were barley loaves (the food of the poor) and that Andrew had found a small boy with them. Evidently they were the boy's own food supply. It was not much in the face of the multitude. The alternative to sending the people off was *to go and buy food*. But the disciples saw this as impossible, both because they were so distant from sources of supply and because they did not have the necessary financial resources (Philip pointed out that two hundred denarii would not be sufficient, Jn. 6:7).

14, 15. Luke now tells us that there were *about five thousand men* in the crowd (the use of *andres* points to men in distinction from women and children, though there were probably not very many of these). Jesus told the disciples to get them seated in groups of about fifty, evidently for convenience in serving.

16, 17. Jesus began in the way the Jews normally began a meal: He took the food and 'said the blessing' (NEB), looking up to heaven as He did so. The verb *blessed* does not mean that He somehow imparted a blessing to these physical objects. Such an idea is nowhere found in Scripture. The meaning is that Jesus said a prayer of thanksgiving, a prayer that would begin with, 'Blessed art Thou, O Lord,' followed by mention of that for which thanks were offered, in this case the loaves and fishes. Bread was often broken during the saying of this prayer, though here it will refer also to the breaking in pieces for distribution to the people. Jesus gave the food to the disciples and they to the people until all *were satisfied*. That is to say, they had a full meal and not simply a token. When the meal was over the disciples gathered up what was left and took up *twelve baskets of broken pieces*. Though there was abundant supply there was to be no waste.

x. Discipleship (9:18–27)

At this point Luke omits the whole section Mark 6:45 – 8:26.[1] Whatever the reason for this it yields an interesting sequence, as Leaney points out. Herod has asked, 'Who is this?' (9). Some answers are suggested by the feeding of the multitude (*cf.* Jn. 6:14f.), the disciples cite three other answers given by the people, then Peter adds one of his own (19f.). The climax comes with an awe-inspiring answer from God (35). We should also notice another sequence here: the disciples' recognition that Jesus is the Messiah is followed immediately by the teaching that this means a cross for Him, and a cross, too, for them.

i. Peter's confession (9:18–20).

Matthew and Mark locate this incident in the vicinity of Caesarea Philippi, near the foot of Mount Hermon. This was heathen territory, the worship of the great god Pan being especially prominent. Jesus had withdrawn from Herod's dominions and from the crowds that had been thronging Him. Here He could talk quietly with the disciples and have opportunity for undistracted thinking. Luke characteristically tells us that Jesus was *praying alone*. Then He started a conversation by asking the disciples, *Who do the people say that I am?* Their answer is much the same as the reports that reached Herod (7f.). The Greek appears to mean that the answer generally given was *John the Baptist*, though some people had other ideas (so Goodspeed). Elijah or another old-time prophet was suggested. Jesus goes on, *But who do you say that I am?* In all three Synoptists His *you* is emphatic. In distinction from others, He is saying, what do *you* think? The knowledge of Christ is always a personal discovery, not the passing on of a report learnt from other

[1]See Introduction, pp. 51f.

people. As often, Peter is the spokesman. He speaks for them all when he says, *The Christ of God*. For *Christ* see the note on 2:11. Peter is saying that Jesus is the Deliverer for whom the people of God had been looking for so long. That he and his companions had come to see this was not a human discovery, but a revelation (Mt. 16:17). But what 'Messiah' really meant they did not know. So Jesus went on to explain that it involved suffering and death. It was a lesson they found hard to learn. Indeed, they had still not learnt it when Jesus was crucified.

ii. A prophecy of the passion (9:21, 22). Jesus' response to Peter's words is a very firm instruction to silence. *He charged and commanded them*, or, as NEB puts it, 'gave them strict orders'. The reason is surely the near certainty of misunderstanding if it was spread abroad. The Jews detested their state of subjection to the Romans and longed for deliverance. They were ready to follow almost anyone who claimed to be Messiah and in fact there were many petty revolts. Had Jesus been hailed widely as Messiah, people would have understood it as a political and military claim. They would have completely missed what He was teaching them.

22. Jesus proceeded to explain a little of what being Messiah meant. He *must* suffer. Suffering, for Him, was no accident, but a compelling divine necessity. The cross was His vocation. In accordance with this, of the *many things* He would suffer Jesus speaks only of the final rejection. The word *rejected* seems to be a technical term to denote rejection after a careful legal scrutiny held to see whether a candidate for office was qualified (see LS). It implies here that the hierarchy would consider Jesus' claims but decide against Him. The one article in the expression *the elders and chief priests and scribes* points to the fact that the three formed a single group in the Sanhedrin. There was, of course, only one high priest, and the plural signifies all the members of the high-priestly families. It was the nation's leaders who would be foremost in rejecting Him. Nor would this be merely a matter of words. He would *be killed*. Jesus left them in no doubt but that being Messiah meant a cross. But the cross is not the whole story. *On the third day* the Son of man will *be raised*. The resurrection was as certain as the crucifixion.

iii. Taking up the cross (9:23-27). Jesus immediately followed the announcement of the cross with a reference to another cross, this one to be carried by His followers. There is, of course, a difference. Their cross was not literal and their sufferings not atoning. But it was (and is) real.

23. The follower of Jesus must *deny himself*. There is nothing self-indulgent about being a Christian. The disciples had probably seen a man *take up his cross*, and they knew what it meant. When a man from one of their villages took up a cross and went off with a little band of Roman soldiers, he was on a one-way journey. He'd not be back. Taking up the cross meant the utmost in self-denial. This is Luke's first use of the word *cross* and it comes with striking effect. Christ's follower has died to a whole way of life (*cf.* 14:27). Luke tells us that this is not something that can be finished and got out of the way: it must be done *daily*. So, says Jesus, will he *follow me*.

24, 25. Paradoxically a man can lose his life trying to save it (*cf.* 17:33; Mt. 10:39; Jn. 12:25). *Would save* is rather 'wills to save'. It points to the attitude of the man who puts his emphasis on getting the best out of life for himself. That way means certain loss. It is the man who *loses his life* (not 'wills to lose', but actually loses) for Christ's sake who saves it. When he gives up all for Christ he finds that he has entered that life which is life indeed. Barclay finely says, 'The Christian must realize that he is given life, not to keep it for himself, but to spend it for others; not to husband its flame, but to burn himself out for Christ and for men.' Life cannot be measured in terms of material things. In a magnificent hyperbole Jesus asks what is the profit if a man *gains the whole world*, but *loses or forfeits himself*. Nothing material can compensate for the loss of the self.

26. Jesus reinforces this with a reference to eternal issues. He now speaks of a time when He will come in glory and in *the glory of the Father and of the holy angels*. This clearly refers to the end of this world-order and the breaking in of something quite new, the final state of things. To be ashamed of Jesus and His teaching now, He says, is to ensure that He will be ashamed of us in that glorious day.

27. The paragraph is rounded off with a mysterious saying. Some of those present *will not taste of death before they see the kingdom of God*. *Taste of death* surely means 'die', but it is not clear what the coming of *the kingdom of God* means in this context. Some maintain that Jesus is referring to the *parousia* and that He was mistaken. But this does not fit the language used. If some will not die *before* (or 'until', as TEV; *heōs an*) the event in question, the implication seems to be that they will die after it, which is impossible of the *parousia*. But in any case this line is too simple. Plummer notes seven possible interpretations of the words: the transfiguration, the resurrection and ascension, Pentecost, the spread of Christianity, the internal development of the gospel, the destruction of Jerusalem and the second advent. He holds that the reference to *some standing here* means that some (viz. those present on that particular occasion) have special privilege as opposed to men in general. This rules out all of the seven except the transfiguration and the destruction of Jerusalem, of which Plummer prefers the latter. He may be right, for that coming in judgment suits the words as well as any. But there are many ways in which the kingdom comes and there is much also to be said for the view that Jesus is referring to the critical time of the crucifixion, resurrection and the coming of the Spirit. The saying is complex and without further information it is impossible to be sure of the precise meaning intended.

y. The transfiguration (9:28–36)

It is not easy to see exactly what happened at the transfiguration or why it occurred. We may see it as a revelation of the glory of the other world and perhaps this is meant as an encouragement to the disciples after the hard words about cross-bearing. The combination of glory and the conversation about the death of Christ will also be a way of teaching the disciples that true glory and the cross are not incompatible. But we should also understand it all as having significance for Jesus Himself. In the quietness He had doubtless thought long about the outworking of His vocation. He was about to go up to Jerusalem and die for men. This vision on the mountain set the seal of divine approval on the step He was about to take.

28, 29. Traditionally Mount Tabor has been understood as the place where the transfiguration occurred, but this is almost certainly wrong. It is too far away from Caesarea Philippi and it appears to have been occupied at the time. It would thus not have afforded the solitude into which Jesus took His followers to pray. There is more to be said for Mount Hermon, but that is far from certain. Characteristically Luke tells us that Jesus went to the mountain *to pray* (see Introduction, p. 46). As He prayed His whole appearance was altered. Luke does not give us much detail, but we learn from the other Evangelists that Jesus' face shone like the sun and that His clothing became whiter than any earthly laundryman could make it.

30, 31. All three Synoptists agree that Moses and Elijah *talked with him*, the great lawgiver and a great representative of the prophets. Together they point to the hour of fulfilment of all that the Old Testament foreshadows. Only Luke tells us that the subject of the conversation was Jesus' *departure*, *i.e.* His death (*cf.* 2 Pet. 1:15). That such a topic was chosen at such a time shows how central the death of Jesus is.[1] The use of the word *exodos* for death is unusual and we should probably discern some Exodus typology. The Exodus had delivered Israel from bondage. Jesus by His 'exodus' would deliver His people from a far worse bondage.

32, 33. The disciples 'were sound asleep, but they awoke' (TEV). It may well have been night (37; *cf.* 6:12). Evidently as Jesus prayed the disciples fell asleep, but they were awakened by the shining of the light. They saw Jesus' glory and the heavenly visitants. When Moses and Elijah were beginning to leave, Peter tried to retain the experience by making for them *booths*, *i.e.* leafy shelters or huts of a temporary kind; the word is commonly used for a tent or tabernacle. Peter did not really know what he was saying. The experience was overwhelming.

34, 35. Now *a cloud came and overshadowed them*. In the Old Testament a cloud is sometimes associated with the presence

---

[1] H. Conzelmann comments, 'The purpose behind the heavenly manifestation is the announcement of the Passion, and by this means the proof is given that the Passion is something decreed by God' (*The Theology of St Luke*, p. 57).

of God (*e.g.* Ex. 40:34f.) and we need not doubt that this is the case here, especially in view of the heavenly voice. It is not quite clear who entered the cloud. RSV gives the impression that the disciples were included. But it seems more likely that the cloud enveloped Jesus and the heavenly visitants;[1] *cf.* Knox, 'they saw those others disappear into the cloud, and were terrified.' That the disciples were outside the cloud seems indicated by the fact that the voice came to them *out of* (*ek*) it. The voice said, *This is my Son, my Chosen; listen to him!* The other Gospels have 'my beloved Son', as do some MSS of Luke. *Chosen* emphasizes another aspect of Jesus' Person, rather like Messiahship. God chose and anointed Jesus for His ministry. This clearly and emphatically differentiates Him from Moses and Elijah (against the views in 8, 19). To Him, men must give heed.

36. That ended the vision. Luke passes over Jesus' coming to them and touching them as they lay prostrate. He simply says that after the voice *Jesus was found alone.* He adds that *in those days* the disciples told nobody about the vision. It had been a wonderful experience, but it was not the kind of thing that encouraged idle chatter.

z. Jesus and the disciples (9:37–50)

Luke now brings together four short incidents in which he shows the disciples' lack of faith, their slowness to learn, their pride and their intolerance. It is an impressive sequence and makes a sad conclusion to his Galilean section. The disciples have much to learn.

i. The demon-possessed boy (9:37–43a). The mountain-top experience is followed in all three Synoptists by the distressing inability of the disciples to deal with a case of demon possession. The contrast is striking. On the one hand we have those who rejoiced in the light of God on the mountain top, on the other those defeated by the powers of darkness on the plain. But the supremacy of Jesus is evident in both places.

37. Luke says that this incident took place *the next day.* He omits the discussion about the coming of Elijah and goes

---

[1] So A. Oepke, *TDNT*, iv, p. 908.

straight on to the boy with the demon. *A great crowd* was with the lad and now met Jesus.

38–40. A man in the crowd called loudly to Jesus, explaining his need. He had an only son (*cf.* 7:12; 8:42), who from time to time was seized by a demon. The symptoms sound much like those of epilepsy and many class the illness as such without further ado. As, however, it is attributed to demon possession, this may be a trifle too confident. The man concludes his tale of woe by telling Jesus that he had begged the disciples to deal with the demon but unfortunately *they could not.* It is not clear whether these *disciples* included some of the apostles or not. Since only three of the twelve were with Jesus presumably they did. In that case there is a problem, for they had successfully coped with demons on their preaching tour (9:1–6). Now the power had left them. There must have been some failure in their spiritual life (Mk. 9:29 refers to the necessity of prayer).

41. It is not easy to see to whom Jesus addresses the words, *O faithless and perverse generation* (*cf.* Dt. 32:5). There seems no reason for thinking of the father, for in the first instance he was not a 'generation', and in the second he had brought his son for cure in faith, even if imperfect faith (Mk. 9:24). But some may well have come in the spirit of 'Let us see what these disciples can do' and perhaps, even, 'what they can't do'! This seems to be the point of the argument between the scribes and the disciples (Mk. 9:14). We should take the address then as 'to all people who are present and had failed to show faith enough for the healing of the boy' (*THB*). The words are important, for Luke has made them central by greatly abbreviating the narrative. He has omitted very interesting sayings like Jesus', 'All things are possible to him who believes' and the father's, 'I believe; help my unbelief!' (Mk. 9:23, 24). The question, *how long,* . . . ? (*cf.* Nu. 14:27), shows that Jesus was concerned at the lack of faith and purpose of which He speaks. People were seeing the miracles as wonders, but not as signs of God's presence and of His demand for repentance. But immediately Jesus turns to the man and His need and asks him to bring the boy along.

42, 43a. As the boy came the demon made his final outburst. He *tore him* (better, 'threw him down', Knox, or 'knocked him to the ground', TEV) *and convulsed him*. Mark relates a short conversation that followed, but Luke, like Matthew, concentrates on the cure. Jesus *rebuked the unclean spirit* (*cf.* 4:35, 39, 41; 8:24) and healed the boy. His concern for persons comes out again as He *gave him back to his father*. The miracle brought astonishment *at the majesty of God*. Jesus did not attract attention to Himself, but brought glory to the Father.

ii. Another prophecy of the passion (9:43b–45). Jesus turned the disciples' attention from *marvelling at everything he did* to the passion. *Let these words sink into your ears* is a call to pay close attention. It is addressed specially to the disciples as the emphatic 'you' ('For your part', JB) indicates. The disciples are set in contrast to the general public who did no more than wonder at the miracles. After this solemn introduction Jesus tells His followers that He will be *delivered into the hands of men*. This is not very specific, which may be part of the reason why *they did not understand this saying*. But more importantly, *it was concealed from them*, which may mean that there was opposition from the forces of evil. Luke goes out of his way to emphasize their inability to grasp the saying, for his words are much stronger than those in the other Gospels. They *were afraid* to ask Jesus about it. This attitude is all the more unaccountable in that Jesus had spoken of the same things not so very long back (22). But they had not understood Him then either, and this saying is shorter and perhaps more mysterious. On the other side of the cross it must have been terribly difficult to grasp the truth that Jesus' Messiahship meant His death.

iii. The disciples' pride (9:46–48). Ryle reminds us that pride keeps recurring in man, though 'Of all creatures none has so little right to be proud as man'. He adds, 'of all men none ought to be so humble as the Christian.'

46. How far the disciples were from the spirit of Jesus comes out in their *argument* (the word can mean 'thought' or 'reasoning') *as to which of them was the greatest*. Jesus had just spoken of His sacrificial death for men. They were speaking of their pride of place. This may be part of the reason for their inability to understand. They were thinking of themselves, He of others.

47, 48. Jesus knew *the thought of their hearts* (the word translated *thought* here is rendered 'argument' in the previous verse). So He rebuked them by setting a little child (for Jesus' attitude to children *cf.* 10:21; 17:2; 18:16) beside Him and saying, *Whoever receives this child in my name receives me*. The child stands for the helpless and the unimportant. The test of loving service is that we receive such in the name of Christ. To receive the child is to receive the Christ and to receive the Christ is to receive the Father (notice the reference to mission in the words, *him who sent me*). True greatness is not earthly greatness but its antithesis. The really great man is the lowly one. Jesus is not saying that the great man is one who is ready to serve his stint in a lowly place. Rather the one *who is least* is the one *who is great*. He does not say 'greatest'. In the kingdom men do not compare themselves with one another. True greatness consists in lowly service.

iv. The strange exorcist (9:49, 50). Jesus' ministry had attracted wide interest and some who had never attached themselves to the circle of the disciples were prepared to serve God in His name. One such attracted the attention of the apostles with his casting out of demons.

49. John *answered*, which means that he responded to Jesus' words. He may mean, 'But surely there are limits. This would not apply to a case like this.' Or perhaps he had seen that his actions came under condemnation and his conscience was troubled. For whatever reason he now told Jesus of a man they had seen *casting out demons* in Jesus' name. Some commentators reject this, saying that exorcism in the name o Jesus is unlikely to have been carried out in His lifetime. They think Luke is reading back the experience of the church into the time of Jesus. But this seems superficial. When Jesus was as successful in casting out demons as the preceding chapters show, nothing is more natural than that someone should attempt the same in His name. But John and whoever else is included in his *we* told him to stop (the imperfect may mean 'we tried to stop him' or 'we kept stopping him') *because he does not follow with us*. Luke does not say that the man claimed to be a disciple. He only cast out demons in Jesus' name. But for these disciples it was not enough that he should be able to do in the name of Jesus what they had so recently and so conspicuously failed to do (40). He had to follow with them. This has been the error of Christians in every age and it is interesting to see it in the very first generation of Jesus' followers.

50. But the Master would have none of it. *Do not forbid him*, He said. He added the important rule, *he that is not against you is for you*. There can be no neutrality in the war against evil. The man who opposes demons in Jesus' name is to be welcomed, not opposed. He is on the right side. Plummer aptly points out that this gives the test a man should apply to others, whereas the saying, 'He who is not with me is against me' (11:23) he should apply to himself.

V. FROM GALILEE TO JERUSALEM (9:51 – 19:44)

There is no real parallel to this section in any of the other Gospels, though some parts of it are like passages in Matthew and, after 18:15, in Mark also. Luke speaks of Jesus as travelling to Jerusalem; but His ministry is far from over and there is much that He has yet to teach the disciples. This section is largely (though not exclusively) concerned with teaching, just as the preceding one has concentrated on Jesus' deeds. There can be no doubt about the idea of a journey. Luke speaks specifically of Jesus as travelling to Jerusalem a number of times (9:51, 53; 13:22, 33; 17:11; 18:31; 19:11, 28) and there are other, less specific, indications of a journey (9:57; 10:1, 38; 14:25). But a problem arises when we try to trace its course. From 9:51ff. Jesus appears to be going by the shorter route through Samaria, but later we find Him passing through Jericho (19:1) which lay on the longer route through Perea. In 10:38 He is at the village of Martha and Mary, *i.e.* Bethany (Jn. 11:1), only a couple of miles from Jerusalem. But in 17:11 He is 'between Samaria and Galilee'.

Godet thinks all this hangs together. He sees it as all part of one leisurely journey from Galilee to Jerusalem, during which Jesus gave a good deal of teaching. Others think there are two distinct journeys, seeing that begun in 9:51 as perhaps the journey for the feast of Tabernacles (Jn. 7), while Jesus' last journey to the capital is commenced in 17:11 (where see note). Some think that Luke was acquainted with two traditions of Jesus' last journey to Jerusalem (9:51 – 10:42 and

17:11 – 19:28) and that he has put in between some interesting matter for which he lacked information about dates or places. Others think the 'journey' quite artificial and hold that Luke has inserted here a good deal of miscellaneous matter which did not obviously belong anywhere else. Probably most scholars take the journey motif to have theological significance, though there is dispute as to precisely what. Thus W. G. Kümmel cites seven different scholars with six different opinions about this theological significance. It cannot accordingly be maintained that any one tendency is strongly marked. In view of these varied assessments of the evidence it is difficult to see how Kümmel's conclusion is to be resisted, when he says no more than that in this section 'the Lord, who goes to suffer according to God's will, equips his disciples for the mission of preaching after his death'.[1] The appeal to the Galileans is over. The passion lies before Jesus and He journeys steadily towards it. But until it comes He must continue His work.

a. More lessons in discipleship (9:51–62)

i. Rejection by the Samaritans (9:51–56).
Luke highlights the contrasting attitudes of Jesus and His followers to the refusal of some Samaritans to receive them.

51. With His ministry drawing to a close Jesus *set his face* towards Jerusalem. The expression *to be received up* is unusual. It is actually a noun ('the days of his receiving up'), which occurs here only in the New Testament. The corresponding verb is used a number of times in Acts, sometimes of Jesus' ascension. Some see in the word an oblique reference to Elijah's being taken up into heaven. This is reinforced by the reference a little later to calling down fire from heaven as Elijah did (54; *cf.* 2 Ki. 1:10, 12). Whatever the truth in this, Luke will have in mind the consummation of Jesus' work in the crucifixion, resurrection and ascension. But first in this sequence is the cross, and there is courage accordingly in the fact that Jesus *set his face to go to Jerusalem.*

---

[1] W. G. Kümmel, *Introduction to the New Testament*, p. 99.

52, 53. It is not said who Jesus' messengers were, but probably they were some of the Twelve who went on ahead to prepare lodgings for the little band. A group of a dozen or so would strain the resources of a small village if they arrived unexpectedly; and, of course, there may have been more. We do not know how many 'disciples' were with Him. But the Samaritan villagers, seeing that *his face was set toward Jerusalem*, would have nothing to do with Jesus. Their feud with the Jews was so bitter that they would not help anyone travel to Jerusalem, though apparently they did not mind receiving Galileans as such. Josephus tells us that Samaritans were not averse to ill-treating pilgrims going up to Jerusalem, even to the extent of murdering them on occasion (*Bellum* ii. 232; *Antiquities* xx. 118; this latter passage tells us that it was the custom of the Galileans to pass through Samaria at festival time).

54. This surly attitude was too much for James and John. These 'Sons of thunder' (Mk. 3:17) asked whether Jesus wanted them *to bid fire come down from heaven and consume them*. There is great faith in Jesus in this question. In the face of the insult to their Master they felt they had only to call for the fire in Jesus' name and it would be given. But this is more credit to their zeal and their devotion to Jesus than to their understanding of the nature of Christian service.

55, 56. Jesus *rebuked them*. That is not the way His followers behave. And without taking any steps in opposition to the Samaritans they went on to another village, perhaps a Jewish one. The words in RSV margin should probably not be read. They are found in the bulk of the late manuscripts and in a few early ones, mostly Western. But they are absent from the papyri and the great uncials. Most scholars regard them as a scribal insertion.

ii. Whole-heartedness (9:57–62). This paragraph is located simply 'along the road'. As Jesus journeyed Luke tells us that some announced their readiness to follow Him. They were clearly well-intentioned, but had not realized the nature of the demands the kingdom makes on men.

57, 58. The first man expresses his readiness to follow Jesus. There is nothing wrong with the way he puts it: he is ready to go anywhere Jesus leads. But the reply shows that he has not reckoned with what this means. Animals and birds have their places of habitation, *but the Son of man has nowhere to lay his head*. This is an incidental glimpse of the cost of the incarnation. And it shows that the follower of Jesus must not reckon on luxurious living.

59, 60. The second man was called by Jesus. In response he asked leave first to bury his father. Some hold that, had the father been a corpse at home, the man would probably not have been with Jesus at all; he would have been occupied with duties connected with the funeral. On this view his request was to stay at home until his father died. This might have meant an indefinite delay and the affairs of the kingdom cannot be put off. But the words have an even greater urgency if the father was dead. The Jews counted proper burial as most important. The duty of burial took precedence over the study of the Law, the Temple service, the killing of the Passover sacrifice, the observance of circumcision and the reading of the Megillah (*Megillah* 3b). But the demands of the kingdom were more urgent still. Jesus could not wait while the man got through all that burial meant. So He says, *Leave the dead to bury their own dead*. Jesus has called the man. He is to *proclaim the kingdom of God*. Let those without spiritual insight perform the kind of duties they so well can do. Burial is very much in keeping for the spiritually dead. But the man who has seen the vision must not deny or delay his heavenly calling.

61, 62. The third man, like the first, offered his services. But he interposed the condition that he *first say farewell* to those at home. This seems not unreasonable (*cf.* 5:29). But in this case it evidently concealed some reluctance to take the decisive step. Jesus points out that the kingdom has no room for those who look back when they are called to go forward.

b. The mission of the seventy (10:1-24)

Luke alone tells of the sending out of this large band of disciples. Some of the instructions are similar to those in Matthew's account of the sending out of the Twelve. This leads some scholars to the view that this passage is no more than a variant of Matthew's charge to the Twelve. This, however, in Plummer's phrase, 'will not bear criticism'. Luke's recording of this mission in such close proximity to that of the Twelve (which he has in 9:1-6) shows that he regarded them as distinct. Each is intelligible in its own place. And, as Manson points out, it is probable that Jesus utilized the services of others than the Twelve and equally probable that this would later be largely forgotten in view of the place given the Twelve in Christian recollection.

i. The mission and the message (10:1-12). Luke records Jesus' instructions to the larger group much more fully than those earlier to the Twelve.

1. One of the most difficult textual problems in the New Testament is that of the number of people Jesus sent out on this mission. Many good MSS read *seventy*, as RSV, but there are many also which read 'seventy-two' as mg. With the evidence at our disposal certainty is impossible (though I think 'seventy-two' is slightly more likely). The number appears to be symbolic of the nations of the world, a view the Jews based on Genesis 10, where there are seventy names in the Hebrew text and seventy-two in LXX. The gospel is for the whole world. Others, however, associate the number with that of the elders appointed by Moses (Nu. 11:16f., 24f.; seventy-two with the two who remained in the camp). They see Jesus as the second Moses. Others again think of the seventy members of the Sanhedrin, the religious leaders who should have been preparing for the coming of the Messiah. Whatever the truth behind these conjectures, Jesus sent the disciples ahead of Him in pairs. Such a large group of forerunners shows that He had a busy itinerary ahead of Him.

2. Jesus began His instructions with words He apparently used on more than one occasion in slightly different forms (*cf.* Mt. 9:37f.; Jn. 4:35). That *the harvest is plentiful* means that there is much work to do; that *the labourers are few* that they must not delay. It means also that they must look to *the Lord of the harvest to send out labourers into his harvest,* as well as for their own strength and guidance. Prayer for more workers for God is a duty resting on those who labour for Him.

3, 4. They go to no easy task. *Lambs in the midst of wolves* are in no enviable situation. The simile points both to danger and to helplessness. God's servants are always in some sense at the mercy of the world, and in their own strength they cannot cope with the situation in which they find themselves. They must look to God. So Jesus tells them to take no equipment (*cf.* 9:3). The *purse* (*ballantion*) is a money-bag. The word is used only by Luke in the New Testament. The *bag* (*pēra*) is a traveller's bag (see on 9:3). That they are to carry *no sandals* probably means, not that they are to go barefoot, but that they are not to take a spare pair. They are to go as they are. *Salute no one on the road* is not an exhortation to impoliteness: it is a reminder that their business is urgent and that they are not to delay it by dallying with wayside acquaintances. Eastern salutations can be elaborate and time-consuming.

5, 6. When they *enter* a house will refer to taking up lodgings when they come to a town or village. They are to give the greeting of peace. If the householder is *a son of peace* (a man characterized by peace, according to a Semitic idiom; we would say 'a man of peace'), their peace will *rest upon him*. A state of harmony will exist. But if he is not, *it shall return to you*. This is figurative language which assures the disciples that they will not be trying to convey a blessing to someone who does not wish to receive it. God's good gifts are not given by magic.

7. The Twelve were told to remain in the one house in any one town (9:4) and this applies to the seventy also. They are to have no compunction about receiving their meals free, for *the labourer deserves his wages* (*cf.* 1 Tim. 5:18). This is a principle of wide application that has sometimes been overlooked in Christian activities. But if the labourer is worth his wages he is not worth more. The disciples are not to *go from house to house*. That would mean engaging in a social round and being entertained long after they have done their work. There is an urgency about their mission. They must press on.

8, 9. Jesus now gives the procedure to be followed when the preachers are welcomed. They are to accept hospitality, eating what is put in front of them. In the area beyond Jordan to which they were apparently going there were many Gentiles. Food might not always satisfy the rigorist for ceremonial purity. They were not to be sidetracked into fussiness about food. They were to heal and to preach, the content of their message being, *The kingdom of God has come near to you*. The message must be accepted and acted on by those who received it. But the kingdom is *near*. This is their day of opportunity.

10-12. Perhaps a town will not receive them. Then they are to *go into its streets* with their message. They are to tell the people two things. The first is that they wipe the dust off their feet against them (for this symbolical action see the note on 9:5). This tells the citizens in symbol that they have placed themselves outside the people of God. The second is that that does not alter the realities. Their rejection of it does not alter the fact that it was nothing less than *the kingdom of God* that had *come near*. In rejecting the preachers they were rejecting not simply a couple of poor itinerants, but the very kingdom of God, and that has serious consequences. The people have drawn down judgment on themselves. *That day* is not explained, but clearly it means the dreadful day of judgment (*cf.* 21:34; Mt. 7:22; 2 Thes. 1:10; 2 Tim. 1:12, 18; 4:8). Then it will be *more tolerable . . . for Sodom* than for the offenders. The destruction of Sodom (Gn. 19:13, 24f.) led to that city's becoming proverbial for the judgment by God of wicked men. The guilt of those who rejected the messengers of God's kingdom is emphasized by the allusion.

ii. The doom of the Galilean cities (10:13-16). Mention of those who might reject Jesus leads naturally to the mention of those who had already done so. These words may or may not have been spoken on the same occasion (Matthew has them in a different context, 11:20-24). But they suit the theme of judgment.

13, 14. *Woe* is not a call for vengeance, but an expression of deep regret, 'Alas' (*cf.* 6:24-26). The mention of the towns *Chorazin* (in the New Testament only here and in the Matthean parallel) and *Bethsaida* brings home the fact that we know little of Jesus' life. Nothing at all is known of His ministry in the former town and very little of that in the latter. But these words show that He had worked extensively in both places and done miracles there. Indeed the *mighty works* He did had been of such a character that they would have produced repentance in *Tyre and Sidon*. Those cities, situated on the coast to the north

of Galilee, had formed the heart of the Phoenician empire.
They were great commercial centres, but had sinned grievously and had been the object of God's appeal through the prophets and of His judgment when they would not respond (*cf.*
Is. 23; Ezk. 26–28). Yet these cities would be better off *in the
judgment* than Chorazin and Bethsaida. So serious is it to
reject the Son of God.

15. *Capernaum* was the city where much of Jesus' ministry had
been exercised. So much was He there that it could be called
His own city (Mt. 9:1). It had seen miracles and heard teaching. But it had remained largely unmoved. Evidently the
citizens of Capernaum thought well of themselves and spoke
in terms of being *exalted to heaven.* But this was not to be the
fate of their city. It would be *brought down to Hades* (*cf.* Is. 14:13,
15). Clearly *heaven* and *Hades* are here used for the height of
glory and the depth of degradation. 'Jesus predicts the future
humbling or death of the city . . . Today the deserted site of
Capernaum bears its eloquent, silent testimony to his prophecy' (Ellis).

16. Jesus on a number of occasions spoke words like this
little saying (Mt. 10:40; Jn. 13:20). Luke evidently puts it here
because of its general appropriateness and not to indicate that
it was necessarily spoken at this time. It emphasizes the
importance of the messengers Jesus sent out. When He
authorizes a man to speak, that man speaks with authority.
He who hears him hears Jesus and he who rejects him rejects
his Lord. This puts a great responsibility on all who hear the
message. But it does not stop there. The man who rejects Jesus
rejects also, and in that act, *him who sent* Him. Jesus' messengers
then go forth with the fullest accreditation. Their message is
to be taken with full seriousness.

iii. The return of the seventy (10:17–20). In due course
the preachers returned. Luke does not tell us how long they
were away or where they reported back, but in due course
they linked up with Jesus again.

17. The MSS are divided over *seventy* and 'seventy-two' in
much the same way as in verse 1 (where see note). The group
returned *with joy.* Their experience had evidently not included

too many rejections and they were happy as they reported in. The one thing they mention in particular is that the demons were subject to them in the name of Jesus. Presumably this means that they cast demons out of sufferers, and they felt that they were sharing in Jesus' triumph over the evil ones. As this is not mentioned in their commissioning, they may not have been expecting it and it came as a joyful extra.

18. It is not easy to see the meaning of the words, *I saw Satan fall like lightning from heaven. Heaven* will stand here for the height of power (so Plummer; *cf.* Is. 14:12). It may be that in the mission of the seventy Jesus saw the defeat of Satan, a defeat as sudden and unexpected (to the forces of evil) as a flash of lightning. To the casual observer all that had happened was that a few mendicant preachers had spoken in a few small towns and healed a few sick folk. But in that gospel triumph Satan had suffered a notable defeat. Another view takes the words to refer to Satan's fall which Jesus saw in pre-incarnation times. On this view the disciples are being warned not to be proud as a result of their successful mission: they should remember that even Satan fell. But the former view is to be preferred.

19, 20. To the seventy Jesus has given *authority* (the word points to the right to exercise power rather than simply to power) *to tread upon serpents and scorpions* (*cf.* Ps. 91:13; Mk. 16:18). They were immune from harm from such sources while they were doing the work to which they were sent. It is not certain whether the words are to be taken literally or figuratively. It is probably the latter, for there is no record of a Christian preacher treading on literal snakes or scorpions without taking harm (though once Paul escaped when a viper fastened on his arm, Acts 28:3–5). More, they had authority *over all the power of the enemy.* Satan himself could not prevail against them. Their security is emphasized with *nothing shall hurt you.* All this makes a dazzling picture for such humble people. But Jesus goes on to teach that they must get their priorities straight. Their real ground for rejoicing is not their victory over *the spirits.* The men from whom they had expelled demons would in due course pass away, as would even this earth, the scene of their triumph. Much more important is it that their names *are written in heaven* (*cf.* Ex. 32:32; Dn. 12:1;

Heb. 12:23; Rev. 3:5, *etc.*). Jesus turns their attention to permanent realities.

iv. Jesus' joy (10:21-24). Caird speaks of this as 'an inspired and exultant utterance by Jesus, which contains a succinct summary of most of his teaching'. The section is so much like much in John that it has been called 'a Johannine thunderbolt from the Synoptic blue'. It is a reminder that the style in John is not as alien from that of the Synoptists as some have maintained.

21. *Rejoiced* is far too colourless a translation for *ēgalliasato*, which means a positive exultation ('thrilled with joy', Moffatt). Typically Luke says that this was *in the Holy Spirit*. The prayer is one of thanksgiving. God is addressed both in His compassion (*Father*) and His greatness (*Lord of heaven and earth*). Jesus goes on to thank God for His revelation. What it is that is revealed He does not say, but we would naturally refer *these things* to what the seventy have just learnt. The revelation has been made on grounds other than human wisdom and it is for this that Jesus gives thanks. The *wise and understanding* often feel themselves so superior that they cannot receive the revelation. But God has spoken to the lowly, those who are no more than *babes*.

22. *All things have been delivered to me by my Father,* Jesus goes on (*cf.* Jn. 3:35; 13:3). He has the supreme place, lacking nothing. But this is not at all obvious. No-one knows *who the Son is except the Father*. There are depths in the being of our Lord that His followers cannot plumb. Jesus calls Himself *the Son* in the Synoptic Gospels only here (together with the Matthean parallel) and in Mark 13:32, though the expression is common in John. It goes with this that no-one knows *who the Father is except the Son*. But there is an important addition, *and any one to whom the Son chooses to reveal him*. It is through Jesus and only through Jesus that men come to know the Father as He is. 'The God and Father of the Lord Jesus' (2 Cor. 11:31) is an expression with a very full meaning. That God is as Jesus revealed Him is a most important truth.

23, 24. After His prayer Jesus had a word for the disciples. He spoke to them *privately*, which implies that the previous words were uttered in the hearing of more than the disciples. But these words are for them alone. Jesus tells them that they are really blessed in seeing what they see. *Many prophets and kings* desired to see and hear what they saw and heard, but without doing so. Jesus was the long-expected Messiah, the One who had been before the spiritually great in their expectation and longing. But it was given to the disciples to see the fulfilment of all this and it was not given to any previous generation.

c. The parable of the good Samaritan (10:25-37)

This parable is peculiar to Luke. There are parallels to the conversation with the lawyer that introduced it, especially the summary of the law in the command to love (Mt. 22:34-40; Mk. 12:28-31). But there are differences, notably in timing and in the fact that in the others the summary is given by Jesus, here by the lawyer. We should not think of dependence.

25. At some unspecified time *a lawyer stood up* (which presupposes that people were seated; evidently Jesus had been teaching). A *lawyer* would be concerned not with secular studies, but with the Law in the Jewish sense, the first five books of the Old Testament. Arising from that he would have studied the rest of Scripture and matters incidental. He was thus a man who might be expected to be both interested in and knowledgeable about religious affairs. He *put* Jesus *to the test*. That is to say he asked his question, not in the search for information, but to see what kind of answer Jesus would produce. He may even have been hoping that Jesus would do badly and that he would have the opportunity of showing Him up. His question, *what shall I do . . . ?* shows that he was thinking of some form of salvation by works and had no understanding of divine grace. *Eternal life* means life that is proper to the age to come. It denotes life that will never end, but, in the Christian understanding of it, the more important thing is that it is life of a particular quality, that life that is the gift of God.

26, 27. The questioner was a lawyer and it was highly appropriate that Jesus simply referred him to the Law. He answered with a combination of passages which Jesus Himself also used to sum up the Law's requirements (Dt. 6:5; Lv.

19:18; *cf.* Mk. 12:30f.). Both the Hebrew and LXX (and also
Mt. 22:37) have three faculties with which men should love
God, while both here and in Mark there are four. But the
difference does not seem important. Both ways of putting it
mean that a man should love God with all he is. The whole of
his nature is included. The lawyer clearly had a deep insight
into the Scriptures when he could sum up the Law in this way.
The *neighbour* (*ho plēsion*) means more than the man who lives
nearby (which is *ho perioikos*, used, for example, in 1:58). There
is the thought of community, of fellowship.

28. Jesus commended the answer and went on, *do this, and
you will live.* Some see in this a formal commendation of the way
of works. If you want a way of salvation by doing, this is it
(with the implication that you won't be able to do it). It is
perhaps more likely that it is a repudiation of works. It is not
what we do, considered as a meritorious work, that matters,
but our attitude. If we really love God in the way of which
Jesus speaks, then we rely on Him, not ourselves. This kind of
love is our response to God's love for us, not the cause of His
acceptance of us (*cf.* 6:47–49). Jesus is not commending a new
system of legalism somewhat different from the old, but pointing to the end of all legalism. The lawyer wanted a rule or a
set of rules that he could keep and so merit eternal life. Jesus
is telling him that eternal life is not a matter of keeping rules
at all. To live in love is to live the life of the kingdom of God.
Arndt points out that the saying 'recognizes the importance
of the realm of the soul and spirit; if that area is sound, the
whole person is well'. Our attitude to God determines the rest.
If we really love Him we love our neighbour too (1 Jn. 4:20).

29. But the lawyer would not let it rest there. He wanted *to
justify himself.* His basic attitude was still wrong: he had not
understood the implication of his own words. So he went on to
ask, *And who is my neighbour?* He saw that it meant more than
the man next door. But how much more? There were different ideas among the Jews on this point, but they all seem to
be confined to the nation Israel; the idea of love towards mankind had not reached them.[1] As we approach the parable we
must bear in mind that it is told to the lawyer in answer to the

[1]See SB, i, pp. 353ff.

question, 'Who is my neighbour?' not, 'What must I do to be saved?'

30. Jesus did not answer the question directly but told a story. The traveller in the story is clearly a Jew, but no stress is put on this. He is called simply *a man*. It is the need of our neighbour and not his nationality that is important. The road *from Jerusalem to Jericho* runs down a steep descent through desolate country. The distance is about seventeen miles and the road descends more than 3,000 feet. It is the kind of wild country in which robbers might well be safe. Jesus does not say that the *robbers* of his story robbed the man: that would be understood. He concentrates on their violent ill-treatment of the traveller. They left him *half dead*.

31. It happened that *a priest* came by while he was still lying there. Since the man was 'half dead' the priest would probably not have been able to be certain whether he was dead or not without touching him. But if he touched him and the man was in fact dead, then he would have incurred the ceremonial defilement that the Law forbade (Lv. 21:1ff.). He could be sure of retaining his ceremonial purity only by leaving the man alone. He could be sure he was not omitting to help a man in need only by going to him. In this conflict it was ceremonial purity that won the day. Not only did he not help, he went to the other side of the road. He deliberately avoided any possibility of contact. Other factors may have weighed with him, such as the possibility that the robbers might return, the nature of his business, and so on. We do not know. We do know that the priest left the man where he was in his suffering and his need.

32. Much the same happened when *a Levite* came by. He also was a religious personage and might be expected to be interested in helping a man in need. But he also was a man interested in matters of ceremonial purity. He also thought it better not to get involved. And he also *passed by on the other side*.

33, 34. The audience would have expected a priest and a Levite to be followed by an Israelite layman. They would almost certainly now be expecting a story with an anti-clerical twist. Jesus' introduction of the Samaritan was thus devastating. In view of the traditional bitterness between Jew and Samaritan, *a Samaritan* was the last person who might have been expected to help. But this man *had compassion* on the sufferer. He attended to him as best he could on the spot. *Wine* would have been used for cleansing the wounds (the alcohol in it would have had an antiseptic effect though, of course, the man could not know that; he knew only that it helped). *Oil, i.e.* olive oil, would have eased the pain. The two appear to have been widely used by both Jews and Greeks. The wounded man was too weak to walk, so the Samaritan *set him on his own beast* (which must have meant that he himself walked), and so *brought him to an inn*. There he *took care of him*. What this meant is not spelt out, but the Samaritan did not regard his duty as done when he had brought the man to shelter. He continued to look after him.

35. He continued his kindness even when he had to leave. He gave the innkeeper *two denarii* on account, and instructed him to look after the man. According to the historian Polybius,[1] a man could secure accommodation in inns in Italy in his time (*c.* 150 BC) for half an *as* a day, *i.e.*, 1/32 of a denarius. If rates in Palestine at this period were comparable, the Samaritan was paying for about two months' board. However, J. Jeremias brings forward evidence to show that a day's rations cost a twelfth of a denarius at this time.[2] If this be accepted the period for which the Samaritan was paying is correspondingly reduced. But it was still a worth-while period. Nor was that all, for whatever more the innkeeper might have to spend the Samaritan undertook to refund on his way back. It is a most attractive picture of a man who did more than the minimum. He saw a man in need and did all he could.

36, 37. Jesus did not answer the lawyer's question but asked him, *Which of these three . . . proved neighbour to the man who fell among the robbers?* The answer, of course, is not in doubt. Jesus drove home the lesson with the command, *Go and do likewise.* The man had asked, 'Who is my neighbour?' Jesus faced him with the question, 'To whom am I neighbour?' He was an expert in the Law. Now he must think whether the priest and

---

[1]Polybius, ii. 15.6.
[2]J. Jeremias, *Jerusalem in the Time of Jesus* (London, 1969), p. 122.

the Levite, who scrupulously retained the moral purity required by the Law, really kept the Law, which likewise en-
joined love of the neighbour.

Throughout the centuries some have delighted to see in the
good Samaritan a picture of Jesus. Undoubtedly a moving
devotional study can be made centring on Jesus as the good
Samaritan of men's souls. It is even possible that Luke himself
thought of Jesus in this way. But it is another thing altogether
to see this as the meaning Jesus intended. That seems impossible to maintain.

d. Martha and Mary (10:38-42)

This story is found nowhere else. Luke appears not to have
placed it in chronological sequence, for Bethany was near
Jerusalem and at a later time Jesus was still far from the
capital (17:11). He may have placed it immediately after the
preceding parable as a safeguard against any of his readers
coming under the misapprehension that salvation is by works.
He makes the point that waiting quietly on the Lord is more
important than bustling busy-ness.

38. Both time, *as they went on their way*, and place, *a village*,
are left vague. Elsewhere we find that Martha and Mary lived
at Bethany (Jn. 11:1), about two miles from Jerusalem. Here
the house is said to be Martha's and the impression we get is
that she was the elder of the sisters and the hostess.

39, 40. Mary (the name is 'Mariam', the Greek form of the
Hebrew 'Miriam') *sat at the Lord's feet and listened to his teaching*.
She was taking full advantage of her opportunity. Martha,
distracted with much serving, did not approve. We get the impression that she wanted to do something special for Jesus.
The result was unnecessarily elaborate provision and *much
serving*. Hard-working Martha was *distracted*. When she could
stand it no longer she asked Jesus to intervene. There is
reproach of Jesus in her *do you not care . . . ?* and of Mary in *my
sister has left me to serve alone*. Her solution is, *Tell her then to help
me.*

41, 42. Jesus' reply is tender. *Martha, Martha* perhaps shows
that Jesus tended at times to use doubled words (*cf.* 22:31;

Jn. 1:51, *etc.*). He contrasts Martha's 'fretting and fussing about so many things' (NEB) with the *one thing* that is really needful. Some good MSS read 'few things are needful, or only one'. Whichever reading we adopt, Jesus is saying that Martha is worried over too many things. Life has few real necessities and at need we can do without much on which we lavish time. The *one thing* is not defined, but clearly it finds expression in Mary's sitting at Jesus' feet, learning from Him. It is the attitude of dependence on Jesus that matters. Some commentators refer it to food: they think Jesus is saying that one dish is all that is needed, instead of Martha's elaborate meal. But the language does not support this, especially that referring to Mary's choice. She has chosen *the good portion, which shall not be taken away from her*. The right spiritual attitude is a possession we need never fear losing.

e. Prayer (11:1-13)

Luke has a deep interest in prayer (see Introduction, p. 46). Here he brings together the Lord's pattern prayer and some teaching about prayer.

i. The Lord's prayer (11:1-4).

The relationship of this to the fuller version of the prayer in Matthew 6:9-13 has been the subject of a good deal of discussion. Some think that Jesus taught the prayer more than once. They point out that this is inherently likely. In Matthew it is delivered during the course of a sermon early in the ministry. Here it is apparently much later and is Jesus' response to a request from a disciple, who may well not have been present on the earlier occasion. Variation would be natural if Jesus was interested in a pattern rather than a rigid insistence on one form of words. Others hold that Jesus gave the prayer once only (I wonder why; if Jesus meant it as a pattern it seems curious that He should not repeat it). They usually think the shorter Lucan version the more original, but hold that Matthew has in places retained more of the flavour of the Aramaic original. Recent scholars often see the prayer as primarily eschatological. They regard 'Thy kingdom come' as the central petition and the others as elaborating aspects of the coming kingdom. On this view the prayer asks God to hallow His Name by the final destruction of all His enemies, then looks for the bread of the Messianic banquet, for the forgiveness God will give on judgment day, and for deliverance from the final time of trial. This, however, seems an unnatural interpretation of the language used and it is better to take the prayer as one Christians should pray as they seek God's help in ordinary daily life. It is, of course, not impossible that Christians (who see themselves as living in the 'last days') should combine the everyday and the eschatological meanings. But I see no reason for holding the eschatological view to be sufficient of itself. A final point to notice is that, while it can be prayed privately, it is essentially a corporate prayer. All the pronouns are plural.

1. Impressed with something about the way Jesus prayed, *one of his disciples* asked for guidance of the kind John the Baptist had given. Religious leaders of the day often taught their followers how to pray (see SB). His request, *Lord, teach us to pray*, might mean that he wanted a form of words he could use, or a pattern on which to model prayers, or some general instruction in the subject.

2. Jesus replied by delivering a form of words. His opening, *When you pray, say*, shows that He intended the prayer to be used just as it stands. In Matthew it is introduced with, 'Pray then like this', which makes it a model on which we can base other prayers. Christians have found both approaches helpful. Jesus begins with the simple address, *Father*. This corresponds to the Aramaic *abba*, the address of a child to its parent. In prayer the Jews used the form *abinu*, 'Our Father' (found, for example, in the fourth and sixth of the 'Eighteen Benedictions'), normally adding 'in heaven' or the like. This tended to put men at a distance from the great God, whereas Jesus taught His followers to think of God as their Father (that they learnt the lesson is seen from Rom. 8:15; Gal. 4:6).

Hallowed means 'made holy', 'reverenced'. The *name* in antiquity stood for far more than it does with us. It summed up a person's whole character, all that was known or revealed about him. The prayer concerns more than the way people take the name of God upon their lips (though this is included). It refers to all that God is and has revealed of Himself and prays for a proper attitude in the face of this. It is not likely that the prayer is to be taken in the sense that God should sanctify His name (*cf.* Ezk. 36:23). Rather men should show reverence for God. It is a prayer that 'God shall be God, that man shall not whittle God down to a manageable size and shape' (Melinsky).

Thy kingdom come looks for the bringing in of the kingdom that was the constant subject of Jesus' teaching. There is a sense in which it is realized here and now, in the hearts and lives of men who subject themselves to God and accept His way for them. But in another sense it will not come until God's will is perfectly done throughout the world (*cf.* the addition in Matthew, 'Thy will be done, on earth as it is in heaven'). It is this for which we pray.

3. The next petition is for *bread*, *i.e.* the provision of our daily needs. The continuous present, 'keep giving', and the *each day* make it clear that we should look to God constantly, not ask for provision for a lengthy period and then proceed to forget Him. Christians live in a state of continual dependence on God. But the precise meaning of *epiousios*, *daily*, is not clear. It is a very rare word and most discussions centre on possible derivations, since there is practically no usage to appeal to (see AG,MM). The most favoured meanings are *daily* (RSV), 'for the morrow' (Moffatt), and 'the food we need' (TEV; *i.e.* 'the bread for existence'; *cf.* Pr. 30:8). The first mentioned fits the term and harmonizes best with the tenor of the prayer.

4. The prayer, *forgive us our sins*, is followed by the assertion that we forgive those who sin against us (*every one who is indebted to us* refers not to financial transactions but to sin, here regarded as a debt). This does not make a human action, the forgiveness of others, the ground of forgiveness. The New Testament is clear that forgiveness springs from the grace of God and not from any human merit. Rather the thought moves from the lesser to the greater: since even sinful men like us forgive, we can confidently approach a merciful God. Some take *lead us not into temptation* in the sense of NEB, 'do not bring us to the test'. But this is to be preferred only if we take the whole prayer as eschatological. The word *peirasmos* is the normal word for 'temptation' (though it can mean 'test') and *temptation* is surely correct here. This does not imply that God does sometimes cause man to be tempted and in fact James assures us that He never does (Jas. 1:13). Rather Jesus is encouraging an attitude, the attitude that flees from temptation (*cf.* 1 Cor.

6:18; 10:14; 1 Tim. 6:11; 2 Tim. 2:22). The Christian recognizes his weakness, recognizes also the ease with which he gives way to the temptations of the world, the flesh and the devil. So he prays to be delivered from them all.

ii. The parable of the friend at midnight (11:5-8). Jesus follows with a humorous parable which drives home the point that prayer must be persistent and that God is always ready to give.

5-7. The setting is a small village where there are no shops. A household would bake its bread each morning. Jesus pictures a man whose household has used its supply and on whom a journeying friend makes an unexpected call. It is *at midnight*, which probably means that the friend had travelled after dark to avoid the heat. The man must feed his friend, for hospitality was a sacred duty. So he goes to another friend for *three loaves, i.e.* three small loaves which would suffice for one man. But this second householder has shut his door and gone to bed with his children. Evidently he was a poor man living in a one-roomed house. The whole family would sleep on a raised platform at one end of such a room, possibly with the animals at floor level. A man in such a situation could not get up without disturbing the whole family. He raises no difficulty about giving the bread, but the bother of getting up is quite another matter. It is much easier to stay where he is.

8. But the man is persistent. He will not go away, nor will he let his friend go back to sleep. And where friendship cannot prevail, *his importunity* (lit. 'shamelessness') wins the day. The lesson is clear. We must not play at prayer, but must show persistence if we do not receive the answer immediately. It is not that God is unwilling and must be pressed into answering. The whole context makes it clear that He is eager to give. But if we do not want what we are asking for enough to be persistent, we do not want it very much. It is not such tepid prayer that is answered.

iii. Asking and giving (11:9-13). The parable leads naturally into the way God gives to those who seek.

9, 10. Jesus tells His followers to *ask*, to *seek* and to *knock*. He assures them that in each case there will be the appropriate response. All three verbs are continuous. Jesus is not speaking of single activities, but of those that persist. He is speaking of a similar attitude to that taught by the parable. The repetition in verse 10 underlines the certainty of the response. Men ought not to think of God as unwilling to give: He is always ready to give good gifts to His people. But it is important that they do their part by asking. Jesus does not say and does not mean that, if we pray, we shall always get exactly what we ask for. After all, 'No' is just as definite an answer as 'Yes'. He is saying that true prayer is neither unheard nor unheeded. It is always answered in the way God sees is best.

11, 12. This is driven home with a couple of illustrations from human conduct. Jesus asks what father will give harmful things, *a serpent* or *a scorpion*, when his child asks for something to eat.

13. It is unthinkable that men should give such evil gifts to their children. On the contrary they give good gifts, even though they *are evil*. Even when He is talking of the good that men do, Jesus is not unmindful of the fact that they are evil. 'Innate human sinfulness is for Jesus a basic presupposition' (Ellis). But if evil men do not harm their children but, on the contrary, do them good, *how much more* will God do good to His children? The good that God will do is not left in general terms: He will give *the Holy Spirit*. Luke is interested in the work of the Spirit and here he sees the gift of the Spirit as man's highest good. There seems no reason for understanding this in terms of the 'charismatic' gifts. The reference is rather to the Spirit's work in the Christian's life generally, as in Romans 8.

f. Jesus and the evil spirits (11:14–26)

i. The Beelzebul controversy (11:14–23). All three Synoptists depict the conflict between Jesus and the forces of evil in part by showing that He constantly expelled demons. That He exercised power over the evil spirits does not seem to have been doubted, even by His enemies. But they did try to discredit Him by saying that the source of His power was not God but the devil. Luke gives us this example of the criticism and the way Jesus met it.

14. The incident is not placed in the chronological sequence with any precision. Luke simply tells us that Jesus was healing a demoniac, a man who was dumb (Matthew says he was blind as well). After the exorcism *the dumb man spoke*. The emphasis is on the controversy that followed, so Luke tells the story of the miracle very briefly and adds no more than that *the people marvelled*.

15, 16. *But some of them* attributed the miracle to *Beelzebul, the prince of demons*. Matthew adds the information that these people were Pharisees, and Mark that they were scribes from Jerusalem. The name of the demon prince is given in some manuscripts as 'Beezebul' (apparently no more than an easier way of pronouncing the same name), and in the Vulgate as 'Beelzebub'. It seems fairly clear that the name was 'Beelzebul'. But why it was applied and what it means are difficult questions. The form 'Baalzebub' occurs as the name of the god of Ekron (2 Ki. 1:2, 3, 6, 16; this is in the Hebrew text, not LXX). This means 'lord of flies' and may well be a Hebrew pun on a similar sounding Philistine name (like the Ras Shamra name noted below). Some suggest that the Jews further corrupted this into the similar sounding 'Baalzebul', 'lord of dung', as a way of referring to the heathen god, and then transferred this name to a demon. But the form 'Baalzebul' also occurs in the Ras Shamra tablets as the name of a Canaanite deity, the term apparently meaning 'lord of the dwelling' or 'lord of the high place'. Our best understanding of the evidence seems to be that the Jews took this name of a heathen god and understood it in terms of the similar sounding Hebrew, 'lord of dung'. They applied it to a prominent demon, perhaps to Satan himself. Jesus clearly understood it as referring to Satan.

Other people took a somewhat different line. They tested Jesus by seeking *a sign from heaven*. This is not essentially different, for it means that they did not regard the exorcism they had just seen as a sign of the kingdom. Jesus deals with the Beelzebul accusation straight away and comes to the demand for a sign in verse 29.

17, 18. Apparently the comments were made privately, not to Jesus. But He knew what these people were thinking. So He pointed out that, if they were right, the forces of evil would be destroying themselves. He reasons from the universal rule, *Every kingdom divided against itself is laid waste.* Mark adds a similar comment about a house (*i.e.* household) and Matthew includes a city as well. Luke's *a divided household falls* seems to be an explanation of the preceding. When a kingdom is destroyed by disunity 'house after house falls down' (Moffatt). From the general Jesus moves to the particular with the question, *if Satan also is divided against himself, how will his kingdom stand?* The forces of evil are destructive of good, not of one another.

19. Jesus clinches His argument with an appeal to the practice of Jewish exorcists. If casting out demons means a league with the devil, then Jewish practitioners of the art are in the same case. The argument proves too much. *Your sons* is strongly emphatic. It may refer to the actual sons of the people to whom Jesus was talking, or the expression may mean 'your own people' (Rieu) or 'your followers' (TEV).

20. It is *by the finger of God* (*cf.* Ex. 8:19) that Jesus performs His exorcisms and He invites His enemies to contemplate the consequence. Incidentally, it is rather curious that Luke reads *finger of God* where Matthew has 'the Spirit of God', for Luke generally emphasizes the Spirit. Both ways of putting it emphasize that Jesus' power over the demons comes from God and no-one else. And if this is so, then *the kingdom of God has come upon you.* The presence of the kingdom is to be seen, not in good advice nor in pious practices, but in the power that expels the forces of evil.

21, 22. Jesus hammers this home with a little picture of Satan as the 'strong one' guarding his possessions, *i.e.* the man under his power. Satan is in control and at peace. But the strong one can be defeated. When *one stronger* overcomes him, as Jesus has just done in casting out the demon, the whole situation is altered. Satan's armour is taken away. His *spoil* (probably what he has taken from his captives) is divided. Both terms are pictorial and they stand for the complete inability of Satan to stand in the face of God. Evil has a strong grip on men. But that strong grip is broken decisively when the kingdom of God comes in. The kingdom is not beautiful words; it is the overthrow of evil.

23. There can be no neutrality about this. When a man sees what the kingdom means he must be either for it or against it. The man who does not side with Christ in the battle against evil is against Him. If he does not *gather* with Christ he *scatters* (the imagery is from gathering a flock together).

ii. The return of the evil spirit (11:24–26). Jesus adds a little story to show that He is not talking about some temporary moral reformation, but a complete and final defeat of evil by the power of good.

24. Here *the unclean spirit* has not been expelled from the man. It has simply left. Desert places were popularly regarded as the haunts of evil spirits and Jesus pictures this one as wandering through such waterless regions without finding *rest*. So it decides to go back to the place it came from. Though it has left the man, it still calls him *my house*.

25. When it comes back it finds the house *swept and put in order*. Without the evil spirit the man's life is better. He is able to order things properly. Jesus describes a moral tidying up.

26. But the wicked spirit now brings *seven other spirits more evil than himself* and they all come and live in the man. *Dwell* (*katoichei*) means 'settle down', 'live permanently'. Now inhabited by eight spirits the man is in worse case than at the beginning when he had but one. When a man gets rid of an evil spirit but puts nothing in its place, he is in grave moral danger. No man can live for long with his life a moral vacuum. The kingdom of God does not bring about such a vacuum in a man. It means such a victory over evil that evil is replaced with good and with God.

g. Jesus teaches the people (11:27 – 12:59)

At this point Luke has a considerable section of teaching, including some interesting controversial passages. There is little indication of time or place, though some of the sections are linked to one another.

i. True blessedness (11:27, 28). Typically it is Luke alone who tells us of this spontaneous exclamation from a woman in the crowd. The lady apparently thought how wonderful it would be to have a son like Jesus and she pronounced a blessing on her who had borne Him. Her words involve a recognition of His Messiahship and are in part a salutation of Jesus. He did not reject the woman, but proceeded to something more significant. The word *menoun*, translated *rather*, 'does not question the truth of the preceding statement, but emphasizes the greater relevance of what follows' (*THB*). It is not physical relationship to Jesus that is supremely important, but one's attitude to God's word. What matters is hearing and keeping the word of God. This points to patient, unspectacular religious practice. *The word of God* came to the men of that day through the teaching of Jesus as well as through the study of Scripture. They had a certain advantage over others, but Jesus is saying that wherever men have Scripture the path to blessing is open.

ii. The sign of Jonah (11:29–32). People had asked Jesus for a sign (16) as well as asserting that He exercised power over the demons with the help of Beelzebul. He dealt with the Beelzebul accusation first, but now He comes to the request for a sign.

29. Jesus' response to the demand for a sign was given as *the crowds were increasing*. Evidently it was a widespread demand and He regards it as characteristic of *this generation*. But in that it seeks a sign it is *an evil generation*. Men should trust God and not seek miracles. A *sign* is not defined, but clearly it means some miraculous divine activity. Such a sign will not be given. The only sign these men would have would be *the sign of Jonah*. In Mark's account Jesus says simply, 'no sign shall be given' (Mk. 8:12), which conveys essentially the same meaning. J. Jeremias remarks, 'Materially, there is no discrepancy between the absolute refusal to give a sign (Mk. 8:11) and the intimation of the sign of Jonah. Both statements make it clear that God will not give any sign that is abstracted from the person of Jesus and that does not give offence.'[1]

30. Jesus explains. Jonah had been *a sign to the men of Nineveh* and He Himself will be one *to this generation*. It seems best to understand this of the resurrection, as is made clear in

[1] *TDNT*, iii, p. 410.

the corresponding passage in Matthew. Jonah had been in the whale for three days (Jon. 1:17) before, so to speak, coming to life again. For the Ninevites the sign was the reappearance of a man who had apparently been dead for three days. For the men of Jesus' day the sign would be the reappearance of *the Son of man* on the third day after His death. Many recent scholars think that the sign here is not the same as in Matthew, but a simple appeal to the fact that Jonah preached the authentic word of God and the Ninevites recognized the fact and repented. Similarly Jesus proclaimed the word of God and men ought to repent. One difficulty in the way of accepting this commonly held view is that of seeing in what sense preaching can properly be called a *sign*. A second is that Jesus does not speak of Jonah's and His own words as signs, but of Jonah and Himself. The sign in each case is the person. A third is the use of the future tense. Jesus does not say that He is a sign, but that He *will be* a sign. This fits in with Matthew's account and also with the fact that John tells us that, when Jesus was asked for a sign on another occasion, He pointed forward to the resurrection (Jn. 2:19). Jesus then makes it clear that when He gives a sign it will be one of His own choosing, not one given at the demand of an unbelieving generation.

31. He hammers home the guilt of that generation by referring to the queen of Sheba. Though almost certainly a heathen, she had been prepared to make a long and difficult journey (Sheba was in southern Arabia, the modern Yemen) *to hear the wisdom of Solomon. At the judgment* (*i.e.* on judgment day) the men of Jesus' generation would stand condemned by such an example. They had no journey to make, for Jesus was in their very midst. In a day of male supremacy the use of the term *andrōn* for *men*, rather than the more general *anthrōpōn*, is probably important. She was but a woman, where they were men. But they did not respond. *Something greater* (the Greek neuter means more than 'someone greater') seems to stand for all that is involved in the coming of Jesus and the inauguration of the kingdom. This is an action of God mightier by far than anything He had done in Solomon.

32. The men of Nineveh will also condemn Jesus' contemporaries, for they repented at the preaching of the prophet.

And just as God's action in Christ was greater than Solomon, so was it *greater than Jonah*.

iii. The light that is in you (11:33-36). Jesus proceeds to some teaching on light. He starts with physical light and goes on to speak metaphorically of the light within a man.

33. The function of light is to shine. Nobody kindles a lamp and then places it where it cannot be seen. On the contrary, it is put where its light may be seen to the best advantage (*cf.* 8:16).

34. The eye is the organ that receives light and Jesus speaks of it as *the lamp of your body*. When the eye is reacting to light in the normal manner, the whole body gets the benefit. A man can perform almost any bodily function when he has good illumination. But if his eyes are impaired so that he cannot make use of the light, almost every function is impaired. The failure of the eyes affects for the worse everything the man does. There is a spiritual parallel. It is possible for the eye to be *sound*, where the Greek means 'single'. A man's eye may be single-mindedly fixed on the good: then the whole man is *full of light*. But when the eye is *not sound* (the Greek word can mean 'evil'), when the man's attention is focused on evil, then the whole man is corrupted. He is *full of darkness*.

35, 36. Since the whole life is concerned and may be given to right or to wrong, men must take care lest the light in them *be darkness*. That is the ultimate disaster. Then the good in the man is wholly corrupted. But Jesus finishes with the encouragement that a man may be *full of light, having no part dark*. He will then be *wholly bright*. The shining lamp is an example of this.

iv. True cleansing (11:37-41). Jesus' acceptance of a Pharisee's invitation to a meal at his home leads to teaching in which Jesus is sharply critical of certain aspects of Pharisaic practice.

37, 38. Luke mentions briefly the Pharisee's invitation to a meal and Jesus' acceptance (*aristaō* means 'to have lunch' rather than *to dine*). The reason for the invitation is not given.

But as it came after an address (*while he was speaking*, besides being improbable, overlooks the aorist; better is JB, 'He had just finished speaking'), it is a fair inference that the host was interested in Jesus' teaching. When Jesus came in, the Pharisee *was astonished* that He did not wash (the verb is *baptizō*) before the meal. This had nothing to do with hygiene, but was a rule made in the interests of ceremonial purity. Before eating anything, scrupulous Jews had water poured over their hands to remove the defilement contracted by their contact with a sinful world. The quantity of water and the manner of washing are prescribed in minute detail in the Mishnah (*Yadaim* 1:1ff.). The Pharisee clearly expected that Jesus, as a noted religious teacher, would conform to the accepted practice.

39-41. It is not recorded that the Pharisee said anything. But Jesus discerned his astonishment and made His comment. He stressed the importance of the inward where the multitude of the rules, so dear to the Pharisees, concerned themselves only with the outward. The result of this was that they could keep their rules and still be *full of extortion and wickedness*. They were concerned with what a man does, Jesus also with what he is. Forthrightly He castigates them as *fools*. He goes on to an instruction about almsgiving, the precise meaning of which is disputed. RSV's *give for alms those things which are within* is a fairly literal rendering. But what are the *things within*? Some understand it of the things within the *cup* and the *dish*. The expression then means that men should give food to the poor rather than feast luxuriously themselves. *Cf.* NEB, 'let what is in the cup be given in charity, and all is clean.' Others take the *cup* and *dish* as symbolizing possessions in general, as Knox, 'you should give alms out of the store you have, and at once all that is yours becomes clean.' Others see the saying as ironical, 'As regards the soul (the things within), give alms and everything is clean (so you think).' Moffatt has 'Better cleanse what is within'. This gives good sense, but it rests on a conjecture about the meaning of the underlying Aramaic. Such meanings cannot be dismissed as impossible. But it seems that Jesus is stressing the importance of the inward over against the outward, and it is better to take the words as referring to the importance of a right inward state when we give alms. We must give our hearts and not just make an outward gesture. 'The gift without the giver is bare' (Lowell, cited in Arndt).

When a man gives from his heart, *everything is clean*. No amount of pouring of water can make up for a wrong state in the inward man.

v. Woe to the Pharisees (11:42-44). Jesus proceeds to other Pharisaic practices in which the emphasis on the outward leads to error.

42. *Woe* is an expression of regret, not of vindictiveness, with a meaning like 'Alas' (see on 6:24-26). Jesus grieves over the Pharisees for their tithing practices. Tithing was commanded in the Law (Lv. 27:30; Dt. 14:22, *etc.*). It was meant to be a joyful offering of love, but this calculation of one tenth of all the stalks of garden herbs made a burdensome mockery of it. Actually this kind of detail was not required by the Law, while the Mishnah expressly lays it down that rue, at any rate, was exempt from the tithe (*Shebiith* 9:1). The Pharisees were going beyond what was required. There was nothing actually wrong in doing this and Jesus does not say that they should not have done it. But when men concentrate on the trivial they are apt to overlook the important. The condemnation of the Pharisees lay, not in the fact that they tithed herbs, but that in their zeal for trifles they neglected *justice and the love of God*.

43, 44. A further result of Pharisaic preoccupation with the outward was the love these men showed for being in the public eye. They liked to get *the best seat in the synagogues, i.e.* a seat at the front, facing the congregation. Anyone sitting there was prominently in view and was seen to be a man of distinction. *Salutations in the market places* were plainly elaborate greetings in public places which marked the recipients as men to whom deference should be shown. All this hindered rather than helped ordinary men. Jesus regretfully goes on to liken the Pharisees to *graves which are not seen*. To come into contact with a grave was to incur ceremonial defilement. A problem was posed by the fact that men were sometimes buried in unmarked graves. The unwary traveller could easily walk over such a grave and all unwittingly contract ceremonial defilement. There is irony in the comparison of the religious Pharisees, who thought so well of themselves, to these unsuspected sources of defilement. Men who walked over unmarked graves became ceremonially unclean. And men who walked in the teaching and ways of the Pharisees became morally unclean.

vi. Woe to the lawyers (11:45-54). The lawyers, as we have noticed before, were men who gave themselves over to the study of the Old Testament Law. They were religious men and many of them were Pharisees. There was a difference in that the lawyer as such was a member of a learned profession and the Pharisee of a religious party. There was a link in that the essential Pharisaic position was based on a close study of the Law.

45. It is not clear what made the lawyer think that Jesus' words were not meant to apply to him and his fellows. But the reference to tithing (which has a legal flavour) may have seemed a possible source of misunderstanding. Since in his view Jesus could not possibly have meant to include the lawyers in His denunciation, he gave Him the opportunity of excepting them. *You reproach us* is scarcely strong enough. The verb means 'insult'.

46. But Jesus had no intention of letting the lawyers off. He proceeded to single them out for special criticism. The first count is that they asked others to do difficult things and did not help them. The *burdens hard to bear* were the scribal interpretations of the Law and the traditions of the elders. These were taken with the utmost seriousness. The Mishnah lays it down that it is more important to observe the scribal interpretations than the Law itself (*Sanhedrin* 11:3). The reasoning is that if it was a serious matter to offend against the Law which was sometimes hard to understand, it was a much more serious matter to offend against the interpretation which, the scribes thought, made everything clear. The lawyers ought to have expounded God's Law in such a way that it helped and inspired men. Instead they made it a wearisome burden. The lawyers' failure to *touch the burdens with one of your fingers* may mean that they did not move a finger to help other people, or that their interpretations enabled them to escape themselves. They did not need even to use one finger. Perhaps we can see something of the situation by considering an example. On the sabbath, they taught, a man may not carry a burden 'in his right hand or in his left hand, in his bosom or on his shoulder'.

But he may carry it 'on the back of his hand, or with his foot or with his mouth or with his elbow, or in his ear or in his hair or in his wallet (carried) mouth downwards, or between his wallet and his shirt, or in the hem of his shirt, or in his shoe or in his sandal' (*Shabbath* 10:3). Multiply this by all the regulations of the Law and ordinary people have a burden beyond bearing even to know what they might do and might not do. But there is also a multitude of loopholes for a lawyer who knew the traditions which enabled him to do pretty well what he wished.

47, 48. A second count was the treatment the lawyers accorded the prophets. They held that they were honouring those heroes of the faith by building splendid tombs for them. But really they were doing no more than complete the work of those who killed them. The same spirit actuated both. Their action gave an unconscious assent to the murders. It is always easier to honour dead saints than living ones. The lives of the builders of the prophets' tombs showed all too clearly that they were at one with the murderers.

49-51. It is not clear what book Jesus is quoting, if any, for the words of *the Wisdom of God*. The saying is not found in the Old Testament, but some hold that Jesus is quoting a non-canonical book. It is, of course, impossible to disprove this. But we should bear in mind that in no other place does Jesus quote from such a book and no book is known which has these words. Moreover the reference to *apostles* is more likely to come from Jesus than from a non-canonical book. Perhaps He is not quoting, but saying in effect, 'This is in accordance with God's wisdom' (*cf.* 7:35). It was in the purpose of God to send *prophets and apostles*. Thus was God's will and God's word made known to men. But, though God knew that men would reject His messengers, that rejection is not blameless. The men of *this generation* are castigated because they rejected the essential position of the prophets and aligned themselves with all those who had persecuted and killed them. Thus *the blood of all the prophets* would be *required* of them. *Abel*, of course, was the first martyr (Gn. 4:8; it is not clear why he should be called a prophet). *Zechariah*'s death was the last death of a prophet mentioned in the Old Testament, taking the books in their normal Hebrew order (2 Ch. 24:21f.). Jesus is saying that the blood of all those slain for their faithfulness to God will be required. It is laid at the door of *this generation*, because the men of the day fully share in the attitude that brought about the deaths of the prophets.

52. The final *Woe* reveals another paradox. The lawyers professed to expound the meaning of the law and thus to be the teachers of the people. But in fact they have *taken away the key of knowledge*, *i.e.* the key that unlocks the meaning of Scripture and brings men to the knowledge of God. Their methods were such that people could not get at the essential meaning of God's word. Instead of opening up the treasures of knowledge, the lawyers closed them fast. They turned the Bible into a book of obscurities, a bundle of riddles. Only the experts could understand it. And the experts themselves were so pleased and preoccupied with the mysteries they had manu-factured that they missed the wonderful thing that God was saying. They neither entered themselves nor allowed others to enter. There were ordinary people on their way to the know-ledge of God until their teachers turned them away.

53, 54. Jesus' opponents were incensed. The *scribes* (another name for the lawyers) *and the Pharisees* tried to trap Jesus. That they *began to press him hard* shows their intensity and their vehemence. Their method was to try to provoke Him into some indiscreet saying which could be used against Him. The word rendered *catch at* is *thēreusai*, which is used of hunting wild beasts. It is a vivid word for intense opposition.

vii. The leaven of the Pharisees (12:1–3). The saying about the leaven is in all three Synoptic Gospels, but that about revealing what is covered is lacking in Mark and is found in a different context in Matthew. This should not trouble us greatly. There is no reason for holding that the selection or arrangement of material must be the same in all three Gospels. And in any case there is every reason for think-ing that Jesus repeated His teaching on different occasions with slight variations.

1. Only Luke speaks of *so many thousands* as having gathered. The word *murias* means properly 'ten thousand' (in Acts 19:19 five 'myriads' amount to 50,000). But the term is often used indefinitely of a large crowd and that will be the meaning here. The article with it in the Greek may mean 'the usual large crowd'. Luke also is the only one to tell us that the people *trod upon one another*, the press was so great. Though there can be no doubt that Jesus wished the crowd to hear what He said, He addressed His teaching to the disciples *first*. Those who profess to follow Jesus cannot sit back comfortably and listen while Jesus makes demands on people outside their number. Disciples must see the Master's teaching as addressed to them in the first instance, whatever applications it may have to outsiders. Jesus *began* on this occasion with a warning against *the leaven of the Pharisees*. The metaphor would have been more obvious then than now, for people tended to make their own bread and everyone would be familiar with the way a little yeast slowly transforms a large lump of dough. Leaven speaks of a penetration that is slow, insidious and constant. In this case the leaven is *hypocrisy*. The practice of saying one thing and doing another eats at the moral life like a canker.

2, 3. Many things could be said about hypocrisy, but on this occasion Jesus chooses to point out that it is a short-sighted policy. In the end everything will become known. The art of being a hypocrite depends on the ability to keep some things concealed. When concealment is no longer possible the hypocrite is inevitably unmasked. At present the Pharisees may have certain things *covered up*, or *hidden*. But in the end, on judgment day, all will be known. Men may think they have said things safely in secret, but all will be brought into *the light*. They have *whispered in private rooms*. The latter are really 'store rooms', but, where walls could be easily dug through, store chambers tended to be inner rooms well away from exterior walls and thus the secondary meaning 'inner rooms' developed. But what has been whispered so secretly will be *proclaimed upon the housetops*. A housetop would give a public speaker a first-rate platform from which his voice could sound out; so Jesus is referring to the fullest publicity.

viii. Be ready for judgment (12:4–12). The teaching about the Pharisees and the judgment leads naturally into a more general section on judgment and the importance of being prepared for it.

4, 5. Jesus calls the disciples *friends* here only in the Synoptic Gospels (but *cf.* Jn. 15:14). First He warns them that they must get their values straight. There is a natural tendency to fear men who may *kill the body*. The end of this life seems to men the ultimate disaster and they commonly fear it. But Jesus points out that men who kill can do no more. Death is their ultimate achievement. Their power extends no further. We should not fear those whose powers are so limited. Rather we should fear God whose authority extends beyond death and who has *power to cast into hell*. The fear of God is rather out of fashion these days. We much prefer to stress the love of God. But, while there is a sense in which perfect love casts out fear (1 Jn. 4:18), there is another in which fear is quite compatible with love. This kind of fear is continually regarded in the Bible as a necessary ingredient in right living. It is an attitude compounded of a recognition of the greatness and the righteousness of God on the one hand and our readiness to sin on the other. Fear of this kind guards against presumption and must find its place in a right faith. *Hell* here is *Gehenna*, which is not to be confused with *Hades*, also translated 'hell' in the older versions. *Hades* is a general name for the place of departed spirits, whereas *Gehenna* carries the notions of punishment. The word derives from the Hebrew *gē Hinnōm*, 'the valley of Hinnom'. This was a valley adjacent to Jerusalem where in earlier days children had been offered in sacrifice to the god Molech (Lv. 18:21; 1 Ki. 11:7, *etc.*). Josiah ended all this (2 Ki. 23:10), but the valley was regarded as accursed (Je. 7:31ff.; 19:6). One ancient writer at least saw this as permanent: 'This accursed valley is for those who are accursed for ever' (1 Enoch xxvii. 2). In New Testament times the place was used as a rubbish tip and no doubt a fire was always burning there. The associations of the term made it a fitting symbol for the perpetual torment of hell. A few commentators have held that the one with power to cast into hell is Satan, but this should certainly be rejected. The evil one can operate only within the limitations God assigns him and there is no indication that God ever gave him this power. Moreover we are not to fear Satan but to resist him (Jas. 4:7; 1 Pet. 5:9). It is God who has power over the eternal issues and Jesus repeats, *yes, I tell you, fear him!*

6, 7. But His basic concern is to reassure His friends, not to frighten them. He goes on immediately to the care God has for His people. He illustrates from the little birds. *Five sparrows* were sold for *two pennies*. Matthew tells us that two sparrows went for a penny. Evidently one was thrown in for nothing when two pennyworth were bought. But *not one of them* (not even the free one!) *is forgotten before God*. God takes notice of the commonest and cheapest of birds. Much more, then, will He be concerned for men. Jesus brings out this point with the information that the hairs of our heads are all numbered. The importance of this does not lie in the actual count, but in the fact that God cares enough about His people to know the minutest detail about them. He knows things they do not know about themselves. So those who are *of more value than many sparrows* should face life without fear.

8, 9. Our attitude to Jesus is all important. If a man *acknowledges* Him before men, Jesus will acknowledge him before *the angels of God* (Matthew has 'before my Father who is in heaven'). This is warm encouragement for judgment day. But the man who *denies* ('disowns', NEB) Jesus will face the ultimate denial. He has refused to number himself among Jesus' followers. When he stands before God his choice will be ratified. Jesus leaves His hearers in no doubt but that eternal issues are involved in their attitude to Him. Moorman reminds us that there is more than one way of denying Jesus. These days, he thinks, we are unlikely to deny Him in the same way as Peter, for example, did. But we may deny 'the unique authority of his teaching, imagining that, on some points, we know better than he did, or that much of what he said can be explained away'. We may also deny His divinity and repudiate His claims. 'In either case it is the sin of pride and self-assurance, man's . . . ultimate denial of the supremacy of Christ and of God.'

10. This leads to the solemn thought that there is a sin so serious that it cannot be forgiven. Jesus introduces this with the statement that a word spoken against Himself can be forgiven. This does not mean that such a word is a trifle. The preceding verse has shown something of the dignity of the Son of man: He is not to be taken lightly. Yet even sin against this august personage may be forgiven. Men may blaspheme but then repent; the blasphemy is not their final word. But *he who blasphemes against the Holy Spirit* is in a much worse case. We must understand this, not of the uttering of any form of words, **but** of the set of the life. This blasphemy is so serious because it concerns the whole man, not a few words spoken on any one occasion. Matthew and Mark put these words in connection with the Beelzebul controversy and this helps us to get the meaning. Then Jesus' opponents attributed His works of mercy to the devil. They called good evil. Men in such a situation cannot repent and seek forgiveness: they lack a sense of sin; they reject God's competence to declare what is right. It is this continuing attitude that is the ultimate sin. God's power to forgive is not abated. But this kind of sinner no longer has the capacity to repent and believe.[1]

11, 12. But we should not think of the Holy Spirit primarily or only as One whom we must be careful not to blaspheme. He is our Helper. He is present with God's people, especially with God's persecuted people, to give them the assistance they need when they stand before the authorities. Jesus speaks first of being brought before *the synagogues*, which points to persecution by the Jews. The synagogue could be a court or a school as well as a place of worship. He speaks also of *the rulers and the authorities*, a comprehensive expression which might refer to Jews or Gentiles or both. Being accused in this way could be a terrifying experience. But Jesus tells His own not to be anxious at such a time about what they are to *answer* (the Greek term is often used in the technical sense of 'make a legal defence'). The reason? *The Holy Spirit will teach you in that very hour what you ought to say* (*cf.* 21:14f.). Notice that the Spirit's teaching will come at that moment. He will not instruct men some time beforehand. What you *ought* to say might well be rendered 'what you must say'. Jesus is concerned with the duty that rests compellingly on believers even in such a time of danger. He is not telling them how to secure acquittal. He is telling them how they may best serve God in their trying situation. The Spirit will inspire them with such a defence that through it the gospel will be proclaimed and God's purposes be set forward.

ix. The parable of the rich fool (12:13–21). An interruption from the crowd gives the opening for some teaching on the right use of material possessions.

---

[1]See further, Leon Morris, *Spirit of the Living God* (London, 1960), pp. 48ff.

13, 14. One of Jesus' hearers was having trouble with his brother about the proper division of an *inheritance*. Jewish laws of succession covered most cases (*cf.* Dt. 21:17), but there was sometimes room for doubt and in this case the man who spoke up felt that an injustice was being done. His brother was clearly in possession and he wanted Jesus to persuade him to disgorge. He does not ask Jesus to decide between the merits of two claims: he asks for a decision in his own favour. He seems to be acting unilaterally. Nothing indicates that the brother had agreed to have Jesus try the case. The man simply called on Jesus to intervene on his behalf. In this he is taking Jesus as a typical rabbi, for the rabbis customarily gave decisions on disputed points of law. Jesus, however, refused to have anything to do with it. His form of address, *Man*, is far from cordial (*cf.* Bengel, 'He addresses him as a stranger'). He came to bring men to God, not to bring property to men. In this situation He was concerned with the attitudes of the people involved, not with who got what.

15. Jesus issues a strong warning against *all covetousness*. He introduces it with *Take heed, and beware*, which surrounds the injunction with a solemn seriousness. Actually *beware* scarcely does justice to the force of *phulassesthe*, which is rather 'guard yourselves' (TEV): it is the taking of positive action to ward off a foe. Jesus follows with a statement of principle, *a man's life does not consist in the abundance of his possessions*. It is an important warning for men who live in an age of affluence.

16, 17. Characteristically Jesus hammered the point home with a parable. He pictures a wealthy farmer with a good harvest. His stores are full and he has nowhere to put this latest bumper crop.

18, 19. So what does he decide to do? Pull down his barns and build bigger ones. That will take care of the storage problem. With enough of everything laid by he can relax and enjoy his wealth. He looks forward to years of pleasure. Notice the repeated *my* which points to an ingrained selfishness. The man is not concerned to use his wealth wisely. He is not trying to help other people. He is not even concerned to have a richer and fuller life for himself. He is concerned only with self-indulgence.

20. *Fool!* says God. A man's life is an uncertain thing at best and no man has the assurance that he will live the years he would like. The really stupid thing was the rich man's easy assurance that the future was in his control. God said to him, *This night your soul is required of you.* The verb is literally, 'they require', a construction common among the rabbis to denote an action of God (SB), *i.e.* 'God requires your soul'. Man whose life hangs by a thread and who may be called upon at any time to give account of himself is a fool if he relies on material things.

21. Jesus rounds this off with a contrast between laying up treasure for oneself and being *rich toward God* (*i.e.* rich 'where God is concerned', Phillips). It is the latter that matters. Men are fools to settle for less.

x. Seek the kingdom (12:22-34). From the sins of greed and selfishness Jesus turns to that of worry, which in a way is connected with the other two. 'Greed can never *get* enough, worry is afraid it may not *have* enough' (Arndt). Wealth can represent a danger to those who do not have it as well as to those who do. Jesus emphasizes the importance of trust in God and detachment from things.

22, 23. The previous words were addressed to the crowd, these to Jesus' *disciples*. What Jesus now says arises from His previous words, as *Therefore I tell you* shows. But this is not teaching for the masses. It is to His own that Jesus says, *do not be anxious about your life*. The believer may take reasonable forethought for his needs, but he is not to worry about food or clothing. Life is bigger than such things (*cf.* 12:15).

24. Jesus reinforces this with an appeal to *the ravens* (or 'crows', Goodspeed, TEV), mentioned here only in the New Testament (they are the objects of God's care in Ps. 147:9). Birds do not engage in agricultural activities, but they do not lack for all that. God feeds them. There is possibly significance in the fact that the ravens were unclean (Lv. 11:15). God makes provision even for these unclean birds. And Jesus goes on to remind His hearers that they are of more value than birds (*cf.* verse 7).

25. In any case men are limited. It is not quite clear what the limitation is that Jesus singles out: the word *hēlikia* can refer either to age (Jn. 9:21) or to stature (19:3). A *cubit* is a measure of length (the distance from the tip of the fingers to the elbow). But measures of length were occasionally applied to time (*e.g.* 'handbreadths' in Ps. 39:5). So the expression might mean 'add a short period to his life' or 'add eighteen inches to his height'. Those who favour the former meaning hold that few men worry about increasing their height by eighteen inches, but many worry about lengthening their life. The rich fool could not add one moment to his span of life when God's summons came. They hold also that this fits better with the reference to a 'small' thing in the next verse. Though an increase in the span of life seems a large matter to us, it may well be the point that it is small to God. Those who see a reference to height point out that this fits better with the growth of plants in the context. Plants do not worry, but they make great increases in height. The more natural use of the terms seems to favour this second view.

26. The point is driven home. If men cannot do such a small thing, then why should they be anxious about other things? God who takes care of our growth will take care of all our needs.

27, 28. Jesus has appealed to the birds; now He turns to plant life. The *lilies* are probably not lilies in our sense of the term. AG suggest that the autumn crocus may be in mind, or the Turk's cap lily or the anemone or the gladiolus. Shewell-Cooper adds the iris and the Martigon lily.[1] In the Old Testament it is used of the colour of the lips (Ct. 5:13), which leads some to favour the scarlet anemone. But clearly there is great uncertainty and there is much to be said for the view that the term is not specific. Jesus then is referring in a general way to 'flowers'. These do not manufacture cloth as men do, but God clothes them with a beauty that even Solomon's gorgeous robes could not match. Yet the flowers, now spoken of as *grass* (which supports the view that no particular plant is in view), are very temporary. They live today and are burnt tomorrow. The argument is irresistible. If God does all this

[1] W. E. Shewell-Cooper, *Plants and Fruits of the Bible* (London, 1962), p. 7.

for the flowers that disappear so quickly, *how much more* will He clothe His people? *O men of little faith* shows that some of the disciples had shown anxiety. It is needless.

29, 30. Jesus commands (not advises) His followers not to worry. Worry is a great inhibitor of action: to live in worry is to miss what life is all about. The disciples are not to *seek* food and drink. This, of course, does not exclude legitimate effort, but it does prohibit concentration on these items. Phillips gets the meaning with 'You must not set your heart on what you eat or drink' (*cf.* the rich fool, 12:16–20). Similarly the disciples are not to be *of anxious mind*. Worry about food and clothing may befit *the nations of the world* (a common rabbinic designation of the Gentiles; see SB), but it is not proper to God's people. *Your Father knows that you need them*; and He who knows the need will supply it.

31. From the negative Jesus turns to the positive and instructs the disciples how to live. They are to *seek his kingdom*, which points to a concentration on all that the kingdom involves. Disciples have pledged themselves to their Master. They must accordingly spend their time in doing His work and seeking His kingdom. This will mean trying to produce in their own lives conduct appropriate to those who have accepted the rule of God. It will also mean trying to bring others into a like way of living, for it is in this way that the kingdom grows. Jesus adds the information that when His followers concentrate on the kingdom, *these things shall be yours as well*. When men truly honour God, God honours their faith. His servants may not grow wealthy as the world understands riches, but they will not lack.

32. *Little flock* is an unusual form of address, found only here in the New Testament. It speaks of the small number of true disciples, but also of the care they may expect from their Shepherd. Indeed Jesus goes straight on to speak of the Father's gifts to His people. These are not wrung from Him as though He were unwilling to give: it is His *good pleasure* to give. And His gift is *the kingdom*, that very kingdom they have just been told to seek.

33, 34. Jesus reverts to the comparison of earthly and heavenly riches. He counsels His followers to concentrate on the real riches, heavenly treasure. This can involve selling earthly *possessions* and giving the proceeds away. But we should not understand the words as though they meant that all Jesus' followers must sell all their possessions. To produce a class of holy paupers in this way would be to sin against love, for these paupers would become a charge on their neighbours. In any case it is relevant to recall that Jesus was entertained in Martha's house (10:38), and that He later commended Mary to the beloved disciple who took her into his home (Jn. 19:27). In neither case did Jesus rebuke His follower for owning possessions. Indeed, Jesus and the apostles themselves had money which they used to buy food and to give alms (Jn. 13:29). It seems clear that Jesus is not excluding private ownership; but He is emphasizing that believers must not be dominated by their possessions. Trust in riches prevents trust in God. When this takes place, possessions become a fatal barrier to life. Real riches are *a treasure . . . that does not fail*, found in *purses that do not grow old*. Such riches are secure from robbery and from moths (which eat away at some forms of earthly riches, *e.g.* costly robes). The *heart* and the *treasure* go together. A man's heart, the concentration of his energies and his interests, is always with his treasure, *i.e.* the things he values most.

xi. The coming of the Son of man (12:35–40). Jesus reinforces His teaching on the right use of wealth with the reminder that earthly things are temporary and the coming of the Son of man sure. We naturally interpret this of the second coming, but many scholars feel that this would have been incomprehensible to Jesus' hearers. They hold that Jesus is warning them to be ready for a crisis, which is probably to be seen in the events surrounding the crucifixion. It is hard to exclude such a meaning. And there is a permanent application in that Jesus' followers must always be ready to face the crises of life in the spirit of true discipleship. But it is impossible to hold that this exhausts the meaning. There will also be a fuller reference which looks forward to the second coming.

35, 36. Jesus calls on the disciples to be ready. *Your* is emphatic and there is an emphatic 'you' with 'you be . . .'. Whatever others do, you must be ready. The girding of the loins is a step towards preparedness. The long, flowing robes of the Easterner were picturesque, but apt to hinder serious labour, so when work was afoot they were tucked into a belt about the waist. Jesus goes on to picture servants whose master has gone to a marriage feast and who expect him back at any moment. They will not be found unready, but will open the door as soon as he knocks and show themselves prepared for whatever service he wants.

37. The *master* who finds his servants in such a state of readiness is pleased. This one is so pleased that he reverses the normal roles and has them sit at table while he serves them a meal. This unexpected twist cannot be taken from life, but is something extra provided for God's people (*cf.* 22:27). But then the reward of God's people is never commonplace: it is always the unexpected.

38-40. The importance of being ready, whenever the Son of man comes, is now stressed. Jesus pronounces a blessing on the servants who are ready when the master comes *in the second watch, or in the third*. The Romans divided the night into four watches, but the Jews into three (*cf.* Jdg. 7:19). Thus Jesus is speaking of servants who watch throughout the night for the coming of their lord. They do not know the time of the master's return, but they know that it may well be long delayed. A change of imagery reminds us that no householder would suffer loss if he knew when the burglar was coming. The house in mind is one of mud brick which could be 'dug through' (*broken into*). The householder must be ready: that is the only way he can be secure from such robbery. Jesus rounds off this section with the explicit statement that the disciples do not know when the Son of man is coming. That coming is certain, but the time is not known to the sons of men. It will be *at an unexpected hour*. They must therefore live in constant readiness, as the whole of the foregoing section has made clear.

xii. The responsibility of servants (12:41-48). Peter's question may be meant to raise the question of the privileges and responsibilities of the apostolate. It certainly has relevance to the work of the ministry, a topic that would have been important to Luke's readers. Jesus does not answer directly, but draws attention to the responsibility of all servants. He stresses that the greater the privilege the greater the responsibility.

41–44. Only Luke tells us that it was Peter who asked, but the question is quite in character. As He often did, Jesus countered with another question to make His questioner think. The *steward* was a slave (he is called *doulos* in verse 43), to whom was given the task of managing the whole estate. This freed the owner from routine administration and it meant that the steward necessarily had considerable freedom of action. If he was *faithful and wise* he would see that the estate was properly run, which included making sure that all members of the household were duly fed. Jesus speaks of a situation wherein the *master* is absent but returns unexpectedly (43). A diligent steward, whom his master found working efficiently when he thus returned suddenly, would be promoted (44).

45, 46. But the master's prolonged absence might lead a careless steward into a false sense of independence. There was nothing to stop him from indulging his whims. After all, he was in charge. When a steward abused the trust reposed in him the master's return would surprise him. The result would be the punishment and downgrading of the unreliable manager. *Punish* is a picturesque word (see mg.) and points to a severe penalty. That Jesus is thinking primarily of His followers and not of the setting of the little story is seen in the putting of the offender *with the unfaithful*. This would not worry a self-indulgent steward very much (unless we take it in the sense 'servants being punished for their unfaithfulness'), but it would matter to a Christian.

47, 48. Jesus rounds off this section with a warning of the certainty of punishment for those who fail to do their duty. Responsibility rests on those who have received much (*cf.* Am. 3:2). Notice that men are punished not simply for doing wrong, but for failing to do right (*cf.* Jas. 4:17). It is important that Jesus' servants be active in doing His will. We are apt to be disturbed by the thought that a man who sinned in ignorance will be punished (48). Here we must bear in mind that 'there is no such thing as absolute moral ignorance (Rom. i. 20, ii. 14, 15)' (Farrar), and again, 'Our very ignorance is part of our sin' (Ryle). The emphasis is, of course, on the fact that the beating is *light*. But we should not minimize the importance of doing God's will. God's servant must make every effort to find out what God's will is and do it. We are all accountable.

xiii. Fire on the earth (12:49–53). There is a sense in which Jesus came to bring peace. But some things are more important than peace, and sometimes His message and the way it is received means division. Jesus spells this out.

49, 50. The meaning of this passage is far from obvious. Some have taken *fire* to mean division, others holiness or faith. But the term more often stands for judgment and that is probably the sense of it here. Jesus' coming means judgment, for example on unbelief. He looks forward to its being *kindled*, *i.e.* at the cross, the focus of all His activities. Some, it is true, take the words in the sense, 'And what do I want, if it is already kindled?' (Rieu). But this seems a less likely understanding of the Greek, and of the parallelism with the following. Jesus is saying that God's plan for men is salvation that involves judgment. But it is a judgment that the Messiah will bear for others, not one He will inflict on others. It is not an attractive prospect, but Jesus longs for it to come, for only so can the saving work be accomplished. He goes on to the thought of the cross as a *baptism*, a figure He uses elsewhere (Mk. 10:38f.). It fits in with the frequent link of 'baptism' and 'baptize' with death.[1] We catch a glimpse of the cost of the cross to Jesus in His comment, 'what constraint I am under until the ordeal is over!' (NEB). The shadow of the cross hung over Him. He knew it was inevitable: it was the very purpose of His coming. But though He accepted its inevitability nothing could make it attractive.

51–53. To the question whether we think Jesus came to bring peace most of us would unhesitatingly reply 'Yes'. But Jesus' *No* is emphatic (*ouchi*). There is, of course, a sense in which He does bring peace, that deep peace with God which leads to real peace with men. But in another sense His message is divisive. The cross challenges men. Jesus calls on His followers to take up their own cross as they follow Him (9:23ff.;

[1]See J. Ysebaert, *Greek Baptismal Terminology* (Nijmegen, 1962), ch. III.

14:27). When men do not rise to this challenge they not uncommonly become critical of those who do. The divisions that thus arise may run through families (*cf.* Mi. 7:6). Incidentally, the *five* of verse 52 has not grown to six in the next verse, for the *mother* and the *mother-in-law* are identical. The family is father, mother, son, son's wife (who would come and live with them), and daughter.

xiv. The signs of the times (12:54–59). It is not clear whether these words were spoken on the same occasion as the preceding. There is no obvious connection, and Matthew gives a similar saying in response to a request for a sign. Probably Luke is reporting a saying without indicating its context.

54, 55. Jesus comments on the ability of His fellow-countrymen to forecast the weather. They had learnt how to interpret the clouds and the winds and their forecasts were accurate.

56. But they were *hypocrites*. They concentrated on the superficial. They gave attention (*dokimazein*) to the weather that they found interesting, but ignored what was important. 'They were unable to see the true character of the times because they did not want to see it' (Arndt). Weatherwise they were, but they could not discern the storm clouds that were even then rising and were to burst into the cataclysm of AD 66-70. They understood the winds of earth, but not the winds of God; they could discern the sky, but not the heavens. Their religious externalism prevented them from seeing the significance of the coming of Jesus.

57-59. Jesus encourages His followers to make their peace with God. In earthly matters men get the best settlement they can out of court instead of insisting on seeing through a hopeless case. Or, in a land like Judea where there were two jurisdictions, the Roman and the Jewish, a man who was likely to be in trouble in one jurisdiction might appeal to the other successfully. But sinners should not be lulled into a sense of false security, thinking that, though their case against God is hopeless, they have a good one in earth's jurisdictions. If they rely on this they will finally lose everything before the one tribunal that matters, that of God, for ultimately they cannot avoid His jurisdiction. They should spare no effort accordingly to get right with God. When He finally condemns a man the penalty will be inflicted to the uttermost.

h. Repentance (13:1-9)

i. Men who perished (13:1-5). Luke does not tell us why certain people informed Jesus of the slaughter of the Galileans. But they may have been Judeans who cited it more or less approvingly as an example of the kind of judgment of which Jesus has just been speaking. Jesus does not go along with this, but uses the occasion to drive home the urgent need for repentance.

1. This incident is not known to us from any other source, but it fits in with what we know of Pilate's character. Some men from Galilee had evidently gone up to Jerusalem to worship and had been put to death by the governor as they were in the act of offering sacrifice. That their blood had mingled with that of their sacrifices was a particularly horrible detail. It is difficult to see what could justify an execution at such a moment.

2, 3. It was commonly held that disaster was a punishment for sin (*cf.* Jn. 9:2). So Jesus immediately makes the point that these Galileans had not been singled out for a horrible death because they were worse sinners than others. He calls on His hearers to repent, otherwise they will *all likewise perish*. Plainly He does not see any need to argue that they are *all* sinners and need repentance. As elsewhere, He takes universal sinfulness as basic. His *likewise* can scarcely mean that they will be killed in exactly the same way. Perhaps the thought is that the manner of the death of the Galileans gave them no time to repent. Jesus' unrepentant hearers were setting themselves on a course which meant unrepentant death in due course. Or the point may be the execution by Romans. Unless His hearers repented they would suffer likewise at the hands of the Romans.

4, 5. Jesus goes on to speak of another disaster in Jerusalem, also unknown to us apart from this reference. His hearers are not to suppose that the eighteen people who had been killed when *the tower in Siloam* fell were *worse offenders* (really 'debtors';

men owe God obedience) than others. But their fate is a warning to His audience of the urgency of repenting. Luke uses a present imperative (with continuous force) in verse 3 and an aorist (of a single decisive action) here. Repentance is both a once-for-all thing that shapes the whole subsequent course of the life and a day-by-day affair that keeps putting sin away.

ii. The parable of the man seeking fruit (13:6–9). Luke proceeds to a parable that brings out both the need for repentance and the slowness of God to punish. The preceding passage has stressed the importance of repenting and this one highlights the fact that opportunity does not last for ever.

6, 7. Jesus sets the scene with a fig tree in a vineyard (and thus in fertile soil). The owner has been looking for fruit for three years, which seems to indicate a well-established tree. A failure to bear for three years sounds ominous. It was unlikely that such a tree would bear again. So the owner gives the command, *Cut it down*. Not only was it not bearing fruit, it was taking up ground that might otherwise be productive.

8, 9. The vinedresser counsels patience. Perhaps treatment of the soil and the application of manure for a further year will bring results. It will give the tree one last chance to produce. But the vinedresser recognizes facts. If it still does not bear, that is the end of the matter. Yet even so he does not say 'I will cut it down', but *you can cut it down*. He will take no initiative in destruction. Jesus teaches that to the end God is merciful.

i. Healing the bent woman (13:10–17)

The right use of the sabbath was a continuing source of controversy between Jesus and His opponents. Luke tells of a healing on the sabbath which provoked a dispute about the right use of that day.

10, 11. Neither the time, other than that it was on the sabbath, nor the place, except that it was a synagogue, is indicated. This is the last time Jesus is recorded to have taught in a synagogue or even to have been in one. The woman's deformity is described by A. Rendle Short as 'spondylitis deformans; the bones of her spine were fused into a rigid mass'.[1]

12, 13. There is no indication that the woman believed in Jesus, or indeed that she knew Him at all. Jesus Himself took the initiative. He pronounced her cured, laid His hands on her and she was *made straight*. Jesus did not usually lay hands on people when performing exorcisms. Perhaps Luke means that the spirit (11) was already cast out (12) and that Jesus now completed the cure with the laying on of hands. It is interesting that the woman's gratitude is shown in her praising of *God*, not Jesus.

14. The cure annoyed *the ruler of the synagogue* (for this official see on 8:41). Luke's explanation puts emphasis on the day: 'it was on the sabbath that Jesus had healed'. The ruler may also have felt that there was an invasion of his prerogative, for he directed what went on in the synagogue and this took place without reference to him. He did not rebuke Jesus, but spoke to the people at large. He took the fourth commandment to prohibit such healings as this. People should get themselves healed on six days.

15, 16. Jesus' plural, *hypocrites*, castigates not only the ruler but all who agreed with him as well. His hypocrisy consisted in his talking to the crowds when he really aimed his rebuke at Jesus, but even more in his professed zeal for the law in objecting to a deed which fulfilled the spirit and the purpose of the law. Jesus chose to rebuke the hypocrisy of this approach by pointing to the Jewish practice of looking after animals. The rabbis were greatly concerned that animals be treated well. On the sabbath, animals could be led out by a chain or the like as long as nothing was carried (*Shabbath* 5:1). Water could be drawn for them and poured into a trough, though a man must not hold a bucket for the animal to drink from (*Erubin* 20b, 21a). If animals may be cared for in such ways, much more may *a daughter of Abraham* be set free from Satan's bondage on the sabbath. In fact Jesus uses a strong term and says she 'must' (*dei*) be loosed. The afflicting of the woman was due to Satanic activity and Satan must be overthrown.

---

[1] A. R. Short, *Modern Discovery and the Bible* (London, 1947), p. 91.

This does not, of course, mean that the woman was wicked. She was attending worship, and Jesus' description of her seems to show that she was pious. But her illness was evil.

17. The effect was twofold. Jesus' *adversaries were put to shame* and *all the people* kept rejoicing (the tenses are continuous). Evidently public opinion was solidly on Jesus' side. And people were impressed not only by this one miracle, but by *all the glorious things that were done by him.*

j. The kingdom of God (13:18-30)

The two short parables that begin this section form a pair also in Matthew (that of the mustard seed, but not the leaven, occurs in Mark).

i. The parable of the mustard seed (13:18, 19). Luke's *therefore* shows that this teaching arises out of the preceding. The opposition of the ruler of the synagogue and his friends did not mean that the kingdom would fail of its consummation. The warm welcome the multitude gave Jesus' retort to the ruler and their joy in all His works (17) showed that the kingdom was making its impact. Matthew and Mark place the parable differently, but this should not be taken as a reason for rejecting Luke's setting. This is the kind of pithy story that might easily be repeated and used in different ways. In fact in Matthew and Mark the contrast between the tiny size of the mustard seed and the big plant that results is the point. Luke, however, does not even mention the size of the seed. Here the point is the end result: the plant grows so big that the birds nest in its branches. The precise plant in mind is not known for certain, but most think of the *sinapis nigra*. This is not really a tree, but under favourable conditions it grows to a height of ten or twelve feet. The birds roosting in the branches are often a symbol for the nations of the earth (Ezk. 17:23; 31:6; Dn. 4:12, 21). The kingdom will be universal. Men from all nations will find themselves therein.

ii. The parable of the leaven (13:20, 21). The previous parable was concerned with the kingdom's extension through the world; this one rather with its transforming power. Where home-made bread was common people would grasp the point

more easily than we do today. There seems no emphasis on the fact that the woman used *three measures* of meal, though this is the quantity used by Sarah (Gn. 18:6). It may have been the normal quantity, but it was not a small amount (*cf.* NEB, 'half a hundredweight of flour'). Only a small amount of yeast is needed to make a large quantity of dough rise. *Leaven* is often used in Scripture to denote a bad influence, but there seems no reason for taking it in such a way here. The point is that a small quantity of yeast makes itself felt throughout a much larger mass. So with the kingdom. Yeast works quietly and unseen, and the kingdom works through Christ's influence on the hearts of men, not in anything merely external and visible. It is perhaps worth noting also that yeast works from inside: it cannot change the dough while it is outside. But it is also important that the power to change comes from outside: the dough does not change itself.

iii. Who are in the kingdom? (13:22-30). The next incident to be narrated took place on another occasion, but it is connected in subject. Jesus makes it clear that there will be many surprises in the membership of the kingdom.

22, 23. The impression Luke conveys is that Jesus journeyed on towards Jerusalem without haste, and with many pauses for teaching in both large towns and small villages. Somewhere someone asked, *Lord, will those who are saved be few?* The question was very relevant in view of the confused religious state of the day. There is evidence that it was discussed (*e.g.* 4 Ezra vii. 55ff.), and that the rabbis held widely differing views (*e.g. Sanhedrin* 97b). But it seems to have been firmly held that all Israel would be saved, except for a few blatant sinners who excluded themselves (*Sanhedrin* 10:1).

24, 25. Jesus does not answer directly, but urges His questioner and others (*Strive* is plural) to make sure that they are in the number, however large or small it proves to be. This is much more important than doing some arithmetic on those rescued from eternal loss. *Strive* is a word denoting whole-hearted action. It is a technical term for competing in the Games (see LS), and from it we get our word 'agonize'. It points to no half-hearted effort. This does not mean that human achievement merits entrance into the kingdom: it is the attitude that is in mind. The *narrow door* is not explained, but it is plainly the door into salvation. The *many* who will be unable to enter are those who do not try to get in until too late. There is significance in the future, *will seek*, which contrasts with the present, *Strive*. Those who strive now enter. Neither here nor elsewhere is there any indication that genuine seekers find themselves excluded from the kingdom. But there is inevitably a time-limit on the offer of salvation. When the door of opportunity is finally shut it will be too late. Men must strive to enter now.

26. Jesus envisages some of those rejected as pleading that they had known the Lord. They *ate and drank* where He was; He taught where they were. Incidentally, some rabbis forbade teaching in the open street (*Moed Katan* 16a), but not Jesus. He opened His teaching to all men, wherever they were. But these men plead no more than physical proximity. They cannot claim that they have ever entered into sympathetic understanding of what He was teaching.

27. In consequence they will know complete rejection. The householder says that he does not know where they come from and he brands them as *workers of iniquity* (*cf.* Ps. 6:8). No specific evil deed has been mentioned. But in the end there will be only two classes, those inside and those outside. Since these people did not take the necessary steps to get inside, they are to be numbered with the evildoers outside.

28. They will wail (thus expressing their grief) and *gnash* their *teeth* (in rage). This marks the ultimate in frustration and disappointment. But these men will feel no less when they see the great heroes of the faith in the kingdom they had always thought they would share, while they find themselves *thrust out*. This last expression seems to indicate the use of some force. The end result of their attitude is to bring upon them the active opposition of God.

29, 30. The paragraph closes with the thought that there will be many surprises in the final membership of the kingdom. Men will come from the four corners of the earth, which means that the Gentiles will be well represented (*cf.* Is. 45:6; 49:12). This will surprise those Jews who think they have a mortgage on the kingdom. *Sit at table* employs the imagery of the Messianic banquet, a symbol of the joy of the end time greatly beloved of the Jews. It must have astounded them to hear of Gentiles taking part in it all, while they themselves were excluded. There is a double mortification: being excluded themselves and seeing the despised Gentiles included. The reversal can be complete, as the words about the *first* and the *last* amply demonstrate. God's ways are not men's ways.

k. Prophets perish in Jerusalem (13:31-35)

i. That fox Herod (13:31-33). 31. It is curious to find *some Pharisees* warning Jesus against Herod. Though they were vigorously opposed to much that He said and did, they perhaps recognized that they stood much closer to Him than they did to Herod. It is perhaps more likely that they were Herod's witting or unwitting agents. After his experience with John the Baptist the tetrarch may not have wanted the murder of another prophet on his conscience; but he did want to be rid of Jesus. So he used the Pharisees to pass on a death threat to Jesus. They may have been ready to co-operate in the hope of frightening Jesus into moving out of Perea into Judea, where they had more power.

32. The *fox* was used by the Jews as a symbol of a sly man, but more often for an insignificant or worthless person (SB). It was sometimes a symbol of destructiveness. T. W. Manson says, 'To call Herod "that fox" is as much as to say he is neither a great man nor a straight man; he has neither majesty nor honour.'[1] The expression is thus contemptuous. Herod is the only person Jesus is recorded as having treated with contempt. Later we read that he wanted to see Jesus perform a miracle, and that when Jesus stood before him the Master said nothing to him at all (23:8f.). When Jesus has nothing to say to a man that man's position is hopeless. That Jesus tells the Pharisees to go to Herod may support the view that they had some connection with the tetrarch. But it may be no more than His way of making the point that it does not matter to Him if Herod comes to hear what He has to say. The casting out of demons and healing mean that Jesus will continue His ministry. But He makes it clear that this will not last

[1] *SJ*, p. 276.

indefinitely. The *third day* means 'in a short time', or 'at the
end of a definite time', or both. Then Jesus will 'be finished'.
The word (*teleioumai*) might denote the end of His work in that
region or the completion of His work of redemption. Jesus is
saying that He will complete His allotted course. God, not
Herod, will determine when He is to die.

33. The same time-note with the same problem of interpretation (and the same solution) occurs again. Jesus follows
the path God maps out for Him. This is strengthened with the
word *must* (*dei*), which points to the divine necessity that
dictated Jesus' movements. The verse comes to an ironical
climax, 'it would never do for a prophet to perish except in
Jerusalem!' (Moffatt). The capital was the heart of the nation.
It was there that its destiny and that of its prophets were
wrought out. It was there, before the Sanhedrin, that trials of
prophets took place. It was there that the nation's attitude to
Jesus would take its final shape and that death take place that
would accomplish God's purpose for His Messiah.

ii. Lament over Jerusalem (13:34, 35). It is possible
that Luke records the lament over Jerusalem at this point
simply because of its kinship with the subject-matter. It seems
more probable that it occurred as Jesus approached the city,
as Matthew says it did. The alternative is that Jesus uttered
the words twice, which does not seem likely. The tender
address shows that Jesus was deeply concerned about the final
fate of the city. It shows also that He must have had more
dealings with Jerusalem than are indicated in the Synoptic
Gospels, for *How often* would be a curious way of referring to
the few contacts with the city of which they speak. Jesus
describes Jerusalem as habitually rejecting, even killing,
God's messengers, be they prophets or others (*cf.* 2 Ki. 21:16;
2 Ch. 24:21; Je. 26:20f., *etc.*). Yet even so she was not rejected
out of hand. The Son of God would often have *gathered* her
children together, but they would not come (for a contrasting
attitude *cf.* Ps. 57:1). There is tenderness in the imagery of the
hen and its chicks. The responsibility of the Jews for their fate
is sheeted home with the final *you would not!*

35. The nation has invited the final result. When a nation
or a man persists in rejecting God the end is inevitable. So

Jesus says *your house is forsaken*. Many hold the *house* to be the Temple, but it is more probably Jerusalem as a whole. Whatever the truth of this, the important thing is that it is *forsaken* (*cf*. Je. 22:5). God no longer lives there: that is the final disaster. Jesus goes on to say that the city will see Him no more until it greets Him in the words of Psalm 118:26. Some see in this a reference to the triumphal entry when these words were used about Jesus. But this seems an inadequate fulfilment of such a solemn prediction. And in any case it was not the men of the city but the Galilean pilgrims who uttered the words then. Moreover Matthew records Jesus' prediction after the entry (Mt. 23:39; the entry is in Mt. 21:1–11). Others think of the words as the response of believing Jews at some future conversion of Jerusalem, but it is hard to see this either in the words themselves or in history. It is better to think of the second advent. Jesus' return in splendour will draw from Jerusalem this recognition, however unwilling, of His Messiahship.

1. Dinner with a Pharisee (14:1–24)

Luke may have put together here a number of 'feast' narratives, as some scholars think. But it is not at all impossible that he is in fact narrating what happened at a more than usually interesting meal.

i. Healing a man with dropsy (14:1–6). Once again we
have a healing on the sabbath (see on 4:31ff.). As in the case of the man with the withered hand (6:6ff.), Jesus disarmed criticism by first asking whether it was lawful to heal on the sabbath or not.

1. Neither place nor time (other than the sabbath) is indicated. Jesus' host was an important man. The Greek may mean *a ruler* (perhaps a member of the Sanhedrin) who was also a member of the Pharisaic party. Or it can signify 'a leading Pharisee' (NEB). Either way he was an important figure. Dinner on the sabbath seems often to have been a rather special meal (the food having all been prepared beforehand) and it was common to invite guests. Jesus' enemies were present in full force and *they were watching him*. Clearly they were hoping to find Him doing something for which they could bring a charge against Him.

2–4. It is possible that the presence of the man with dropsy was a trap set by enemies who hoped Jesus would break the law. Support for this is sometimes found in the use of the verb 'answering' (*apokritheis*; AV is correct, RSV has *spoke to*). No-one had spoken so Jesus was answering the action, or perhaps the thought of His enemies, or the man may have entered the house looking for help so that his very presence was a mute appeal to which Jesus 'replied'. Luke does not tell us. He simply says 'lo, he was there'. We must, of course, bear in mind that on occasion 'answered' can be used in a Hebraistic sense which does little more than carry on the narrative. But it seems more likely that here Jesus was 'answering' the opposition of the enemy. Before He took action Jesus asked whether it was lawful to heal on the sabbath. It was an awkward question to answer. According to the rabbinic regulations it certainly was not lawful; healing could take place on the sabbath only when there was danger to life. In this case the man would probably not have died if the case had been stood over until sundown. To agree to healing under these circumstances could lead to an accusation that they were 'soft' on law enforcement. But on the other hand *lawful* might mean 'contained in the law of Moses'. There is nothing in Scripture to forbid such healing. It was the rabbinic interpretation of Scripture that was the source of the rule. To insist publicly on this interpretation might lead to a charge of indifference to human suffering. Small wonder then that *they were silent*. But their silence before the miracle made it more than difficult for them to complain afterwards. Jesus healed the man and dismissed him.

5, 6. He proceeded to justify His action by appealing to their own procedure. It is not certain whether Jesus refers to *a son* or to 'an ass'. If we accept the latter reading (with RSV mg.), Jesus is appealing to their practice with animals. It is true that the men of Qumran at least in some cases refused to pull an animal out of a ditch on the sabbath.[1] But this seems

---

[1] In the Damascus (or Zadokite) Document. See T. H. Gaster, *The Scriptures of the Dead Sea Sect* (London, 1957), p. 87.

not to have been the normal Jewish custom, which was marked rather by concern for animals. I am not aware of any regulation which specifically deals with the case Jesus mentioned, though it is provided that bedding or the like should be thrown into a pit to enable an animal to scramble out on the sabbath (*Shabbath* 128b), and there is a discussion of how the hauling out of certain animals on the sabbath may be justified (*Shabbath* 117b). Jesus probably means that in the absence of a regulation a man would find some way of justifying his procedure. He would not leave an animal in a pit on a sabbath. But on the whole it seems that the textual point should be resolved in favour of *son*, when the meaning will be, 'Which of you, having a son or even an ox . . .?' And even the men of Qumran did not teach that a man should leave his son in a well should he chance to fall into one on the sabbath. The clear implication of all this is that deeds of mercy are in order on the sabbath. Jesus' critics *could not reply*. Conceivably they might have argued that He was talking about unusual emergencies, while their objection was to a routine cure. But they may have perceived that His case was based on the fact that the sabbath was instituted for man's good. Their emergency procedures gave testimony to this, just as did Jesus' works of healing.

ii. Invitation to a banquet (14:7–14). The behaviour of guests at banquets gave Jesus the opening for a lesson on humility.

7. At banquets the basic item of furniture was the couch for three, the *triclinium*. A number of *triclinia* were arranged in a U-shape. Guests reclined on their left elbows. The place of highest honour was the central position on the couch at the base of the U. The second and third places were those on the left of the principal man (*i.e.* reclining behind him) and on his right (*i.e.* reclining with the head on his bosom). After this there seems to have ranked the couch to the left, its most honourable occupant being in the middle, with the next places behind and before him as on the first couch. The third couch, with a similar arrangement of its occupants, would be on the right of the first, the fourth to the left of the second, and so on.[1]

[1] SB, iv, p. 618.

Many commentators take up Plummer's view that we cannot be certain about seating arrangements in view of the very different customs among Jews, Greeks, Romans and others. That there was variety is probable, but there is no reason to doubt the accuracy of the information about Jewish custom given in rabbinic sources (even though they are later than our period). Nor should we doubt that a leading Pharisee would follow Jewish rather than foreign custom. At this particular feast there was an undignified scramble for the places of highest honour and Jesus commented on it.

8, 9. He began by referring to an invitation to *a marriage feast*. This was probably more formal than most meals, but the words apply to any banquet. Jesus pointed to a danger in the scramble. When a man succeeds in securing a place of honour he runs the risk that a later guest will have more claim to it. When the host insists that he vacate his position he may find all the other places occupied, so that the only course open to him is *to take the lowest place*, with all the shame and loss of face implied (*cf.* Pr. 25:7).

10. It is better to go to the lowest place first. The way to get to the top is to start at the bottom. If a man chooses the lowest place, the only way he can go is up. R. Akiba is reported to have advised guests to take a place two or three seats lower than that to which they are entitled. He says, 'Better that people say to you "come up, come up," and not say to you, "go down, go down" ' (*Leviticus Rabbah* I. 5). But Jesus is not giving a piece of worldly advice: He is teaching men to be genuinely humble. He reminds us that the truly humble man will finish up where he ought to be and receive the honour that is due. Godet points out that, in following Jesus' advice, 'we run no other risk than that of being exalted'.

11. The principle that should govern our conduct occurs a number of times in slightly different forms (18:14; Mt. 23:12; *cf.* Mt. 18:4; 1 Pet. 5:6). To exalt oneself means ultimate abasement. The way to true exaltation is humility.

12. Jesus has some advice for the host: he should not confine his guest-list to friends, relations and rich neighbours. If these are the only objects of his bounty he will suffer the

terrible fate of receiving return invitations! In this way he will
be repaid. It scarcely needs pointing out that Jesus is not forbidding normal social life; but He is emphasizing that there
is no generosity in giving to people who will make a recom-
pense.

13, 14. It is otherwise with *the poor, the maimed, the lame, the
blind*. Such people cannot repay their hosts. To give them a
feast is an act of pure generosity. This kind of thing will be
recognized at *the resurrection of the just*, not the conviviality that
arises from celebrations among boon companions.

iii. The parable of the excuses (14:15-24). This story
of a banquet emphasizes the truth that men are saved, not by
their own effort, but by responding to the invitation; if they
are lost, however, it is by their own fault. It is tragically
possible to reject the gracious invitation. In this parable there
are resemblances to that of the great feast (Mt. 22:1-14) and
some see this as a variant of the same story. But the differences
are as striking as the resemblances and it is better to see the
two as distinct.

15. Jesus' reference to resurrection sparked off a pious
ejaculation from one of the guests: *Blessed is he who shall eat
bread in the kingdom of God!* Clearly he had no doubt that he
would be there, whatever the fate of others. Jesus' parable
challenges his sincerity. When the critical time came, would
he really accept God's invitation? Or would he be too busy
about some activity affecting his more immediate interests?

16, 17. Jesus' story is about a man who *invited many* to *a great
banquet*. It seems that they accepted the invitation. At any rate
none of them is said to have declined. When the banquet was
ready a slave was sent to announce the fact. In an age when
people had no watches and time was fairly elastic, and when
a banquet took a long time to prepare, the precaution must
have been helpful to all. We see the double invitation in the
Old Testament (Est. 5:8; 6:14), while a remark in the Midrash on Lamentations shows that much later the men of
Jerusalem took it very seriously: 'None of them would attend
a banquet unless he was invited twice' (on La. 4:2).

18. But the prospective guests began to excuse themselves (the Greek may mean either *all alike* or 'at once'). Jesus gives a sample of the kind of thing they said and begins with a man who said he had bought a field and must see it. The excuse is transparently false. No-one would buy a field without careful prior inspection. And if by any chance a man did this, there was no hurry. The field would be there tomorrow. It is plain that the man did not want to come.

19. So with the second man. He had bought *five yoke* (*i.e.* five pairs) *of oxen*. His *I go* means 'I am going', 'I am on my way', and his verb *examine* (*dokimasai*) should probably be understood as 'to test them' or 'to prove them'. No-one would buy oxen without first satisfying himself that they would do the job. And if he did, there was no hurry for his testing. The oxen would keep.

20. The third man's excuse is certainly original. He could back it up with an appeal to Scripture, for the Old Testament envisages that a man will be at home during the first year of married life (Dt. 24:5). But that is a regulation aimed at freeing him from military service, not at isolating him from social contacts. This excuse is as transparent as the others. Marriage certainly involves obligations, but it does not cancel out other obligations, especially things of which due notice has been given.

21. The *master* was angry at his slave's report. He was clearly determined to hold his banquet at the set time and not allow the makers of excuses to disrupt his plans. So he sent his slave to the poorer quarters of the city to bring in *the poor and maimed and blind and lame* (the very classes named in verse 13).

22, 23. But the search through the city did not yield enough guests. The slave did as he was told and reported that there was still room. So his master sent him out to *the highways and hedges*. These are the major roads outside the city and the hedges alongside them in which derelicts might find shelter of a sort. It would not be as easy to find people there, since they would be spread over a greater area. The extension of the search to such unpromising fields is a way of showing that the master meant business. So does the use of the word *compel* (*anagkason*). This does not countenance the use of force: only one slave is in question and he could not bring force to bear. The use of this verse to justify persecution is illegitimate. The point is that wanderers in such places would take a lot of convincing that they were really wanted at a banquet in the city. The slave was not to take 'No' for an answer; the house must be filled. There seems little doubt that we should see a reference to the mission of the church. God's invitation had gone out to the people through the prophets. Now in Jesus the second invitation was given. When the religious élite refused it, the church was to bring in both those within the city (the Jews) and those outside (the Gentiles). The slave is not said to have fulfilled the commission to those outside. Bringing in the Gentiles was still future when Jesus spoke and for that matter for the most part when Luke wrote.

24. The parable concludes with a sombre verdict on those who were first invited and who made their excuses. There would be no second chance for them. They had squandered their opportunity and they would get no other. Once again we see Jesus stressing the urgency of the situation. God is gracious and will receive all who come to Him. But men may not dilly-dally. Those first invited might not take up the invitation but others would, both Jew and Gentile. God's purpose may be resisted, but it cannot be overthrown.

m. Discipleship (14:25-35)

i. The cost of discipleship (14:25-33). 25. Jesus is still on His journey. That *great multitudes* followed Him may be held to support the view that He was travelling through Perea, an area where as far as we know He had not been previously. There would be curiosity to see the Teacher from Nazareth. But Luke does not say where this teaching took place, only that Jesus *turned* (*cf.* 7:9; 9:55; 10:23; 22:61; 23:28) and spoke to them.

26. Discipleship means giving one's first loyalty. There is no place in Jesus' teaching for literal hatred. He commanded His followers to love even their enemies (6:27), so it is impossible to hold that He is here telling them literally to hate their earthly nearest (*cf.* 8:20f.). But hating can mean something like loving less (Gn. 29:31, 33; Dt. 21:15, where the Hebrew means 'hated' and not 'disliked', as RSV). Jesus' meaning is surely that the love the disciple has for Him must be so great that the best of earthly loves is hatred by comparison (*cf.* Mt. 10:37). The listing of the nearest and dearest spells this out with solemnity. A man must not set store even by *his own life* (*cf.* Jn. 12:25). Devotion to Christ cannot be anything less than whole-hearted.

27. For this saying see note on 9:23, where we have the positive form of what is put negatively here. Cross-bearing is of the essence of discipleship.

28–30. Jesus does not want disciples who do not realize what they have let themselves in for. Counting the cost is important. He uses twin parables (a device He employs often) to drive the point home. A man who decides to *build a tower* must first think. To get no further than the foundation is to invite mockery. The man must therefore first *sit down* (the matter is not to be decided in a hurry) *and count the cost*. Only then can he expect success.

31, 32. A second illustration comes from kings at war. It is not easy with *ten thousand* soldiers to defeat one who attacks with *twenty thousand*. A king in such a position thinks hard. If he cannot see his way through the problem he does not tamely wait for defeat: he arranges a peace while the enemy is still *a great way off*.

The two parables are similar but they make slightly different points. The builder of the tower is free to build or not as he chooses, but the king is being invaded (the other *comes against him*). He must do something. *Cf.* A. M. Hunter, 'In the first parable Jesus says, "Sit down and reckon whether you can afford to follow me." In the second he says, "Sit down and reckon whether you can afford to refuse my demands." '[1] Both ways of looking at it are important.

33. The lesson is plain. Jesus does not want followers who rush into discipleship without thinking of what is involved. And He is clear about the price. The man who comes to Him must *renounce all that he has*. For the third time we have the

[1] A. M. Hunter, *Interpreting the Parables* (London, 1960), p. 65.

solemn refrain, he *cannot be my disciple* (26, 27). These words condemn all half-heartedness. Jesus is not, of course, discouraging discipleship. He is warning against an ill-considered, faint-hearted attachment in order that men may know the real thing. He wants men to count the cost and reckon all lost for His sake so that they can enter the exhilaration of full-blooded discipleship.

ii. The parable of the salt (14:34, 35). He adds a little parable about salt. *Salt is good*, though Jesus does not indicate which qualities of salt He has in mind. Commentators point to its preservative and flavouring values. It is, of course, impossible for salt (sodium chloride) to lose its taste, but the salt in use in first-century Palestine was far from pure. It was quite possible for the sodium chloride to be leached out of the impure salt in common use so that what was left lacked the taste of salt. It was literally useless. It could not fertilize the land or even decompose usefully on the manure heap. *Men throw it away*. There is an astringent quality about discipleship. If a man lacks it, then whatever other qualities he may have, as regards discipleship he is useless.

n. Three parables of the lost (15:1–32)

This is one of the best-known and best-loved chapters in the whole Bible. Three parables bring out the joy of God when the lost sinner is found.

i. Sinners gather (15:1, 2). The *tax collectors* were not highly regarded, for they both helped the hated Romans in their administration of conquered territory and enriched themselves at the expense of their fellow-countrymen. They were ostracized by many and regarded as outcasts by the religious. The *sinners* were the immoral or those who followed occupations that the religious regarded as incompatible with the Law. *The Pharisees and the scribes* objected to Jesus receiving such people. SB cite an old rule, 'One must not associate with an ungodly man', and point out that this was taken so seriously that the rabbis would not associate with such a person even to teach him the Law (*cf*. Acts 10:28). Eating with these people was regarded as worse than mere association: it implied welcome and recognition. Jesus did not let the

Pharisaic censure interfere with His ministry. He had come to help sinful men, which He could scarcely do if He did not meet them. We should not let the modern chapter division make us miss an important point. Jesus has just made an uncompromising demand for whole-heartedness as He showed what following Him meant. He finished with 'He who has ears to hear, let him hear'. Luke's very next words inform us that these sinners came near *to hear him*. Whatever the case with the Pharisees and their like, these sinners had been challenged. They knew what discipleship meant. They were called on to hear. And they heard.

ii. The parable of the lost sheep (15:3-7). A great Jewish scholar, C. G. Montefiore, saw here a distinctive and revolutionary note: God actively seeks out sinners and brings them home. The rabbis agreed that God would welcome the penitent sinner. But it is a new idea that God is a seeking God, a God who takes the initiative.

3, 4. Jesus appeals to custom. Should one sheep stray, any shepherd would leave *the ninety-nine* who were safe and look for the missing one. The ninety-nine are in no danger; they are found. But the safe possession of ninety-nine is no substitute for the loss of one. So the shepherd keeps looking *until he finds it*. He makes more than a token search. He wants his sheep. He looks till he finds it.

5, 6. Finding the lost is a joyful experience. The shepherd happily brings the sheep home *on his shoulders*. There is no grumbling about having to carry the animal: the shepherd is *rejoicing*. The joy of finding his lost one overshadows all else. In his overflowing happiness he calls in others to share his joy.

7. The application brings out the *joy in heaven* over one repentant sinner. Edersheim quotes a Jewish saying, 'There is joy before God when those who provoke Him perish from the world'.[1] But Jesus has a very different concept of God. He rejoices over the returning penitent more than over many safely in the fold. There is joy over these, but *more joy* over the repenting sinner.

[1] *LT*, ii, p. 256.

iii. The parable of the lost coin (15:8–10). Again we
have twin parables. In this second story Jesus speaks of a
woman *having ten silver coins*. The coin is the Greek *drachma*
(only here in the New Testament), which was the wage paid
to a labourer for a day's work. The ten coins may represent a
poor woman's savings, or, as some think, they may have been
strung together as an ornament. The point is evidently not
significant. Either way the loss of a coin would be a serious
matter for a poor woman. So she searched for it determinedly.
An Eastern house would have no windows, or very small ones,
so the lighting of the lamp was necessary for a close search
even in the daytime. The woman sweeps and seeks till she
finds it. And, like the shepherd, she shares her joy when she
is successful. This time Jesus speaks of joy *before the angels of
God* (previously 'in heaven'), but the meaning is much the
same. Among the rabbinic writings there is the lost coin motif,
but it is used very differently. If a man keeps seeking for a lost
coin much more should he seek for the Law, said the rabbis
(*Canticles Rabbah* I. 1.9). There is no rabbinic equivalent to
God's seeking of sinners.

iv. The parable of the prodigal son (15:11–32). Many
regard this superb story as the finest of all the parables. It is
certainly among the best-loved of them all. The human heart
responds to the message of God's forgiving love for sinners so
plainly set forth. Jesus is not dealing here with the whole gospel
message but with the one great fact of the Father's pardoning
love. The story is not 'a complete compendium of theology'
(T. W. Manson). Some hold that, since it has no atoning
sacrifice, no atonement is necessary. But this is a precarious
conclusion. To cite Manson again, 'If the carrying out of the
purpose of God leads, as in fact it did, to the Cross, then it
becomes the business of Christians to include the Cross in the
purpose of God and to think out, as best they can, how the
death of Christ is involved in God's purpose of saving sinners.'[1]
This is not to diminish the importance of the parable, but to
see it as powerfully setting forth the love of God for sinners,
the mainspring of the gospel.

It has sometimes been argued that the concluding section
(25ff.) should be deleted as no part of the original parable.

[1]*SJ*, p. 286.

No good reason is put forward and there is much against it. There is not the slightest evidence that the parable ever existed without it, and the point it makes is important. Indeed it is quite possible to hold that the main aim of the parable is to contrast the reactions of the father and the elder son to the prodigal. And in the situation in which Jesus found Himself, while it was important to make the point that God welcomes sinners, it was also important to emphasize that those who reject repentant sinners are out of line with the Father's will. The parable says something to 'the tax collectors and sinners'. But it also has a message for 'the Pharisees and the scribes'.

11, 12. We should not overlook the opening reference to *two sons*. The elder brother is in the story from the beginning. The younger son asked for *the share of property that falls to me*. Deissmann notes this as a technical formula, used in the papyri of 'the paternal inheritance'.[1] A man might leave his goods to his heirs by last will and testament (*cf.* Heb. 9:16f.), in which case he was bound by the provisions of the Law. This meant that the first-born received two thirds of the whole (Dt. 21:17). But he could make gifts before he died and this gave him a freer hand (SB). The rules for disposing of property are given in the Mishnah (*Baba Bathra* 8). If a man decided to make gifts, he normally gave the capital but retained the income. He could then no longer dispose of the capital, only of his interest in the income. But the recipient could get nothing until the death of the giver. He could sell the capital if he chose, but the buyer could not gain possession until the death of the donor. We see this in the elder brother. The father clearly retained the managership of the property and the use of the proceeds. But he can say, 'all that is mine is yours' (31). The son of Sirach thought it unwise to give property away too early and he warns against it (Ecclus. 33:19–21). But his warning shows that the practice existed. What is unusual about the son's request is that he sought the use of the capital immediately. This could be given, and it was given in this case. But it was far from common.

13. The younger son gave no reason for his request, but when the father consented it quickly became apparent. Once he had control of his inheritance he soon set out to see the

[1] *BS*, p. 230.

world. He *gathered all he had*: he left nothing that would serve as an anchor and bring him back in due course. With ample funds at first and with much to see and do he *squandered his property*. RSV says this was *in loose living*, but the adjective rendered *loose* should probably be understood as 'reckless'. Phillips gives the sense of it with 'he squandered his wealth in the wildest extravagance'.

14. Two disasters struck him simultaneously—he ran out of money and he ran into a famine. The first was entirely his fault. It does not need vast experience to know that when capital is expended without return it must eventually be dissipated. The famine was not his fault but it increased his difficulties. People who might have helped him would find their own circumstances more straitened. Food was short and consequently would be high priced. It gave people the perfect excuse for refusing to help. So the young man *began to be in want*. He lacked even the necessities of life.

15. He had to get a job; but in a time of famine employment was not easy to come by. Only this explains why he attached himself to a local citizen who *sent him into his fields to feed swine*. For a Jew no occupation could have been more distasteful. A rabbinic saying runs, 'Cursed be the man who would breed swine' (*Baba Kamma* 82b). The pig was unclean (Lv. 11:7) and the Jew under normal circumstances would have nothing to do with it at all. The young man must have been in desperate straits even to consider this job.

16. It is not clear what he ate. Jesus says that he *would gladly have fed on the pods that the swine ate* (these *pods* being the seeds of the carob tree). But did he? *No one gave him anything* seems to indicate that he did not, especially if we understand it to mean that no-one gave him any of the pods (so TEV). Some conjecture that since no-one gave him anything, he must have stolen in order to keep alive. If so he was sunk in moral as well as physical degradation. But it does not follow. His master may well have provided his rations. It would be strange if he did not. That no-one helped him shows the low esteem into which he had fallen. Pigs were more valuable than he.

17. Disillusionment set in. The young man 'came to his senses' (NEB). Hardship has a wonderful way of bringing men to face facts. The prodigal reflected on the contrast between the starvation he was experiencing and the full and plenty enjoyed not by his father and brother alone but by his father's *hired servants*. Even for them there was *bread enough and to spare*.

18, 19. The young man resolved to go home. If his initial motive was not particularly lofty (the desire to be better fed, 17), the confession he planned to make is a classic. He expressed sorrow not for what he had lost but for what he had done: he had sinned. He recognized that his sin was first against God, *heaven* being a reverent periphrasis for the divine name (unless we take *eis ton ouranon* to mean that he saw his sins piling up on high till they reached heaven, *cf*. Ezr. 9:6). Sin is always sin against God before anyone else. But this young man had also sinned against his father and he saw this, though without specifying exactly what he had in mind. It may be that he saw it as wrong to spend everything without leaving something to provide for his father in his old age. Or perhaps he saw that his whole attitude had been wrong: he had failed to honour his parent according to the commandment. He recognized that he had forfeited all claim to be treated as a son and he looked only for the possibility of being made like one of the paid servants, *i.e.* he would ask for a job. At least then he would get a living wage in congenial surroundings.

20. So he went back. Significantly Jesus does not say to his own village or even to his home, but *to his father*. Plainly the old man had hoped and watched for such a return. Jesus emphasizes the welcome the father gave his unworthy son. He saw him while he was still *at a distance*, he *had compassion*, he *ran* (which was striking in an elderly Oriental), he *embraced him* ('fell on his neck') and he *kissed him* (*cf*. David's forgiving kiss of Absalom, 2 Sa. 14:33). This last verb, *katephilēsen*, may mean 'kissed him many times' or 'kissed him tenderly'. Even if no special significance is to be attached to the compound form, at least the verb points to a sincere greeting and not to perfunctory politeness.

21. It is not clear whether when the time came the son could not bring himself to utter the words about being like a hired servant (19), or whether his father was so intent on his welcome that he did not give him time to finish. Probably it was the latter. But at any rate the son got out the words that expressed his sense of sin and unworthiness.

22–24. The father sent his slaves scurrying. The *best robe* was a sign of position and the *ring* also, especially if, as many hold, a signet ring is meant (*cf.* Gn. 41:42). Such a ring conveyed authority. In his destitution the son went barefoot. But this was fitting only for a slave and the *shoes* marked him out as a freeman. The *fatted calf* was clearly an animal carefully looked after for some special occasion. Its use now showed that the father felt that there could scarcely be a more special occasion than this. The old man's overflowing joy finds expression in his memorable opposition of *dead* to *alive again* and of *lost* to *found*. In the feast where *they began to make merry* perhaps the younger son found some of the solid pleasure he had looked for in vain in the far country.

25, 26. There can be no doubt that in the father's welcome of the younger son Jesus is teaching that the heavenly Father welcomes returning sinners. When Jesus turns to the elder brother we should see His concern for the Pharisees and their like. The nation's religious leaders had not so far shown any of the divine compassion to penitent sinners. This section is needed for the full lesson that Jesus is teaching. He pictures the *elder son* as *in the field*, evidently at work, while all this was going on. The sound of the celebrations he heard as he neared home puzzled him and he sought information from one of the servants. The *music and dancing* would have been performed by entertainers, not the banqueters.

27. The servant gave a concise report of the state of affairs. He confined himself to the return of the younger brother and the killing of the fatted calf. He adds that the reason for this latter is that the father *has received him safe and sound*.

28–30. The elder son's reaction was anger. He would have no part in all this and he *refused to go in*. The likeness to the Pharisees is unmistakable. We can easily imagine the elder brother saying of his father, 'This man receives sinners and eats with them' (15:2). But there was no false pride about the father. He had already gone out to meet one son and he now went out to plead with the other. But he was met by a torrent of words as the pent-up feelings of years came tumbling out. The elder son was conscious of his own rectitude. He was completely self-righteous. He saw himself as always the model son. But his use of the verb *douleuō* 'to serve as a slave' (*cf*. NEB, 'I have slaved for you all these years') gives him away. He did not really understand what being a son means. That is perhaps why he did not understand what being a father means. He could not see why his father should be so full of joy at the return of the prodigal. He complains that the father has never given him *a kid* (let alone a calf) for a feast with his *friends* (who would have been respectable people and not like the other boy's associates). The proud and the self-righteous always feel that they are not treated as well as they deserve. He cannot even refer to the prodigal as his brother but as *this son of yours*. Let the father welcome him if he wanted to: he disowned him. He speaks of the younger man as having spent the father's money on *harlots*, which goes beyond anything said previously and may be his own invention. He comes to his climax that it was *for him* that the father killed the fatted calf.

31, 32. To this son as to the other the father's words are tender. They are both sons and he loves them both. He makes it clear that he appreciates this son's constant attendance. He says plainly that the property settlement stands: *all that is mine is yours*. He does not propose to interfere in any way with the rights and possessions of the faithful elder son. We may perhaps infer that that son was in error in saying that he had never had a kid wherewith to entertain his friends. He had it all. But he, like the Pharisees, did not realize the extent of his privileges. But when all this is said the father does not back down in the slightest in his welcome for the younger brother. *It was fitting* is not strong enough for his word *edei*, which means 'It was necessary'. The welcome to the younger son was not simply a good thing which might or might not have occurred. It was the right thing. The father had to do it. Joy was the only proper reaction in such a situation. Notice that he does not speak of 'my son' but of *your brother*. The older boy might try to overlook the relationship, but it was still there. The father will not let him forget it. And he finishes by repeating the wonderful thing that has happened: the dead has come to life, the lost is found.

Jesus does not go on to tell us whether the elder son responded or not. Nor does He say how the younger son lived in
response to his father's welcoming love. In leaving these points
unresolved He throws out a challenge to all His hearers, be
they like the elder or like the younger. We tend to see ourselves as the prodigal and rejoice in the welcoming love of God.
This is good, and it is even better if we go on to make the
appropriate response to that love. But we might also profit-
ably reflect that, unless we are very unusual, we can also see
ourselves in the elder brother. It is a common human failing
to think that we are not appreciated as we should be, that
people do not give us credit for what we have done. And
whether we be religious or irreligious, we are usually somewhat censorious towards those we see as having failed to live
up to our standards, even if our standards are not theirs. That
Jesus leaves the elder son's reaction open is encouraging. We
can still do the right thing. God's love is a continuing challenge
to all our self-seeking.

o. Teaching, mostly about money (16:1-31)

i. The parable of the unjust steward (16:1-9). This is
notoriously one of the most difficult of all the parables to
interpret. The root problem is the commendation of the
steward who is so plainly dishonest (8). The usual way of
explaining this is that the steward is commended, not for his
dishonesty, but for taking resolute action in a crisis. The
coming of Jesus forced men to decision. When even dishonest
worldly people know how and when to take decisive action,
much more should those who follow Him. It is the astuteness
of the steward that is commended, not his commercial practices. T. W. Manson reminds us that there is a world of difference between 'I applaud the dishonest steward because he
acted cleverly' and 'I applaud the clever steward because he
acted dishonestly'.[1] This view is often held in conjunction
with the idea that Luke has appended applications to the use
of money which were not original. It is perhaps more likely
that we should understand the parable in the light of commercial practices of the day. Jews were forbidden to take
interest from fellow-Jews when they lent them money (Ex.

[1]*SJ*, p. 292.

22:25; Lv. 25:36; Dt. 23:19). Those who wished to make money from loans evaded this by reasoning that the law was concerned to prohibit the exploitation of the poor. It was not meant to forbid innocent transactions that were mutually beneficial and where the payment of interest amounted to the sharing of the profits. If a man had even a little of a given commodity he was not destitute and thus lending to him was not exploitation. As almost everyone had a little oil and a little wheat, the way was open for widespread use of a legal fiction. Whatever was borrowed was given a value in oil or wheat (say, eighty measures of wheat), the interest added on (say, twenty measures), and the bond made out for the repayment of the total in terms of wheat or oil (in this case one hundred measures). The transaction was usurious, but the bond gave no indication of this. Commonly these transactions were carried on by stewards, ostensibly without the owners' knowledge. Understood in this way, the parable presents us with a steward who, faced with the loss of his employment, protected his future by calling in the bonds and getting the debtors to rewrite them so that they no longer carried interest. He looked to their gratitude to express itself by their taking him into their homes. His action put the owner in a difficult position. He would have the greatest difficulty in establishing his claim to the original amounts now that the first bonds were destroyed. In any case he could not repudiate the steward's action without convicting himself of taking usury. It would be extremely difficult to obtain his legal rights and in the process he would convict himself of acting impiously. So he put the best face possible on the situation and 'commended' the man. Thus he secured an undeserved reputation for piety. The steward was now conforming to the law of God and the owner was seen as applauding it. Both were acting decisively in a difficult situation.[1]

1, 2. This story is addressed to *the disciples*, whereas the previous trio was aimed at the Pharisees (15:2f.). But the Pharisees are still in the background, for they scoffed at what Jesus said (14). *Steward* is perhaps not a good translation of *oikonomos* (*cf.* 12:42), but a better is not easy to find, for we no

---

[1] See further, J. Duncan M. Derrett, *Law in the New Testament* (London, 1970), pp. 48–77.

longer have the office (though I am informed that the Scottish 'factor', as Moffatt translates, still exists and performs the same function). It usually denoted a slave who was put in charge of an estate to relieve the owner of routine management. In this story the steward must have been a freeman, not a slave, for he could enter into agreements that bound his master and a slave could not do this. He was the manager of his master's estate. The man was accused of *wasting* his master's *goods*. The nature of his job made it easy for him to misappropriate funds for his own purposes. The owner evidently thought the charge well founded, for he informed the steward that he was dismissed and instructed him to prepare a final accounting.

3, 4. This gave the steward time to think up a plan of action. The loss of *the stewardship* meant the loss of his livelihood. He glanced at digging, but abandoned the idea on account of his physical limitations. He thought of begging, but was ashamed (*cf*. Ecclus. 40:28, 'it is better to die than to beg'). *I have decided* renders an aorist with a meaning like 'I've got it!' There is the thought of a sudden inspiration. He sees a way of being kept by his master's creditors.

5, 6. He quickly puts the plan into action. He deals with the debtors *one by one*. Secrecy was essential. The first owes him *a hundred measures of oil*. The *measure* is the *batos*, mentioned here only in the New Testament. From a reference in Josephus (*Antiquities* viii. 57) we find that this was about eight and threequarter gallons. The debt was thus for about 875 gallons of oil (Jeremias makes it about 800 gallons and sees this as the yield of 146 olive trees;[1] it was thus a considerable debt). The steward tells him to write another bill, substituting *fifty*.

7. A second example is given. This man is allowed to substitute a bill for eighty measures of wheat in place of one for a hundred. The measure here is the *koros*, about ten bushels, making the total approximately 1,000 bushels. Jeremias sees this as the yield from about 100 acres.[2] Clearly quite large amounts were involved. The steward varied his rate of discount perhaps because of the difference in the commodities.

[1] J. Jeremias, *The Parables of Jesus* (London, 1954), p. 127.
[2] *Ibid*.

It was comparatively easy to adulterate olive oil, so the rate of interest on transactions involving oil was high. Derrett points out that 'where a debtor has nothing left to offer, short of his self and family as slaves, but an amount of natural produce, and where this is a fluid like olive-oil, he must pay dearly for the risks to which he submits his creditor.'[1] It was much more difficult to adulterate wheat and the interest was correspondingly lower. We should probably understand that the steward continued the process with the other debtors. These two examples are sufficient to indicate his general line.

8. The *master* was in an awkward position if the steward had been getting rid of usurious contracts. To repudiate him would be to declare himself an irreligious and oppressive man. The only thing to do was to make the best of the situation by praising the steward and thus endorsing his action. This would redound to his credit. It might be presumed that the steward had entered the usurious contracts without his knowledge and now he piously praised their cancellation. That the steward is called *dishonest* may be the master's protest against the way he had been deprived of his money in these transactions, or it may indicate his conviction that the steward had been dishonest from the beginning (1f.). If it is not a matter of usurious contracts, we must feel that the master appreciated that he had been outwitted by a smart rogue and paid his tribute to the wisdom, though not the morality, of the act. He did not say that he was pleased. He simply admired the astuteness of the steward while doubtless deploring its effect on himself. The worldly-minded (*sons of this world*) are wise by their own lights. *Cf.* Moffatt, 'the children of this world look further ahead, in dealing with their own generation, than the children of Light.' The *sons of light* are the servants of God. Well-intentioned as they are, they often lack the wisdom to use what they have as wisely as the worldly use their possessions for their very different ends.

9. Jesus adds the instruction to use *unrighteous mammon* wisely. *Mammon* is our transliteration of an Aramaic expres-

---

[1] J. D. M. Derrett, *op. cit.*, pp. 71f. He also points out that there are many parallels in Indian custom and he cites a rate of as much as 800% over six years and eight months for oils and wines, an annual rate of something over 100% (*ibid.*, p. 71).

sion, of uncertain derivation, which is used to denote money
or wealth generally. The adjective reminds us that all too
often this is acquired in unworthy ways. The exact expression
'the mammon of unrighteousness' does not seem to be paralleled elsewhere.[1] Jewish writings, however, do contain a contrast between 'false mammon' and 'true mammon',[2] which
indicates that possessions might be acquired honestly or the
reverse. Jesus' use of the term may imply that there is commonly some element of unrighteousness in the way men ac-
quire possessions. Jesus' followers must use their money for
their spiritual purposes just as wisely as the children of this
world do for their material aims. As our goal is 'treasure in
heaven', we should use money for purposes such as almsgiving. This will gain us friends and it will stand us in good
stead when money *fails*, *i.e.* when we die and money is of no
more use. The meaning of *they may receive you into the eternal
habitations* (*cf.* Jn. 14:2) may be that the friends thus made will
welcome us in heaven. More probably we have a common
Jewish use of the plural to mean 'God' in accordance with a
tendency to avoid use of the divine name (SB). It is God who
receives men into heaven.

ii. God and mammon (16:10–13).

Jesus takes men's
attitude to money as a means of teaching the lesson that
discipleship must be whole-hearted.

10. First the principle is laid down. Faithfulness is no
accident: it arises out of what a man is through and through.
What a man does with the small things of life he does also
in the big things. His faithfulness or his dishonesty appears
throughout. Life is a unity.

11, 12. Jesus contrasts *the unrighteous mammon*, earthly
riches, with *the true riches*, the heavenly riches that God alone
can give. In accordance with the principle laid down in the
previous verse the man who uses his money in the wrong way
shows himself unfitted to handle more important things. He
must not be surprised if God keeps them from him. The same
truth is put in a highly paradoxical way. We would say that,

[1]*SJ*, p. 293.
[2]*TDNT*, iv, pp. 388ff.

249

if we are not faithful in our own things, we are not fit to handle those of others. Jesus reverses this. The money we think we own is not really ours. It is always what we have from God (1 Ch. 29:14) and we are no more than stewards of it. We cannot take it with us when we die. If we handle it badly we show that we are unfitted to use the true heavenly riches which will otherwise be given us as our permanent possession (*cf.* Mt. 25:34).

13. *Servant* is a household slave and *serve* (*douleuein*) means 'serve as a slave'. Nobody can be a slave to two masters at once. He may try, but only one will get his full devotion. So is it with *God* and *mammon*. A man can devote himself whole-heartedly to the service of either, but not both (*cf.* Col. 3:5).

iii. The covetous Pharisees (16:14, 15). This sharp anti-thesis did not please the Pharisees. The covetous like to disguise their sin and see their money as evidence of the blessing of God on their activities. So the Pharisees *scoffed*. Jesus contrasts the outward justification before men (which was all that the Pharisees could rise to) with the state of heart. *God knows your hearts* ('sees through you', NEB) is a frightening prospect for the lovers of money. The corollary of this is that what pleased the Pharisees so much and which men in general admire is no more than *an abomination in the sight of God*.

iv. The law and the prophets (16:16, 17). The coming of Jesus marked a watershed. Up till then God's revelation had been made in *the law* (strictly the books Genesis to Deuteronomy) *and the prophets*. The combined expression stands for the whole Old Testament. This operated right up to the time of John the Baptist. Conzelmann places great significance on this passage. He sees 'the period of Israel' as lasting up to this point, including John's ministry. He puts more stress on this than Luke's words require, but there is an undoubted emphasis on the new state of affairs brought about by Jesus' coming. Now *the good news of the kingdom of God is preached*. The kingdom is Jesus' favourite topic of teaching (see on 4:43). It stands for the rule of God in all of life. There is a problem with the phrase *every one enters it violently*. Some see the meaning as 'every one treats it violently', but this seems unlikely. There may be the thought of pressing into the kingdom 'with the greatest earnestness, self-denial and determination, as though with spiritual violence' (Geldenhuys). Or Jesus may mean that those pressing into the kingdom must be at least as much in earnest as the violent men of Palestine who tried to bring in the kingdom by force of arms. In the context we may think of men like the astute steward. When they see the value of entrance to God's kingdom they are ready to force their way in, in contrast to the Pharisees who did not make use of their opportunity. Knox translates, 'all who will, press their way into it'.

17. It might be thought then that the Law was over and done with. Jesus however assures His hearers that it does not lack fulfilment. It outlasts *heaven and earth*. Jesus never cast doubt on the validity of the Law. It was the way it was interpreted, particularly by the Pharisees, that drew His criticism. The *dot* was the tittle, a small projection on some Hebrew letters. Its use indicates that the Law will be fulfilled right down to the minutest particular.

v. Divorce (16:18). This saying finds its place here apparently because it helps us see from another angle the place of the Law. The Law allowed men to divorce their wives (Dt. 24:1ff.), though women could not divorce their husbands. Some of the Pharisees were very permissive, allowing men divorce on the most trivial grounds. Thus Hillel thought it enough if a wife spoiled her husband's dinner and Akiba went so far as to permit divorce if the man found someone prettier than his wife (*Gittin* 9:10). This was to make a mockery of the Law. Jesus taught that the aim of the Law was not divorce. God instituted marriage so that the two should become one (Gn. 2:24). Divorce was no more than a provision for man's 'hardness of heart' (Mk. 10:5). Marriage was meant to be a life-long union. Thus the man who divorces his wife and remarries *commits adultery*, as does the man who marries a divorcee. Jesus is not here suggesting a law for society at large. He is saying that this is how God's people regard marriage. Some hold that He is making a public criticism of Herod Antipas, who had divorced the daughter of Aretas and married the divorcee Herodias. He was thus guilty on both counts. Jesus' words certainly apply to Herod, but it is difficult to think that they were aimed primarily at him.

vi. The parable of the rich man and Lazarus (16:19–31). This parable is peculiar to Luke. Many see it as an adaptation of a popular folk-tale, perhaps originating in Egypt, which contrasted the eternal fates of a bad rich man and a virtuous poor man (see Creed). If Jesus has taken over a popular tale, He has given it a stamp of His own. As it stands it marks the contrast with the attitude inculcated in the parable of the unrighteous steward. Perhaps we can go further back and say that this chapter challenges the elder son of the previous parable and with him all the respectable to act in the spirit of the unrighteous steward. They should repent and then help others with their money. The alternative is to use their money in such a way as to secure eternal condemnation.

19. Jesus pictures a rich man. *Purple* was cloth dyed with a very costly dye (obtainable from the shellfish murex). It would be used for the outer garment and the *fine linen* for the undergarment. The combination stands for the ultimate in luxury. *Feasted* (*euphrainomenos*) sounds the note of happiness, for the same verb is used of merriment in 12:19; 15:23, 32. This man had all he asked in life and lived a life of enjoyable ease. He is not said to have committed any grave sin, but he lived only for himself. In that lay his condemnation.

20, 21. In contrast is the *poor man*, called *Lazarus* (*i.e.* Eleazar; the name means 'God has helped' and may be significant; certainly man did not help this unfortunate). This is the only character given a name in Jesus' parables. Sometimes the rich man is called 'Dives', but this is simply the Latin for 'rich man'. Lazarus lay at the *gate* of the other, the word denoting a large gate or portico like that of a city or a palace. The house was a grand one. *Full of sores* points to physical misery and this is emphasized with the detail that the pariah dogs licked his sores. His destitution comes out in the information that he *desired to be fed* (not necessarily was fed) *with what fell from the rich man's table*. The one man had all he wanted; the other had nothing.

22. Nothing has been said about the religious state of either. But Lazarus was evidently a faithful servant of God, for when he died the angels took him to *Abraham's bosom*. The expression is not common, but plainly it denotes felicity. Some see in it the relationship of child to parent (*cf.* Jn. 1:18). But it gives a better antithesis to the table at the opening of the story to see Lazarus at table with Abraham (for seating at table see note on 14:7). The bliss of the saved is pictured as a great feast in which the favoured one reclines with his head on the bosom of the great patriarch (in the manner of Jn. 13:23; *cf.* Mt. 8:11). There is no corresponding joy for the rich man after his death.

23. *Hades* is normally a colourless term. It signifies the abode of all the departed, whether good or bad. In the New Testament, however, it is never used of the saved. Here it seems to be equivalent to Gehenna, the place of punishment, for the rich man was *in torment*. Not only so, but he was able to see Lazarus and to note his felicity.

24. The rich man's attitude to the great patriarch is deferential, for he addresses him as *Father Abraham* and words his request humbly enough. But there is a note of unconscious arrogance in his attitude to Lazarus, for he assumes that he can have the poor man sent across to do him a service (unless his words mean no more than that he was ready to accept the slightest alleviation from any source). He has not realized that earth's values no longer apply.

25, 26. Abraham gives a reasoned refusal of the request. His address, *Son*, is tender. But he points to a reversal. In life the rich man had had his good things. The adjective *your* is significant. He had had what he chose. He could have spent time with the things of God and delighted in the word of God. He could have engaged in almsgiving (Lazarus had been close enough!). For him *good things* had been purple and fine linen, daily merriment and feasting. He had chosen what he wanted as his good things and now he must abide by his choice. Lazarus had received *evil things*. In this case there is no 'his'. Lazarus had not been responsible for the evils he had suffered.

Now, Abraham points out, a different set of values operates.

The balance is redressed. Justice is done. And there is another factor, the *great chasm . . . fixed*. This is no doubt a pictorial detail, but it means that in the afterlife there is no passing from one state to the other (the Greek implies that this is the purpose and not simply the result of the great chasm). The rich man can know how it is with Lazarus (and vice versa), but there is no crossing the chasm on the part of either. Some Jewish writings speak similarly of a permanent separation in the afterlife, *e.g.* 1 Enoch, where interestingly the righteous have 'the bright spring of water' (1 Enoch xxii. 9).

27, 28. For the first time in the story the rich man shows some interest in others (though still not of the poor; he sticks to his own). He asks that his *five brothers* may be warned of what awaits them. Once again he assumes that Lazarus may be despatched on his errand: his deep-seated sense of superiority remains. He also implies that he had not been treated fairly. If he had really been given all the information he needed, he would have acted differently. In contrast is Lazarus's impressive silence throughout the parable. He does not speak at all. He neither complains of his hard lot on earth, nor gloats over the rich man after death, nor expresses resentment at the latter's endeavours to have him sent on errands. Throughout he accepts what God sends him.

29-31. Abraham points to the Scriptures. *Moses*, of course, means 'the writings of Moses', and the combination with *the prophets* points to the whole of Scripture, as in verse 16. The Bible, reasons Abraham, gives the brothers all they need. There is an implication that the rich man's unpleasant situation was due not to his riches (after all, Abraham had been rich), but to his neglect of Scripture and its teaching. But the rich man does not agree. He knows how he had reacted to the possession of the Bible. So he says that *if some one goes to them from the dead* things will be different. That will bring them to repentance. Such is the fallacy of the natural man. The parable concludes with Abraham's solemn affirmation that the appearance of one risen from the dead will bring no conviction to those who refuse to accept Scripture. 'If a man (says Jesus) cannot be humane with the Old Testament in his hand and Lazarus on his doorstep, nothing — neither a visitant from the other world nor a revelation of the horrors of Hell—will teach him otherwise.'[1] In the context the one risen from the dead must be Lazarus. But Luke's readers could scarcely help thinking of Jesus. He rose. But those who refused to see Him in the Scriptures and to heed what is written refused to be convinced by One risen from the dead.

p. Teaching about service (17:1-10)

In this chapter connections between the various paragraphs are not obvious. It is possible that Luke has gathered fragments of Jesus' teaching too valuable to be lost, but of which he did not know the historical context. On the other hand a connection may be present, as is indicated in the notes. At the very least this may show why Luke put the teaching in this order.

i. Forgiving others (17:1-4). The connecting link here may be that of the attitude of the religious leaders. They were in danger of using their wealth wrongly, and they were also in danger of leading their lesser brethren astray. The temptation would be present to *his disciples* as well as to people like the Pharisees. The saying begins with the inevitability of *temptations to sin*. The word *skandala* is perhaps not quite as specific as this translation. It means the bait-stick of a trap, that which triggers off trouble (the corresponding verb is found in 7:23). Moffatt renders 'hindrances'. All hindrances to the spiritual life are included, but temptations to sin are clearly the worst of these. These are inevitable, but this does not mean that a man who causes them is blameless.

2. Jesus does not tell us what his fate will be. The 'woe' of the previous verse shows that it will not be pleasant and now we find that it would be better for him to be drowned here and now. A *millstone* was a heavy stone used for grinding grain. A horrible death is preferable to causing spiritual harm to even *one of these little ones*. This term may refer to infant believers, but it is also possible to see it as a description of believers of any age (*cf.* Mk. 10:24; Lk. 10:21), helpless as they are apart from God's aid.

3, 4. Far from bringing about sin, the follower of Jesus will

[1] A. M. Hunter, *Interpreting the Parables*, p. 84.

oppose it. When someone sins he will *rebuke him*. This does not
mean that he will adopt an attitude of censoriousness, for the
context stresses forgiveness. It means that, though he will be
compassionate, he will not be weak. He cannot be indifferent
to evil, but this does not mean that he will bear a grudge. If the
offender repents, the believer must *forgive him*. And his forgiveness must be without limit. When Jesus speaks of *seven times in
the day* He does not, of course, mean that an eighth offence
need not be forgiven (*cf.* Mt. 18:21f.). He is saying that
forgiveness must be habitual. From the world's point of view a
sevenfold repetition of an offence in one day must cast doubt
on the genuineness of the sinner's repentance. But that is not
the believer's concern. His business is forgiveness.

ii. Faith (17:5, 6). Apparently the apostles think a lot of
faith is needed to forgive like that. So they say, *Increase our
faith*. This could possibly mean, 'Give us also faith' (Barclay),
i.e. 'Give us faith in addition to other gifts'. But probably RSV
is right. The apostles want more faith. Jesus' answer turns them
from the thought of a less and a more in faith to that of its
genuineness. If there is real faith, then effects follow. It is
not so much great faith in God that is required as faith in a
great God. The *mustard seed* was proverbial for its small size.
It is uncertain what tree the *sycamine* was, but most think of the
black mulberry. Whatever it was, the rabbis held that its roots
would remain in the earth for six hundred years (SB). Clearly
it was held to be very firmly rooted, so that removing it would
be very difficult. Jesus is not suggesting that His followers occupy themselves with pointless things like transferring a tree
into the sea. His concern is with the difficulty. He is saying that
nothing is impossible to faith: 'genuine faith can accomplish
what experience, reason, and probability would deny, if it is
exercised within God's will' (Miller).

iii. Unprofitable servants (17:7-10). When men have
such faith they may be tempted to spiritual pride. Jesus
inculcates humility by referring to standard practice with
slaves. At the end of the day's work the master does not call
the slave to have dinner (though our Master does that and
more! 12:37; 22:27). Rather he calls on the slave to serve him
while he eats. And he does not thank the slave for doing what
he is told (9). That is no more than his duty. So with God's

servants ('slaves'). We are required to be perfect (Mt. 5:48). Whenever we complete a task we cannot claim that we have done more than we should. *Unworthy* (*achreioi*) is a difficult word, but it seems to mean 'not yielding gain' (*cf.* its use of the man who hid his talent, Mt. 25:30). Our best service does not give us a claim on God (*cf.* 1 Cor. 9:16). At best we have done only *what was our duty*. In the same spirit Rabbi Johanan b. Zakkai is reported to have said, 'If thou hast wrought much in the Law claim not merit for thyself, for to this end wast thou created' (*Aboth* 2:8).

q. The ten lepers (17:11–19)

11. It is not easy to see why Jesus should have been *passing along between Samaria and Galilee* at this stage of the narrative (see on 9:51). The words denote a journey in the border area between the two provinces. AV has 'through the midst of Samaria and Galilee', but that order points to a journey in a northerly direction, whereas Jesus appears to be going the other way. The problem is posed by the fact that He seems to have reached Perea before this time. It may be that Luke is not placing everything in chronological sequence and that the story is that of an incident that took place earlier. Alternatively after a journey through Perea Jesus went back to this area again. Arndt points out that Jesus went to a town called Ephraim after the raising of Lazarus (Jn. 11:54), this being about twenty miles north of Jerusalem. He suggests that when the Passover approached Jesus continued in a northerly direction to join the Galilean pilgrims going up to Jerusalem and that this is where and when our incident is to be located. This is supported by the fact that on His last trip to Jerusalem Jesus went by way of Perea (Mt. 19:1; Mk. 10:1), which would be the natural continuation of the journey Luke describes here. The suggestion cannot be proved, but there is nothing improbable about it.

12, 13. Luke does not tell us where this miracle took place, other than that it was at the entrance to *a village*. The *lepers* were compelled by law to keep their distance (see on 5:12) and these did. But they came as near as they dared and shouted an appeal for help. They did not ask specifically for healing, but simply for *mercy*. However, in the circumstances, there could be little doubt as to the direction in which they hoped that mercy would operate.

14. Apparently Jesus did not see them at first, but when He did He responded. He did not come to them or touch them. He did not even say, 'You are cured!' He told them, leprous as they were, to go and show themselves to the priests. This was the normal procedure when a leper was cured. The priest acted as a kind of health inspector to certify that the cure had in fact taken place (Lv. 14:2ff.). Jesus was putting their faith to the test by asking these men to act as though they had been cured. And as they obeyed so it happened: *as they went they were cleansed*.

15, 16. The cure immediately awoke a chord of gratitude in one of the ten. He did not wait to be certified fit to rejoin the community, but returned to Jesus when he saw that he was cured. His *praising* of *God* shows that he saw the hand of God in the cure and that he was ready to let everybody know about it. When he came to Jesus he acted with humility, prostrating himself in lowly homage as he thanked the Master. Luke now adds the information that *he was a Samaritan*. Normally Jews and Samaritans had little to do with one another and it is a mark of the horror of leprosy that those suffering from this disease had lived together, ignoring distinctions they would otherwise have seen as compelling. It might have been expected that this Samaritan would have been the last to give thanks to a Jewish healer. Luke notes that he was the first, and evidently the only one. If men do not give thanks quickly, they usually do not do so at all.

17, 18. In a series of questions Jesus expresses disappointment in the nine. All were cleansed and had an equal motive for gratitude. It might have been expected that all would *give praise to God*. But apparently the nine were so absorbed in their new happiness that they could not spare a thought for its source. The one exception was *this foreigner*, a man who did not even belong to the chosen people. His behaviour shows up that of the healed Jews.

19. Jesus had a word of encouragement for the man who came back. He told him to get up and go on his way and assured him that his faith had *made* him *well*. Presumably the nine had faith also, for this was the common (though not invariable) prerequisite of Jesus' miracles. But certainly this Samaritan had faith and he had gratitude. It is possible that we should take the verb to mean more than cure: it is literally 'has saved you'. It may be that Jesus recognized in this man the attitude that brings salvation and sent him off with the assurance that it was well with his soul as it was with his body. Full restoration means a saved soul as well as a sound body.

r. The coming of the kingdom (17:20–37)

Luke has here some sayings peculiar to this Gospel and some shared with Matthew 24. The passage stresses the certainty of judgment and the importance of being prepared.

20, 21. The Pharisees may have asked their questions out of a genuine interest in the subject. Or, since they knew Jesus often spoke of the kingdom, they may have been interested in finding out His views on the point. Jesus' reply makes it clear that the kingdom is unlike any kingdoms with which the Pharisees were familiar. Its coming cannot be observed. It is *in the midst of you* (*entos humōn*), an expression for which a number of meanings have been suggested. *a.* The kingdom is essentially inward. But this would be unparalleled in the Gospels (though *cf.* Rom. 14:17). *b.* The words prophesy the way the kingdom will come: 'The kingdom will suddenly appear among you.' This is possible, but the words in that case bear a somewhat unnatural sense. *c.* The kingdom is 'within your reach', *i.e.* it is attainable if you go the right way about it. But Jesus usually regards the kingdom as God's gift, not man's attainment. *d.* The kingdom is 'among you', *i.e.* it is present in the Person and ministry of Jesus. This seems the way the words should be taken.

22. Jesus now speaks *to the disciples* on the future of the kingdom. Men cannot control it. They may desire to see it, but they will not succeed. *The days of the Son of man* is not a self-explanatory expression. It may be a designation of the times of the Messiah (so SB). Some think that in later years the disciples will look back and long for one of the days when Jesus was with them. Or they may look forward to heaven and long for one of the days with Him there. Bengel thinks of the days preceding the coming of the Lord and he cites 9:51 for a similar construction, 'the days . . . for him to be received up' (on verse 26). In addition it is possible to take *one* as a Semitism with the meaning 'first' (as in Jn. 20:1). In that case the words point to the inauguration of the Messianic era, the second coming. On the whole it seems best to take it of the times of the Messiah. Men will long for the Messianic kingdom.

23–25. People will think they see the coming of the Son of man and will call on the disciples to see it their way too. The implication is that the kingdom is present in some secret, unexpected way. Jesus flatly rejects this. Such peering into corners will not be necessary, for when the Son of man comes His coming will be as obvious as the lightning. In any case other things must happen first. Immediately ahead is something very different: His suffering and rejection at the hands of *this generation*.

26, 27. Till the Son of man comes life will continue normally. It will all be like the times of Noah. Noah's contemporaries were sinful men, but it is not this that Jesus stresses. There is nothing sinful about the activities He lists; they are the stuff of ordinary human life. But that is just the point. Those men of old were so taken up in the ordinary affairs of life that they took no notice of Noah. The result was that they were overtaken in the destruction that they might have avoided.

28, 29. A similar warning is drawn from Lot's experience. In his day, too, people went on with the business of living and took no heed to his example and teaching. But the fact that they ignored the man of God did not bring them exemption from the judgment of God. One day God brought Lot out of the city and that day Sodom was destroyed. T. W. Manson reminds us that neither Noah nor Lot was a 'paragon of the virtues'. But 'both realised that the catastrophe must come, and both took means to save themselves. The Christian message is not for those who think that they deserve a better fate than their neighbours, but for those who, in the midst of universal indifference and complacency, realise the desperateness of their situation, and ask, "What must I do to be saved?" '[1]

[1] *SJ*, p. 144.

30. Jesus applies this to *the day when the Son of man is revealed*. People will be condemned not because they are sinners above all sinners, but because they have been self-centred. Men like this are so taken up in their own concerns, in the ordinary business of life, that they have no time and no attention to spare for the warnings that come to them from God.

31. When that day comes the situation will be urgent. Jesus brings this out by speaking of two things men might be tempted to do. A man on a housetop might think of saving something from his house; a man in the field might turn back for a similar reason. These are natural and harmless acts. But in the day of the Son of man this kind of thing will be out of place. Then men must give their whole attention to the Son of man, not to their goods. The equivalent words in Matthew and Mark refer to flight at the fall of Jerusalem and some scholars hold that Luke has taken the saying out of its context and applied it to a situation where flight is impossible. But surely Luke was intelligent enough to see that! It is much better to hold that, whether Jesus uttered the words on more than one occasion or whether Luke is correctly applying them to another situation, they really do apply to the day when the Son of man comes. They inculcate a whole-hearted devotion to the Son of man uncomplicated by a desire for material possessions.

32. *Lot's wife* came as close to deliverance without achieving it as was possible. She was brought right out of the doomed city and set on the way to safety. But she looked back and lingered, evidently in longing for the delights she was leaving behind. In the process she was caught up in the destruction that overtook Sodom and she perished with the city (Gn. 19:26).

33. Jesus has already spoken about saving and losing the life (9:24, where see note). In this context the thought will be that the self-affirming life of the men of Noah's day and of Lot's day (26-29) will prove self-destroying when the Son of man comes. By contrast the man who is willing to lose his life now will save it then.

34, 35. That day will mean separation between those who are for the Son of man and those whose lives show that they are against Him. Physical proximity will mean nothing. Of two in one bed, one will be taken but not the other. Some translations read 'two men', presumably because in the Greek the masculine gender is used in both *one* and *the other*. But this gender would be employed also if the two were man and wife, for the man might be either (*cf.* 24:25). It is likely that man and wife are meant. Again, of two women grinding grain together one will be taken and the other left. Jesus does not explain what He means by *taken*, but evidently it means taken to be with Him (*cf.* 1 Thes. 4:17).

37. AV includes verse 36, but it has inferior MS attestation and most agree that it has been taken over from Matthew 24:40 (though some argue that a scribe may have omitted it on the grounds that a daytime activity is incompatible with the 'night' of verse 34). Jesus' hearers want to know where all this is to take place, but He does not answer directly. He seems to be citing a proverb setting out the truth that it is the dead body that attracts the vultures (so, as mg., rather than *eagles*; the Greek word could mean either, but eagles do not eat carrion nor congregate in flocks). Where the spiritually dead are found, there inevitably will there be judgment.

s. Two parables about prayer (18:1–14)

i. The parable of the unjust judge (18:1–8). Jesus is not, of course, likening God to an unrighteous judge. The parable is of the 'How much more . . .' variety. If a wicked man will sometimes do good, even if from bad motives, how much more will God do right.

1. There is no indication of time, but the last chapter is concerned with the second advent and *told them* may indicate the same audience. The story relates to prayer in the long interval (there is a similar link between prayer and the parousia in 21:36). When praying men see no sign of the answer they long for, it is easy for them to be discouraged. But they must pray on and not *lose heart*. Jesus' teaching goes beyond that of the Jews, who tended to limit the times of prayer lest they weary God.[1] Three times a day (on the model of Dn. 6:10) was accepted as the maximum.

[1] SB, i, p. 1036.

2, 3. A judge who *neither feared God nor regarded man* (contrast 2 Cor. 8:21) was controlled only by his own ideas and inclinations. The *widow* was almost a symbol of helplessness. She was in no position to bribe the judge and she had no protector to bring pressure to bear on him. She was armed with nothing but the fact that right was evidently on her side (she asked not for vengeance but for justice) and her own persistence.

4, 5. But what she had she used. Her persistence eventually wore the judge down. In the end he did as she asked for no higher motive than the desire to be rid of her. He did not want her to *wear* him *out*. The verb is a picturesque one meaning, literally, 'give a black eye'! Clearly it is used metaphorically here.

6, 7. Since even an unjust judge can sometimes do justice, much more must we expect that the righteous God will vindicate *his elect*. This word emphasizes His choice, though we should bear in mind that the elect are called for service. Often we speak as though the term was concerned exclusively with privilege. The elect *cry to him day and night*. They pray with unwearied persistence. They realize that they are in great need and they recognize that their one hope is in God. Earthly resource will not do. RSV may be right in translating *Will he delay long over them?* The meaning will then be that the elect will be vindicated very soon. But the Greek is difficult and it may be understood as AV, 'though he bear long with them'. In this case the thought is that God delays the vindication, probably for a gracious purpose in strengthening His own as they endure hardship. Some scholars think the *them* refers to the oppressors, as Moffatt, 'Will he be tolerant to their opponents?' But there is nothing in the Greek to correspond to 'opponents'. More plausible is the view that the words render a Semitic expression meaning 'He postpones His wrath', *i.e.* God's delay in vindicating the elect is in order to give men the opportunity to repent. Either way the delay is seen then as part of God's gracious purpose, but whether this is the purpose of strengthening the elect or of giving opportunity to the wicked to repent we cannot be sure.

8. Vindication will be done *speedily*, but we should understand this in terms of God's time (in which one day is as a thousand years and a thousand years as one day, 2 Pet. 3:8). Jesus is speaking of the certainty of speedy action when the time comes. When He asks whether the Son of man will *find faith on earth*, he is not suggesting that there will be no believers. He is saying that the characteristic of the world's people at that time will not be faith. Men of the world never recognize the ways of God and they will not see His vindication of His elect.

ii. **The parable of the Pharisee and the publican** (**18:9–14**). This parable follows as giving the spirit in which men should pray. It is also an emphatic repudiation of any suggestion that a man may be saved by acquiring merit. What the Pharisee said about himself was true. His trouble was not that he was not far enough along the road, but that he was on the wrong road altogether.

9, 10. Luke does not identify the recipients of the parable. The error denounced is typical of the Pharisees, but by no means confined to them. In *the temple* public prayers were offered, but men might also pray there privately, and this is evidently the case in the parable. The *Pharisee* was a religious man whom one would expect to find in these surroundings engaged in this activity. The *tax collector* was an unlikely candidate for religious exercises, being normally both dishonest and a betrayer of his own countrymen.

11, 12. The Pharisee *stood*, which was the normal posture for prayer (Mt. 6:5; Mk. 11:25). His prayer was uttered in a spirit of pride, but it seems that this kind of prayer was not unknown. For example, R. Nehunia used to pray,

> I give thanks to Thee, O Lord my God, that Thou hast set my portion with those who sit in the Beth ha-Midrash (House of learning) and Thou hast not set my portion with those who sit in (street) corners, for I rise early and they rise early, but I rise early for words of Torah and they rise early for frivolous talk; I labour and they labour, but I labour and receive a reward and they labour and do not receive a reward; I run and they run, but I run to the life of the future world and they run to the pit of destruction.[1]

[1]Talmud, *Berakhoth* 28b (Soncino translation).

The Pharisee in the parable speaks first of some vices from which he abstains and then of some pious practices in which he engages. The Law provided for but one fast, that on the Day of Atonement, so his fasting *twice a week* was a work of supererogation. The pious were in the habit of fasting more often than the Law required and fasting on Monday and Thursday is attested (*e.g. Taanith* 10a, 12a). The Pharisee also went beyond the Law's requirements in his tithing. The Law prescribed that certain crops be tithed (Dt. 14:22), but it was a Pharisaic practice to tithe even garden herbs (11:42). What this Pharisee said about himself was strictly true, but the spirit of his prayer was all wrong. There is no sense of sin nor of need nor of humble dependence on God. The Pharisee came short of congratulating God on the excellence of His servant, but only just. 'He glances at God, but contemplates himself' (Plummer). After his opening word he does not refer to God again, but he himself is never out of the picture.

13. The *tax collector* was clearly under great conviction of sin. Lifting up the eyes to heaven when praying was normal, but his sense of unworthiness prevented him from doing this. He kept beating his breast (the tense denotes continuous action), a sign of sorrow. His prayer is simple, *God, be merciful to me a sinner!* The verb *be merciful* is *hilasthēti*, 'be propitiated', 'let thine anger be removed'. Even as he looks for forgiveness he recognizes what he deserves. And he calls himself not 'a' but 'the' sinner. He, too, put himself in a class of his own, but how differently from the Pharisee! He has nothing to plead in extenuation. He can only throw himself on God's mercy. 'This publican was a rotter; and he knew it. He asked for God's mercy because mercy was the only thing he dared ask for.'[1]

14. His is the plea that is accepted. The tax collector went home *justified*, reckoned as righteous, 'acquitted of his sins' (NEB). This is a great Pauline word, seen here in the teaching of Jesus. The principle behind it all is that he *who exalts himself will be humbled*. No man has anything of which he can boast before God. By contrast, *he who humbles himself will be exalted* (*cf.* 14:11). The penitent sinner who humbly looks for God's mercy will find it.

[1] T. W. Manson, *SJ*, p. 312.

t. Jesus and the children (18:15–17)

After the long section from 9:51, in which there are practically no Marcan parallels, Luke now rejoins Mark.

15. We are not told who brought the children. We usually assume that it was the mothers, but the pronoun translated *them* is masculine and probably includes the fathers as well. We must take *touch them* in the sense 'lay his hands on them', a natural action in blessing. It is not clear why the disciples rebuked those who brought the children. They may have thought that Jesus was too busy or too tired to be bothered with children. Or they may have thought that children were too insignificant for the Master's notice, for it is a fact that few of the world's great religious teachers have been greatly concerned with children. Jesus is different.

16, 17. The Master *called* the children and made them welcome. He went on to point out that it is the childlike to whom *the kingdom of God* belongs. It is not a proud recital of virtues (*cf.* the Pharisee, 11f.) that brings men into the kingdom, but whole-hearted trust like that of a child. The negative is also true. Unless a man receives the kingdom *like a child* he will never enter it. Children show us the way in their utter dependence, their unworldliness, their openness, the completeness of their trust.

u. The rich young ruler (18:18–30)

18. Luke alone tells us that this man was *a ruler*. The term is a very general one and, according to Gerhard Delling, 'denotes Roman and Jewish officials of all kinds'. In this Gospel he sees the rulers as a group of people distinguished from the elders, scribes and high priests.[1] We cannot thus be specific and suggest for example that he was a ruler of the synagogue (in any case, as Matthew tells us that he was young, this is unlikely). But at least he was among the ruling classes. His greeting, *Good Teacher*, was not in use among the rabbis because it ascribed to man an attribute possessed only by God (according to Plummer there is not one example in the whole Talmud of a rabbi being addressed in this way). It was a piece of

[1] *TDNT*, i, p. 489.

thoughtless flattery. He proceeded to ask what he must do to get *eternal life*. He assumed that eternal life must be earned and that some work he was not at present doing was required.

19. Jesus proceeds to show the shortcomings in the young man's position. *No one is good but God alone* is not to be understood as a repudiation of the epithet *good* as applied to Himself. If that was His meaning, Jesus would surely have said plainly that He was a sinner. Rather He was inviting the ruler to reflect on the meaning of his own words. What he had just said had implications for the Person of Jesus. If He was good and if only God was good, as all rabbinic teaching agreed (see on verse 18), then the ruler was saying something important about Him. So far from repudiating the deity of Jesus, as some hold, the question seems to invite the young man to reflect on it.

There is probably also a further depth of meaning in Jesus' question (as scholars such as Caird and Ellis hold). Jesus invites the young man to reflect on what he was asking for himself. The eternal life he was seeking was life in the presence of the awe-ful purity of God. If he would only reflect on what that meant, he would surely see that he was totally unfitted for the blessing he sought. He would then cry out for mercy, not complacently seek reward. It is the tragedy of the young man that he did not see the drift of the comment, let alone respond to it.

20, 21. The ruler had asked what he should do, so Jesus answers in terms of doing. He directs him to the commandments. If he will not reflect on the implications of the goodness of God, perhaps he will think of how he stands over against the demands of the law? When a man takes seriously the requirements of the law he is on the way to coming to Christ (Gal. 3:24). Jesus quotes five commandments dealing with our duty to our fellowmen, but none with that to God. He will bring that out in another way. The young man sees nothing new in the commandments and he is sure he has kept them ever since he was a boy. The rabbis held that the law could be kept in its entirety, and for example R. Eliezer could ask, 'Akiba, have I neglected anything of the whole Torah?' (*Sanhedrin* 101a). The young man's claim was thus not outlandish, even if superficial.

It showed that he had not thought deeply enough about what keeping the commandments meant.

22. The ruler had not reflected on what God's goodness meant, nor had he measured himself against God's commandments closely enough to see his failure to reach God's standards. Now Jesus issued a challenge which showed that he came short of what was required. But the call to give everything away was more than simply a dramatic challenge: it showed that the man had not understood the commandments he professed to have kept. The first of them enjoins the worship of one God. But when he was faced with the choice he found that he could not serve God by parting with his money. It was not really God that had first place in his heart.

23-25. Luke does not actually say that the young man refused, only that he *became sad*. But the refusal to rise to the challenge is implied. Jesus went on to point out that it is *hard* for the rich to enter the kingdom. The affluent are always tempted to rely on things earthly and they do not find it easy to cast themselves on the mercy of God (contrast verse 13). The same is true, of course, of those whose riches are other than material, the intellectually outstanding, those rich in moral or artistic achievement and the like. Such always find it difficult to rely on God rather than on their own efforts. Attempts have been made to explain Jesus' words about the *camel* and *the eye of a needle* in terms of a camel shuffling through a small postern gate, or by reading *kamilon* 'cable' for *kamēlon*, 'camel'. Such 'explanations' are misguided. They miss the point. Jesus is using a humorous illustration.

26, 27. All this represents a reversal of accepted ideas. It was commonly held that riches were a sign of God's blessing, so that the rich man had the best opportunity of the good things of the next world as of this. So Jesus' hearers ask, *Then who can be saved?* They do not ask, 'What rich man?' but, 'Who (of any kind)?' If the rich with all their advantages can scarcely be saved, what hope is there for others? Jesus makes it clear that there is none. But what man cannot do God can. Salvation, for rich or poor, is always a miracle of divine grace. It is always God's gift.

28–30. This leads Peter to say, *we have left our homes and followed you*. Some take Jesus' reply as humorous: 'Whimsically Jesus promises that those who have left home and family for the service of the kingdom will find themselves caring for a far bigger family than the one they left' (Caird). Most, however, take the words to mean that God is not under obligation to any man. If a man gives up anything for God he will be repaid *manifold more in this time*, to say nothing of *eternal life* in the coming age. It would be quite out of harmony with this whole passage to understand these words to mean that men may follow Jesus with a view to worldly benefits. If gain is their motive they have not begun to understand what discipleship means. They must renounce all worldly things. But that does not mean that God will bless them grudgingly. Where there is the genuine spirit of self-sacrifice, there God supplies all His servant needs (*cf.* Phil. 4:19). Ryle thinks we should take the words in a spiritual sense, for 'The wisdom of God is sometimes pleased to allow a converted man to be a loser in temporal things by his conversion.'

v. Another prophecy of the passion (18:31–34)

This is often spoken of as Jesus' third prediction of His suffering, but it is in fact the seventh that Luke records, following others in 5:35; 9:22, 43–45; 12:50; 13:32f.; 17:25.

31. Luke does not tell us when these words were spoken. He simply gives the prophecy, and he includes the assurance that *everything that is written of the Son of man* will be fulfilled. The purpose of God will be worked out. In the end it is not what men please but what God pleases that will be done.

32, 33. Jesus speaks of being *delivered to the Gentiles*, the first time this note has been sounded. He does not specifically refer to crucifixion, but He does refer to insult and injury and death. He does not leave it at that, however, but goes on to speak of rising again on the third day. The passion is not defeat but victory.

34. On the other side of the cross such sayings must have been very difficult. The disciples did not understand. Jesus said many paradoxical things and they probably reasoned, 'He cannot mean that He will literally die and rise. This must be something like the dying in order to live that He demands of us' (*cf.* 17:33). It took the cross and the empty tomb to make them understand. For the present *this saying was hid from them*, which may mean that they were prevented from understanding. If so, the thought will be that their failure to grasp it had its place in God's purpose.

w. A blind man receives sight (18:35-43)

Matthew speaks of two blind men being healed as Jesus went out of Jericho (on which Farrar remarks that it is unlikely that a blind man would have been quite alone). Mark has one blind man, whom he names as Bartimaeus, healed as Jesus went out of this city. Luke does not name the man and he locates the miracle at Jesus' entry into the city. There is little doubt that all three refer to the same incident, but with our present information it may be impossible to give a satisfactory explanation of these differences. Some think there were two blind men of whom Bartimaeus was the more prominent or the better known in the church. It is also pointed out that there were two Jerichos, the old one, famous in the Old Testament, and the new one established nearby by Herod the Great. Some hold that the healing took place as Jesus was leaving one city and entering the other.

35-37. Jesus' journey took him to Jerusalem by way of Jericho, a city near the Jordan and about 700 feet below sea level. As He neared the city the crowd with Him attracted the attention of a blind man who inquired about the excitement and was told, *Jesus of Nazareth is passing by*.

38, 39. Luke does not tell us how the blind man might have expected that Jesus would help him. Evidently His reputation had preceded Him. The blind man seized his chance and called on Jesus as *Son of David*, the only one in this Gospel to address Jesus in this way (the expression is found also in 20:41; Mark has a similar usage, but the title is used more often in Matthew). The title is Messianic and Jesus' healing of the man in response to its use looks like an acceptance of its implications. In that case He admitted His Messianic destiny as He went up to Jerusalem where He was shortly to die as

Messiah (*cf.* 22:67ff.). The blind man was persistent, for when he was told to desist *he cried out all the more*. He was not half-hearted; he would not forgo his opportunity.

40, 41. Jesus did not let his plea go unheeded. He had the man brought before Him and asked what he wanted. So far the man had simply requested mercy, and mercy might take any one of a number of directions. Asked to put his desire into words, the man crystallized his longing, *Lord, let me receive my sight*.

42, 43. Matthew tells us that Jesus touched the men's eyes, but Luke records no action. He mentions only the healing words, to which Jesus added, *your faith has made you well*. This does not mean that the man's faith created the cure, but that it was the means by which he received it. When he got his sight he followed Jesus, *glorifying God*. Jesus did not fasten attention on Himself, but turned men to the Father, and this is seen again in the reaction of the people who saw the miracle. They, too, gave praise to God.

x. Zacchaeus (19:1–10)

The story of Zacchaeus stands in marked contrast to that of the rich young ruler. Coming so soon after the emphatic statement about the difficulty of the salvation of the rich (18:24f.), this incident must be seen as a striking manifestation of God's grace (18:27).

1–3. Evidently Jesus did not intend to make a stay in Jericho. He was just *passing through*. But this gave Zacchaeus the opportunity of seeing Him. The name is Hebrew with the meaning 'pure' or 'righteous'. The man is unknown to us apart from this incident. He was not simply a tax collector like others we have met in this Gospel (see on 3:13; 5:27), but *a chief tax collector* (*architelōnēs*). This title is not found anywhere else, so its precise significance is not known, but it seems to point to the head of the local taxation department. Zacchaeus would employ others to do the actual collecting of the taxes, while he passed on what the Romans required. Jericho must have been a good spot for a tax man. An important trade-route from Jerusalem to the East passed by it, and it was the centre

of a good deal of local wealth, as, for example, from the
famous balsam groves that abounded. It is no surprise that
Zacchaeus was *rich*. In this spot with this occupation he could
scarcely be anything else. But he must have been unpopular
and would have had little social life. This man heard of Jesus
and wanted to see Him. But he had a problem, for he was
small of stature. He could not see over people's heads, and few
would make room for such an unpopular man.

4. But Zacchaeus was clearly a man of resource (he had not
become chief tax collector for nothing), and he was untroubled
by any concern for dignity. So he ran on ahead and *climbed
up into a sycamore tree*. This was a tree 'very closely related to the
mulberry. It certainly is an easy tree to climb and is often
planted by the roadside'.[1] Thus ensconced, he was in a good
position to see the Teacher from Nazareth as He passed by.

5, 6. But Jesus did not pass by: He stopped and called
Zacchaeus down. He did not say, 'I would like to stay at your
house', but *I must stay*. This is a strong expression. Jesus saw
His visit to Zacchaeus as part of His divine mission. Zacchaeus
responded with alacrity. He descended from the tree quickly
and received Jesus *joyfully*.

7. The crowd disapproved and Luke's *all* shows that the
disapproval was general. *Murmured* refers to the low muttering
that goes through a crowd when it is complaining. They
'grumbled'. They condemned Zacchaeus out of hand as *a
sinner* and they criticized Jesus for being the guest of such a
man.

8. *And* should rather be 'But' (*de*). Zacchaeus is set in
contrast to the grumblers. He *stood*, which may mean that he
took up his stance. There is a note of formality about it
which fits the important announcement Zacchaeus was about
to make. He proceeded to give striking evidence of what Jesus'
visit had done for him by announcing the gift of half his goods
for the poor and a fourfold restitution to any he had defrauded.
Where voluntary restitution was made the Law required no
more than the original amount plus one fifth (Lv. 6:5;

[1] W. E. Shewell-Cooper, *Plants and Fruits of the Bible*, p. 120.

Nu. 5:7), so that Zacchaeus was cheerfully agreeing to do more than was necessary. He was doing what was laid down for theft with killing or selling of an animal (Ex. 22:1; 2 Sa. 12:6; there is mention of sevenfold restitution in Pr. 6:31, but it is not clear that this was ever required). Josephus speaks critically of Herod for selling thieves abroad and he says that 'the laws' require no more than a fourfold fine (*Antiquities* xvi. 1–3). Zacchaeus's *if I have defrauded* implies that this was indeed the case. Considering the way he had made his money it was unlikely that this would be a short list. Notice that he uses the present tense in his verbs. He is so firm in his resolve that he says he is about his giving already. NEB's 'I am ready to repay' misses this.

9, 10. Jesus' reply makes it clear that Zacchaeus has been saved, but there are problems in detail. *Salvation has come to this house* must refer primarily to the tax collector, but the household is not overlooked. *A son of Abraham* will mean a true Jew, one who follows the faith of Abraham (*cf.* Rom. 4:12), and not simply a lineal descendant of the patriarch. All Jews could claim this, but not all Jews were saved. There may possibly also be a reference to Zacchaeus as a true member of Abraham's family against slanders that he was a renegade. Jesus adds that He had come *to seek and to save the lost*. This incident shows this plainly. Jesus sought Zacchaeus. He made the contact, not Zacchaeus. That man was certainly among the lost. But Jesus did not leave him there. He saved him.

y. The parable of the pounds (19:11–27)

There are resemblances between this story and the parable of the talents in Matthew 25. Some see these as variants of one original, but the differences make this hazardous (see the discussion in Arndt). It is more likely that Jesus made more than one use of the basic idea. In Matthew He is concerned with men of different abilities to whom are assigned tasks according to their capacities. The sums are large and represent the discharge of serious and important tasks. Here the sums are small and the same amount is given to all. The servants are being tested to see whether they are fit for larger tasks. The Matthean parable reminds us that we all have different gifts, the Lucan that we all have one basic task, that of living

out our faith. The Matthean story concentrates on the servants
and their trading, but Luke has references to a nobleman
receiving a kingdom and the attitude of his subjects. Some hold
that this means a conflation of two originally separate parables
either by Luke or his source. This is possible, but the parable
can be readily interpreted as it stands.

11. For some time Luke has been describing a journey to
Jerusalem (see on 9:51). Jericho is about seventeen miles from
Jerusalem, so the journey was nearly over. This led some to
think that the climax was at hand and that *the kingdom of God*
would *appear immediately*. The climax was indeed at hand,
but it would be of a very different kind from the one these
people imagined. The parable was to help put them right.

12. The *nobleman* going to *a far country to receive a kingdom*
reminds us irresistibly of a vassal making the pilgrimage to
Rome to be made king. Herod the Great had received his
kingdom that way. In his will he divided his realm between
three of his sons, all of whom in due course went to Rome to
press their claims. Archelaus had been left Judea with the title
king, but the people detested him and sent representatives to
ask that he be not given the kingdom. He had given them good
reason for hating him. At the first Passover after his accession,
for example, he had massacred about 3,000 of his subjects
(Josephus, *Bellum* ii. 10–13). He was a thoroughly bad ruler.
But the emperor confirmed him in the place of authority,
though he denied him the title 'king' until he should prove
worthy of it (which he never did). There would be special
fitness in an allusion to Archelaus in this region, for he had
built a magnificent palace in Jericho and also made an
aqueduct for irrigation purposes (Josephus, *Antiquities* xvii.
340). We should probably take the references to the kingdom
allegorically. Jesus was about to finish His course at Jerusalem
and that meant leaving this earth. But He would return in
due course, having been given the kingdom. The reference to
a far country shows that He cannot be expected to return very
soon.

13. The nobleman made arrangements for his business
affairs to be carried on during his absence by entrusting money
to *ten of his servants* (not slaves, for a slave would not have the

authority needed for the business transactions envisaged). *Pound* renders *mna*, a Greek coin worth a hundred drachmas (a drachma was a labourer's wage for a day's work). The servants were told to trade and evidently each had a pretty free hand, though they all knew that in due course they must give account of themselves.

14. The king motif reappears. The people subject to the nobleman did not like him, so they took what steps they could to prevent him from obtaining kingly authority. In the case of Archelaus they were justified, though unsuccessful. We cannot transfer this to the allegory, for Jesus is the perfect King and nothing can interfere with His Kingship. But we should not miss the point that men rebel against all He stands for.

15-19. The nobleman got his kingdom and came home. He now called his servants, who had been trading, to render their accounts. The first and second had gained 1,000% and 500% respectively. Neither claims credit, but each modestly ascribes the increase to the money the nobleman had left them, *your pound has made.* . . . Both are commended and promoted, being given cities in proportion to their profits. The reward is not rest, but the opportunity for wider service.

20, 21. Only one more servant is dealt with and we are left to imagine what happened to the other seven. But this is sufficient, as in the end there are only two classes: those who made good use of the money and those who did not. This third man did nothing with his pound but laid it away *in a napkin*. This did not comply even with the minimum requirements for safety which required burial in the earth (Talmud, *Baba Metzia* 42a). His declared motive was fear. He described his master as *a severe man*, using the adjective *austēros* whose meaning is ' "strict, exacting," a man who expects to get blood out of a stone' (MM). Taking up what one did not put down and reaping what one did not sow are evidently proverbial expressions for making gain through other people's efforts.

22, 23. The master made the servant's words the basis of his condemnation. If the servant really believed what he said about his master, he ought to have done something.

Without risk he could have put the money *into the bank*, where it would have earned interest. There were, of course, no banks in our sense of the term and the Greek means 'on the table', *i.e.* the table of the money-lender (in passing we notice that the English word 'bank' derives from 'bench', the money-lender's bench). It would have been possible to put the money to use, but the frightened servant did nothing.

24–26. So the money was taken from him and given to the man who had proved that he could make good use of it. It is not clear whether the listeners who interject (25) are Jesus' hearers or the other servants in the story. Nor is it quite certain whether the following words (26) are those of the nobleman or of Jesus. In either case they lay down the principle which the parable exemplifies. Jesus is not saying that the rich will get richer and the poor poorer. The words must be seen in their context. It is the man whose abundance shows that he has made good use of what he has who will get more. The man whose lack shows that, like the third servant, he has made no use of his opportunities will lose what little he has. *Cf.* 8:18. It may be objected that there was no point in giving one pound to a man who already had ten and also authority over ten cities. But there is a principle involved. The smallest gift must be put to good use. In the Christian life we do not stand still. We use our gifts and make progress or we lose what we have.

27. The story finishes on a note of frightening severity. Those who rejected the nobleman and sent their embassy after him (14) are not forgotten. Safely installed in his kingdom and with accounts with his trading servants finalized, the nobleman commands the destruction of those he calls plainly *these enemies of mine*. They have set themselves in opposition to him. They must take the consequences. T. W. Manson has possibly the best comment on this: 'We may be horrified by the fierceness of the conclusion; but beneath the grim imagery is an equally grim fact, the fact that the coming of Jesus to the world puts every man to the test, compels every man to a decision. And that decision is no light matter. It is a matter of life and death.'[1]

[1]*SJ*, p. 317.

z. The triumphal entry (19:28–44)

Strictly Luke does not tell of Jesus' entry to Jerusalem, triumphant or otherwise. But he does describe the approach, and the term 'entry' may be used without being misleading. Luke adds to what we read in the other Gospels by telling of Jesus' lament over the city.

i. The approach in triumph (19:28–40).

There is an audacity about this whole procedure. The authorities were hostile and had already given an instruction that anyone who knew where Jesus was should inform them so that He could be arrested (Jn. 11:57). But, far from hiding in fear, Jesus came to Jerusalem publicly and triumphantly. For the present His popularity among the people prevented action being taken against Him (48). But we should overlook neither the bitter hostility of the high-priestly party nor the courage manifested by Jesus and His friends.

28. Apparently Jesus took His departure from Jericho immediately after telling the parable just narrated. He strode on ahead of the disciples (just possibly the Greek means 'he went forward', as Leaney holds; but *cf.* Mk. 10:32). Luke tells us again that He was going *to Jerusalem* in keeping with the emphasis he has placed on the city as the object of the journey.

29. *Bethany* was a village about two miles from Jerusalem on the eastern slopes of the Mount of Olives. The location of *Bethphage* is not known for certain, but clearly it was nearby. In the Talmud it is apparently a suburb of Jerusalem, being regarded as the outer limit of the city. The Greek rendered *Olivet* may mean 'of olives' or 'Olive-Orchard' (Moffatt; the difference is only one of accent). *Olivet* is from the Latin *olivetum*, 'olive orchard'.

30, 31. Jesus instructs two of His disciples to go into a village and get a donkey for Him. He does not name the village and speaks of it only as *the village opposite*. Some hold it to be Bethphage, but we cannot be sure. There, Jesus said, *you will find a colt tied*. The word could denote the *colt* of a horse or of an ass and Luke never says which it is. Matthew and John, however, both make it clear that it was an ass, and in the LXX the word is regularly used without qualification to translate a Hebrew term meaning an ass. Luke is simply following LXX usage. He tells us that nobody had ever ridden it. The thought may be that the animal was thus unspoiled by previous use and was suitable for sacred purposes (cf. Nu. 19:2; 1 Sa. 6:7). Jesus adds the password to be used if anyone hinders them, *The Lord has need of it*. A problem is posed by the fact that it seems to be Jesus who needs the animal, but the expression 'the Lord' seems to have been used of Him very rarely if at all during His ministry. It is thus doubtful whether an unexplained reference to 'the Lord' would have been sufficient to indicate Jesus. Some think we should understand 'the Lord' to be God, *i.e.* the animal is needed in God's service. This is possible, but it is hard to see how the bystanders would have extracted this meaning from the words. Linguistically the expression could mean 'Its owner needs it'. This would be a possible meaning if there was one owner and he was with Jesus. But verse 33 shows that there were more owners than one and that they were with the ass, not Jesus. On the whole it seems best to understand the expression as a pre-arranged password. When the animal's owners heard these words they would know the ass was for Jesus and would let it go.

32-34. The disciples obeyed instructions and the colt's owners responded to the information that the Lord needed the animal. The plural, *its owners*, may point to poverty. Even so small an animal was shared.

35, 36. They put *their garments* on the animal, plainly as a kind of saddle. Luke does not say that Jesus mounted the colt, but that the disciples *set* Him on it. They took the initiative. They, or others, followed this up by spreading *their garments on the road*, thus making a triumphal carpet on which Jesus rode (cf. 2 Ki. 9:13). Luke says nothing about the spreading of branches as well, though all the other Evangelists mention this (John says they were palm branches).

37. *The whole multitude of the disciples* joined in the enthusiasm *at the descent of the Mount of Olives*. It was a happy scene as the disciples *began to rejoice*. They praised God *for all the mighty*

works that they had seen, *i.e.* those miraculous deeds that Jesus
had done throughout His ministry which showed so plainly
that He had come from God. Luke nowhere explains the
enthusiasm, but Matthew and John both quote the prophecy of
Zechariah 9:9 which speaks of Zion's king as coming on an
ass's colt. There can be no doubt but that the multitude saw
Jesus' entry to the city in the light of this prophecy and greeted
Him as king. Now a king on an ass was distinctive. The ass
was the mount of a man of peace, a merchant or a priest.
A king might ride an ass on occasion, but he would be more
likely to appear on a mighty warhorse. Zechariah's prophecy
saw Messiah as the Prince of peace. The Galilean disciples,
now streaming up to Jerusalem for the Passover, knew that
Jesus had done many mighty works. They had for a long time
watched and waited for Him to proclaim Himself as the
Messiah of their hopes. Now they saw Him as doing so. He was
riding into the capital in a way that fulfilled the prophecy.
He was showing Himself to be the Messiah. They did not stop
to reflect that He was also proclaiming Himself a man of
peace and giving no countenance to their nationalistic fervour.
They wanted a Messiah. And now they saw one.

38. All four Evangelists tell us that the crowd cried *Blessed*
and *he who comes in the name of the Lord* (*cf.* Ps. 118: 26), but only
Luke and John that they called Jesus *the King* (John adds 'of
Israel'). Mark refers to the kingdom but not the King. But,
expressed or not, this is implied. The crowd wanted to see the
Messiah claim His kingdom and their delighted delirium
arose from the fact that they saw Him as doing this. Luke
alone tells us that the acclamation included *Peace in heaven*
(*cf.* 2:14). 'God is reconciled to the human race' (Arndt), and
thus His glory is demonstrated. There may also be a reference
to the situation resulting from Satan's defeat (10:18). Luke
omits the foreign word 'Hosanna' (found in the other Gospels)
and substitutes *glory*.

39, 40. We owe to this Evangelist the information that some
of the Pharisees in the crowd (pilgrims from Galilee?) said,
Teacher, rebuke your disciples. They would have objected to the
enthusiasm on general principles and they certainly did not
want to see Jesus proclaimed as Messiah. They were not in
favour of the use of force unless the practice of their religion

was directly involved, and they would have opposed anything that might provoke Roman intervention. There was no hope of stilling the tumult by appealing to the people, so they ask Jesus to calm them down. In a striking saying Jesus affirms that the shouting is inevitable. If the people were to keep quiet *the very stones would cry out*, which may have been a proverbial saying (*cf.* Hab. 2:11).

ii. The lament over Jerusalem (19:41-44). This short section is peculiar to Luke. It shows that Jesus knew what the enthusiasm He was witnessing was worth. The words are taken by some scholars as a late composition, written after the destruction of the city, on the ground that they are too detailed **to** have been uttered in Jesus' time. But, setting apart for the moment the extent of Jesus' prophetic powers, there is nothing here that is not common to the siege techniques of the day and much that is already found in the Old Testament. There is no reason to be apprehensive about the authenticity of the paragraph. *Cf.* T. W. Manson: 'To describe these verses as a Christian composition after the event is the kind of extravagance that brings sober criticism into disrepute.'[1]

41, 42. The lament took place near the city, but Luke does not say precisely where. It forms a striking contrast to the joy of the crowd. *Wept* might be rendered 'wailed'. Jesus burst into sobbing. He lamented lost opportunity. The Jerusalemites did not know *the things that make for peace*. Especially important in the Hebrew understanding of *peace* (which carries over into the New Testament) is its emphasis on peace with God, right relationship between the creature and the Creator, as a necessary ingredient in true peace. It was this that the men of Jerusalem had failed to come to know. And their failure to get to grips with the message of God was now final. These things, Jesus says, *are hid from your eyes*.

43, 44. The destruction of the city is inevitable. Jesus describes a typical siege when He speaks of the *bank* the enemies would cast up (as a protection for themselves and a base from which they could launch their attacks) and of the city as being completely surrounded (*cf.* Is. 29:3). The word *charax*, rendered *bank*, means basically a stake (for example used for supporting vines). It comes to mean timber used in fortifying a camp. The singular here is collective and denotes a palisade encircling a city. Josephus tells us that when the Romans besieged Jerusalem they set up siegeworks (*Bellum* v.262, 264). There must have been a good deal of timber in them, for the Jews destroyed them with fire (*Bellum* v.469ff.; the Romans replaced them with a wall). Jesus says further that the enemy will *dash you to the ground, you and your children within you* (*cf.* Ps. 137:9). This means complete overthrow. Not only will the city be captured but it will be totally destroyed. The repetition of *you* (ten times in two verses) makes it all very personal. Jesus finishes with the reason, *because you did not know the time of your visitation*. This last word is quite general. It could mean any visit, for blessing or for cursing. But in the context there can be no doubt that it is the divine visitation in the presence of God's Messiah among them that the people had failed to know, 'God's moment', as NEB translates. There is an ignorance that is innocent, but there is also an ignorance that is culpable. These men had the revelation God had made known in the scriptures of the Old Testament. They had the continuing evidence that God was active in the life and ministry of Jesus. They could see in Him that God had not forgotten His people. There was every reason for them to have welcomed Jesus as His disciples did. But they refused to accept all this evidence. They rejected God's Messiah. They would now have to live with the consequences of their rejection. It is this that brought forth Jesus' tears.

VI. JESUS IN JERUSALEM (19:45 – 21:38)

We have nearly reached the passion narrative. After Jesus came to Jerusalem He continued to teach for a short time and Luke relates some of the things He said and did in those days. But all this is really no more than a prelude to the passion.

a. The cleansing of the Temple (19:45, 46)

All four Gospels have a story of Temple cleansing, though John places his at the beginning of Jesus' ministry, whereas the other three have it at the end. There is reason for thinking that there

were two cleansings.[1] Luke's account is the shortest of them all.
He follows the Marcan line, the only difference (as opposed to
omissions) being that where Mark has Jesus' words, 'My house
shall be called a house of prayer . . .' Luke has 'My house shall
be a house of prayer . . .'. Curiously Luke omits the words
'for all the nations', though they fit well with his universalism.
Perhaps he thought that the Gentiles would worship elsewhere
(*cf.* Jn. 4:21).

45, 46. From Mark we find that this incident took place on
the day following the triumphal entry (Mk. 11:11f., 15).
Jesus found traders in the Temple. Some were changing
money (only Tyrian coinage was accepted for the Temple
offerings, and other coins had to be changed into this currency);
others were selling sacrificial animals. They were apparently
plying their trade in the court of the Gentiles, the only place
in the Temple where a non-Jew could go to pray and to
meditate. If the Temple system was to carry on it was necessary
that such facilities be provided. But it was not necessary that
they be in the Temple precincts, and it is this to which Jesus
took exception. He *began to drive out those who sold*. Luke does not
mention those who bought nor the money-changers, but
Matthew and Mark tell us that He dealt with them as well.
Jesus upbraided the traders by pointing out the difference
between their dishonesty (*cf.* Je. 7:11) and the true nature of
the Temple as *a house of prayer* (*cf.* Is. 56:7).

b. Teaching in the Temple (19:47, 48)

During His time in Jerusalem Jesus taught daily in the usual
place for such activity, *the temple*. Luke tells us that His
enemies tried *to destroy him*. The scribes and the high priests we
have met before, but *the principal men of the people* is an intriguing
new expression. It indicates that Jesus was finding enemies
among the ruling classes generally. But, though there was
the will to take extreme measures on the part of His varied
enemies, there was not the opportunity. In the afterglow of the
triumphant entry the people at large were too fond of Jesus for
action to be taken against Him. Eagerly they listened to Him.

---

[1]See my commentary, *The Gospel according to John* (*New London Commentary*), pp. 188–191, and more fully in *Explorations, Ridley College Papers:
1971* (Melbourne, 1971), pp. 22–28.

c. Jesus' authority (20:1-8)

1, 2. The character of Jesus' teaching at this time appears in the reference to *preaching the gospel*. At the very time His enemies were plotting against Him, He was bringing God's good news to the people. He was interrogated by *the chief priests and the scribes with the elders*, which looks like an official inquiry from the Sanhedrin. Jesus' recent activities had not endeared Him to officialdom; so a deputation came to question Him. They were concerned with the authority under which He had acted. Their question refers quite generally to *these things*, but they were doubtless primarily concerned at the cleansing of the Temple. What authority could justify a man in acting like that? Perhaps He would say 'The authority of Messiah'. Then who had given Him that authority?

3, 4. Jesus countered with 'I will ask *you* for a statement' (Rieu). John the Baptist had been a considerable religious figure and it was legitimate to expect the ecclesiastical authorities to pronounce on the origin of his baptism. Moreover the answer to Jesus' question would have given the answer to theirs, for John had testified that He was the Messiah. But if they did not believe John's prophecy of the approaching kingdom, they could not be expected to hail its presence in Jesus.

5, 6. Jesus' question put His opponents on the horns of a dilemma. Interestingly they do not seem to have concerned themselves with the facts of the case. They concentrate on the effects, not the truth of the answers they see as possible. They had never accepted John's message. Accordingly to say that his baptism was of heavenly origin would be to leave them wide open, for if that were the case they should have believed him and have followed him enthusiastically. Had they done this they would have had the answer to their question, for they would have recognized that Jesus derived His authority from the same heavenly source as did John. There can be no doubt but that they would have liked to say, *From men*. That was what they believed. But John's popularity with the people made it an answer impossible to give. They feared being stoned.

7, 8. So they gave no answer. Accordingly Jesus gave none to them. He did not say that He had no authority. Throughout the whole of the four Gospels it is clear that He is very conscious of possessing the highest authority. But He will not speak about it to men who will not answer a plain question to which they know the answer.

d. The parable of the wicked husbandmen (20:9-18)

We should see this story as in part an allegorical setting out of Jesus' relationship to the Jewish leaders. He saw Himself as making God's last appeal to them. Systematically the religious leaders of the Jews have rejected God's messengers (*cf.* Ne. 9:26; Je. 7:25f.; 25:4-7; Mt. 23:34; Acts 7:52; Heb. 11:36-38). Now the climax is at hand. Not a prophet, but the Son of God is among them. They face the most critical decision of their lives.

9. Jesus describes what was evidently a quite common action on the part of a property owner. He *planted a vineyard* and *let it out* before going abroad. At the same time the language is reminiscent of Old Testament language about Israel (*cf.* Is. 5:1ff.). The *tenants* (*geōrgoi*) were 'farmers'.

10-12. In due course the owner sent a slave to collect the rent, which was evidently to be paid in kind. But, instead of paying what they owed, the farmers reacted with violence. Each slave who was sent was treated worse than the previous one, and none collected what was due. The farmers appear to us to have behaved unreasonably and outrageously. But J. Duncan M. Derrett thinks some reason can be given for their conduct.[1] He points out that a vineyard would produce very little revenue during the first few years, while the vines were establishing themselves. During this period it was even possible than an owner might on balance owe the tenants money. He would be responsible for expenses such as the purchase of stakes, which might conceivably exceed the income. If the tenants in this story were rejecting the owner's account and claiming that he owed them something, their ill-treatment of the messengers would be an emphatic registering of their protest. They sent them back 'empty' (so, rather than *empty-handed*), which may mean that they took what they could

---

[1] J. Duncan M. Derrett, *Law in the New Testament*, pp. 296ff.

from the slaves to go towards what they claimed from the
owner. This is possible, but there is no hint in Jesus' story
that the tenants were claiming anything. They simply rejected
the messengers. Jesus is picturing a nation which is obdurate
and a God who is compassionate in the face of unreasonable
truculence. Instead of punishing those who rejected the
prophets He gave them further opportunities by sending other
servants.

13. In real life *the owner* would surely have taken strong
action. He had the law on his side and he would have dealt
severely with the offenders. But Jesus is depicting a God who
loves beyond measure and is compassionate where He has
every right to be severe. So He speaks of the owner as thinking
the matter over and deciding to send his *beloved son* (language
which reminds us of the description of Jesus in 3:22). Perhaps
they will respect him. *It may be* translates 'an urbane expression
of one's reasonable hope' (GT).

14. But *the tenants* react unreasonably. They decide to kill
the heir (and thus go one worse than with any of the slaves).
Their idea is that the vineyard will then be theirs. There are
various possibilities here. They may have thought that the
landlord had died and that the son had come to take possession. Or the appearance of the son may have given them the
idea that the father had transferred title in the vineyard to the
son. Tenants were known to claim possession of land they had
worked for absentee landlords (Talmud, *Baba Bathra* 35b, 40b).
In a day when title was sometimes uncertain, anyone who had
had the use of land for three years was presumed to own it in
the absence of an alternative claim (Mishnah, *Baba Bathra*
3:1). The tenants were clearly relying on the fact that the
owner was a long way away (9). They seem to have thought
that with all the trouble the vineyard was causing him, he
would not bother to press his claim. They would claim that the
vineyard was theirs, as their occupation of it during the
preceding years, during which they had paid rent to no-one,
plainly showed. They would doubtless represent the killing of
the heir as self-defence. They were only repelling a robber who
had come to take their land from them. In such ways men
justify wrongdoing. The allegorical application shows that
Jesus knew what fate awaited Him. The nation was acting

towards Him in the same outrageous way as the tenants behaved towards the heir.

15, 16. The tenants carried out their plan. They threw the heir out of the vineyard and killed him. Derrett maintains that it was important that they did not kill him in the vineyard, for this would have defiled the ground with the corpse and made it more difficult for them to sell their produce. He thinks that Mark's account means that the murder was carried out in the 'tower', where the son could be cornered after his attendants were ejected. 'The death-blow would be delivered inside in the hope that the body could be carried alive as far as the wall.'[1] Luke gets the same effect with the death taking place outside the vineyard. But the tenants did not reckon with the determination of the owner. He would neither condone nor overlook this last deed. It must be punished. And since the crime was extreme, so would the punishment be. The tenants would be destroyed and the vineyard given *to others*. In the application this must refer to the Gentiles. But to Jesus' enemies it was unthinkable that the privileges of the Jews as God's chosen people could under any circumstances be given to the Gentiles. They interject, *God forbid!* (the only occurrence of this strong expression anywhere in the New Testament outside the Pauline writings). The words express their sense of outrage and horror as they break in, in the manner of the listeners in 19:25.

17. Jesus points them to Scripture. What is written there must be fulfilled. If the destruction of which He has spoken is not to occur, then how do they explain Psalm 118:22 (incidentally a favourite text in the early church; *cf.* Acts 4:11; 1 Pet. 2:7)? *The head of the corner* was clearly an important stone, but it is not certain where it was. It may have been a large stone set at a corner in the foundations. In this way it would determine the position of two walls and so shape the whole building. Or it may have been a stone at the top of the wall binding the whole together and consummating the work. Either way it is of great importance. Jesus is saying that, though men might reject Him, He is accepted by God whose acceptance is what counts. Even though the Jews make the

[1] J. Duncan M. Derrett, *op. cit.*, p. 307.

same kind of mistake as the builders and reject Him, God's
purposes will be fulfilled.

18. The imagery changes. Now it is not the value to be
placed on the stone that is in mind, but the destructive power
of a stone as against flesh and blood. To fall on the stone or
have the stone fall on one in either case means destruction.
People may reject and oppose Jesus but it is they, not He,
who will suffer. The second part of the saying will refer to the
future judgment. It will be their attitude to Jesus that will
mean the final destruction of the men of His day. The imagery
here is derived from Isaiah 8:14f. (*cf.* also Dn. 2:34f.).

e. Attempts to trap Jesus (20:19-44)

The parable sparked off opposition to Jesus. But in view of the
people's attitude violence was risky. It might provoke a riot
and no-one could tell where a riot would end. The Romans
would intervene and the privileged would lose their privileges.
So Jesus' enemies chose another method: they tried to
discredit Him.

i. Tribute to Caesar (20:19-26). Nobody liked paying
taxes to the Romans. A question on taxation seemed certain
to result in an answer which would bring Jesus into trouble
with either the Romans, who wanted the taxes paid, or the
Jews, who did not. The question was thus aimed at alienating
Jesus' support among the people, or alternatively putting
Him in a position where the Romans (not the hierarchy!)
would take action.

19, 20. The authorities tried to arrest Jesus, but neither
Luke nor any of the other Evangelists tells us how far they
went in the attempt. But they all make it clear that the reason
for their failure was not any lack of will. What prevented the
arrest was fear of the people. Arresting Jesus in the face of
current enthusiasm was too risky a business. So they changed
tactics and sent *spies*, people who would not be known as
enemies, but who would try to provoke Jesus into some statement that would make Him fall foul of the Romans. This
would enable them to hand Him over to *the authority and*

jurisdiction of the governor. Jesus would be effectively removed from the scene, but they would not be held responsible.

21, 22. The questioners begin with flattery, doubtless meant to put Jesus off His guard and to give themselves the appearance of sincere seekers after truth who had been impressed by His lack of respect for persons. The question concerns *tribute* (*phoros*; Matthew and Mark have *kēnsos*, 'poll tax'), a personal tax and different from the customs duties which were levied on goods in transit. Nobody ever likes paying this sort of tax and to pay it to the hated Romans must have been particularly distasteful. The questioners ask whether this is *lawful*, *i.e.* in accord with the law of God. It was obviously in accordance with the law of Caesar, but these men were looking for a pronouncement from a religious teacher. As we have already noticed, it must have been confidently expected that Jesus would be in trouble whichever way He answered.

23-25. Jesus was not deceived, but perceived *their craftiness* (*panourgia* carries overtones of unscrupulousness, 'readiness to do anything', AG). He called for *a coin*, *i.e.* a *denarius*. This was a Roman silver coin which had the effigy of the Emperor Tiberius stamped on it. It was required that the tax be paid in Roman coinage. Various other coins, such as Greek and Tyrian as well as Jewish, circulated in Judea at the time and the pious probably avoided using coins with Caesar's head stamped on them as much as possible. But they could produce a denarius at need and when they did they held in their hands the answer to their question, if they only thought hard enough about it. Jesus proceeded to ask whose likeness it was and got the answer *Caesar's*. This gave Him the opening to reply, *Then render to Caesar the things that are Caesar's, and to God the things that are God's*. Derrett sees a reference to the Old Testament (Ec. 8:2) and thinks that the meaning of the words is, 'Obey the commands of the king and obey (thereby) the commandments of God.' He comments, 'Obedience even to non-Jewish rulers is within one's comprehensive obedience to God.'[1] The difficulty in the way of this interpretation lies in seeing why the answer should have had the effect it did. The enemy marvelled and were silenced. This answer would

[1] J. Duncan M. Derrett, *op.cit.*, pp. 335f.

have been serious but not surprising. All three Synoptists make it clear that the reply confounded the critics. It left no room for an accusation of disloyalty to Caesar, but also stressed loyalty to God. Jesus is saying that a man is a citizen of heaven and of earth at the same time. This does not mean dividing life into compartments, as though the duties of either citizenship could be discharged without reference to those of the other. It means that man has more than one loyalty and that he can neglect neither. The State must be respected and its directions complied with in its own proper sphere. It follows that the State rightly collects taxes to discharge its functions. Notice that in response to the admission that the likeness and inscription are Caesar's Jesus says *Then* (*toinun*) *render*. . . . The obligation arises from a recognition of Caesar's place and this is shown by the use of Caesar's coins. It is also worth noting that, whereas the questioners ask whether it is lawful to *give*, Jesus answers that they should *render*, where the verb *apodidōmi* conveys the thought 'pay what is due'. Those who benefit from the State are under an obligation to pay their dues to the State. But as a man renders to Caesar what is Caesar's due, he must always bear in mind that the rights of Caesar are limited. Caesar has no rights in God's domain. The Christian's first and overriding loyalty is to God. This does not justify him in renouncing his loyalty to Caesar, but it does mean that he must always bear in mind that the most significant area of life does not belong to Caesar. If Caesar strays into that area he can command no loyalty.

26. Luke gives a fuller description of the effect on the questioners than do the other Synoptists. They had proved unable *to catch him*. Their question had seemed so certain to produce the desired effect, but it had turned out to be a damp squib. So they were astonished and they were reduced to silence.

ii. The seven brothers (20:27–40). The restless questioning goes on, with a group of Sadducees replacing the discomfited Pharisees. In view of verse 19 some Sadducees may have been included in the earlier group. Be that as it may, they now come with a question of their own.

27. The *Sadducees* are mentioned here only in this Gospel. None of the Sadducee writings has survived so our information

about the sect is fragmentary and we see the Sadducees only
through the eyes of their opponents. The name appears to be
derived from Zadok (*cf.* 1 Ki. 1:8; 2:35), so that they were
'Zadokites'. They were the conservative, aristocratic, high-
priestly party, worldly-minded and very ready to co-operate
with the Romans, which, of course, enabled them to maintain
their privileged position. Patriotic nationalists and pious men
of religion alike opposed them. They are often said to have
acknowledged as sacred scripture only the Pentateuch, but no
evidence is cited for this and it seems highly improbable. The
Septuagint is evidence that before New Testament times the
canon of the Old Testament was practically fixed and there
seems no reason why any major Jewish party should have
rejected most of it. What is attested is that they rejected the
oral tradition that the Pharisees made so much of and accepted
only written scripture (Josephus, *Antiquities* xiii.297). They
denied the whole doctrine of the after life and of rewards and
punishments beyond the grave (Josephus, *Antiquities* xviii.16,
Bellum ii.165; *cf.* Acts 23:8). They probably thought of the
resurrection as a new-fangled idea brought in from Persia
after the Old Testament period.

28. They try to ridicule the idea of resurrection by referring
to levirate marriage. This was a device to prevent a man's
name and family dying out. When a man died childless, his
brother was to take the widow and raise up children to the
deceased (Dt. 25:5ff.). Not many examples of the practice are
recorded and interestingly those few always seem to regard the
child as the child of its natural father and not of the deceased
(*cf.* Ru. 4:5, 21). By New Testament times this custom seems
to have fallen into disuse, so that the question was an academic
one. But the Sadducees could argue that provision was made
for it in the Law, and that the Law accordingly, at least by
implication, rejects the doctrine of resurrection.

29-33. They told a story of seven brothers who all at one
time or another had been married to the same woman, in each
case without her bearing a child. The Sadducees posed the
problem of whose wife she would be when the resurrection
came. Clearly they regarded a definitive answer as impossible
and the impossibility of an answer as showing the impossibility
of a resurrection.

34. Jesus spoke first of the conditions of this present life. *The sons of this age* is an expression found elsewhere in the New Testament only in 16:8, where it is distinguished from 'the sons of light'. Here, however, it denotes all who live in this world. They marry and are given in marriage. A few MSS add 'are begotten and beget' and some hold that this reading was original. It seems unlikely on the evidence, but the reading points to the conditions of this life which are in contrast to that to come.

35, 36. Jesus' questioners had failed to realize that the life to come will be essentially different from this life. Where the doctrine of resurrection was held among the Jews it was usually envisaged as an indefinite prolongation of this life. There would no doubt be modifications and improvements. All enemies would be overthrown and delights would be multiplied. But essentially it would be the same kind of life as the present one. Some were so sure of the continuation of earthly conditions that they seriously discussed whether the resurrected would need ceremonial purification on the grounds that they had been in contact with a corpse (*Niddah* 70b). Jesus rejects all this. Life in heaven will be significantly different from anything on earth. Human relationships are largely a matter of place and time: they are bound to be different when neither of these applies. Jewish thought at its best realized something of this and on occasion rejected the concept of heaven as a place of material delights in favour of the view that it is basically a 'feasting on the brightness of the divine presence' (*Berakhoth* 17a). Jesus speaks only of the saved, not of all the departed. He sees them as *accounted worthy*, which reminds us both that they do not earn their places by their merits and also that they have a high dignity. He goes on to speak of their attaining *to that age and to the resurrection from the dead*. These are not, of course, different, for the resurrection is the means of attaining to that age. Jesus does not speak of the resurrection 'of the dead', the general resurrection, but 'from the dead', the resurrection of the righteous. Of those in this group Jesus says three things. First, marriage does not apply to them. In this world it is a necessary feature of life, but life in the next world is different. Secondly, *they cannot die any more*. The *for* that links this with the preceding is important. People come together in marriage to preserve the human race, but where there is no death this is not necessary. Jesus does not say that they will not die, but that they *cannot* die. The quality of life in the coming age will be such that death cannot touch it. Thirdly, *they are equal to angels and are sons of God*. Luke may have coined the word *isangelloi, equal to angels*, for it is not attested before this passage. Its meaning includes possession of some of the properties of angels, for more than status is involved. It is a question also of nature and function, for marriage is specially in view. There is a sense in which believers are already *sons of God*. They have been born again; they have been adopted into the family in which they can say 'Our Father'. But there is a sense in which their sonship will not be consummated until the age to come and it is this fuller sense that is in view here. The absence of marriage does not mean, so to speak, a levelling down of relations so that life is on a lower level. Rather it is a being taken up into the fullness of life in the family of God. Luke adds the reason, *being sons of the resurrection* (an expression not found in the parallels). Their resurrection is evidence that they possess that quality of sonship that enables them to be compared to the angels.

37, 38. Jesus does not content Himself with parrying the question. He proceeds to show that the resurrection is implied in the Old Testament. Moreover He does not appeal to some obscure verse, hitherto overlooked, but to that passage of central importance in which God revealed His Name, with all that that means. He speaks of *the passage about the bush* (Ex. 3:1–6). The Bible of those days lacked chapters and verses and had to be referred to in terms of content. God is here called *the God of Abraham and the God of Isaac and the God of Jacob*. Each of the patriarchs named had, of course, long been dead when these words were uttered. So the statement that God is *not God of the dead, but of the living* can be true only if they are alive beyond the grave. The alternative is to think of God as the God of non-existent beings, which is absurd. Caird sees the argument as capable of restatement in terms with great force in our age: 'all life, here and hereafter, consists in friendship with God . . . Death may put an end to physical existence, but not to a relationship that is by nature eternal. Men may lose their friends by death, but not God.' Our certainty of resurrection rests not on some speculative doctrine of the immortality of the soul, but on the fact of God's eternal love.

Luke adds some words not in the other accounts: *for all live to him*, or as NEB, 'for him all are alive'. To us they are dead, but not to God. Death cannot break their relationship to Him. There is a roughly contemporary Jewish saying, 'those who die for God's sake live for God' (the construction is identical with that in Luke) 'just as do Abraham and Isaac and Jacob and all the patriarchs' (4 Macc. xvi.25).

39, 40. That ended the Sadducees' questioning. Some of *the scribes, i.e.* members of other parties, in this case probably Pharisees, paid Jesus the compliment of saying that He had spoken well: 'that was a fine answer!' (Moffatt). The Sadducees were not popular and probably many were glad to see them so discomfited that they *no longer dared* to question Jesus.

iii. David's Son (20:41-44). Jesus rounded off the session of questions by asking one Himself. The problem He posed arises from the habit in antiquity of regarding earlier generations as greater and wiser than the present one. David was the ideal king and his descendants were by definition less than he. But he himself referred to the Messiah as *Lord* (Ps. 110:1). How then could He be *David's son*, as the scribes said? Luke does not, of course, mean that Jesus is denying His Davidic descent. He has made that descent plain over and over (1:27, 32, 69; 2:4; 18:38f.) and his story of the virgin birth, from which his readers would see that Christ pre-existed, shows that even on the scribes' premises Jesus was greater than David. But the question arose, 'How did the scribes understand the Psalm?' Jesus is also clearing up a misunderstanding of Messiahship. People who used the title 'Son of David' (18:38, 39; Mt. 21:9) clearly envisaged the Messiah as someone who would defeat all Israel's foes and bring in a new kingdom of David. They thought of David's son as similar to David in being, outlook and achievement. There are not wanting Jewish writings of the period which speak of the Son of David in terms of a narrow nationalism that looked for Israel's triumph over all its foes (*e.g.* the *Psalms of Solomon*). Jesus means us to see that the Messiah was not David's son in that petty sense. He was *Lord*, Lord of men's hearts and lives. To call Him *Lord* meaningfully is to see Him as greater by far than merely another David.

f. Warning against the scribes (20:45-47)

Jesus proceeds to a warning against the scribes. *Long robes* were a sign of distinction and marked the wearers as gentlemen of leisure, for anyone who worked for his living would not be cumbered with such clothing. Public greetings and good places in synagogues and feasts were further ostentatious marks of eminence coveted eagerly by the scribes. But while they liked thus to shine before men, they were careless of how they appeared before God. Their devouring of widow's houses will refer to practices which resulted in loss to widows, the most defenceless group of the day. It was forbidden to scribes to accept money for teaching. They must, and did, make their knowledge available without charge. But there was nothing to stop people making gifts to teachers and this was regarded as meritorious. Evidently some of the scribes encouraged impressionable widows to make gifts beyond their means. A further count against them is that their prayers featured length rather than depth. Such prayers gave the illusion of piety, but as they were offered in *pretence* they availed nothing before God. The scribes' pretended piety and real dishonesty would result in *the greater condemnation*, greater in proportion to the esteem in which they caused people to hold them or greater in proportion to their hypocrisy.

g. The widow's gift (21:1-4)

1, 2. The *treasury* was apparently the name given to a section of the court of the women where there were thirteen trumpet-shaped collection boxes. Each bore an inscription indicating the use to which its contents would be put. Here Jesus saw *the rich* making their gifts. Luke does not say so, but he implies that some at least were giving generously. In contrast is the offering of a certain *poor(penichra) widow*. Luke's word is unusual (here only in the New Testament) and he may wish to emphasize her penurious state by his choice of word. A widow had few ways of earning money in first-century Judea and normally found life very difficult. A poor widow is thus almost proverbial for the poorest of people. This one made a gift of only *two copper coins* (*lepta*). The word denotes a small Jewish coin (incidentally the only Jewish coin mentioned in the New Testament). Its monetary value was slight (*NBD* put it at about a tenth of an

English penny or an eighth of an American cent; currency changes since then mean an even lower value). Commentators often say that worshippers were not allowed to make gifts of less than two *lepta*, so that this represented the minimum offering. But the Talmudic passage bearing on the problem does not say that a gift of one *lepton* is forbidden. It simply says that one should not put one *lepton* into the charity box unless it is under proper supervision (*Baba Bathra* 10b).

3, 4. Jesus shows that the monetary value of a gift is not everything. There is a sense in which the widow made the biggest gift of all. Jesus' words, if taken literally, mean not 'more than any one of them' but 'more than all of them together'. If the measure be what is left over after giving, she certainly outdistanced them all, for they gave *out of their abundance*, and thus had much left over. She gave all she had. This is real sacrifice.

h. The eschatological discourse (21:5-36)

Each of the Synoptic Gospels contains an account of this discourse, though with some differences. There are some puzzling exegetical problems, notably those posed by the fact that part of the address seems to apply to the end of all things and part to the destruction of Jerusalem. In Luke the distinction between the two seems clearer than in the others and some scholars see in this Luke's distinctive contribution to eschatology. Ellis notes that the discourse presents us with problems, but he sees two elements which must be taken into account: Jesus 'did announce a coming end of the world, and he did reckon with a considerable and indefinite interval before the end'. The discourse expresses Jesus' certainty of ultimate triumph, even though there were dark days ahead. And it concludes with a rousing challenge to His followers to be watchful and not let themselves be weighed down with the difficulties of this world. Much of the language is reminiscent of Old Testament passages (*e.g.* 2 Ch. 15:6; Is. 8:21f.; 13:13; Je. 34:17), which may be a way of emphasizing that what Jesus was describing was a divine visitation.

i. The sign (21:5-7). The discourse is introduced by the disciples' request for a sign of the coming destruction. As they were leaving the Temple (Mk. 13:1) one of them commented on the magnificence of the building. The *noble stones* were the great stones used in erecting the building (some huge stones can still be seen in the 'wailing wall', but this was part of the substructure, not of the Temple itself). According to Josephus some of them were as much as forty-five cubits long. The *offerings* would be decorative gifts such as the golden vine Herod gave with 'grape clusters as tall as a man' (Josephus, *Bellum* v.210). Jesus responds by prophesying its total destruction. So the disciples ask when this will happen and what sign will precede it.

ii. Conflict of the nations (21:8–11). Jesus does not give any one sign; but He warns His followers not to be led astray in the tumultuous happenings that would in due course occur.

8. Jesus warns them not to be *led astray* and goes on to speak of false Christs, those who come *in my name*, *i.e.* claiming to be what I am. They will say, *I am he!* Though *he* is not defined it clearly means the Messiah. The claim to Messianic authority is followed with a prediction that *the time*, the end time, the time of national deliverance, is near. The significance of these words should not be overlooked. Jesus was not predicting the end of the world within the lifetime of men then living. He regarded those who make such forecasts as false prophets.

9–11. Not only will there be Messianic pretenders in Judea, but there will be trouble among the nations at large. Jesus warns His followers not to be *terrified* at wars and the like. Such troubles will come, as will physical phenomena such as *earthquakes . . . famines and pestilences*, and unspecified *great signs from heaven*, *i.e.* among the stars.

iii. Persecution (21:12–19). Clearly the troubled times of which Jesus was speaking will be periods of special difficulty for His followers. They will be persecuted; but they will have resources to meet all difficulties.

12. Before world trouble there will be church trouble. Jesus does not say who *they* are who will *lay their hands* on the disciples and *persecute* them. It is a general reference to unsympathetic authorities. We are apt to think of *synagogues* as places of worship, but we should not overlook their wider functions as centres of administration and education. They were the centres of Jewish life, and Jewish law was administered from them as far as applicable (*cf*. 12:11). The use of the term shows that Jesus' followers must expect opposition from the Jews. *Prisons* points to the certainty of condemnation, while the reference to *kings and governors* shows that the persecuting authorities will be Gentiles as well as Jews.

13–15. This is not simple disaster; it is an opportunity *to bear testimony*. This does not mean virtuoso oratorical performances. It means witnessing to what God has done. And God will provide the means whereby they can do this. They are not even to prepare what they will say (the verb *promeletan, meditate beforehand*, is a technical term for preparing an address; see AG). This, of course, has nothing to do with sermons and lectures which the Christian must prepare as faithfully as anyone else. It refers to the replies believers will suddenly be called upon to give to hostile authorities in times of persecution. At such times Jesus will give them *a mouth and wisdom* (*cf*. 12:11f.), both eloquence and understanding. And this will be so effective that the enemy will be unable to withstand or contradict.

16, 17. Jesus does not minimize the seriousness of the trouble. Families will be divided and some will betray relatives to the persecutors, even close relatives. Jesus makes it clear that what He has just said does not mean that believers can rest assured that they will be delivered. Some of them will not. The believer can be sure that God is in control and that He will work out His purpose, but he cannot be sure what place he himself has in that purpose. He may be killed and come to his eternal triumph through death, or he may survive. His certainty is in the triumph of God, not in how this will be realized in his own life. Opposition will come not only from within the family, but also from the world at large. The world will hate Christ's followers just as it hated Him (*cf*. Jn. 15:18ff.).

18, 19. At first sight these words contradict the preceding. The reconciliation lies in the thought of God's overriding sovereignty. The world cannot harm God's servants unless He permits it. *Not a hair of* their *head will perish*. Bengel thinks we see the meaning if we make an addition such as 'without the special providence of God,—without its reward,—before its time'. Some see a reference to spiritual safety (*e.g.* Plummer), but this scarcely fits the language. Others hold that, while individuals may perish, the community of disciples will be safe, but the same objection applies. It seems best to see Jesus as directing their minds to God's control and purpose. In the light of that they are exhorted to endurance and constancy. Perseverance to the end, not some flashy but isolated piece of resistance, is what is required.

iv. The destruction of Jerusalem (**21:20–24**). Luke makes it clear that this section of the discourse refers to the destruction of Jerusalem and not to the end time. He has some matter not in the other Synoptists, while conversely he leaves out things they include, such as the reference to 'the desolating sacrilege' (Mt. 24:15; Mk. 13:14), which would probably not have meant much to his Gentile readers.

20. It is hard to follow the reasoning of critics who hold that this verse shows that Luke was writing after the fall of Jerusalem. The prediction is quite general and there is no indication that Luke had any knowledge of the kind of detail found, for example, in Josephus. It is perhaps significant that, while Caird dates this Gospel later than AD 70, he refuses to see evidence for his date in this prediction. On the contrary he thinks that Luke is using a source written before the destruction of the city. He also says that 'there can be no doubt that Jesus repeatedly foretold the violent end to which Jerusalem was hastening'. The participle translated *surrounded* means 'being surrounded' (*cf.* Rieu, 'When you see armies closing round Jerusalem'). Were the encirclement complete, Jesus' instructions could not be carried out.

21, 22. In time of war country people would come into walled cities for protection. Jesus tells His hearers that in view of Jerusalem's impending destruction they should keep as far from it as they could. The *mountains* would be inaccessible and the safest place. In fact, when the Romans were beginning to invest Jerusalem, the local Christians mostly fled to Pella, one of the cities of Decapolis and situated in trans-Jordan, south of the sea of Galilee (Eusebius says they went in response to 'an oracle given by revelation', which may mean Jesus' words or a later injunction of a similar kind from a Christian prophet; see *Historia Ecclesiastica* III. v. 3). *Days of vengeance*, or 'the time of retribution' (NEB; *cf.* Ps. 94:1; Is. 34:8, *etc.*), are days when people will be punished for their sins. What is to happen to Jerusalem is not arbitrary, but due penalty. The fulfilment of Scripture shows that the divine judgment is being carried out.

23, 24. A siege brought suffering to all, but especially to such people as pregnant women and those with young children. But the destruction will be total. *Distress* will be on all the land (so, rather than *the earth*) and *wrath* on the people. Josephus tells us that 97,000 were taken prisoner throughout the war and 1,100,000 were killed in the siege (*Bellum* vi. 420). Even when we allow for exaggeration it is plain that the loss of life was staggering.[1] Jesus goes on to speak of *the times of the Gentiles*. This is not an easy expression and a variety of explanations has been suggested: the time for the Gentiles to execute God's judgments, or to be supreme over Israel, or to exercise the privileges hitherto belonging to Israel, or to have the gospel preached to them. The reference to these times as being *fulfilled* points to a divine purpose in them.

v. The coming of the Son of man (21:25–28). In the opinion of most scholars attention now moves to the coming of the Son of man. There are, of course, many who hold that the reference is still to the fall of Jerusalem, as Tasker, for example, does in his discussion of the corresponding passage in Matthew.[2] But the language seems more suited to the parousia (*e.g.* verse

[1] It seems that Jerusalem could not hold the numbers of which Josephus speaks. J. Jeremias works on the information that at Passover there were three groups of worshippers coming to sacrifice their animals, the first two crowding the court. Allowing two men (each with his animal) per square metre the court could take 6,400 when jammed full. Since the third group was not so large this would total about 18,000. With ten worshippers per sacrificial victim this yields a total of about 180,000 at Passover time (*Jerusalem in the Time of Jesus*, pp. 77ff.). Without the pilgrims he thinks the normal population about 25–30,000.

[2] See further the discussion in R. T. France, *Jesus and the Old Testament* (London, 1971), pp. 227–239. He is primarily concerned with Mk. 13:24–27, but much of what he says is relevant to the Lucan equivalent.

27; *cf.* 35). Jesus is pointing to signs that will precede His coming and teaching His followers not to be discouraged.

25, 26. In vivid apocalyptic imagery Jesus speaks of heavenly portents. It is not easy to see how literally the words are meant to be taken. Such language is often used in apocalyptic to denote sudden and violent change and the emergence of a new order. In any case this will be the main part of the meaning here. Men will be perplexed and fearful. They will know that strange things are happening, but will not understand what is about to befall them.

27, 28. Jesus says He will come *with power and great glory*. Tinsley and others think this means a going to God (as in Dn. 7:13). But this would be an unnatural meaning for the participle *erchomenon*, which means 'coming' rather than 'going'.[1] Coming with glory points to royal power. Luke alone preserves the command *look up and raise your heads*. When the perplexing signs begin to occur Jesus' followers must not be downcast. Their deliverance is near. *Redemption* means release on payment of a price. There is a sense in which redemption has been finally accomplished on the cross; but the unfolding of its full implications is still future and it is this of which Jesus speaks.

vi. The parable of the fig tree (21:29–33). This little parable is in all the Synoptists, though only Luke adds *and all the trees* to the reference to *the fig tree*. The appearing of leaves on the trees shows that summer is near. Similarly the occurrence of the signs mentioned shows the approach of the kingdom. It is not easy to see what is meant by *this generation* that is not to pass away before *all has taken place*. Some see a reference to the men then living and see the fulfilment in the fall of Jerusalem. The context seems against this, unless, with Plummer, we see the fall of Jerusalem as a type of the end. Many think that Jesus was prophesying the end of all things within a few years and that He was mistaken. In view of His explicit disavowal of knowledge of this point (Mk. 13:32), this seems most unlikely. Moreover, as many critics have pointed out, it is impossible to hold that Luke who recorded these words under-

---

[1] F. F. Bruce argues that the meaning of the word 'coming' in the parallel Mk. 13:26 is a coming to earth, not a going to heaven (*Baker's Dictionary of Theology*, ed. E. F. Harrison (Grand Rapids, 1960), p. 192).

stood them to mean this. In the early church it was often held that the generation of Christ's followers was meant, so that the elect would persist right through to the end. Others see a reference to the Jewish nation (*e.g.* Ryle). Some have thought that Luke means us to understand the term in the sense 'mankind' (Leaney, Harrington). Lenski draws attention to the frequent use of 'generation' in the Old Testament to denote a kind of man, especially the evil (*e.g.* Ps. 12:7), but also the good (*e.g.* Ps. 14:5). Similarly Ellis points out that in the Qumran scrolls the term 'last generation' apparently 'included several lifetimes'. It seems that it is something like this that Jesus has in mind. This unusual use of *generation* concentrates on the kind of people that would persist through to the end. The expression 'means only the last phase in the history of redemption ... The public revelation of the kingdom *is* just around the corner, but its calendar time is left indeterminate' (Ellis). The paragraph concludes with the assurance that Jesus' words have a permanence that does not attach to the material universe.

vii. Be ready (21:34-36). Jesus' followers must live in the light of these exciting events to come and not give way to the temptation to imitate men of the world. *Dissipation (kraipalē)* is properly the hangover after a carousal, 'the vulgar word for that very vulgar experience'.[1] *Dissipation and drunkenness* are sins which are quite out of character for the Christian, but, as Ryle remarks, 'There is no sin so great but a great saint may fall into it: there is no saint so great but he may fall into a great sin.' The *cares of this life* are much more insidious, but either kind of failing can cause a man to be unprepared. Verse 35 makes it clear that Jesus is talking about the end of all things and 36 that His followers have a special responsibility. The prayer He urges involves an attitude of life, an attitude that seeks to flee worldly sins as the believer concentrates on the service of God. *To stand before the Son of man* is to possess the ultimate salvation.

i. Teaching in the Temple (21:37, 38)

Luke rounds off this part of his story by telling us of Jesus'

[1]Henry J. Cadbury, *The Style and Literary Method of Luke*, p. 54.

custom at that time. He taught in the Temple by day and
lodged on *the mount called Olivet* by night. If the verb *ēulizeto* is
used strictly, the meaning will be that Jesus camped out or
bivouacked on the mount. But we cannot insist on this, as the
term is sometimes used of more permanent dwelling and there
were villages in the area.

VII. THE CRUCIFIXION (22:1 – 23:56)

Throughout the crucifixion story Luke has many parallels
with the other Synoptists, but he also has a good deal of
information from his own source. Interestingly he sometimes
shares matter with John. He emphasizes the innocence of Jesus
and the fulfilment of Scripture (which, of course, means the
working out of God's purpose).

a. The betrayal (22:1-6)

1. Strictly *the feast of Unleavened Bread* was distinct from *the
Passover* (Nu. 28:16f.). But the two occurred together and they
could be regarded as the same festival. Josephus sometimes
speaks of them as distinct but, like Luke, he can give the same
name to both (*Antiquities* xiv. 21). All our Gospels agree that
the crucifixion took place on a Friday in the Passover season,
but whether the Passover coincided with the Last Supper
(as it seems to do in the Synoptics) or with the crucifixion
itself (as John seems to say) is one of the most difficult questions in New Testament interpretation. Some see a flat
contradiction and choose between them. Others think the
Synoptic date correct and see John as really agreeing. Others
again think the Johannine view the right one and think the
Synoptists do not differ. Possibly the best explanation is that
there were different calendars in use. Jesus died as the
Passover victims were being slain according to the official
calendar; but He had held the Passover with His followers the
previous evening according to an unofficial calendar.[1] It
agrees with this that, while all three Synoptists speak of the
meal as though it were the Passover, none of them mentions
the lamb or kid which was the central feature of the Passover

[1]May I refer to my discussion of the point in *The Gospel according to John*
(*New London Commentary*), pp. 774–786.

observance (and which could not be obtained without the concurrence of the Temple authorities). Plummer incidentally sees the absence of the sacrificial victim as important, for Jesus was inaugurating something new, not simply carrying on something old (on verse 11).

2. The initiative in opposing Jesus is taken by *the chief priests and the scribes*. In all the Gospels the Pharisees were Jesus' chief opponents throughout His ministry, but the high-priestly party took over at the end. It was they who had the political power. But that power was not unlimited and Luke pinpoints one difficulty: *they feared the people*. An open arrest might well have provoked a riot among the excitable pilgrims, many of whom supported Jesus. The chief priests dared not risk it.

3, 4. Luke explains Judas's treachery by saying that Satan entered him (*cf.* Jn. 13:27). Neither Luke nor any of the other Evangelists vilifies Judas. They simply state the facts and bring out the enormity of the betrayal only by saying that he *was of the number of the twelve*. Judas took the initiative and sought out the hostile party. Only Luke tells us that the *officers* (*i.e.* commanders of the Temple guard) were involved. It is not clear why Judas betrayed Jesus. One motive was disappointed avarice (Mt. 26:14f., which follows directly the story of the anointing with its 'waste'; Jn. 12:6). Some have tried to put him in a better light by suggesting, for example, that he was trying to get Jesus into a position where He would have to exercise His power and bring in the kingdom. Setting aside the not unimportant consideration that this would align Judas with Satan in the temptation narrative, all such attempts are speculation. There is no foundation for them in the texts.

5, 6. Naturally enough the enemy were *glad* at this defection. It simplified their task. They agreed on the price (given only in Mt. 26:15). Since Jesus had such popular support it was important that He be arrested when there were no crowds present to start a tumult.

b. In the upper room (22:7–38)

The fullest account of what took place in the upper room on the night before the crucifixion comes in John. Luke's account is not as full, but it is longer than those in Matthew and Mark, and he has some information of his own.

i. Preparations (22:7–13). The Passover was not just another meal, but a most important festival. It must be eaten reclining, and there were requirements such as the eating of bitter herbs. Thus quite an amount of preparation was necessary. The meal was not a solitary one, but was eaten in companies usually comprising ten to twenty persons.

7. *The day of Unleavened Bread* is an unusual expression, perhaps meaning the day on which all leaven was removed from homes in preparation for the festival. It was the day on which the combined festival began. The opening day was the one on which the Passover victims were killed, as Luke notes. If we are right in seeing a calendrical difference, this will have been not the day on which the victims were actually slaughtered, but that on which they should have been according to the calendar Jesus was following. Both calendars agreed that the victims were to be slain on the first day: the difference concerned which day that was. RSV's *passover lamb* is not correct. The Greek merely says 'passover' and the victim was not necessarily a lamb. It might be, and often was, a kid.

8, 9. Jesus delegated Peter and John to make the necessary preparations for the little company (only Luke names the pair). Not unnaturally they ask where. They were Galileans and would need guidance as to where they should go in Jerusalem. And at this late time there would be few places available, despite the traditional readiness of the Jerusalemites to make such accommodation available without charge.

10, 11. Jesus seems to have made a secret arrangement with the owner of a house. By doing this He prevented Judas from betraying Him prematurely. He would die, but in His own good time, not when His enemies chose. So none of the disciples knew where the meal would be. Peter and John were to look for *a man carrying a jar of water*, which would be distinctive, for women usually carried water jars (men carried water skins). He would lead them to a house where they were to say certain words to the householder, evidently an agreed formula.

12, 13. The householder would show them *a large upper room furnished*. This last word is literally 'spread' and probably means that there would be couches ready with coverings spread over them (Moffatt translates 'with couches spread'). They followed instructions and prepared the meal.

ii. The last supper (22:14–20). There is a textual problem here of great difficulty. In the 'shorter' text, followed by NEB, Goodspeed, where verses 19b–20 are omitted, the cup is given before the bread. In the 'longer' text (RSV, TEV, JB, Common Bible) the cup is mentioned twice. The shorter text is favoured by many on the grounds that the words are not likely to have been omitted if original and that they look like an insertion from 1 Corinthians 11:24f. to bring the passage into line with current liturgical practice. It is countered that the disputed words are found in all Greek MSS save one (Codex D), that Justin Martyr accepted them *c.* AD 150 (*Apology* i. 66; this is older than our oldest Greek MS), and that they may have been omitted by scribes who could not understand two references to the cup. On the whole it seems that the longer text is to be preferred.[1]

14–16. *The hour* is the time for their Passover meal. It is not clear whether Jesus is saying that He has desired to eat the Passover and is eating it, or that despite His desire He will not eat until its fulfilment in God's kingdom. Perhaps the former view is correct. The reference to fulfilment *in the kingdom of God* indicates that the Passover had typological significance. It commemorated a deliverance indeed, but it pointed forward to a greater deliverance, which would be seen in the kingdom of God.

17, 18. At the Passover meal it was obligatory to drink four cups of wine. It seems that this refers to one of these cups, though it is not easy to be sure which. A. Edersheim thinks it was perhaps the first,[2] after which there was a breaking of bread (*cf.* Mishnah, *Pesahim* 10:2f.). But a breaking of bread and a giving of thanks followed the second cup also,[3] so it may

[1] The textual points are summed up in *The Greek New Testament*, ed. R. V. G. Tasker (Oxford, 1964), pp. 422f. See also the note in Ellis.
[2] A. Edersheim, *The Temple* (London, n.d.), p. 205.
[3] A. Edersheim, *op.cit.*, pp. 207f.

305

have been this one. The sharing in the cup was a token of fellowship. Once again Jesus' eschatological interest is revealed as He looks for the coming of the kingdom. The life He had lived with the disciples was at an end. There would be no more familiar intercourse with them until the kingdom came.

19. The taking, breaking and distribution of *bread* were regular features of the Passover observance and would cause no surprise. But as He gave it to His followers Jesus said, *This is my body*. These words have caused tremendous controversy in the church. The critical point is the meaning of *is*. Some argue for a change of the bread into the body of Christ, but the verb can mean very various kinds of identification, as we see from such statements as 'I am the door', 'I am the bread of life', 'that rock was Christ'. In this case identity cannot be in mind, for Jesus' body was physically present at the time. It must be used in some such sense as 'represents', 'signifies' or, perhaps, 'conveys' (*cf.* Moffatt, 'This means . . .'). The statement is a strong one and should not be watered down, but neither should it be overpressed. The addition, *which is given for you*, looks forward to Calvary. It speaks of Jesus' death for men. This is not something that springs from the Passover ritual. That spoke of deliverance but not of vicarious sacrifice. Jesus is interpreting His death in a Passover context and making it clear that it has saving significance. Ellis thinks that His words about the body and blood here 'can be explained only as an implicit reference to the suffering Servant who, as the covenant representative, "poured out his soul to death and . . . bore the sins of many" (Isa. 53.12).' The command, *Do this in remembrance of me*, does not mean, as some claim, that the communion is essentially a pleading of Christ before the Father. It is lest we forget, not lest He forget.

20. The *cup* was evidently not taken immediately, but some little time later, *after supper*. The pouring out points us to the death on the cross where a *new covenant* would be inaugurated. Israel was in covenant relationship with God, but now there would be a new covenant brought about by Christ's blood (*cf.* Je. 31:31). His death would establish a new way of approach to God. *Cf.* Harrington, 'Jesus lets it be understood that his imminent death is going to replace the sacrifices of the Old Law', and Manson, 'The Lord's Supper as thus presented indicates and inaugurates a redemption effected by the death of Christ as a sacrifice.'

iii. Jesus' prophecy of the betrayal (22:21–23). If Luke is writing in chronological order, then Judas was one of those who shared in the first service of holy communion. Doubt is raised because Matthew and Mark have this prophecy of the betrayal (after which Judas presumably left speedily) before the communion. However none of the Evangelists specifically places these events in sequence and we must remain uncertain. Luke's prophecy of the betrayal lacks the reference to dipping in the common dish the others have, but the hand *on the table* presumably means much the same. It is a mark of close fellowship and the betrayal stands out as all the more horrible in the light of it. Jesus goes on to make it clear that His death is in the divine purpose. It has been *determined* (the other Synoptists mention that Scripture is being fulfilled). But this does not mean that the betrayer is guiltless. The fact that God overrules the evil that bad men do as He brings His purpose to pass does not make them any the less evil. They remain responsible men. *Woe to that man* is better 'Alas for that man'. It is not vindictive, but an expression of grief over the undefined but unpleasant future that he has brought down upon himself. Apparently Judas had disguised his thoughts well, for the other disciples *began to question one another* as to whom Jesus meant. No-one seems to have suspected him.

iv. A dispute as to the greatest (22:24–27). Only Luke tells us of this dispute in the upper room. Matthew and Mark have passages that resemble this one, but not in the farewell discourse. John has the feet-washing incident, which presupposes something like the attitude revealed here, but he does not have this quarrel. It is sad that, with Jesus so close to the cross, His most intimate disciples were so far from His spirit.

24, 25. Evidently the disciples thought the establishment of the kingdom was near and they argued about the best place in it. Luke does not say that they were vying for the top place, but they were certainly interested in whose it would be. Jesus rebukes them by drawing attention to the way *the Gentiles* (who here will be all those who are not God's people) live.

Their *kings* are authoritarian. Their men *in authority* 'get themselves called' (*kalountai* is probably middle rather than passive) *benefactors*. In fact a number of kings in the ancient world styled themselves *Euergetēs*, 'Benefactor'. Men of the world like to receive credit for what they have done.

26, 27. The Christian attitude is in sharp contrast. Among Christ's men *the greatest* must *become as the youngest*, *i.e.* he must take the lowliest place. In the ancient world it was accepted that age gave privileges. The youngest was, by definition, the lowliest. In the same spirit *the leader* must be *as one who serves*. The feet-washing that John records was a striking illustration of Jesus' readiness to take the place of *one who serves*. He did this although He was entitled to the supreme place and men naturally esteem the diner as higher than the waiter. All three examples of the word *serves* translate *diakonōn*, a verb which means in the first place the service of the table waiter and thus is very much to the point. From this it came to mean lowly service in general and this is what is in mind here. Jesus is not saying that if His followers wish to rise to great heights in the church they must first prove themselves in a lowly place. He is saying that faithful service in a lowly place is itself true greatness.

v. Twelve thrones (22:28–30). Since a hard and perplexing road lay ahead of them, Jesus proceeds to give His followers some encouragement. First He speaks of them as *those who have continued with me in my trials*. That is to say, they have served faithfully with Him throughout the hardships that His ministry necessarily involved. They had not shunned the difficult or the lowly place. They will in due course enjoy the Messianic banquet with Him. This (with RSV, Rieu, Phillips) appears to be the meaning of the Greek rather than 'I confer a kingdom on you, just as my Father conferred one on me' (JB; similarly NEB, TEV). The royal state they will enjoy is expressed rather in their sitting *on thrones judging the twelve tribes of Israel*, for *judging* is surely used here in the sense 'ruling' (as in the book of Judges). Jesus speaks of all this in the language of covenant. The verbs *assign* and *assigned* both render forms of *diatithemai*, the usual biblical verb for the making of a covenant. The glorious future of which Jesus speaks is as sure as the covenant of God.

vi. Prophecy of Peter's denials (22:31-34). All four Gospels tell us that Jesus predicted Peter's threefold denial and relate how it happened, but they all do it in their own way. For example, Luke alone tells of Satan's part in it.

31, 32. In Satan's prayer *to have you*, *you* is plural and includes all the disciples. The Greek appears to mean 'Satan has obtained you by asking': there is the thought that the petition has been granted. In passing we notice that Satan has no rights here. He may ask, but it is God who is supreme. It follows that the trials and testings that come to God's people are only those which He allows. The metaphor of sifting *like wheat* is unparalleled, but it is obvious that it signifies great trials. There was a turbulent future before the little band and specifically before Peter. Jesus' repetition of His servant's name, *Simon, Simon*, gives the address a solemn emphasis. Jesus goes on to assure Peter that He has prayed for him (*you* this time is singular and indicates prayer specifically for Peter). Notice that the Master did not ask that His servant might be freed from trouble. The undergoing of difficulty and hardship is an integral part of the Christian way. The quality of Peter's faith in such circumstances is important. Now he is given the assurance of mighty intercession on his behalf. Jesus is confident of the ultimate issue and speaks of the time *when you have turned again*, or, as Rieu puts it, 'once you have retraced your steps'. For that time Peter is given the command, *strengthen your brethren*. He who has been through deep waters has the experience that enables him to be of help to others.

33, 34. Peter realizes neither the seriousness of the position nor his own weakness. Brashly he declares his readiness to die for Jesus if need be. But Jesus knew His disciple better than he knew himself. This is the one occasion on which He is recorded as addressing him as *Peter*. Perhaps He has a sorrowful realization that in the immediate future Peter would require but would lack the rock-like quality the name denotes. Jesus prophesies Peter's threefold denial, specifying the number of times and the time-limit set by the crowing of the cock. This is more than human knowledge.

vii. Two swords (22:35-38). Luke concludes his story of the upper room with a further grim reference to trouble ahead. This short section is peculiar to this Gospel.

35. Jesus begins His warning by contrasting what is to happen with happier times in earlier days. When He had sent them off to preach their resources had been meagre (10:4; *cf.* 9:3), but their needs had been supplied. They agree that they had then lacked *Nothing*.

36, 37. Now things will be different. Perilous and difficult days lie ahead. There will be need for *purse* and *bag*, and even for a *sword*. Some think the sword is meant literally (*e.g.* Ellis, Lenski), but it is difficult to see this in view of Jesus' general teaching and of His specific refusal to let Peter use the sword he had (51). Such considerations lead others to think the words are ironical (*e.g.* Tinsley), but it is more likely they are figurative. It is Jesus' graphic way of bringing it home that the disciples face a situation of grave peril. 'Because He was not thinking of their weapons, the disciples require that courage which regards a sword as more necessary than an upper garment and surrenders even its last possession, but cannot give up the struggle' (Schlatter, cited in Geldenhuys). Jesus goes on to inform the disciples that the words of Isaiah 53:12 are about to be fulfilled. This is noteworthy as one of the few places in the New Testament in which that chapter is explicitly applied to Jesus. Jesus sees His death as one in which He will be one with sinners. This surely points to that death as substitutionary. He would take the place of sinful men. Since Jesus is in such a plight the disciples are also in danger. Rieu brings out the extent of the danger both to them and their Lord with his rendering of the last words of this verse, 'Indeed for me the course is run'.

38. The disciples did not understand. They spoke in terms of this world's arms and said they could muster only *two swords*. Jesus' response, *It is enough*, means not, 'Two will be sufficient' but rather, 'Enough of this kind of talk!' It is a way of dismissing a subject in which the disciples were hopelessly astray.

c. The agony (22:39-46)

Luke locates the agony only on the Mount of Olives (Matthew and Mark tell us it was at Gethsemane). His account is quite short. Where the other Synoptists tell us that Jesus went away and prayed three times and record words He spoke between the first and second occasions, Luke condenses the story and gives us just one example of Jesus' prayer. Nor does he tell us of Jesus' singling out of Peter and James and John. But he has matter of his own, as we shall see. Godet sees this incident as very important, for it differentiates the sacrifice of the freely consenting Jesus from those of animals with no say in the matter. 'At Gethsemane Jesus did not drink the cup; He consented to drink it.' The real battle was fought here.

39. Luke tells us neither that Jesus went to a garden, nor that the place was called Gethsemane. He simply says that Jesus went *to the Mount of Olives*. But he adds that this was Jesus' custom. Evidently throughout this week, and perhaps at other times also, it had been Jesus' habit to spend the night on the slopes of this hill.

40. The other Evangelists speak of Jesus' own prayers, but Luke tells us that He first instructed the disciples to pray, *that you may not enter into temptation* (*cf.* 46; in Matthew and Mark this instruction comes between Jesus' first and second times of prayer). This last word may mean temptation to sin, or, as some take it, a time of severe testing, an ordeal. The disciples should seek to be preserved from both.

41, 42. Jesus prayed alone. The custom of the time was to pray standing with the eyes raised to heaven (*cf.* 18:11, 13), but on this specially solemn occasion Jesus *knelt down*. His prayer reveals a natural human shrinking from the awful death that lay ahead of Him and thus He asks that, if the Father is willing, *this cup* be removed. The *cup* in the Old Testament has associations of suffering and of the wrath of God (*cf.* Ps. 11:6; Is. 51:17; Ezk. 23:33). It was no easy task to which Jesus looked forward, but His prayer centres on the Father's will rather than on His being spared. He prays that God's will may be done and specifically He says *not my will*. This does not mean that His will is in opposition to that of the Father: the very praying of the prayer shows that it is not. But this is a strong affirmation of His desire that the Father's will may prevail.

43, 44. A number of MSS omit these verses and RSV[2] puts them in the margin; but the probability is that they should be included. In a day when scribes were sure of the deity of their Lord, some would find difficulty in the thought of His being strengthened by an angel, and they would see the striking details of the agony as pointing to a Jesus all too human. There would be every reason for omitting the words if they were original, but it is difficult indeed to imagine an early scribe inserting them in a text that lacked them. They are well attested and should be accepted. At this critical moment then angelic strength supplemented Jesus' human resources. We get some indication of the intensity of His feeling when we read of sweat *like great drops of blood falling down upon the ground*. The word *agony* is found here only in the New Testament. Why was Jesus in such perturbation as He faced death? Others, including many who owe their inspiration to the Master, have faced death quite calmly. It cannot be death as such that caused this tremendous depth of feeling. Rather it was the kind of death that Jesus would die, that death in which He was forsaken by God (Mk. 15:34), in which God made Him to be sin for us (2 Cor. 5:21).

45, 46. When Jesus returned to the disciples after this harrowing experience He found them *sleeping for sorrow*, 'worn out by grief' as NEB puts it. It must have added to His trial that at this critical moment His closest followers were so insensitive to His feelings and to what was happening about them that they slept instead of praying with and for Him. They have failed this test, and He tells them to pray that they *may not enter into temptation*. The repetition of the instruction (40) gives it emphasis. There will be further tests and they must pray for the right attitude next time.

d. The arrest (22:47-54a)

Luke's account of the arrest is shorter than that of the others, but he yet includes matter of his own, such as the disciples' question (49), the healing of the ear (51), and the reference to the power of darkness (53).

47, 48. The arrest followed immediately upon Jesus' return to the disciples. Judas and his aides came up while Jesus *was still speaking*. Luke contents himself with the mention of *a crowd* and does not tell us, as Matthew and Mark do, of their connection with the Sanhedrin and of the arms they carried (which points come out later), nor of the Romans who were with them, as John does. He confines himself to the essentials. Judas's crime is brought out again only with the reminder that he was *one of the twelve*. Luke says that this disciple approached Jesus *to kiss him*, though he does not mention Judas's actual kiss. Nor does he say that this was the sign Judas had given the soldiers, though this is clear from Jesus' reaction, *Judas, would you betray the Son of man with a kiss?* The kiss was a not unusual form of greeting when men met (*cf.* 1 Thes. 5:26). It was thus a convenient way for Judas to show to the soldiers which of the group was Jesus and to make sure that they did not arrest the wrong man. But the kiss of greeting expressed friendship and esteem and accordingly this method of betrayal has always seemed particularly heinous.

49, 50. The disciples tried armed resistance. Seeing the trend of events they asked Jesus whether they should use force. He had already spoken to them about having swords (36), and elicited their reply that they had two (38). Evidently their minds ran along such lines and they now leapt to the conclusion that they should use what swords they had. One of them (we learn from Jn. 18:10 that it was Peter) did not wait for the question to be answered. He struck out with his sword, though the best he could do was to cut off the ear of the high priest's slave.

51. Jesus promptly forbade this swordplay, though the precise meaning of the words He used is not clear. It is not even beyond doubt whether He was speaking to the disciples or the soldiers (*cf.* Goodspeed, 'Let me do this much!' which presumably is addressed to the arresting party). But the former is nearly certain. Jesus does not speak to the arresting party till verse 52 and His words here 'answer' (RSV omits this verb, but it is in the Greek) the actions of the disciples. They mean something like 'Permit until this', which might mean *No more of this!* (RSV) or perhaps better, 'Let them have their way' (NEB). Some see the meaning as 'Let events take their course', but this is perhaps not quite so likely. At any rate Jesus made it clear that He wanted no fighting and He went on to demonstrate this by healing the wounded man with a touch. This healing is important. Later Jesus was to tell Pilate that His

kingdom is not 'of this world' (Jn. 18:36) and adduce the fact
that His servants were not fighting as proof. Peter's action
might have cast doubt on His words, but the healing of the
wounded ear cancelled out that action and showed un-
mistakably Jesus' concern for peace.

52, 53. If *the chief priests* were in the garden in person it will
indicate the seriousness with which they took the arrest. But
Luke may mean no more than that important men in the
hierarchy, leading men among the priests, represented the
chief priests. The *officers of the temple* will be the captains of the
Temple police and the *elders* lay members of the Sanhedrin.
Their age would probably make them of little use in the arrest,
but their presence lent dignity and weight to the proceedings.
Jesus drew attention to the weapons the party carried, suitable
indeed for those who went *against a robber*, but singularly
inappropriate in the case of one who had been with them
day after day in the temple. The clear implication is that there is
something underhand in this clandestine arrest. *You did not lay
hands on me* might mean 'you did not try to arrest me' (TEV)
or 'you did not raise a hand against me' (Rieu). Jesus sees the
reason for the way they acted in that *this is your hour, and the
power of darkness*. The *hour* in the Fourth Gospel is the destined
hour, the hour of the cross (*cf*. Jn. 17:1) and there may be
something of that here. There is also the thought that the evil
one is implicated in the passion (*cf*. Col. 1:13, where the same
Greek expression is used; *cf*. also Eph. 6:12). In this arrest the
forces of evil are attacking God. Moffatt translates, 'the dark
Power has its way'.

54a. The arrest followed immediately. They *seized him* (the
term has no necessary implication of violence) and took Him
off to the house of the high priest. It was he rather than the
Romans who had taken the initiative in the arrest and it was
to him accordingly that the prisoner was taken.

e. Peter's denials (22:54b–62)

Peter's threefold denial of Jesus is recorded in all four Gospels.
Some problems arise. For example, whereas the Synoptists
record them all together, John interpolates an examination
before Annas between the first and second. This, however,

need mean no more than that the Synoptists complete the account once they have started it. No-one holds that the three denials followed one another immediately. There must have been intervals (*cf.* 58, 59) and there is no reason why things should not have happened during the intervals. Another problem is that, after the first occasion, different people are said to challenge Peter. In Matthew the second denial appears to be elicited by a question from a slave girl different from the first one, in Mark by the same slave girl, in Luke by a man and in John by a number of people. A little reflection shows that in such a situation a question once posed is likely to have been taken up by others round the fire. Different people telling about it would stress different participants in the drama.

54b, 55. Plummer points out that all four Gospels devote more space to Jesus' trial than they do to His crucifixion and the way they do it answers questions which bring out the meaning of the cross. 'Why was Jesus condemned to death by the Sanhedrin? Because He claimed to be the Son of God. Why was He condemned to death by Pilate? Because He claimed to be the King of the Jews.' None of the disciples other than Peter is said to have *followed* Jesus, though John tells us of another who was known to the high priest and who got Peter into the courtyard, apparently that of Annas. Luke does not say how he came to be there. He simply pictures him in the middle of the group sitting round a fire in the middle of the courtyard.

56, 57. All four Gospels agree that the first challenge came from a slave girl, John adding that she was the doorkeeper. She looked hard at Peter (*gazing at him* means 'staring at him'; it indicates a close scrutiny). Then she said, *This man also was with him.* Such a comment from a little slave girl does not amount to a fearsome ordeal. We do not hear of any charges against the disciples, so there is no apparent reason why Peter should not have admitted it. But he was among the enemy, and fearful. He took the easy way out and said, *I do not know him.*

58. The second challenge came *a little later.* Luke does not particularize its source but simply refers to *some one else.* But the masculine gender of his pronoun and *Man* in Peter's response shows that this time a man was involved. He goes beyond what the slave girl had said by affirming that Peter was *one of them*. Peter simply denied it.

59. The third challenge was more serious. It was made more confidently and Luke tells us that the man *insisted* on his point. His statement is not tentative. He begins with *Certainly* and brings up supporting evidence, *he is a Galilean*. This probably means that Peter's accent gave him away. John tells us that this man was a relative of the slave whose ear Peter had cut off, which may have made him take a longer and harder look at Peter than did others, both in the garden and in the courtyard. At any rate his accusation is clear.

60. Equally clear is Peter's repudiation. He addressed him as *Man* and denied all knowledge of what he was saying. Repudiation could scarcely go further, backed up, as Matthew and Mark tell us it was, with a string of oaths. And at that point *the cock crowed*.

61, 62. We do not know where Jesus was at this moment. He may have been in a gallery overlooking the courtyard, or in a room looking out on to it, or even He may have been passing through it on His way from Annas to Caiaphas. At any rate He was in some place from which He could see Peter and He *turned and looked at* him. Only Luke mentions this, but apparently it was this look that awakened in Peter the memory of Jesus' prophecy. Luke reminds his readers of what Jesus had said. They are to be in no doubt about it. The effect on Peter was shattering: he *went out and wept bitterly*.

f. The mockery (22:63–65)

Jesus was evidently committed to a group of soldiers left to guard Him until the formal session of the Sanhedrin. They took advantage of the opportunity to indulge in a little horse-play at the expense of their prisoner. They had gathered that He was supposed to be a prophet, so they blindfolded Him and called on Him to prove His prophetic gifts by naming the person who struck Him: 'Now, prophet, guess who hit you that time!' (Phillips). Luke gives no other details. He tells us only that they added insults to their violence.

g. Jesus before the Sanhedrin (22:66-71)

The details of Jesus' trial are not easy to piece together, for none of the Gospels gives a full account. But it seems clear that there were two main stages. First, there was a Jewish trial in which the chief priests had Jesus condemned according to Jewish law and then tried to work out how best to get the Romans to execute Him. Then a Roman trial followed in which the Jewish leaders prevailed on Pilate to sentence Jesus to crucifixion. The Jewish trial was itself in two or three stages. During the night there were informal examinations before Annas (as John tells us) and Caiaphas (who had some of the Sanhedrin with him). After daybreak came a formal meeting of the Sanhedrin. This was probably an attempt to legitimate the decisions reached during the night. It was not lawful to conduct a trial on a capital charge at night. It was not even lawful to give the verdict at night after a trial had been held during the day. But the Jewish hierarchy was in a hurry, so they rushed Jesus into an examination immediately after His arrest, night-time though it was. To give this an air of legitimacy they proceeded to hold a daytime meeting in which the essentials of the night meeting were repeated and confirmed. Even so they came short of what was required, for a verdict of condemnation could not be given until the day after the trial (Mishnah, *Sanhedrin* 4:1). But they appear to have thought it was worth doing and all three Synoptists tell us of the day meeting (Mt. 27:1; Mk. 15:1). Luke's account is quite short. He tells us only of Jesus' appearance before the formal Sanhedrin.

66. Luke takes up the story at daybreak, when a formal council could legally be assembled. He speaks of the Sanhedrin as *the elders* and goes on to particularize as *both chief priests and scribes* (though some take the Greek to indicate three constituent parts of the Sanhedrin, *e.g.* TEV, 'the elders of the Jews, the chief priests, and the teachers of the Law').

67-69. It is curious that no accusation is brought against the prisoner. Instead the council invites Jesus to incriminate Himself by telling them that He was the Messiah. But it is not as simple as that. As Jesus puts it, *If I tell you, you will not believe.* His understanding of Messiahship was so different from theirs that He could not have given a simple 'Yes', while they would not have believed Him had He made the claim He was entitled to make. He says further, *if I ask you, you will not answer*. On more than one occasion He had asked penetrating questions bearing on Messiahship, but they had failed to reply (20:3ff., 41ff.). If He now tried to bring out the real nature of Messiahship by questions, they would not answer, nor would they believe Him if He simply affirmed His position. *From now on* indicates that a change is imminent. In something like the Johannine manner there is the thought that Jesus' glory has begun (*cf.* Jn. 12:23f.). His death, resurrection and ascension would change everything. And perhaps because discussion of Messiahship was futile Jesus switched to His favourite term, 'Son of man'. *The Son of man*, He says, *shall be seated at the right hand of the power of God*. The right hand was the place of honour and sitting was the posture of rest. His saving work done, He would have the place of highest honour. The other Gospels speak of His being seated at the right hand of the power, but the addition *of God* in this Gospel would certainly make the expression more intelligible to Gentile readers.

70. These words aroused intense interest. *All* joined in the question that followed. Whereas before they had asked Jesus to say whether He was the Christ, now they ask the direct question, *Are you the Son of God, then?* As men are sometimes called sons of God, we must understand the definite article as important. They are asking whether Jesus claims a special relationship to God. His reference to the Son of man and to the place at God's right hand must have seemed to them a claim to a higher place than that which they understood the Messiah to occupy. For them a claim to be Messiah might be a mistake, but it was not blasphemy. But this was something different. Jesus' reply means something like, 'That is your word, not mine. I would not put it like that, but since you have, I cannot deny it.' Moffatt renders, 'Certainly I am', but this is too definite. I. Abrahams denies that the expression renders a rabbinic idiom,[1] and we cannot take it as a common expression. But the context shows that it must be taken as an affirmative. The point is that Jesus' understanding of the term differed

---

[1] I. Abrahams, *Studies in Pharisaism and the Gospels*, ii (New York, 1967), pp. 1ff.

from theirs; but He could not disown it and His answer recognizes this.

71. As far as the Sanhedrin was concerned that ended the matter. Its members were not interested in the qualifications Jesus would prefer to introduce or the way He understood the words. He had accepted them, or at least had not denied them. In their eyes that made Him guilty. And since the words were His own they needed no further witness. They themselves had heard it.

h. Jesus before Pilate (23:1–5)

The Jewish leaders had condemned Jesus from a variety of motives. The Pharisees saw Him as a blasphemer and they smarted under His biting rebukes of their hypocrisy. The high priests doubtless found their revenues hit when He cleansed the Temple. In addition Caiaphas pointed out that His existence was politically inexpedient: He might cause the Romans to take away what little liberty remained to them. So they wanted Him executed, but they lacked the power (Jn. 18:31). Obviously Rome could not allow a subject people to use their own legal processes to kill off her supporters, so the power to inflict the death penalty remained with the governor. In this case the trouble, from the Jews' point of view, was that Jesus' crime was blasphemy, the claim to be the Son of God. This was not in Roman eyes an offence that merited the death penalty. So the Jews had to draw up their accusation in terms which would seem serious to the Romans. They did this by accusing Jesus of being a king, a political revolutionary.

1, 2. The depth of feeling that gripped the Sanhedrin is seen in that *the whole company of them* brought Jesus to Pilate. This was not a matter for a few representatives, though, of course, the formal charge would have been laid by only one or two of them. They accused Him on three counts: *perverting our nation* (a curiously unspecific charge which probably means sedition; cf. JB, 'inciting our people to revolt'), *forbidding us to give tribute to Caesar* (shades of 20:25!), and *saying that he himself is Christ a king* (though Jesus had refused to use the term in their examination of Him, 22:67ff.). Both the second and third charges were serious and Pilate could be expected to take a dim view of anyone guilty of either.

3. Pilate's first question of Jesus is identically worded in all four Gospels and in all four his *you* is emphatic. What the Jews had said had prepared him to meet a resistance fighter, but one glance at Jesus was enough to show the utter absurdity of such an idea and it wrenched this incredulous question from his lips. Once again Jesus used an answer which signifies reluctant assent (see on 22:70). He was *King of the Jews* (a note Luke stresses) and thus could not give a direct negative. But He was not king in the sense Pilate meant.

4. Luke has greatly abbreviated proceedings. Pilate certainly asked more than one question, but Luke passes over the detailed examination and comes to the moment when the governor announced his verdict to *the chief priests and the multitudes* (*i.e.* it is a public statement, not simply a private communication to those who brought Jesus to him). *I find no crime in this man*, he said. Pilate discerned that it was the malice of the Jews and not any capital charge that was the occasion of Jesus' appearance before him.

5. But this did not suit the high priests. They *were urgent*, which points to vehement protest. They complained that Jesus *stirs up the people*, another indefinite complaint. They stress the extent of His influence and include *all Judea* as well as *Galilee*.

i. Jesus before Herod (23:6-12)

This section is peculiar to Luke. Pilate was clearly unwilling to handle the case, a point made plain in all four Gospels. He discerned that the Jews were implacable in their demand for Jesus' death. But he saw also that the prisoner had done nothing that the Romans regarded as meriting that penalty. So Pilate wanted to have nothing to do with the case. It suited him to send Jesus to Herod.

6, 7. The reference to Galilee as the beginning of Jesus' activities was a straw at which Pilate could clutch. He immediately asked whether Jesus came from that province and, receiving an affirmative answer, he sent Him to Herod (for Herod see on 3:1, 19). A trial was usually carried out in the Roman Empire in the province where the offence was committed, though it could be referred to the province to which the accused belonged. Pilate could thus have gone on with the trial. But it was a gracious compliment to Herod to refer the matter to him and it was technically possible because as a Galilean Jesus *belonged to Herod's jurisdiction*. Herod had probably come up to Jerusalem to observe the Passover, a tactic he would expect would please his subjects. He was thus available.

8. The tetrarch was pleased. Jesus' reputation had penetrated into the palace and Herod had long wanted to see Him (9:9). He had also heard of Jesus' miracles and wanted to see one for himself. *Sign (sēmeion)* is often used of Jesus' miracles in John, but the Synoptists prefer *dunamis*, 'mighty work'. The word normally indicates that the miracles had meaning, that they were significant. But Herod would have been thinking only of the miraculous.

9, 10. The interview must have disappointed Herod. He got no answer to his many questions. What could Jesus say to this trifler who wanted nothing more than a mild sensation? He never refused a sincere questioner, but Herod was not in that class. He is the only person to whom Jesus said nothing at all. *The chief priests and the scribes* made vehement accusations. They took no chances on Herod's releasing Jesus. And, of course, if they could get him to condemn the Galilean, so much the better.

11. But Herod met the wishes of neither Pilate nor the Jews. When he could not get his miracle his interest waned. He joined his warriors in mocking the prisoner (*cf.* 22:63ff.), then sent Him back to Pilate. He had no interest in the case and he declined to try it. The *gorgeous apparel* will reflect the accusation that Jesus was a king. The adjective is *lampros*, 'bright', 'shining', which is often used of white garments, but there is no indication of the colour of this one. A cast-off royal robe is probably meant. The mockery made it plain that Herod did not take the charge seriously. That is the really frightening thing about the incident. With the Son of God before Him Herod could only jest.

12. Nothing is known about this quarrel other than what we read here. If it concerned jurisdiction Pilate's readiness to allow Herod to take over a trial would have been a generous gesture. But when Herod declined to act, returning the compliment so to speak, Pilate had no option but to take up the case again.

j. Jesus sentenced (23:13–25)

Luke now shows how Pilate was compelled to sentence Jesus to death. But he makes it clear that this was very much against the governor's wishes, for he recognized that Jesus was innocent. Indeed four times Pilate said this (4, 14, 15, 22; *cf.* Jn. 18:38; 19:4, 6). The pressure of the high priests for sentence against an innocent man posed a terrible dilemma for Pilate, and the Gospels make it plain that he tried hard to avoid making a decision. He started by trying to get the Jews to deal with the whole matter themselves (Jn. 18:31). Later he sent Him to Herod (7). He attempted to get the Jews to accept Jesus as the prisoner to be released at Passover (Mk. 15:6), and he offered to beat Jesus and release Him (16). But in the end he could not avoid making the fateful decision.

13, 14. Pilate's summoning of *the chief priests and the rulers and the people* shows that he was preparing for a public announcement. He proceeded to repeat part of their charge and refer to an examination *before you*. This makes it plain that Luke has omitted much. It makes it plain also that Pilate had had a good look at the charges. And having done so, he found Jesus not guilty.

15. And this verdict was not alone. Herod supported it for, Pilate says, *he sent him back to us.* AV reads 'for I sent you to him', but this reading is based on inferior MSS and we should accept RSV. Pilate reasons that the tetrarch would not have acted as he did unless he was convinced that Jesus was not a malefactor.

16. The suggestion that Jesus should be chastised before being released strikes us as curious. If He was innocent, He should have been released without further ado. But in Roman law a light beating was sometimes given together with a magisterial warning, so that an accused might take greater care for the future. Many commentators speak of this as scourging and remind us that men were known to have died under this punishment. But A. N. Sherwin-White shows that what is meant here is a lighter punishment.[1] Pilate was apparently trying to appease the Jews. If he vented some judicial displeasure on Jesus they might be satisfied and acquiesce in the release of the prisoner.

18, 19. In some MSS the words which appear in AV as verse 17 are found, but they are inadequately attested and appear to be an importation from Mark 15:6. Such an insertion would be favoured by the fact that verse 18 does not follow on very smoothly from verse 16 and a scribe might well try to improve the connection. Luke's narrative is highly compressed. The custom of releasing a prisoner at Passover (Mk. 15:6; Jn. 18:39) is not attested outside the Gospels, but this kind of thing was done elsewhere. There is nothing unlikely about it. When Pilate spoke of release the crowd immediately called for *Barabbas* (the name means 'son of the father'). From the beginning they made it clear that it was this man, not Jesus, whom they wanted. This would no doubt have been partly because the high priests knew how to manipulate the comparatively small number who could crowd round the praetorium, partly because the partisans of Barabbas would have taken advantage of the opportunity to try to get their friend set free, and partly because nobody would have taken seriously the thought that Jesus was a criminal. If they were having a prisoner released, let it be a real one! Barabbas was evidently a member of what we would call the resistance movement, judging from the reference to *insurrection*. No doubt the *murder* (*cf.* Acts 3:14) had taken place in connection with this uprising.

20, 21. Pilate did not give up immediately. But the crowd rejected his approach and called for a crucifixion. This is the first time this ominous shout appears. In all the Gospels the demand for Jesus' crucifixion appeared only after Pilate had proposed releasing Him as the favoured prisoner at the festival.

---

[1] A. N. Sherwin-White, *Roman Society and Roman Law in the New Testament* (Oxford, 1963), p. 27. He makes the further comment, important for Luke's narrative in general, 'Luke is remarkable in that his additional materials—the full formulation of the charges before Pilate, the reference to Herod, and the proposed acquittal with admonition—are all technically correct' (*ibid.*, p. 32).

22. For the *third time* Pilate protested Jesus' innocence (this is actually the fourth occasion, but verse 15 might be regarded as reporting Herod's view). Luke makes it very clear that Pilate was not only convinced of Jesus' innocence but that he also said so repeatedly. Apparently in desperation Pilate now reverted to the suggestion of beating and release that the Jews have already rejected (16).

23. The mob was insistent. Their *loud cries* give the impression that a riot was beginning to build up. It must have been obvious to Pilate that the situation was becoming increasingly ugly. The mob's shouts won the day.

24, 25. Pilate gave his decision. Luke begins and ends by referring to the Jews, first to *their demand* that Pilate granted and finally to *their will* to which he gave Jesus up. We cannot miss the emphasis on the Jews' responsibility for Jesus' death. Luke repeats the information that Barabbas had been imprisoned *for insurrection and murder*, thus highlighting the contrast with the innocent Jesus. There may also be a hint 'at the substitutionary death of Jesus. The one guilty of death is pardoned (*apoluō*; cf. 6.37), and the innocent one dies in his stead' (Ellis). Perhaps we should add that Luke is not being anti-Semitic, much less providing grounds for anti-Semitism in our own day. He is dealing with a specific group of people and maintaining that they brought about Jesus' death. It was not Pilate nor his Romans that called for Jesus' execution: it was the Jewish chief priests and their followers. But this means no more than that one group of men was guilty. Luke is not indicting a race and neither should his readers.

k. Jesus crucified (23:26–49)

i. Simon carries the cross (23:26). It was customary for the condemned criminal to carry either the cross or its cross-bar to the place of execution. Jesus started the journey to Golgotha carrying His cross (Jn. 19:17), but evidently He had been weakened by the scourging that was the normal preliminary to crucifixion, so the soldiers pressed a passer-by to do this service. Luke tells us that his name was *Simon*, that he was from *Cyrene*, and that he was at this time *coming in from the country*. Elsewhere we find that his family was known in the

church (Mk. 15:21; perhaps Rom. 16:13) and it has been
conjectured that he was won that day by the bearing of Him
whose cross he carried.

ii. The daughters of Jerusalem (23:27-31). This incident is found only in Luke. It brings out something of the
sympathy felt for Jesus by many, especially among the women-
folk. We should bear in mind that those who clamoured for
Jesus' execution were not necessarily a great number. They
could crowd in round the judgment hall. There were still many
in Jerusalem who admired Jesus and it is of some of these that
we now learn.

27. Many were saddened by the turn of events. Luke speaks
of *a great multitude* who *bewailed and lamented*. The impression we
get is of a noisy demonstration of deep grief. In keeping with
one of his interests Luke singles out *women* for special mention.

28. Jesus greets them as *Daughters of Jerusalem,* so that it is the
city-dwellers and not the Galileans who had come up for the
feast who made up this group. At this moment, as He goes out
to execution, Jesus thinks not of Himself but of them. He
wants their repentance, not their sympathy. He is not saying
that they were wrong to mourn over Him, but He is thinking
with compassion of the doomed city and its inhabitants.
His words direct the women to the importance of looking
beyond the present moment to the inevitable consequences of
the nation's sins.

29, 30. Such trouble will come that it will be regarded as a
blessing never to have had children, in contrast to the usual
Jewish view that children are God's good gift (*cf.* Ps. 127:3).
For in that day children will suffer grievously and it is better
accordingly to have none. In the words of the prophet, people
will cry out for death in order to escape the coming wrath
(Ho. 10:8; *cf.* Rev. 6:16).

31. This looks like a proverbial saying. Several possible
meanings have been suggested. If the innocent Jesus suffered
thus, what will be the fate of the guilty Jews? If the Romans
treat thus One whom they admit to be innocent, what will they
do to the guilty? If the Jews treat like this Jesus who had come

to bring salvation, what will be their punishment for destroying Him? If the Jews behave like this before their wickedness reaches its consummation, what will they be like when it does? If grief is aroused by the present events, what will it be when the subsequent disaster strikes? None is impossible, but perhaps the first suggestion is to be preferred.

iii. The crucifixion (23:32–38). Very simply Luke tells of the crucifixion of Jesus, the supreme sacrifice for the salvation of mankind. In this form of execution men were fastened to a cross (which might be shaped like our conventional cross or like a T, an X, a Y or even an I) by ropes or nails. Jesus' hands were nailed (Jn. 20:25), and probably His feet also (*cf.* 24:39), though none of the Evangelists says so in set terms. There was a horn-like projection which the crucified straddled. This took most of the weight and stopped the flesh tearing from the nails. The recent discovery of the bones of a man crucified at about the same time as Jesus raises the possibility that the legs may have been bent and twisted and then fastened to the cross by a single nail through the heels.[1] Such a contortion of the body would have added to the agony. Crucifixion was a slow and painful death, but it is noteworthy that none of the Evangelists dwells on the torment Jesus endured. The New Testament concentrates on the significance of Jesus' death, not on harrowing our feelings.

32, 33. There were two others crucified at that time. Luke says only that they were *criminals*, Matthew and Mark say they were thieves. The three were brought to a place called *The Skull* (in Latin, *calvaria*, from which we get 'Calvary'). The reason for the name is not known. It is usually held to be because of the shape of the hill on which Jesus was crucified, but neither Luke nor any of the others speaks of a hill, let alone its shape. All four Evangelists tell us that Jesus was crucified between the other two, evidently a way of bringing out the fact that He was executed as a criminal (*cf.* 22:37). In His death Jesus was in the midst of transgressors.

34. There is textual doubt about this prayer. It is absent from many of the best MSS and some critics argue that it must be

[1]See the article, 'Jesus and Jehohanan' by J. H. Charlesworth, in *ET*, lxxxiv, 1972–73, pp. 147–150.

rejected, since it would scarcely have been omitted if genuine. Against that is the fact that other very good MSS do attest it. Early copyists may have been tempted to omit the words by the reflection that perhaps God had not forgiven the guilty nation. The events of AD 70 and afterwards may well have looked like anything but forgiveness. We should regard the words as genuine. It is Jesus' own spirit that dictates this concern for those who executed Him. He does not define narrowly those for whom He prays and His *them* probably includes both the Jews who were responsible for the crucifixion and the Romans who carried it out (*cf.* Acts 2:23; 3:17; 13:27f.; 1 Cor. 2:8). It was accepted that the clothing of a crucified person was a perquisite of the executioners. On this occasion it was divided and lots cast for the seamless tunic (Jn. 19:23ff.; *cf.* Ps. 22:18).

35. Luke pictures the generality of the people as simply watching. Executions were popular functions and doubtless many attended this one. But it was *the rulers*, not the people, who mocked (*cf.* Ps. 22:6-8). They did not address Jesus but one another as they spoke of His saving activities. They used two epithets, *the Christ of God* and *his Chosen One*. The evidence that Jesus made extensive use of either is lacking, so it is something of a mystery why they speak in this way. But both expressions point to God's special favour and doubtless they were contrasting words which spoke of favour with the actual plight of Jesus, there on the cross.

36, 37. We read of Jesus being offered drugged wine (which He refused) at the beginning of the crucifixion (Mt. 27:34; Mk. 15:23), and of His being given *vinegar* (*i.e.* cheap wine) just before His death (Jn. 19:29), but Luke alone tells us that the soldiers used it in connection with some mockery of their own (*cf.* Ps. 69:21). They called on Jesus, if He was the King of the Jews, to save Himself.

38. All four Evangelists mention the inscription on the cross. Such a placard would announce the crime for which the condemned man was being executed. The inscription over Jesus' head is differently reported in all four Gospels, but as the inscription itself was in three languages (Jn. 19:20; the corresponding words in AV, RSV mg. here are not well attested

and should be rejected) and we have no means of knowing
which any of the Evangelists is following, this is not strange.
What is clear is that Pilate was proclaiming that Jesus died as
King of the Jews. He was taking a grim revenge on the Jewish
leaders who had hounded him. But he was also proclaiming
Jesus' royalty, a theme that meant much to Luke.

iv. The penitent thief (23:39-43). This story is peculiar to
Luke, whereas Matthew and Mark tell us only that the thieves
crucified with Jesus abused Him. Some think those Evangelists
are saying in effect, 'This is the way the criminals reacted'
(perhaps without knowing that one thief repented). Others
think both men began by reviling Jesus, but that one had a
change of heart.

39. This is the attitude we see in the other Synoptists. This
thief asked, *Are you not the Christ?* His question presupposes the
answer 'Yes', but it is bitterly sarcastic. He calls on Jesus to
save them all without believing that He can do it.

40, 41. His fellow turned on him. Bengel thinks that his
situation on an 'exceedingly hard cross' may have had something to do with the changed attitude, for 'Conversion seldom
takes place on a soft and easy couch'. His question should be
understood as 'Do you not even fear God?' (Barclay). He
might have done more than fear God, but in view of his plight
he should certainly have done no less. The changed thief goes
on to make the point that they two are punished *justly*. They
have broken the law and their suffering had to be seen in the
light of that. Not so Jesus: He *has done nothing wrong*. Such a
recognition of Jesus' innocence must have been widespread.

42, 43. Then he spoke to Jesus, asking Him to *remember* him,
i.e. remember him for good. The MSS are divided as to whether
we should read 'in your kingdom' (*i.e.* in the glory appropriate
to royalty; *cf.* TEV, 'when you come as King!'), or 'into your
kingdom' (*i.e.* when you enter into your royal state; *cf.* NEB,
'when you come to your throne'). The former would more
naturally refer to the return of the Messiah to earth in triumph,
the latter to His going through death to a kingdom in the next
world. Both are well supported in the MSS, but perhaps there is
a little more to be said for 'into your kingdom'. It is not easy to

see how fully the penitent thief could have entered into an understanding of Jesus' Person and work. But these words show that he realized at least that death would not be the end of everything for him and that beyond death remained the kingdom. Jesus' words of reassurance gave him more than he had asked for. Not only would he have a place in the kingdom, whenever that should be established, but that very day he would enter Paradise. *Truly* marks the following words as emphatic and important (see on 4:24). *Today* is occasionally taken with the preceding words, but there seems no reason for this. Almost all scholars agree that it refers to being in *Paradise*. This Persian word meaning 'garden' is used in the Old Testament of a number of gardens. Specially important is its use for the Garden of Eden. Perhaps from this the term came to be used of the abode of the blessed in the coming world (*cf.* 2 Cor. 12:3; Rev. 2:7). It is used in this way here. Jesus assures this man of bliss in the immediate future, a bliss closely associated with Himself (*with me*).

v. The death of Jesus (23:44–49). Luke's account of Jesus' death stresses its peacefulness and its effect on those who watched.

44, 45. The *sixth hour* was noon. The day was divided into twelve parts, beginning with daybreak. An hour varied in length at different times of the year, but the sixth hour was always midday. In John's account 'it was about the sixth hour' when Pilate prepared to sentence Jesus (Jn. 19:14). Mark says 'it was the third hour' (Mk. 15:25). We must bear in mind that the ancients were not as precise in their measurements of time as we. Before clocks and watches, how could they be? All times of day in ancient documents tend to be approximate. So John will mean that it was late morning when Pilate gave sentence and Luke that Jesus was on the cross about midday. Mark may mean that the crucifixion took place rather earlier, or he may mean that the morning was getting on when this event took place. Obviously the Evangelists are not merely repeating one another, but there is no essential contradiction. Luke goes on to tell us that for three hours *there was darkness over the whole land*. He does not say what caused it and those translators and commentators are in error who speak of an eclipse of the sun. An eclipse is impossible at the full moon (which, of course, determined the time of the Passover), and Luke's language should not be pressed to mean this. He is surely linking the darkness not to astronomical phenomena but to the sad events leading to the death of Jesus. So with the tearing of *the curtain of the temple*. This was the curtain that separated the holy of holies from the rest of the Temple. It symbolized the separateness, the remoteness of God. The tearing of the curtain at this point gives symbolic expression to the truth that the death of Jesus has made the way open into the very presence of God (*cf.* Heb. 9:3, 8; 10:19ff.). Perhaps also, as Godet thinks, there is the thought that the Temple is no longer God's dwelling.

46. Jesus' last words are a beautiful expression of trust as He commends Himself to the Father in the words of a psalm (Ps. 31:5). Matthew and Mark emphasize the terrible nature of the death Jesus died for sinners with the words, 'My God, my God, why hast thou forsaken me?' (Mt. 27:46; Mk. 15:34). Luke is not denying this insight, but what he stresses is that in that death, paradoxically, Jesus was at one with the Father. He did the will of the Father. The word rendered *breathed his last, exepneusen*, is not the normal one for saying that a man has died. In fact none of the Evangelists says 'Jesus died', which may be part of the way they bring out the truth that in Jesus' death there was something most unusual.

47. Luke proceeds to the reactions of some of those who saw Jesus die. *The centurion*, who would have been in charge of the execution, *praised God*. This seems to mean that his tribute to Jesus was an unconscious act of praise. Jesus 'was righteous' (so, rather than *innocent* as RSV), that is to say, He was acceptable to God. The implication is that the death of the righteous must accord with the will of God. In recognizing the righteousness the centurion was thus praising God. Matthew and Mark have 'Son of God', but the sense in which a Roman would have used the term is better given in Luke's words. Plummer paraphrases, 'He was a good man, and quite right in calling God His Father.'

48. *The multitudes* will be the Jerusalemites who had no great interest in Jesus but who had come to watch the execution. Instead of being entertained they were saddened by it all and went home *beating their breasts* in grief. Many have seen in this reaction a preparation for the successful preaching on the day of Pentecost when three thousand believed in this city (Acts 2:41). Why so many? Part of the answer surely is that many went home from the crucifixion disturbed and thoughtful.

49. Curiously Luke does not mention the effect on Jesus' followers. He tells us that some of them were there and characteristically he singles out certain women for special mention. But he tells us only that these people *stood at a distance* (it may not have been politic to come too close) *and saw these things*.

1. The burial of Jesus (23:50-56)

All the Gospels agree that Joseph of Arimathea took the lead in Jesus' burial and that some women were associated with him. We know nothing of him apart from what we learn from this incident.

50, 51. The location of Arimathea is not known. But as Joseph had a tomb near Jerusalem he had evidently left his home town and come to live in the capital. He was a member of the Sanhedrin (the *council*), but Luke makes it clear that he had not given his consent to the execution of Jesus. He must have been absent, for the vote was unanimous (note the 'all' of 22:70; Mk. 14:64). Luke refers to his good character and to his *looking for the kingdom of God*. This is probably his way of telling us that Joseph was a follower of Jesus (*cf.* Mt. 27:57; Jn. 19:38).

52, 53. It was evidently necessary to get Pilate's permission to bury Jesus and Joseph did this. He took the body from the cross and put it in *a linen shroud* (John speaks of strips or bandages, Jn. 19:40; the shroud would have covered the whole). The tomb was *rock-hewn* and had not been used previously (tombs, being expensive, would tend to be given maximum use; surviving Jewish tombs of the period often have several chambers so that they can accommodate a number of bodies). Elsewhere we learn that Joseph had prepared this tomb for himself (Mt. 27:60).

54. *The day of Preparation* was Friday, the day when men prepared for the sabbath. Work could not be done on the sabbath, so, with Friday nearing its end and with the sabbath beginning when the sun went down, the burial had to be completed with some haste.

55, 56. The faithful Galilean women saw things through to the end. The Jewish custom was to wrap *spices and ointments* with the body, but for this there was not adequate time. Actually it was not forbidden to anoint a body on a festival (*Shabbath* 23:5), but there were other restrictions such as those on preparing a coffin or grave (*Shabbath* 23:4), or on moving even a limb of the deceased (*Shabbath* 23:5). So the burial had to be hurried. They placed the body in the tomb and then the women went off to the places where they were staying and prepared the necessary ingredients for a proper anointing when the sabbath had passed. Their preparations completed, they complied with the Law and rested on the sabbath. In John the spices Nicodemus brought were buried with the body, in Luke the women prepared spices before the sabbath, in Mark they bought them after the sabbath, while in Matthew there is nothing about the spices at all. Perhaps we should understand all this to mean that the burial on the Friday had to be hurried, but that use was made of the spices that were to hand. Then the faithful women, before and after the sabbath, did what was necessary to complete the burial.

VIII. THE RESURRECTION (24:1-53)

None of the four Gospels describes the resurrection, which in any case no man saw. But all emphasize its critical importance, though in widely differing ways. Some things are common to all the accounts, such as the empty tomb, the reluctance of the disciples to believe that Jesus had risen, the fact that the first appearances were to women, and the limited number of appearances. Even when they are talking about the same appearance each Evangelist tells it in his own individual way (*e.g.* Lk. 24:36ff.; Jn. 20:19ff.). This kind of thing makes it difficult to arrange the appearances in a coherent sequence and some critics hold that discrepancies in the various accounts make this impossible. That this is incorrect is demonstrated by the fact that Arndt, for example, has worked out a possible harmony (as have others). We may or may not feel able to accept Arndt's solution, but it cannot be denied that he has worked out a sequence that includes all the appearances mentioned in the accounts. Luke's treasure is the wonderful story of the walk to Emmaus. His other resurrection stories also bear his own stamp and they differ from what we read elsewhere. It is noteworthy that he concentrates on Jerusalem and says nothing about appearances of the risen Lord in Galilee.

a. The appearance to the women (24:1-11)

1. The sabbath was, of course, the seventh day so that *the first day of the week* was our Sunday. The sabbath would have ended at sunset on the Saturday, but little could be done during the hours of darkness. So the women were astir early on Sunday and they set off for the tomb *at early dawn*. That they took with them *the spices* shows that they had in mind the completion of Jesus' burial.

2, 3. Mark tells us that as they went they discussed the problem of moving the heavy stone from the mouth of the tomb. Luke simply says that when they arrived they found it already *rolled away*. When later on the beloved disciple came to the tomb he was diffident about entering it (Jn. 20:5), but the women had no such hesitation. When they went in, however, *they did not find the body*.

4. Not unnaturally, the women were 'utterly at a loss' (NEB). The *two men* who now stood there *in dazzling apparel* (*cf.* Acts 1:10) are evidently to be understood as angels. Matthew speaks of one angel who rolled the stone away and also spoke to the women. Mark refers to a young man in a white robe whom they saw after they entered the tomb. John mentions two angels in white who spoke to Mary Magdalene. It is clear that all these refer to angels. The fact that sometimes we hear of one and sometimes of two need not concern us. As many commentators point out, a spokesman is more prominent than his associates and may be referred to without reference to others. Neither should we be greatly concerned that the angels may be sitting (in John) or standing (here), nor that their words are not identical in the various accounts. It is hypercriticism that does not allow angels to change their position, and there is no reason for holding that they spoke once only. Moreover John speaks of them in connection with a different incident. Problems there undoubtedly are, but the chief thing these minor differences tell us is that the accounts are independent. It is also possible that with angels spiritual perception is presumably required and that all may not have seen the same thing.

5-7. The reaction of the women was fear. Bowing *their faces to the ground* was a mark of respect in the presence of such great ones. The angels first asked, *Why do you seek the living among the dead?* This startling question gets to the root of the matter immediately. Jesus is not to be thought of as dead: therefore He is not to be sought among the dead. The words, 'He is not here, but has risen', are rejected by many critics, since they are not found in one important Greek MS and a few other authorities. It is argued that they might well have been imported from Mark 16:6. But against this, they are attested by an overwhelming majority of MSS including the very old P75. Moreover they seem to be implied by verse 23. They should be accepted. Even if they are not, what they say must be understood. The angels proceed to remind the women that this was in accordance with Jesus' prediction while He was still in Galilee. Then He had said that He would *be crucified, and on the third day rise* (*cf.* 9:22; this teaching continued after Galilee, 17:25, 18:32f.). Matthew and Mark omit this, but they tell us, as Luke does not, that Jesus would go into Galilee before the disciples and that they would see Him there. Perhaps Luke omitted this because he did not propose to include any account of Jesus' appearances in Galilee.

8, 9. They remembered and evidently this brought some measure of conviction to them. They had heard the words before, but Jesus had often spoken metaphorically and they had probably taken the strange words about resurrection in some such way. Now they saw that Jesus had intended to be taken literally. The women went off to *the eleven* with their news and they told it also to *all the rest*, *i.e.* the other followers of Jesus in the locality.

334

10. Luke proceeds to list the names of some of the women. *Mary Magdalene*, the first to see the risen Lord (*cf.* Mk. 16:9), is mentioned in each of the four Gospels in the resurrection narrative. But apart from her connection with the crucifixion and resurrection we hear of her only in 8:2 (where see note). *Joanna* is mentioned only here and in 8:2 (where see note). *Mary the mother of James* (Mk. 16:1) is apparently 'the other Mary' of Matthew 28:1. These and *the other women* (who will include Salome, mentioned in Mk. 16:1) told the apostles what they had seen and heard.

11. But the lordly males were not impressed. They thought the story 'nonsense' (NEB). Luke underlines this by adding, *and they did not believe them*. The apostles were not men poised on the brink of belief and needing only the shadow of an excuse before launching forth into a proclamation of resurrection. They were utterly sceptical. Even when women they knew well told them of their experiences, they refused to believe. Clearly irrefutable evidence was needed to convince these sceptics.

b. Peter at the tomb (24:12)

RSV and many other authorities omit this verse (see mg.), presumably because it is difficult to see why anyone would leave it out if original. But reasons can be suggested. Some scribes may have thought the absence of any reference to John a contradiction of the Fourth Gospel, or they may have found the verse hard to harmonize with verse 24. The verse is read by almost all our best authorities for the text, the Codex Bezae and other representatives of the Western text being the only notable exceptions. The suggestion that it is a quick summary of the appearance narrated by John will not stand up. If that is its origin, why should there be no mention of the beloved disciple, especially since that narrative culminates in his believing (Jn. 20:8)? And as far as Peter is concerned, the important thing in John is that he went into the tomb, which Luke does not mention. On the other hand Luke tells us, as John does not, that Peter went off *wondering at what had happened*. In view of such difficulties it is hard to think that this verse derives from John. And if it does not, then in view of its overwhelming attestation it should be accepted, as it is by Moffatt, Leaney, Harrington, JB, TEV, *etc*.[1] It gives us Peter's characteristic reaction to the news brought by the women. He *ran to the tomb* (which action seems to be referred to in verse 24). He *saw the linen cloths by themselves*, which underlines the fact of the empty tomb. But Peter did not yet believe in the resurrection for he went home *wondering at what had happened*. But at least he had been impressed. Something marvellous had taken place.

c. The walk to Emmaus (24:13-35)

This charming story is one of the best loved of all the resurrection narratives. There is something very moving in one of the risen Lord's few appearances being given to these humble, quite unknown disciples. The story, moreover, has something so vivid about it that some hold that it must have come from one of the participants, perhaps even that Luke himself was the unnamed disciple. Others however regard this as no more than a proof of the literary artistry of this Evangelist.

13, 14. *That very day* ties this story firmly in with the other happenings on the day of the resurrection. Luke does not

---

[1]Ever since Westcott and Hort there has been a strong feeling that a number of passages towards the end of Luke (and elsewhere) are spurious. Westcott and Hort called them 'Western non-interpolations', a curious name for interpolations into their beloved 'neutral' text. Scholars have been swayed by this weighty opinion, by the great antiquity of the Western text and by the difficulty of explaining why scribes should omit such striking passages. Recently, however, attention has been given to the newly discovered papyri, especially the great P75. It is now plain that these readings are as old as or probably older than the Western text and the trend is towards accepting them. See, for example, the article by Klyne Snodgrass, ' "Western Non-Interpolations" ', *JBL*, 91, 1972, pp. 369-379. On the present verse Snodgrass says, 'it is plain that this verse, one of the "most secure Western non-interpolations," belongs to the original text of Luke' (*ibid*., p. 373). Earlier J. Jeremias pointed to a great difficulty in the way of the common attitude to the Western non-interpolations: 'The assumption that the archetype of the group D it vet-syr had suffered some loss is a comparatively easy one, whereas it is exceedingly difficult to visualize the historical evolution of a text where an interpolation could find its way into every Greek MS. with the exception of D only. The originality of the shorter text could be assumed, therefore, only for very cogent reasons' (*The Eucharistic Words of Jesus* (Oxford, 1955), pp. 91f.). K. Aland stresses the importance of P75 in his acceptance of a considerable group of passages (including the present one) rejected by the 'Western non-interpolations' theory (*NTS*, xii, 1965-66, pp. 193-210).

name the disciples of whom he writes, simply referring to *two of them*. He locates Emmaus with precision as sixty *stadia* from Jerusalem (a *stadion* was 606¾ feet). This site cannot now be identified, for there are difficulties in the way of each suggested identification (see AG for suggestions and documentation). Luke does not define the subject of their conversation, but *all these things* must refer to the stories of the empty tomb and of the angels.

15, 16. The verb *drew near* might refer to an approach from any direction, but as the two speak of Jesus as being from Jerusalem (18), the meaning must be that He overtook them as they journeyed. On a number of occasions the risen Jesus was not recognized at first (Mt. 28:17; Jn. 20:14; 21:4): so now. On this occasion the implication appears to be that the disciples were somehow prevented from recognizing Jesus. It was in God's providence that only later should they come to know who He was. Perhaps Luke wants us to gather, as Ford suggests, 'that we cannot see the risen Christ, although he be walking with us, unless he wills to disclose himself'.

17, 18. Jesus' question about the subject of their conversation caused them to stand still, *looking sad*. Clearly they had been deeply moved by the turn of events. *Cleopas*, now introduced for the first time, is not known to us apart from this story. He saw the events of which he had just been speaking with his friend as common knowledge. The stranger, he thought, must be *the only visitor to Jerusalem who does not know* these things. It was evidently a topic much on the lips of all in the capital city at the time.

19, 20. To Jesus' question *What things?* they gave an illuminating answer. They saw Jesus as *a prophet*. Their perception of His Person was limited. Yet in their hope for redemption (21) they must have seen Him as more. At any rate they had been impressed both by His deeds and His words and they characterized them alike as *mighty*. They had seen the power of God in Jesus. But although He had had this character they explained that the Jewish rulers had destroyed Him. Notice that it is not the Romans but *our chief priests and rulers* who both *delivered him up* and *crucified him*. The reference to His being *condemned to death* implicates the Romans, but the chief blame is put squarely on the Jews.

21. The hope of the pair (and perhaps others; *we* may mean 'we Christians') had been that *he was the one to redeem Israel.* They had seen Him as the promised Deliverer. Redemption in the ancient world signified deliverance on payment of a price. It is inconceivable that God should pay a price to anyone, so that where He is the subject the concept is necessarily modified. But close examination of such passages shows that they tend to convey the thought that God saves at cost (He may, for example, be pictured as putting forth a great effort in the interests of His own). Until Calvary no man could know the extent of the cost. But the use of the concept of redemption expresses something of Israel's hope and of the certainty that God cares.

22–24. The travellers single out what they have learnt from the women as the empty tomb and the *vision of angels.* They do not say who went to the tomb to check, but the plural, *some of those who were with us,* shows that they knew that Peter had not been alone. The women's story had been verified, at any rate as far as the empty tomb went. But these two conclude sadly, *him* (there is emphasis on this word) *they did not see.* Apparently those who went to the tomb had hoped to see Jesus; but they did not, and this threw some doubt on what the women had said.

25, 26. Their words drew a rather sharp rebuke from their companion. Perhaps *O foolish men* is a trifle strong for *anoētoi,* and NEB may give the sense better with, 'How dull you are!' But the words certainly fall short of being a compliment, and show that the two had done less than might reasonably have been expected. Incidentally *men* may be more definite than the Greek demands, for the two could have been man and wife (*cf.* 17:34, where see note). Some have thought that Cleopas's companion was Luke himself, others that he was called Simon. But we really do not know. Jesus goes on to point out that the root of the trouble was their failure to accept what is taught in Bible prophecy. The prophets had spoken plainly enough, but the minds of Cleopas and his friend had not been quick enough to grasp what was meant. The word *all* is probably important. They had no doubt seized on the prediction of the glory of the Messiah, but it was quite another thing to take to heart the prophecies that pointed to the darker side of His mission. But the dark side was there, in the prophecies. And this means that the passion was not simply a possibility that might or might not become actual, depending on the circumstances: it was *necessary*. Written in the prophets as it was, it had to happen. The Christ must suffer. But that is not the end of it. He must also *enter into his glory*. God is not defeated. He triumphs through the sufferings of His Christ.

27. Jesus began a systematic Bible study. *Moses and all the prophets* formed the starting-point, but He also went on to the things that referred to Himself *in all the scriptures*. The picture we get is of the Old Testament as pointing to Jesus in all its parts. Luke gives no indication of which passages the Lord chose, but he makes it clear that the whole Old Testament was involved. We should perhaps understand this not as the selection of a number of proof-texts, but rather as showing that throughout the Old Testament a consistent divine purpose is worked out, a purpose that in the end meant and must mean the cross. The terribleness of sin is found throughout the Old Testament and so is the deep, deep love of God. In the end this combination made Calvary inevitable. The two had wrong ideas of what the Old Testament taught and thus they had wrong ideas about the cross.

28, 29. As they neared their journey's end it appeared that Jesus was *going further*. Had they not pressed Him to stay, there is no reason for thinking that He would have done so. We must not interpret the words as pointing to a piece of play-acting. Without the invitation He would not have stayed. But the two had been more than impressed with His exposition of the Bible and accordingly they *constrained him* to stay with them. This probably means in the home of one of them. Some have felt that they went to an inn, but the only evidence is that Jesus took the initiative in breaking the bread (30), which the host would normally do. This scarcely seems adequate and it is much more likely that they went into a home. That it was *toward evening* meant that it was time to stop normal travelling. After dark the going would be difficult on unlit paths and there might be dangers from robbers or wild beasts. It was better to call a halt.

30, 31. At table Jesus went through the motions familiar at the beginning of a Jewish meal, though normally they would have been performed by the host, not a guest. For the procedure see the note on 9:16, 17. *Bread* was commonly broken at the prayer of thanksgiving before a meal. Some have seen here a reference to the breaking of bread in the communion service, but this seems far fetched. It would have been a very curious communion service, broken off in the opening action and as far as we can see never completed. And it would have been quite out of place. In any case the two were not present at the Last Supper (*cf.* 22:14; Mk. 14:17), so they could not have recalled Jesus' actions then. Moreover there is no mention of the wine. However, something in the action awoke a chord, or perhaps they now saw the nail-marks in Jesus' hands for the first time. Or perhaps it was just God's time. *Their eyes were opened* may mean that God chose this moment to make it clear that this was His Son. At any rate *they recognized him*. And as they did so *he vanished out of their sight*.

32. The recognition that it was the Lord with whom they had walked explained to them what had happened on the journey. They remembered how their hearts had burnt within them. Clearly Jesus' exposition had stirred them deeply. They speak of Him as 'opening' the scriptures: when He spoke the meaning hidden in the words of the Bible became clear.

33–35. Their immediate reaction was to tell the other believers. They seem not to have completed their meal, for they left *that same hour* (which means 'straight away' rather than 'within an hour'). The arguments they had used with Jesus about the lateness of the hour apparently did not weigh with them at all now. In Jerusalem they found *the eleven* and other disciples with them, though Luke does not say who they were. But they were full of the news of the resurrection, for the Lord *has appeared to Simon!* (*cf.* 1 Cor. 15:5). They had not been prepared to take the word of the women, but Simon was different. If he said he had seen Jesus, then *The Lord has risen*

indeed. So Cleopas and his friend told of their walk with
Jesus and of His becoming known *in the breaking of the bread*.
The manner of His becoming known had clearly impressed
them.

d. The appearance to the disciples (24:36–43)

It is fairly obvious that this is the same appearance as that
described in John 20:19ff., but the differences between the
two accounts show that they are independent. There is nothing
here about Jesus' breathing on the disciples, no reference to the
Holy Spirit or to the declaration that sins are forgiven or
retained. But both accounts refer to the same time on Easter
Day, in both Jesus shows the disciples the marks of His wounds
and in both probably there is the greeting of peace.

36. This incident follows hard on the return of the two
from Emmaus. It was *as they were saying this* that Jesus appeared.
Luke does not speak, as John does, of 'closed (*i.e.* locked) doors',
but that seems to be the implication of *Jesus himself stood
among them*. The risen Lord was not bound by the limitations
that beset men in general and His sudden appearances and
disappearances underline this. The placing of the greeting,
'Peace to you!" in the margin (RSV) seems another example of
the tendency to accept the Western text too readily. These
words are read by all the important Greek MSS but one, and the
fact that they are found in John (and thus could have been
copied from there by a scribe) is not of itself sufficient reason
for discarding them in the light of their overwhelming attestation. They represent the normal greeting of the day.

37. It is not surprising that the disciples *were startled*. After
all, to have the risen Lord suddenly appear in their midst
must have been something of a shock. That they were *frightened*
is not quite so explicable. They had just been telling the two
from Emmaus that 'The Lord has risen indeed'. But it is one
thing to accept such a statement on the word of someone else
about an absent Person and quite another to accept it for
oneself when the Person is suddenly present despite locked
doors. Small wonder that they *supposed that they saw a spirit*,
i.e. a ghost! Their fear was the natural reaction to the supernatural.

38-40. Jesus proceeded to calm and reassure His followers. First He asked the reason for their being *troubled* and for their *questionings*. It is well to take doubts out into the open and see what causes them. The invitation to handle Him and the reference to *flesh and bones* show that Jesus' resurrection body had physical aspects, or at least that it could conform at Jesus' will to physical laws. *See my hands and my feet* is probably an invitation to look at the marks of His wounds as a means of verifying that it was Jesus Himself who stood before them. To handle Him would show them that He was not a ghost. Verse 40 is yet another passage omitted by RSV (and many others) on the grounds that it is missing from the Western text. Unless we are prepared to give that text a veto the words should be read. They cannot have been derived from John, for His account speaks of Jesus' hands and side (Jn. 20:20). They indicate that Jesus did what His words implied and showed the disciples the places where the nailprints were.

41-43. Now it seemed to the little group that all this was just too good to be true. They *disbelieved for joy*. So Jesus dispelled their unbelief by calling for some food which He proceeded to eat. AV adds 'an honeycomb' to the *piece of broiled fish*, but this is the reading of inferior MSS and should be rejected.

e. The fulfilment of Scripture (24:44-49)

The fulfilment of Scripture is a major theme of Luke's. He sees God as setting out His purpose in those ancient writings and then as bringing to pass what He has foreshadowed. He was not frustrated by the machinations of wicked men.

44. *These are my words* means, 'These happenings, specifically the resurrection, represent the outworking of the things I taught you.' Jesus had included in His teaching enough foreshadowings of the passion and resurrection for His followers not to have been surprised at what had happened. He can say, *while I was still with you*, for His presence now (and on other occasions like this) was exceptional. The definitive break had taken place and He no longer abode on earth. The solemn division of Scripture into *the law of Moses and the prophets and the psalms* (the three divisions of the Hebrew Bible) indicates that there is no part of Scripture that does not bear its witness to Jesus. This incidentally appears to be the only place in the New Testament where this threefold division is explicitly mentioned.

45, 46. As on the road to Emmaus He *opened their minds* (32). He showed that the Bible points to a Messiah who would suffer and rise. Once again Luke makes the fact clear without telling us what the passages were on which Jesus relied to make His point.

47, 48. On this occasion Jesus went beyond showing how prophecy was fulfilled in His passion and resurrection. It follows from His saving acts that *repentance and forgiveness of sins* are to be preached. It is often said that Luke does not see the cross as accomplishing an atoning function, so these words connecting forgiveness with the passion are important. Luke may not stress the atonement in the way some other New Testament writers do, but it is there. *In his name* connects this repentance and forgiveness with what Jesus is and has done. Men are not called to a repentance based on general principles and to receive a forgiveness always available. Luke is speaking about what Christ has done for men and what is available through Him. This Evangelist's universalism comes out in his reference to *all nations*. It is no petty forgiveness available for a few pious or nationalistic souls, but for all men. The next words, *beginning from Jerusalem*, could be taken grammatically either with the preceding or the following. It is more likely to be with the preceding (as RSV), but perhaps there is not in the end a great deal of difference. The gospel is to be preached to all nations and the witness to Christ is to be made. Both are to be performed by men who at this point of time were in Jerusalem. That was where their witness would begin and that was where the evangelization of the nations would begin.

49. The risen Jesus has the power to *send* the Spirit. His authority is not limited as it was during the days of His earthly ministry. *The promise of my Father* is an unusual designation of the Holy Spirit emphasizing the place of the divine promise in His coming. The disciples are not to attempt the task of evangelism with their own meagre resources, but are to await the coming of the Spirit. The equipment He would provide is picturesquely described in terms of the disciples being *clothed with power from on high*. The note of power is significant, and *on high* reminded them (and reminds us) of the source of all real power for evangelism.

f. The ascension (24:50-53)

The ascension is described more fully in Luke's second volume (Acts 1:9-11). Here he is content to give the main fact and to leave us with a picture of the worshipping and rejoicing disciples. The account is quite short. Luke has already written more than most papyrus rolls contained and he is clearly hastening to the end of this volume. He does not explain in detail what he means by the ascension, but it is difficult to believe that he thought that Jesus went up vertically and stopped in a heaven a mile or two above the earth. But plainly he did think of the ascension as something that happened. As C. F. D. Moule maintains, we should be ready to accord to Luke's ascension the same kind of historicity that we accord to the post-resurrection appearances and the transfiguration.[1] And the ascension differs radically from Jesus' vanishing from the sight of the disciples at Emmaus (24:31) and similar happenings. There is an air of finality about it. It is the decisive close of one chapter and the beginning of another. It is the consummation of Christ's earthly work, the indication to His followers that His mission is accomplished, His work among them come to a decisive end. They can expect to see Him in the old way no more.

Theologians also see in the ascension the taking into heaven of the humanity of Jesus. The incarnation is not something casual and fleeting but a divine action with permanent consequences. And Moule argues that if the ascension means the taking of Christ's humanity into heaven, 'it means that with it will be taken the humanity which He has redeemed— those who are Christ's, at His coming. It is a powerful expression of the *redemption* of this world, in contrast to mere *escape* from it.'[2]

50, 51. Jesus took the initiative and *led* the disciples *as far as*

---

[1] *ET*, lxviii, 1956-57, p. 208.
[2] *Ibid.*, p. 209 (Moule's italics).

Bethany. There is no time note and some have thought that
Luke is picturing the ascension as taking place on Easter Day.
But, quite apart from the difficulty inherent in the idea that
Jesus would have led His followers from Jerusalem to the
Mount of Olives late at night for this purpose, we should not
see a contradiction of Luke's own words in Acts 1:3. There we
learn that forty days elapsed between the resurrection and the
ascension. *Bethany* was on the slopes of the Mount of Olives
and the ascension took place from somewhere on this hill.
Luke describes this event very simply. He speaks only of Jesus
as being parted from the disciples during the act of blessing
them. NEB and others omit the words 'and was carried up into
heaven', the Western text being supported on this occasion by
one other Greek MS. But the words should be read with the
vast preponderance of authorities. They may readily have
been omitted by a scribe anxious to avoid the impression that
the ascension took place on Easter Day. But the omission
leaves us with no explanation of the disciples' joy. There is then
no reference to the ascension and the words seem to indicate a
disappearance in the manner of that in verse 31.

52, 53. Here once more we should accept the reading of all
the Greek MSS except one (the Western text again!) and read,
'they worshipped him' (mg.). Whatever their view of His
Person during His ministry, the passion and resurrection and
now the ascension had convinced them that He was divine.
He was worthy to be worshipped and they gave Him His due.
Worship is their response to His ascension. It is interesting that
their feeling at this final parting was not one of grief but of
great joy (*cf.* Jn. 14:28). They were understanding more than
they had previously. Luke began his Gospel in the Temple
(1:5). Now he brings it to an end with the disciples *continually
in the temple blessing God*. It is a fitting acknowledgment of the
grace that God has shown so singularly in the events he has
narrated.

A TABLE OF PARALLEL PASSAGES

This table will enable the student to find passages in the other Synoptists which parallel those in Luke. I have included passages which deal with the same subject but which are not in the strict sense literary parallels (*e.g.* Mt. 1:18–25 and Lk. 2:1–7). The table will also enable the student to see at a glance which passages are peculiar to Luke and it will help him see how the order of the narratives in this Gospel resembles and differs from that in each of the other Synoptists.

	Matthew	Mark	Luke
Preface			1:1–4
The birth of John foretold			1:5–25
The birth of Jesus foretold			1:26–38
Mary's visit to Elizabeth			1:39–45
The song of Mary			1:46–56
The birth and naming of John			1:57–66
The song of Zechariah			1:67–80
The birth of Jesus	1:18–25		2:1–7
The angels and the shepherds			2:8–20
The circumcision			2:21
The presentation in the Temple			2:22–24
The song of Simeon			2:25–32
Simeon's prophecy			2:33–35
Anna's thanksgiving			2:36–38
The return to Nazareth			2:39–40
The boy Jesus in the Temple			2:41–52
The ministry of John the Baptist	3:1–12	1:2–8	3:1–20
Jesus' baptism	3:13–17	1:9–11	3:21–22
Jesus' genealogy	1:1–17		3:23–38
Jesus' temptations	4:1–11	1:12–13	4:1–13
Jesus in Galilee	4:12–17	1:14–15	4:14–15
Jesus at Nazareth	13:53–58	6:1–6	4:16–30
The man with an unclean spirit		1:21–28	4:31–37
Peter's mother-in-law	8:14–15	1:29–31	4:38–39
Many healings	8:16–17	1:32–34	4:40–41
A preaching tour	4:23	1:35–39	4:42–44
The miraculous catch of fish			5:1–11
Healing a leper	8:1–4	1:40–45	5:12–16
Healing a paralytic	9:1–8	2:1–12	5:17–26
The calling of Levi	9:9–13	2:13–17	5:27–32
Fasting	9:14–17	2:18–22	5:33–39
Lord of the sabbath	12:1–8	2:23–28	6:1–5
Healing the withered hand	12:9–14	3:1–6	6:6–11
Choosing the Twelve	10:1–4	3:13–19	6:12–16

347

A TABLE OF PARALLEL PASSAGES

	Matthew	Mark	Luke
The sermon on the plain			
The multitude		3:7–12	6:17–19
The beatitudes	5:3–12		6:20–23
The woes			6:24–26
Love	5:38–48		6:27–36
Judging other people	7:1–5	4:24	6:37–42
The tree and the fruit	7:16–20; 12:35		6:43–45
Foundations	7:21–27		6:46–49
Healing the centurion's slave	8:5–13		7:1–10
The widow of Nain's son			7:11–17
John the Baptist's questions	11:2–19		7:18–35
The anointing of Jesus by a sinful woman			7:36–50
Women who helped Jesus			8:1–3
The parable of the sower	13:1–23	4:1–20	8:4–15
The lamp and the cover	5:15; 10:26	4:21–22	8:16–17
To him who has . . .	13:12; 25:29	4:25	8:18
Jesus' mother and brothers	12:46–50	3:31–35	8:19–21
The stilling of the storm	8:23–27	4:35–41	8:22–25
The Gerasene demoniac	8:28–34	5:1–20	8:26–39
The daughter of Jairus	9:18–26	5:21–43	8:40–56
The mission of the Twelve	10:1–15	6:7–13	9:1–6
Herod the tetrarch	14:1–2	6:14–16	9:7–9
The feeding of the five thousand	14:13–21	6:30–44	9:10–17
Peter's confession	16:13–19	8:27–29	9:18–20
A prophecy of the passion	16:20–23	8:30–33	9:21–22
Taking up the cross	16:24–28	8:34 – 9:1	9:23–27
The transfiguration	17:1–9	9:2–10	9:28–36
The demon-possessed boy	17:14–21	9:14–29	9:37–43a
Another prophecy of the passion	17:22–23	9:30–32	9:43b–45
The disciples' pride	18:1–5	9:33–37	9:46–48
The strange exorcist		9:38–41	9:49–50
Rejection by the Samaritans			9:51–56
Whole-heartedness	8:18–22		9:57–62
The mission of the seventy			10:1–12
Doom of the Galilean cities	11:21–24		10:13–16
The return of the seventy			10:17–20
Jesus' joy	11:25–27; 13:16–17		10:21–24
The parable of the good Samaritan			10:25–37
Martha and Mary			10:38–42
The Lord's prayer	6:9–13		11:1–4
The parable of the friend at midnight			11:5–8
Asking and giving	7:7–11		11:9–13
The Beelzebub controversy	12:22–30	3:22–27	11:14–23
The return of the evil spirit	12:43–45		11:24–26
True blessedness			11:27–28
The sign of Jonah	12:38–42	8:11–12	11:29–32

	Matthew	Mark	Luke
The light that is in you	5:15; 6:22–23	4:21	11:33–36
True cleansing			11:37–41
Discourse on the Pharisees and the lawyers			
Woe to the Pharisees	23:6–7, 23, 27		11:42–44
Woe to the lawyers	23:4, 13, 29–36		11:45–54
The leaven of the Pharisees	10:26–27; 16:5–6	8:14–15	12:1–3
Be ready for judgment	10:28–33, 19–20; 12:31–32	3:28–30	12:4–12
The parable of the rich fool			12:13–21
Seek the kingdom	6:25–33, 19–21		12:22–34
The coming of the Son of man	24:42–44		12:35–40
The responsibility of servants	24:45–51		12:41–48
Fire on the earth	10:34–36		12:49–53
The signs of the times	16:1–3; 5:25–26		12:54–59
Repentance			13:1–5
The barren fig tree			13:6–9
Healing the bent woman			13:10–17
The parable of the mustard seed	13:31–32	4:30–32	13:18–19
The parable of the leaven	13:33		13:20–21
Who are in the kingdom?			13:22–30
That fox Herod			13:31–33
Lament over Jerusalem	23:37–39		13:34–35
The man with dropsy			14:1–6
Invitation to a banquet			14:7–14
The parable of the excuses	22:1–14		14:15–24
The cost of discipleship	10:37–38		14:25–33
The parable of salt	5:13	9:49–50	14:34–35
The parable of the lost sheep	18:12–13		15:1–7
The parable of the lost coin			15:8–10
The parable of the prodigal son			15:11–32
The parable of the unjust steward			16:1–9
God and mammon	6:24		16:10–13
The covetous Pharisees			16:14–15
The law and the prophets	11:12–13; 5:18		16:16–17
Divorce	19:9	10:11–12	16:18
The parable of the rich man and Lazarus			16:19–31
Forgiving others	18:6–7, 15, 21f.	9:42	17:1–4
Faith	17:20	11:23	17:5–6
Unprofitable servants			17:7–10
The ten lepers			17:11–19
The coming of the kingdom	24:23–41		17:20–37
The parable of the unjust judge			18:1–8
The parable of the Pharisee and the publican			18:9–14

	Matthew	Mark	Luke
Jesus and the children	19:13–15	10:13–16	18:15–17
The rich young ruler	19:16–30	10:17–31	18:18–30
Another prediction of the passion	20:17–19	10:32–34	18:31–34
A blind man receives sight	20:29–34	10:46–52	18:35–43
Zacchaeus			19:1–10
The parable of the pounds	(25:14–30)		19:11–27
The triumphal entry	21:1–9	11:1–10	19:28–40
Lament over Jerusalem			19:41–44
The cleansing of the Temple	21:12–17	11:15–17	19:45–46
Teaching in the Temple		11:18–19	19:47–48
Jesus' authority	21:23–27	11:27–33	20:1–8
The parable of the wicked husbandmen	21:33–44	12:1–12	20:9–18
Tribute to Caesar	22:15–22	12:12–17	20:19–26
The seven brothers	22:23–33	12:18–27	20:27–40
David's Son	22:41–46	12:35–37	20:41–44
Warning against the scribes	23:1–7	12:38–40	20:45–47
The widow's gift		12:41–44	21:1–4
The eschatological discourse	24:1–34	13:1–37	21:5–36
Teaching in the Temple			21:37–38
The betrayal	26:1–5, 14–16	14:1–2, 10–11	22:1–6
Preparations for the Passover	26:17–19	14:12–16	22:7–13
The last supper	26:26–29	14:22–25	22:14–20
Prophecy of the betrayal	26:21–25	14:18–21	22:21–23
Dispute about status	20:24–28	10:41–45	22:24–27
Twelve thrones	19:28		22:28–30
Prophecy of Peter's denials	26:31–35	14:27–31	22:31–34
Two swords			22:35–38
The agony	26:36–46	14:32–42	22:39–46
The arrest	26:47–57	14:43–53	22:47–54a
Peter's denials	26:58, 69–75	14:54, 66–72	22:54b–62
The mockery	26:67–68	14:65	22:63–65
Jesus before the Sanhedrin	26:59–66	14:53–64	22:66–71
Jesus before Pilate	27:1–2, 11–14	15:1–5	23:1–5
Jesus before Herod			23:6–12
Jesus sentenced	27:15–26	15:6–15	23:13–25
Simon carries the cross	27:32	15:21	23:26
Daughters of Jerusalem			23:27–31
The crucifixion	27:33–37	15:22–26	23:32–38
The penitent thief	27:44	15:32b	23:39–43
The death of Jesus	27:45–56	15:33–41	23:44–49
The burial of Jesus	27:57–61	15:42–47	23:50–56
The women at the tomb	28:1–8	16:1–8	24:1–11
Peter at the tomb			24:12
The walk to Emmaus			24:13–35
The appearance to the disciples			24:36–43
The fulfilment of Scripture			24:44–49
The ascension			24:50–53